A Special Relationship

A Special Relationship

Anglo-American Relations
from the Cold War to Iraq

2nd edition

John Dumbrell

First published 2006 by
PALGRAVE MACMILLAN
Houndmills, Basingstoke, Hampshire RG21 6XS and
175 Fifth Avenue, New York, N.Y. 10010
Companies and representatives throughout the world.

PALGRAVE MACMILLAN is the global academic imprint of the Palgrave Macmillan division of St. Martin's Press, LLC and of Palgrave Macmillan Ltd. Macmillan® is a registered trademark in the United States, United Kingdom and other countries. Palgrave is a registered trademark in the European Union and other countries.

ISBN-13: 978–1–4039–8774–7   hardback
ISBN-10: 1–4039–8774–2   hardback
ISBN-13: 978–1–4039–8775–4   paperback
ISBN-10: 1–4039–8775–0   paperback

This book is printed on paper suitable for recycling and made from fully managed and sustained forest sources. Logging, pulping and manufacturing processes are expected to conform to the environmental regulations of the country of origin.

A catalogue record for this book is available from the British Library.

A catalog record for this book is available from the Library of Congress.

Printed in Great Britain by the MPG Books Group, Bodmin and King's Lynn

Contents

Preface to the Second Edition

The controversies and passions surrounding the foreign policy of the administration of President George W. Bush, and London's response to it, set the context for this second edition. A by-product of the War on Terror has been a resurgence of serious academic interest in the US–UK 'special relationship' which has made the subject matter of this book much more of a hot topic than it was when the first edition was published. Transatlantic conferences and academic journals in recent years have reflected a rebirth of interest in what was once considered the worthy, but slightly dull and dated, topic of Anglo-American (more properly, US–UK) relations. To some degree this rebirth is the result of the natural process of archive release, with a generation of younger scholars becoming attracted to 'new' documentary evidence as the basis upon which to challenge traditional or consensus views. The rebirth is also, at least arguably, connected to the problems of contemporary transnational governance in general, and of the European Union in particular. The international era of the War on Terror has seen something of a general reprioritization of bilaterals: of US foreign policy being conducted in terms of relations with particular countries, rather than via regional or global transnational groupings. More obviously, current interest in US–UK relations derives from the outpouring of debate about the UK's supposed subservience to Washington – 'poodle studies', if you will – which accompanied London's decision to participate in the 2003 invasion of Iraq.

In short, the period between the publication of the first and second editions of *A Special Relationship* witnessed a transformation in the popular, and indeed academic, saliency of the study of US–UK relations. The second edition has, in consequence, involved a virtually complete rewriting. Like the first edition, the new version deals in detail with the period since 1960. Even the narrative of the years between 1960 and 2001, however, has been rewritten to take account of new scholarship. There are completely new sections on transatlantic attitudes, on London and the George W. Bush foreign policy, on the Iraq invasion and subsequent conflict, on post-2001 nuclear and intelligence cooperation, on recent European integration, and so on. Recent events have indeed called for a rethinking of all aspects of the 'special relationship'.

The US–UK 'special relationship', defined primarily in terms of close and 'special' military and intelligence cooperation, survived the end of the Cold War. The assumption of this book's first edition was that it would not survive long into the new century, or at least that it would be transformed by the process of European integration. That assumption no longer seems so secure. US–UK special relations, in the traditional sense of intimacy in matters of defence and intelligence, were rather spectacularly revived after the 11 September 2001 terror attacks on New York and Washington. Substantial sections of the new edition are concerned with the implications of that revival.

As with the first edition, this new version of *A Special Relationship* does not define 'special relations' entirely in terms of bombs and secrets. Space is also found for cultural relationships. The Anglo-American cultural 'special relationship' is sustained still by history and language, though it is continually prey to false understandings and the pitfalls of confident over-familiarity. The second edition is again structured in terms of both narrative and thematic chapters. Like its predecessor, the new edition draws particular attention to Irish issues in the context of the developing relationship between Washington and London.

I have presented academic papers on topics relevant to the concerns of this book at various conferences and seminars: at the Society for Historians of American Foreign Relations conference in Washington DC; at Hofstra University, New York; at the London School of Economics; and at the American Politics Group annual colloquium at the US Embassy in London. I would like to thank all those who offered comments and advice on these occasions. I would also like to thank colleagues in the Department of Politics and International Relations at the University of Leicester. Special thanks also, for his patience and professionalism, to Steven Kennedy at Palgrave.

JOHN DUMBRELL

List of Abbreviations

ABM	Anti-Ballistic Missile Treaty
ANF	Atlantic Nuclear Force
ANIA	Americans for a New Irish Agenda
BIS	Information Service British
BRIAM	British Advisory Mission (Vietnam)
CF	Country File
CIA	Central Intelligence Agency
CND	Campaign for Nuclear Disarmament
COCOM	Coordinating Committee
CRS	Congressional Research Service
CSCE	Conference on Security and Cooperation in Europe
EFTA	European Free Trade Area
ERW	enhanced radiation weapon (neutron bomb)
ESDI	European Security and Defence Identity
FCO	Foreign and Commonwealth Office
FO	Foreign Office
ICC	International Criminal Court
INC	Irish National Caucus
MLF	Multilateral nuclear force
NATO	North Atlantic Treaty Organisation
NIF	New Ireland Forum
NORAID	Irish Northern Aid Committee
NSA	National Security Agency
NSC	National Security Council
NSF	National Security File
OAS	Organisation of American States
OECS	Organisation of East Caribbean States
PIRA	Provisional Irish Republican Army
RRC	Rapid Reaction Corps
SACEUR	Supreme Allied Commander in Europe
SALT	Strategic arms limitation talks

SBIRS	Space-based infra-red systems
SDI	Strategic Defence Initiative
SEATO	Southeast Asia Treaty Organization
SIGINT	Signals intelligence
SIOP	Single Integrated Operational Plan (US)
SNF	short-range nuclear force
WEU	Western European Union
WHCF	White House Central File
WMD	Weapons of Mass Destruction

1
Introduction

President George W. Bush Visits London

When Queen Victoria visited Dublin in 1901 during the Boer War, she was famously greeted by a resentful, sullen and silent city. Over one hundred years later, in November 2003, President George W. Bush visited London on what was, rather extraordinarily, the first official state visit accorded to an American president during the reign of Queen Elizabeth II. Bush's visit, like Victoria's, had the trappings of an imperial progress. Some 14,000 British police officers were reportedly assigned to cover the London stage of the presidential trip. An excursion to Prime Minister Tony Blair's constituency in Sedgefield cost the Durham police authorities over one million pounds. Disagreements were reported between British and American security personnel, with the latter requesting that large sections of London's West End be sealed off to traffic. The Queen apparently vetoed the positioning of a Black Hawk helicopter over Buckingham Palace. This particular feature of the US security presence was deemed by royal decree to be 'too noisy' (Oborne, 2003, 14).

In 2003, of course, President Bush found, not a silent city, but one seething with noisy protest against the direction of US foreign policy and against what was widely seen America's neo-imperialist relationship with Britain. Like Victoria in 1901, he was also forced to defend an unpopular war. Some nine months before the Bush visit, prior to the invasion of Iraq, London had witnessed the largest anti-war demonstration in British history. A public opinion poll published in *The Sunday Times* on 16 February 2003 had seen roughly equal numbers of respondents citing Bush and Iraqi dictator Saddam Hussein as the 'greatest threat to world peace'. Bush's

1

November 2003 trip to London had been arranged well before the March 2003 invasion of Iraq: an invasion, of course, in which British forces had participated. The day before the visit, on 18 November, Lindis Percy, a veteran peace protester, clambered up the gates of Buckingham Palace to unfurl an inverted American flag replete with anti-Bush slogans.

The 2003 state visit was the occasion of an extraordinary outpouring of a range of anti-Bush and anti-American emotion. Rational condemnation of the invasion became obscured in raw hatred of the US president, often also by a vaguer, generalized anti-Americanism and a visceral resentment of British subservience. On 17 November, the *New Statesman* editorialized: 'Nobody should apologise for being anti-American; if you don't like what America does, wear the badge with pride.' Playwright Harold Pinter addressed George W. Bush: 'I'm sure you'll be having a nice little tea party with your fellow war criminal, Tony Blair. Please wash the cucumber sandwiches down with a glass of blood, with my compliments' (*The Guardian*, 18 November 2003). A Merseyside hospital porter interviewed by *The Observer* (16 November 2003) identified the 'thing that really needles me' as the fact that 'Britain has become America's tart'.

Yet, even in this emotional and sometimes hysterical national response to the 2003 Bush visit, the complexity of US–UK relations, not least in the realm of sentiment, had to be recognized. The 16 November *vox pop* exercise by *The Observer* elicited the following comment from a Liverpudlian secretary: 'My Nan remembers the Americans coming here in the war to rescue us, and I think we owe them.' Many Iraq War critics were keen to distance themselves from comprehensive anti-Americanism. Polly Toynbee insisted that she was an opponent of the president, not a foe of his country: 'Apart from the left fringe and the mohican fringe, we are broadly pro-American and always have been. No, this is personal.' Timothy Garton Ash, looking forward to the 2004 US presidential elections, estimated that 'perhaps one in twenty British people … are in some meaningful sense "anti-American" '. He advised Bush that Britain simply hated conservative America: 'Most of the people on the streets of London, whether actively demonstrating or privately muttering, are not against America; they just want the other America. Think of them as Democrats, casting an early overseas vote' (*The Guardian*, 18 November 2003). It should also be remembered that the visit was by no means the utter disaster that Downing Street must have feared. The sting of the protests was drawn to some degree by the simultaneous bomb attacks on British economic targets in Turkey. Public opinion, as revealed in polls published around the time of the visit, remained stubbornly complex. General British approval ratings of the US certainly dropped significantly (from about 75 to 40 per cent) at the time of the Iraq invasion; by the Summer of 2003, however, they had returned to around 70 per cent (*The Observer*, 9 November 2003). A poll published in *The Guardian* on 18 November saw a majority of Labour voters actually welcoming the Bush visit and 62 per cent of all respondents believing the US to be 'generally speaking a force for good, not evil, in the world'.

A Special Relationship

The early years of the twenty-first century saw an extended debate about the nature of the relationship between the United Kingdom and the United States. The controversies surrounding the foreign policies of the first George W. Bush Administration, and the Blair government's support for them, generated degrees of passion which cried out for rational, historical analysis of Anglo-American relations. It is the prime purpose of this book to provide such an analysis.

A few fairly obvious points will set this analysis in motion. The United States in the early part of the new century was indeed a formidable power: in some senses, probably the most powerful nation state in world history. As Robert Cooper, sometime foreign policy adviser to Tony Blair and subsequently a senior European Union diplomat, put it in 2003, there 'is an imperial tinge to American policy', even if 'America is not imperial in the usual sense' of seeking annexation and formal domination of territory abroad. It is certainly hegemonic'. To quote Cooper once more: 'The hegemony is essentially voluntary, part of a bargain in which America provides protection and allies offer bases and support' (Cooper, 2003, 48). Despite the abuse hurled at him on the streets of London in November 2003, George W. Bush was an emperor in no formal sense. Quite unlike Victoria in 1901, he had no formal, juridical authority over the country he was visiting. The United

States and the United Kingdom are sovereign allies, not states bound together by the imperial knot. Blair's support for Bush's foreign policy was certainly at one level the product of the historic habits of cooperation between London and Washington which are a major subject of this book. London's support, however, was also freely given and was, as much as any other factor, the result of Blair's personal belief both about the obligations surrounding the US–UK 'special relationship' and about the fundamental rightness of the George W. Bush administration's reaction to the terror attacks of 11 September 2001. Blair's support was neither inevitable nor determined by the prior history of US–UK relations. What is clear, however, is that little sense can be made of contemporary transatlantic controversies without a prior understanding of the various forces that have tended to bind Britain and America together over the past half century.

Though drawing on prior cultural, linguistic and historical links, the roots of the 'special relationship' between the United States and Britain which is the subject of this book are widely and correctly seen to lie in the period of collaboration between the allies during the Second World War. Following the Arcadia conference with Franklin Roosevelt in 1942, Winston Churchill told King George VI that 'Britain and America were now married after many months of walking out.' On his way to meet the US president, Churchill put it even more colourfully: 'Previously we were trying to seduce them. Now they are securely in the harem' (Jenkins, 2001, 676). After 1945, the relationship, by turns, developed, thrived and stuttered against a background of an, admittedly, frequently strained community of interests in the conditions of the Cold War. Shifts in international power necessitated a reworking of the power relationships as understood by Churchill. By 1960, London was certainly not in the business of running international harems. Though driven by common interests – essentially common perceptions of the Soviet communist threat – the relationship was nevertheless sustained by cultural sharing, by personal friendships, by institutionalized exchange of information and by complex and sturdy networks of military and diplomatic cooperation.

The main concern of this book is with the later Cold War and the immediate post-Cold War era. Detailed attention is given particularly to events after 1960. The post-1960 era constitutes a distinct phase of the 'special relationship' and a phase which, in comparison to the well-researched period of 1941–60, has not yet received its fair share of scholarly attention. The restoration of close US–UK cooperation following the 1956 Suez crisis inaugurated a distinct stage in the relationship. Especially, but not entirely, in nuclear issues, the era of President John Kennedy and Prime Minister Harold Macmillan (the years 1961–3) began a period of Anglo-American closeness which lasted, albeit in attenuated form, into the post-Cold War years. Major tensions in the relationship emerged in the later 1960s and early 1970s, with firm and close leader relations being restored to some degree in the late 1970s, but fully re-established only in the 1980s with the coming to power of President Reagan and Prime Minister Margaret Thatcher. This book reviews the apparent peaks and troughs in the Cold War relationship. It argues that, even in the conspicuous peaks of closeness – the eras of Kennedy and Macmillan and of Reagan and Thatcher – there were significant misunderstandings, squabbles and, indeed, near breakdowns in the relationship. By the same token, in periods of apparent coolness, for example, in the early 1970s, networks of bureaucratic cooperation continued to flourish.

We will also assess the evolution of the US–UK relationship through not one, but two fundamental international transformations: the end of the Cold War and the onset of the post-9/11 War on Terror. The Cold War's end removed much of the rationale for intimate and 'special' US–UK cooperation. The sharpening, in the 1990s and into the twenty-first century, of the European integration agenda also set what remained of the 'special relationship' in a new and unpredictable environment. By 2003, however, with the two allies engaged in the conflict in Iraq and Tony Blair widely regarded as by far the most influential of foreign leaders in Washington, obsequies for the relationship seemed very premature. A major purpose of this book is to explain the continuation of close relations in international conditions very far removed from those to which the 'special relationship' traced its origins and initial sense of purpose. At various stages in its recent evolution, the US–UK relationship has been surrounded by 'end of the affair' literature. The Cold War's end stimulated one such eruption. At one level, perceptions of the US–UK affair ending were bound up with European integration. In the mid-1990s, Margaret Thatcher began publicly to bemoan the fact that John Major, her successor as British prime minister had 'chosen' Europe over America to the extent that the 'special relationship' was now marginalized, if not actually destroyed (Gilmour, 1995). Many observers argued that, following the Cold War, Washington no longer had any need for special relations with London. For John Dickie (1994), the demise of the Cold War had removed the fundamental purpose of the alliance. Another rash of 'end of the affair' commentary emerged at the very time that Blair was offering close support to the US in Afghanistan and Iraq. It was now argued that, far from demonstrating the resilience of special relations, Blair's policies represented a stubborn refusal to recognise that times had changed. As David Marquand (2004) put it: 'Europe no longer needs a guardian angel. There is nothing to guard against.' Perhaps future historians will come to see the Blair-George W. Bush relationship as something of a last hurrah for Anglo-American closeness. From the perspective of the early years of the twenty-first century, however, it is the resilience of the closeness, not its demise, which requires emphasis and explanation.

A major preoccupation in the ensuing pages is with the interplay between culture, sentiment and interests in the later Cold War and post-Cold War eras. To numerous commentators, the US and UK are united primarily by values and habits of outlook and attitude: by, for example, attachment to the rule of law, including of course property rights, to religious toleration, basic human freedoms of expression. For Raymond Seitz, US ambassador to London in the early post-cold War years, 'end of the affair' jeremiads were inappropriate because the shared Anglo-American 'joint moral perspective', despite the different 'constitutional and structural expression' each country gives to their belief in 'tolerance and equity' and 'the basic freedoms' (Seitz, 1993, 86). It will be argued below that shared culture (especially, but not entirely, shared elite culture) has been an important and sustaining influence in the 'special relationship': not in some quasi-mystical sense of a sentimentalized 'Anglo-America', but as a practical and quotidian bolster to cooperation rooted in interests. The book is concerned also with the degree to which the 'special relationship', in its Cold War and post-Cold War incarnations, has signified partnership and mutuality, rather than simple US dominance.

By way of background to further explanation of the 'special relationship' in recent history, the next section of this chapter provides a brief, thumbnail review of Anglo-American relations up to 1945.

Anglo-American Relations to 1945

The English were not the first Europeans to settle in North America. The first attempt by English settlers to found an American colony took place on Roanoke Island, off the coast of present-day North Carolina, in the 1580s. This was one hundred years after Christopher Columbus's voyage of discovery and after a Spanish empire had been established in the Americas. In 1607, English settlements were established in Virginia, at Jamestown and Sagadahoc. English religious dissenters had a unique role in founding and shaping the emerging colonial, and especially the New England, identity. In 1620, the *Mayflower* landed at Massachusetts Bay. The *Mayflower* pilgrims, who founded the colony of Plymouth Plantation, were Puritans who had separated from the established Church of England and who had subsequently sought refuge in the Netherlands. For English Puritans, New England would be, in John Winthrop's famous phrase, a godly 'city upon a hill': a model for the world. Between the mid-seventeenth and mid-eighteenth centuries, however, colonial society did become increasingly heterogeneous. In 1700, the English and Welsh population made up 80 per cent of the population in the British American mainland colonies; by 1755, the percentage had dropped to 52. Germans, Scots-Irish, Irish and African slaves all grew in number.

The revolution against British rule famously involved the airing of political ideas derived from the English radical and republican traditions. It rested on a growing sense of nationhood and impatience with London's imperial tug. The year 1776 saw the publication of both the Declaration of Independence and of *Common Sense*, the radical republican tract written by Thomas Paine, an Englishman who had come to America two years previously. The outbreak of war between Britain and France in 1803 began an era of trade disputes between London and the (neutral) United States of America. The War of 1812, between the US and Great Britain, grew out of trade and territorial disputes, as well as grievances resulting from the Royal Navy's continued impressment of American seamen. The War of 1812 resulted in a new awareness on London's part of the degree to which the US now had to be taken seriously as a territorial and trading competitor. The two powers clashed over access to Latin American and West Indian trade, and over the future of the Canadian provinces. By 1850, various accommodations had been made concerning these issues, along with Anglo-American tension over Central America, Oregon and British efforts to suppress the slave trade. Benjamin Disraeli gave his opinion of American territorial expansion in 1856; it was 'not injurious to England ... (let me say this in a whisper lest it cross the Atlantic) – more than that – it diminishes the power of the United States' (Campbell, 1974, 94–5). The years immediately preceding the American Civil War were actually ones of considerable Anglo-American amity and interdependence.

During the American Civil War (1861–5), the Confederacy made several attempts to win British support. In 1861, the British vessel, *Trent*, which was carrying Confederate emissaries to London, was intercepted by the US Navy. The South's 'cotton diplomacy' – using Britain's needs for southern cotton to extract recognition from London – collapsed. London increasingly judged that the Southern cause would fail and Britain was able to buy cotton from non-American sources. Following the war, however, anti-British feeling in the Northern states was intense. This was linked to the fact that Southern warships had been constructed in British shipyards, as well as to the growing influence of Irish-American republican groups. 'Old' immigration from Northern and Western Europe, including Britain, did continue. English immigrants arrived in considerable numbers in response to economic depressions in 1873 and 1883. From the mid-1890s, however, 'new' immigration, from Southern and Eastern Europe, permanently changed US demography.

Partly in reaction to this putative 'de-Angloing' of America, elites on both sides of the Atlantic in the 1890s advanced ideas of the desired unity of English-speaking peoples and of 'Anglo America'. Such ideas profoundly influenced the young Winston Churchill. In 1898, US Secretary of State Richard Olney wrote that Anglo-American 'close community', based on 'origin, speech, thought, literature, institutions, ideals', would obviate any future conflict between the two countries, and would indeed cause them to stand together against common enemies (Campbell 1974, 201). The Spanish American War of 1898 and the Second Boer War (1899–1902) saw a considerable degree of Anglo-American cohesion. The period between 1894 and 1914 involved new accommodations, especially during the expansionist presidency of Theodore Roosevelt (1901–9). The rise of US power, despite Roosevelt's global ambitions, was still primarily in the Western hemisphere and limited – in Anne Orde's words – 'so far, to areas where British interests were not thought vital' (Orde, 1996, 40). John Young (1997, 26) describes a new 'policy of friendship', despite 'the fact that, in some ways, the US represented a potential threat'. By 1907, in tonnage terms at least, the US was the world's second largest naval power. By 1900, America had overtaken Britain in terms of share of world manufacturing output.

Between 1914 and 1917, Woodrow Wilson (president, 1913–21) urged Americans to be neutral in thought and action as Europe abandoned itself to war. Cultural and economic links between the US and Britain were strong, and consciously emphasized by London. There was in Washington a clear 'British party', which felt American entry into the conflict on Britain's side to be inevitable. Robert Lansing (US secretary of state, 1915–19) certainly saw an Allied victory over Germany as a vital American interest, yet the US remained neutral for the first three years of the First World War. Neutrality was generally supported by the American public (not merely by German-Americans and Irish-Americans). The route to American intervention was punctuated by various German violations of American neutrality rights (as defined by Wilson) and the granting to Britain of American loans. The Zimmerman telegram, given by London to Wilson, raised tension further in February 1917. The telegram, from Germany's foreign secretary, proposed an anti-US alliance of Germany, Mexico and Japan in the event of American entry into the conflict. During 1917–18, US and British naval forces operated under a joint (British) command, yet wartime relations were strained by personal rivalries and by differing British and American views on the future world order.

The stage for the postwar era was set by the US Senate's 1919 rejection of the Treaty of Versailles and by American non-participation in the League of Nations. Anglo-American relations in the 1920s focused on issues of war debts and naval rivalry. The Washington Naval Arms Conference of 1921–2 involved an agreement by the US, Britain and Japan to reduce battleship tonnage. John Callaghan (1997, 43) comments: 'Economy and *realpolitik* ruled out a war with the United States and this was what really mattered to the British decision-makers, though some of them indulged in the rhetoric of "Anglo-Saxondom".' The issue of belligerent maritime rights raised tensions in the late 1920s and dominated the 1929 meeting between President Herbert Hoover (1929–33) and Ramsay MacDonald

(Labour prime minister, 1924, 1929–35). This period of Anglo-American relations was ended by the onset of global economic depression and the rise of international trade protectionism: notably, the 1930 Hawley-Smoot Act in the US and the British 'imperial preference' system, adopted in 1932.

The rise of fascism in Germany, Italy and Japan took place against a background of Anglo-American introversion and unwillingness to act in defence of European or Far Eastern security. Neville Chamberlain (Conservative prime minister, 1937–40) was personally distrustful of the US and rebuffed a suggestion in 1938 by President Franklin Roosevelt (1933–45) that a conference be organized by the world powers on disarmament and economic cooperation. Writing in January 1937, however, British Ambassador to Washington R.C. Lindsay offered an upbeat assessment of Anglo-American relations as Europe began its slide into war. Debts and reparations deriving from World War One constituted 'the only actively sore place in Anglo-American relations'. Regarding future European conflicts, he wrote that it was 'widely held in America that the issue in Europe is the clash between the democratic and the totalitarian or autocratic philosophies of government, and on that question every American is whole-heartedly in sympathy with the former' (Adams (ed.), 1995, Annual Report for 1936, 290–91). Lindsay wrote as if US engagement on Britain's side in a future war against Britain was inevitable. It was not. The US was brought into World War Two by the Japanese attack on Pearl Harbor in December 1941. As late as 1939, the American pro-Hitler German-American Bund held a rally in New York City which attracted over 20 000 people. However, following the 1939 outbreak of war, and especially following his victory in the 1940 presidential election, Franklin Roosevelt's own course did seem clear. US defence spending increased. In December 1940, FDR declared that the US would be the great arsenal of democracy. The destroyers-for-bases deal of September 1940 and, especially, Lend Lease (the aid for Britain programme begun in March 1941) ended US neutrality well before Pearl Harbor.

Anglo-American cooperation in war conditions was organized almost immediately at the White House Arcadia conference between Prime Minister Winston Churchill and Roosevelt. At this conference, Churchill also disclosed the degree to which Britain in the ULTRA programme had broken German ciphers. Only in the

Pacific theatre did General Douglas MacArthur succeed in keeping Anglo-American cooperation at relative arm's length. The intensity and success of wartime cooperation did not mean that tensions were absent. There were disputes over the South American naval block-ade and over the Middle East. Churchill resisted American pressure to dismantle the imperial preference trading system. Roosevelt felt, with some justification, that London was excessively preoccupied with rescuing and enhancing its control of the Empire. The two allies clashed over future roles for Britain in the Balkans. Though Churchill was to emerge in the late 1940s as a strong advocate of high-level negotiation with Moscow, his attitude towards the Soviet Union and its intentions was consistently more antagonistic than Roosevelt's, and his view of the future role of the United Nations more sceptical. The British leader's opinion of President Harry Truman (1945–53) was little short of openly contemptuous. US wartime and immediate post-war diplomacy was increasingly geared to the achievement of a liberal world order, with consequent opposition to British economic protectionism a clear part of Washington's agenda. American use of atomic weapons in Japan in August 1945 seemed to symbolize US domination of a world order in which Britain could enjoy only a junior role. Britain had collabo-rated in the Manhattan Project, the wartime programme to develop the atom bomb, but in a clearly subordinate capacity.

Special Relations

The term 'special relationship' appears to have been coined during the Second World War. Prime Minister Winston Churchill used it in 1943 in a private communication. Foreign Secretary Lord Halifax wrote in July 1940 about 'the possibility of some sort of special association' between Britain and the US. It was, of course, in Churchill's 'iron curtain' speech, delivered at Fulton, Missouri, on 5 March 1946, that the term came to public attention. The British ex-prime minister advocated 'the fraternal association of the English-speaking peoples'. This involved 'a special relationship between the British Commonwealth and Empire and the United States'. The US–UK relationship constituted one of 'three circles of influence' for Britain. Within these circles – the other two involved Britain's relationship with the Commonwealth and with Europe – the

UK could operate as a swing power: not totally integrated into any one circle, but wielding power as a fulcrum within a wheel (Reynolds, 1989, 94). 'Three circles' thinking, which has been enormously influential for the development of post-1945 British foreign policy, tends to insist that the UK does not need to choose between the circles. Successful policy results rather from the simultaneous commitment to all three dimensions. In the post-1960 era, the 'Commonwealth circle' has tended to be replaced by a commitment to influence on a global scale beyond Europe. Andrew Gamble has also made the point that there were always four circles rather than three: 'Once the automatic identity of England and Britain is broken the assumption that the British state is a permanent and inviolable unity dissolves, making the British Union itself a fourth circle of England, and the first in time' (Gamble, 2003, 30). However conceptualized, 'circles' thinking has greatly contributed to the idea that, for British foreign policy, closeness to Washington serves always to enhance, not to destroy, other dimensions of international British influence.

Churchill foresaw the fact but not the extent of the post-war decline in Britain's international power. As America negotiated the early Cold War treaty system, it, not Britain, emerged as the swing power: the centre of the non-communist wheel. Churchill's vision, however, provides the essential starting point for discussion of Anglo-American relations since 1960. Churchill was, as John Charmley (1995, 3) has put it, 'fugleman and midwife' for the Anglo-American alliance. The present book is concerned with various themes which flow from these early visions of Anglo-America and the 'three circles': the nature of the Cold War 'special relationship'; the balance within it between interests and sentiment; the degree to which the relationship, though profoundly asymmetrical, embodied mutuality; the rise of the 'European circle'; and prospects and developments after the Cold War and in the era of the global War on Terror.

This study contends, rather uncontroversially, that a 'special' US–UK relationship did exist, certainly in the Cold War era. Its heart lay in defence and intelligence cooperation, but the relationship extended also to foreign policy. Here it is important to distinguish the 'special relationship' as policy and the 'special relationship' as a state of international interaction. 'Special relationship' as policy has always been almost entirely a British affair.

For David Reynolds (1989, 95–6), the 'special relationship' was largely a British diplomatic strategy to cope with and benefit from American power. As such, it dated back to the turn of the nineteenth and twentieth centuries: 'the use of the special cultural connection to help manage this new and unpredictable actor on the world stage'. It is also salutary to appreciate that the value (real or perceived) of the 'special relationship' was greater to London than to Washington. In 1942, Churchill wished to entice Roosevelt into the British harem, not *vice versa*. It certainly is the case that US–UK closeness is resented by other American allies. French suspicion of 'Anglo-Saxonism' is a long standing diplomatic reality. Adolfo Aguilar Zinser, Mexican ambassador to the United Nations, declared in 2003 that, compared to its 'special' commitment to Britain, America saw its relations with Mexico as '*un noviazgo de fin de semana*' ('a casual weekend fling') (*The Economist*, 18 June 2005, 91). Washington has long enjoyed 'special relationships', in various senses, with many countries: Israel, as well as Mexico, springs to mind. The US certainly has 'special' security and intelligence closeness to Canada. Despite all this, and especially during the Cold War, there certainly was an institutionalized 'special relationship' with Britain, centring on patterns of consultation, nuclear sharing, defence and intelligence cooperation. The Cold War relationship was sustained by what Dean Rusk, US secretary of state under presidents Kennedy and Johnson, called 'the transaction of common business'(Ashton, 2002, 7).

To many diplomats of the Cold War era, the 'special relationship' seemed almost a fact of nature. For James Callaghan (British prime minister, 1976–9) it was obvious after World War Two that 'Anglo-American joint decisions would shape the future' (Callaghan, 1981, 89–90). In the view of Henry Kissinger (national security adviser to President Nixon and secretary of state, 1973–7), the 'special relationship' involved 'a pattern of consultation so matter-of-factly intimate that it became psychologically impossible to ignore British views' (Kissinger, 1979, 90). For Kissinger, the 'special relationship' was 'not a favour the United States granted to the British; rather it was earned, first by conduct during the war and later by the enormous contribution in helping shape the Marshall Plan, the North Atlantic Treaty Organization (NATO), and what generally came to be identified as the Cold War pattern of international relations'. To the conduct of Cold War international relations, according to Kissinger, Britain brought 'experience in a multipolar world, a global orientation of mind, an experienced leadership, a commitment to security, overseas ties of not insignificant proportions, and the English language' (Kissinger, 1995, 99).

The 'special relationship' was not a fact of nature. It was constructed at a particular historical period, the Second World War and continued, indeed thrived, in the conditions of the Cold War. It was certainly rooted in interests. In 1952, Secretary of State Dean Acheson informed the British-American Parliamentary Group that he would not bother 'language, history and all of that': 'What I do wish to stress is one thing we have in common, one desperately important thing, and that is that we have a common fate' (Danchev, 1996, 739).

The 'special relationship' suited the anti-Soviet foreign policy of both countries. The dominant school of interpretation of the 'special relationship' is what Alex Danchev has called 'functionalist': a view which stresses shared interests, as well as frequent friction and negotiated compromises. 'Functionalists' play down the role of sentiment and shared culture. They tend to align themselves with realist interpretations of international relations: the view, that the consolidation and improvement of their power position constitutes the goal of national foreign policies. For Christopher Thorne, there was no need to pursue explanations for US–UK cooperation which 'wander off, however well-meaningly, into mythology'. Implicit in much mainstream interpretation of transatlantic relations is the view that, without shared interests, or in a situation where shared interests are in steep decline, the Anglo-American relationship becomes one of *mere* sentiment, lacking any substance (Thorne, 1979, 725). The survival of US–UK 'special relations well into the post-Cold War era, of course, runs against the grain of this 'functionalist' mindset.

Despite the grounding of (at least the Cold War) alliance in mutual interests, the account of US–UK relations given in this book actually places quite a deal of emphasis on sentiment. In part, this reflects a reaction against 'functionalism' and a commitment to the view that shared history, culture and language do count for something. 'Functionalism' itself, of course, embodied a response to neo-Churchillian accounts of the 'special relationship' which laid inordinate stress on kinship ties and the whole sentimental paraphernalia of 'Anglo America'. The emphasis on culture and sentiment also reflects the need to account for the manifest survival of the 'special relationship' throughout the international upheavals of the post-1990 period. Those British diplomats who sought to promote the specialness of the London-Washington axis had to start somewhere. They started precisely from culture and sentiment.

Though so much recent writing on Anglo-American relations does bear the imprint of 'functionalism' and the realist calculus of interests, it is worth noting that the more general study of American foreign relations has actually been affected considerably since the 1980s by cultural interpretations. The historian Michael Hunt, for example, whose *Ideology and US Foreign Policy* was published in 1987, explicitly located his work in the tradition of cultural study pioneered by Clifford Geertz. For Geertz (1973, 89), 'the concept of culture denotes an historically transmitted pattern of meanings embodied in symbols, a system of inherited conception expressed in symbolic forms by means of which men communicate, perpetuate and develop their knowledge about and attitudes towards life'. In this tradition, values, ideology and beliefs are components of culture, and are seen as both socially constructed and relatively constant. Interests-based realism, of course, remains strongly influential in the academic discipline of international relations, despite the problems posed for realist thought by the circumstances of the Cold War's end. The perceived view of US foreign policy, however, is now clearly one in which culture, which embraces 'sentiment' and values, is seen as centrally significant, and where culture and interests refuse to be unscrambled. In a sense, and usually from a radically divergent political perspective, recent cultural interpretations of American foreign policy represent a reworking of the 'national mission' approach of older writers like Samuel Flagg Bemis.

Britain obviously does not, and cannot, partake of many key elements in American national culture, notably exceptionalism (the belief that the US has a special destiny, usually linked to international democracy-promotion), missionary optimism and belief in the perfectibility of human institutions. These issues will be discussed further in the following chapter. For the moment, let us simply recall that cultural historians and commentators generally accept that shared language, a certain shared history and the 'Anglo' orientation of traditional American elites do affect US–UK relations. British Conservative John Redwood (2005, 68) notes the extent to which, at least in some ways, 'America has preserved eighteenth-century Britain rather better than Britain herself.' Toll roads in the US are called 'turnpikes'; presidents and judges are 'impeached'. Noah Webster, the great American lexicographer, insisted that what appeared to be vulgar American linguistic coinages were usually correct and authentic examples of English eighteenth century speech (Langford, 2000, 84). Alexander DeConde (1992, 197) noted that 'Anglo Americans' never had to face charges of 'unAmericanism' because 'they had created the national ideology'. By the end of the twentieth century, of course, the demographic base of the United States was once again being transformed; this time by immigration from Asia and Latin America.

Subsequent chapters will demonstrate that the history of recent US–UK relations is not one of unremitting and absolute American domination. It goes somewhat against the grain of respectable academic rigour to argue the case for British influence in this way. The argument always stands in danger of being pushed too far or, as with an emphasis on shared culture, collapsing into sentimentality. For many realists the story of international history is the story of the great powers. Henry Kissinger once famously dismissed claims about the importance of Latin American 'middle powers' to the US by asserting that South America was a dagger pointed at the heart of Antarctica (Gray 1996, 249). Yet Kissinger, as we have seen, was a believer in the 'special relationship'. During the Cold War, 'middle powers' used various strategies to enhance their security without undue sacrifice of sovereignty. Britain chose the 'special relationship' and relied on mutual respect and diplomatic skill to achieve its aims. Most academic discussions of 'middle powers' focus on the possibility of combining diplomatic creativity and some level of credible defence self-sufficiency to maximize interests in a regional order (Lee, 1998).

Emphasis on British influence and 'middle power' status should not be taken as a denial of the undoubtedly high degree to which the American alliance impinged on British sovereignty and freedom of action. Kathleen Burk noted in 1998 the dangers of 'supporting the US even when the US does the seemingly insupportable'. British strategy – 'to ensure that Britain remains the US's most dependable ally, in the hope and expectation that the US will remain Britain's' (*The Independent*, 27 August 1998) – did not always work. The 'special relationship', despite US support for European integration, to some extent deceived British policy makers into believing that there was a non-European home. The 'special relationship' also unquestionably bolstered British pomposity and unrealism during the Cold War, making the management of decline even more problematic. Especially invidious here was the notion of Britain acting as Greeks to America's Romans. Harold Macmillan, British prime minister from 1957 to 1963, famously developed the Greeks and Romans analogy during the Second World War. Here is Macmillan addressing the young Richard Crossman at Allied Force Headquarters in Algiers in 1943:

> We, my dear Crossman, are Greeks in this American empire. You will find Americans much as the Greeks found the Romans – great big, vulgar, bustling people, more vigorous than we are and also more idle, with more unspoiled virtues but also more corrupt. We must run AFHQ as the Greek slaves ran the operations of the Emperor Claudius. (Danchev, 1996, 740)

Macmillan confided to his diary in 1944:

> They either wish to revert to isolation combined with suspicion of British imperialism, or to intervene in a pathetic desire to solve in a few months by the most childish and amateurish methods problems which have baffled statesmen for many centuries. Somehow between these two extremes we have got to guide them, both for their own advantage and ours for the future peace of the world. (Macmillan, 1984, 446)

The 'Greeks and Romans' analogy has in many ways been an impediment to the smooth working of the 'special relationship'. It has certainly fuelled American resentments. It has also unquestionably contributed to British delusion about London's global power. British Greeks can also be British self-deceivers. However, it is part of this book's intention to illustrate that the 'special relationship' was not entirely devoid of mutuality. America's part of the Cold War system was one characterized by 'open hegemony' (Ikenberry, 1998–9) and Britain enjoyed a privileged place within it. Influence could be exerted and shared culture increased the chances of British success. America's post-Cold War policies did indeed, as Robert

Cooper put it, have an 'imperial tinge' to them. However, the pursuit and development of the George W. Bush administration's War on Terror illustrated that effective foreign policy for the US could not be achieved without credible, democratic allies. This reality opened the way, at least in theory, for an effective and redefined British recommitment to the US–UK circle of influence.

This book seeks consciously to combine chronological and thematic approaches to the subject of Anglo-American relations from 1960. Chapter 2 deals with mutual attitudes: the ways in which elites and publics on either side of the Atlantic view one another. Chapters 3, 4, 5 and 6 provide a chronological account of US–UK relations as they developed from the Kennedy-Macmillan to the post-Cold War and post-9/11 eras. The concentration here is on foreign policy. Chapter 7 deals with nuclear, defence and intelligence cooperation – the heart of the Cold War relationship and indeed, albeit in changing strategic and institutional contexts, of the post-Cold War and post-9/11 eras as well. Chapter 8 considers how the alliance faced the test of war: Vietnam, the Falklands, and the 1991 and 2003 Iraq conflicts. The ninth chapter is concerned with the interaction between European integration and the 'special relationship'. Ireland, a subject omitted from many conventional US–UK histories, is discussed in Chapter 10. The importance of Ireland to Anglo-American relations is not a new theme; it did, however, become especially prominent after 1992. The final chapter looks back and forwards to offer some general judgements and observations.

2
Transatlantic Attitudes

The point of this chapter is to examine the complex structure of attitudes, emotions and cultural interactions which surrounds and conditions Anglo-American relations. The lexicon of the 'special relationship' has its own characteristic metaphors, rituals and phrases. The memory of Winston Churchill is invoked to bolster the appearance of transatlantic closeness. Lipservice is paid to mutuality and partnership in the theory and practice of what comic writer Stephen Potter dubbed 'hands-across-the-seamanship'. Key 'special relationship' phrases for Potter were: 'We have a lot in common'; 'After all, we come from the same stock'; and 'We have a lot to learn from each other' (Potter, 1970, 263; Danchev, 2005). In fact, every aspect of Anglo-American relations in the later twentieth and early twenty-first centuries has been affected by the radical asymmetry of power which lies at the heart of the relationship. Baldly put, this means that Britain has been far more preoccupied with the US – its impact on and power over the UK – than America has with Britain. For this reason, this chapter will be more concerned with British than with American attitudes.

Much of this chapter is concerned with Anglo-American tension and mutual irritation. To head off false impressions, it should be emphasized that it is extremely easy to find examples of mutual admiration, esteem and profound knowledge of each other's history, politics and culture. American respect for British tradition is balanced by British approval of American inventiveness and democratic purpose. Labour politician Richard Crossman in 1964 recalled his Second World War experience: 'the American military mind delights in innovation, like the American civilian mind' (Howard, 1990, 101). For American historian Warren Kimball, positive feelings are guaranteed by a fundamental convergence of outlook. He quotes Churchill: 'The British and American peoples come together naturally, and without the need of policy and design …. They can hardly help agreeing on three out of four things. They look at things the same way' (Kimball, 2005a, 1). Perusal of the US War Department's 1942 guide to Britain for American servicemen, one is struck as much by its good sense as by its moments (certainly from a distance of over 60 years) of hilarity. American servicemen were informed about the 'orderly and polite' crowds at English soccer matches; according to the War Department, the British 'bobby' is 'not in a hurry' and will 'take plenty of time to talk to you'. Yet it was also emphasized that 'our common speech, our common law, and our ideals of religious freedom were all brought from Britain when the Pilgrims landed at Plymouth Rock'. Most importantly: 'you are higher paid than the British "Tommy". Don't rub it in'. It is 'always impolite to criticize your hosts; it is militarily stupid to criticize your allies' (War Department, 2004).

At elite levels, various institutions and traditions have operated to foster transatlantic closeness. The Rhodes scholarships, for example, were founded in 1902 to facilitate US postgraduate entry to Oxford University. Reviewing British scholarship on the US, Richard Pells (1997, 422) concluded: 'British intellectuals and scholars tended to be more knowledgeable and more dispassionate about the United States than did their colleagues on the Continent.' British Americanists, especially in the Cold War era, benefited from American cultural diplomacy. British specialists on America, 'long distance observers of the US', have also tended to be caught between a desire to write as informed 'insiders', and a felt responsibility to offer comparative and self-consciously 'European' perspectives on the United States (Adams, 1989; Badger, 1992). On the American side, academic work on Britain has often been of very high quality, with important sections of US academic opinion expressing approval for various British institutions and practices. An example is the school of American political scientists who have recommended adoption in the US of British parliamentary and 'responsible party' models.

Americans View Britain

Some traces of the old imperial relationship do remain. Villains in Walt Disney films frequently have English accents. These accents, according to Jonathan Freedland (1998, 73), 'strike a chord with an American audience, reminding them of life before the republic, when they were the subjects of a faraway crown'. When Americans jokingly accept the label 'colonial', it is often not without a considerable degree of archness. When President Reagan wished to indicate his support for his friend Prime Minister Margaret Thatcher, he would refer to America as 'the colonies' (Thatcher, 1993, 435).

During the first half of the twentieth century, references in the US to British imperialism showed no such lightness of touch. The quasi-fascist 'radio priest' Father Charles Coughlin in the 1930s condemned the League of Nations as the 'catspaw of the international bankers of the British Empire'. In granting loans to Britain in 1946, Adam Clayton Powell, the black congressman from Harlem, argued that the US would be 'placing our approval on hypocrisy, imperialism, colonialism and broken pledges'. Hostility to Britain was a central aspect of the pre-1940 US populist tradition, as well as an aspect of particular American ethnic group belief systems (Moser 1999, 94, 181; Moser, 2003). American literary Anglophobes included major figures such as H. L. Mencken and Edmund Wilson. In the 1920s and 1930s, popular anglophobia underpinned an Anglo-American geopolitical rivalry which, at least to some contemporary observers, had the potential to develop into actual warfare (Williams, 2003). Lingering distrust of British imperialism endured on even into the post-1960 era: for example, in the lack of American sympathy for British attachment to the Commonwealth.

By the second half of the century, of course, the pendulum of power had swung westwards. The putative 'American empire', rather than the disintegrating British one, held attention. Writing in 1974, the British poet and critic Stephen Spender (1974, 3) recalled that, one hundred years previously, Ralph Waldo Emerson had described 'the immense advantage' which England enjoyed over America. American thoughts, wrote Emerson, were English thoughts. Now, argued Spender, the reverse was true: 'European thoughts are American thoughts.' The reversal was 'the result of the great, inevitable, ever-predictable shift in wealth, power and civilization from the eastern to the western side of the Atlantic'.

Anglo-American elite and public attitudes have been moulded, especially since the middle years of the twentieth century, by this shift in power. As Colonel Robert R. McCormick of the *Chicago*

Tribune remarked, in an anecdote related by John Kenneth Galbraith: 'The British are no longer important enough for me to dislike' (Galbraith, 1981, 294). For Dean Acheson, American secretary of state from 1949 to 1953, Britain was the country which had lost an empire and not found a role. Readers of the (American) Council on Foreign Relations journal, *Foreign Affairs*, were informed in 1968 that Britain's 'root problem' was that 'she has been attempting for too long to do more than her own capabilities, as currently mobilized and motivated, could support or afford' (Roosa, 1968, 503). Rather poignantly, when the debate over *American* international decline erupted after the defeat in Vietnam, US commentators looked to Britain as a power which had trod this road before. It was even an Englishman, Paul Kennedy, the Yale historian, who gave the most prominent notice of decline in his 1988 book, *The Rise and Fall of the Great Powers*. Samuel Beer (1982, xi), the Harvard University authority on British politics, related the reason given by one of his students for enrolling on one of Beer's courses. The student's father had advised: 'Study England, a country on its knees. That is where America is going.' William Leuchtenberg (1979, 2) wrote in the late 1970s of 'a reversal of our historical relationship'. Where Britain used to perceive the US as the land of the future, the US now looked to Britain for 'experience with a diminished world role and limited economic growth'. Some American critics of the neo-imperialist thrust of post–9/11 US foreign policy urged Washington against replicating the trajectory of Britain's empire (Elkins, 2005).

American populist anglophobia had largely disappeared by about 1960. The explanation for this no doubt is linked into the World War Two and Cold War alliances. The wartime and indeed post–1945 'occupation' of Britain by the US military had complex effects. David Reynolds in his study of the period 1942–1945 noted the very complex results of the mass military experience. It contributed to the 'Americanisation of the United States' – a sharpening of American sense of identity – as much as to the Americanization of the UK (Reynolds, 1995). However, direct US experience of life in Britain was almost bound to call into question the crude certainties of populist anglophobia. The most persuasive explanation for changing American perceptions, however, probably lies in McCormick's remark about Britain being too weak to hate. John Moser (2003, 64) links this point into arguments about the manners of American elites: 'Since Great Britain seems to have lost its cultural monopoly over elite culture in America, it should not be particularly surprising that neither the anti-corporate populists of the Left nor the anti-intellectual populists of the Right bother employing anti-British rhetoric in pursuit of their political goals.'

Despite the decline of populist anti-British feeling in the US, traces of earlier resentments, many of them no doubt richly deserved, do remain. American commentators frequently criticise the 'Anglo' orientation of American foreign policy elites. Eric Alterman, for example, saw 'the driving force' behind US reactions to the 1982 Falklands conflict between Britain and Argentina as 'ethnic solidarity' with the former. According to Alterman, foreign policy 'establishment organizations' like the Council on Foreign Relations and the State Department itself 'remain under the purview of the old Anglo-American elite' (Alterman, 1998, 148). In this updated version of the old anglophobia, Britain may or may not be aggregated into the putative cultural snobbery of European elites. Michael Kelly of the *Washington Post* wrote in 13 June 2001 that Europe's 'elite class' had 'generally cherished a sneering and jingoistic contempt for America and American values'. For Kelly, this attitude 'fulfils an obvious psychological need: as the former ruling class of Europe saw America emerge overwhelmingly superior in economic, political, military and cultural terms, a natural response is to insist on Europe's moral and intellectual superiority'. American commentary on Britain typically invokes class distinction, elitist social rituals and general 'uptightness' as forces worthy of criticism. Donald Rumsfeld, President George W. Bush's secretary for defence, once reportedly found himself, during a NATO summit, being required to sit through a modern dance and poetry performance. When asked for his reaction, he replied: 'I'm from Chicago' (Macintyre, 2005). Admittedly, the summit was in Prague; but Rumsfeld's reaction would scarcely have been different, even if it had been in London – or, indeed in New York. A 1990 piece in the *Washington Post* entitled 'Uptight Little Island', compared the crowd at Royal Ascot to 'the Cherokee medicine men on their reservations who, for a small fee, dress up in funny costumes and dance for rain' (Stephens, 1990). In this immediate post-Cold War period there was actually something of a modest revival in journalistic Britain-bashing. James Fallows, for example, wrote about the 'British con', a phenomenon which apparently stretched from 'status names' for American babies like Simon and Nigel, to the journal, *The Economist*. Who, asked Fallows, 'are the Brits to give economic advice to anybody?'(Lewis, 1991, 9).

US perceptions of Britain are greatly complicated by the problem of 'British', 'English', and 'Anglo' identity. As Andrew Gamble (2003, 42–3) reminds us, the Roman term, 'Britain' was revived in the sixteenth century as a synonym for 'England' and in the twentieth century as a term designating England, Scotland and Wales, possibly Northern Ireland as well. The term 'Kingdom of Great Britain' came into use after 1707. The 'United Kingdom of Great Britain and Ireland' was formed in 1801 and the 'United Kingdom of Great Britain and Northern Ireland' in 1921. It is all very confusing, and the various terms defy serious unscrambling. However defined, the 'British' imprint on American society, beliefs and institutions is strong. It is important to appreciate that Scots, Irish, Welsh and, to add to the confusion, Scots-Irish immigrants from Ulster all played important roles in the American founding and development. David Hackett Fisher (1989) has analysed late twentieth century society in terms of original (largely British) settler 'folkways': Puritan, Quaker, Cavalier, and Scots-Irish. Ulster actually had a special role in American political development, with five men with roots in the Irish province signing the Declaration of Independence. Andrew Jackson, James Polk, Ulysses S. Grant, Grover Cleveland, William McKinley and Woodrow Wilson are just some of the US presidents with direct Ulster descent. It is also important to remember, as Arthur Schlesinger (1996) reminds us, that 'America was a multi-ethnic society from the start.' In the late eighteenth century, Hector St John de Crevecoeur described his fellow settlers: 'a mixture of English, Scotch, Irish, French, Dutch, Germans and Swedes'. We read in William Bradford's *of Plymouth Plantation*, written between 1630 and 1650: 'Our fathers were Englishmen which came over the great ocean, and were ready to perish in this wilderness'. At one level at least, the American War of Independence was fought for 'English' values. As Benjamin Franklin put it: 'It was a resistance in ... favour of the liberties of England' (Huntington, 2005, 47). Scots-Irish and English identities are frequently intermingled. The elite American Anglophile, patron of English institutions, is an easily identified twentieth-century phenomenon. Paul Mellon donated millions of dollars to Cambridge and Oxford universities, to the Royal Veterinary College, the Tate

Gallery and the Fitzwilliam Museum in Cambridge. A graduate of Clare College, Cambridge, Mellon became a leading collector of English rural painting and an honorary member of the Jockey Club. Paul Mellon's grandfather had actually emigrated to the US from Northern Ireland. One of the best known recent American Anglophiles was John Paul Getty III, widely known as an extraordinarily generous patron of English cricket. Figures like Mellon and Getty, albeit in extreme form, personify America's 'Anglo' culture. Twentieth-century Anglo-American elite connections were anchored in formal and informal networks such as the Ditchley conferences and in figures such as Marietta Tree, born a Peabody from New England, whose Anglo-American connections almost defined a generation. John Jay wrote in the second *Federalist*, in 1789, of America's connectedness to 'the same ancestors', seeing this as a strong and happy force for social cohesion (Rossiter (ed.) 1961, 9).

Despite the self-consciously 'Anglo' orientation of many traditional American elites, it should be clearly recognized that by the middle of the twentieth century less than half the US population were of British stock. By the first decade of the following century, 'deAngloing' and wider demographic change were at the centre of national debates about identity, purpose and international orientation. By the year 2000, only about one in ten of the population actually claimed any British ancestry. According to President Bill Clinton, the US actually needed a 'third revolution', in the wake of the American Revolution and the civil rights movement, to 'prove that we literally can live without having a dominant European culture' (*The Economist*, 13 November 2004, 56). We do not need to enter the debate about what Samuel Huntington (2005) sees as the erosion of foundational 'Anglo-Protestant culture' to appreciate that demographic change does have implications for American attitudes towards Britain (Coker, 1992; Citrin *et al.*, 1994).

To many Americans in the post-1960 era, Englishness – or, perhaps, the 'English' element in 'Britishness' – has tended to evoke images of a kind of haughtiness in rags: a refusal to acknowledge that the days of empire were spent. George Ball, adviser to Presidents Kennedy and Johnson, was an anglophile of British descent, yet he recorded in his memoirs his impatience at British attitudes after 1945: British diplomats 'thought of their country as on a different level from the nations of the continent; being a co-victor (of the Second World), it should deal with the United States as an equal'. Ball also recorded his irritation at the way British people tend to view American English as a 'quaint variant of their own language' (Ball, 1982, 81, 209). The 'haughtiness in rags' theme also appears in the account given by George Shultz, President Reagan's Secretary of State, of British reactions to America's failure to follow London's bidding on a United Nations vote on the Falkland Islands. According to Shultz (1993, 152), Sir Oliver Wright, Margaret Thatcher's ambassador to Washington, 'on instructions, read me off like a sergeant would in a Marine Corps boot camp'.

American public attitudes to the UK are generally positive. A 1976 Gallup poll revealed 87 per cent of American respondents declaring a 'favourable' opinion of the UK. In 1989, a parallel poll found 86 per cent still expressing their positive view. In both polls, Britain was beaten only by Canada, which had 91 per cent 'favourable' in 1976 and 92 per cent in 1987. Mexico had scores of 75 in 1976 and 62 in 1989. A 1996 Gallup poll had Britain cited as 'very favourable' by 30 per cent. Again Britain was beaten only by Canada. In 1996, France and Germany achieved 'very favourable' rates of 15 and 17 respectively. In 1994, 54 per cent of Americans saw the UK as a 'very valuable ally'. France achieved a score of 19, Germany 15 and Japan 9 (*The Gallup Poll*, 1990, 98; 1997, 174; 1995, 93). British support for the post-9/11 War on Terror, and especially participation in the 2003 invasion of Iraq, was reflected in clear pro-British (and decidedly anti-French) sentiment in subsequent polling.

Over the years, Gallup has also conducted occasional polls in the US which touch on Anglo-American relations in specific or quirky ways. In 1982, of those who knew about the Falklands crisis – the poll was taken in April – 2 per cent of Americans wished to aid Argentina and 17 per cent wished to help Britain, while 65 per cent wished to stay out altogether. Overall, 15 per cent 'sympathized' with Argentina, with 50 per cent supporting Britain. A 1984 poll had 60 per cent of Americans believing that Britain enjoyed 'a great deal of freedom', compared to 44 per cent believing that the same was true for France. In 1995, when Americans were asked to rate countries on a one-to-one scale in terms of freedom of the individual, 22 per cent scored Britain at nine or ten, a total beaten only by Canada (36 per cent) and the US itself (51). A 1994 poll, taken on the fiftieth anniversary of D-Day asked both the British and American public to name the nation – the US, the USSR or the

UK – which had contributed most to victory in the Second World War. Britons voted 18 per cent for the US, nine per cent for the Soviet Union and 37 for the UK. Americans opted 13 per cent for Britain, 11 for the USSR and 65 per cent for America. When, also in 1994, Americans were asked whether they thought Britain spied on the US, 43 per cent replied in the affirmative (the figure for Japan was 79 per cent); 17 per cent felt that the Central Intelligence Agency should spy on Britain (*The Gallup Poll* 1983, 99; 1985, 21; 1996, 251; 1995, 93, 37).

American mass attitudes towards Britain appear considerably more consistent than British attitudes towards the US. Events and personalities in Britain occasionally cause ripples in American public opinion. Margaret Thatcher was unquestionably the most well recognized and popular British leader of the later Cold War era. Generally, however, events in the UK rarely permeate through to US public opinion in a way that will alter long held views. Chicago Council on Foreign Relations surveys reveal that Americans certainly see the US as having 'a vital interest' in the alliance with Britain, although, as with virtually all countries, policy leaders see more 'vital' an interest than do the general public. The CCFR also conducted 'thermometer' ratings, testing public 'warmth' towards various countries, in 1982, 1986 and 1990. In each year Canada was the only country to exceed the temperature achieved by the UK (Rielly, 1991, 85, 88). Yet, as the Gallup poll on the Falklands crisis indicated, Americans, certainly in the pre-9/11 era, tended to be very cautious about troop commitment, even to help a valued ally. The Vietnam War was the clear watershed here. A 1975 Gallup poll, taken in the year of South Vietnam's defeat, showed only 18 per cent of Americans favouring troop commitment even if England were invaded by 'communists' (*The Gallup Poll*, 1978, 473).

As already indicated, American attitudes towards Britain during the post-9/11 era were strongly influenced by the Blair government's forthright foreign policy and military support for the War on Terror, and especially for the war in Iraq. Since public attitudes are fairly predictably positive in any case, the 'Blair effect' was perhaps most conspicuous at elite levels. GlobeScan and University of Maryland polling in 2005 revealed an American public which still had an overwhelmingly positive attitude towards the UK. Only 15 per cent of those Americans polled saw Britain as having a generally nega-tive influence in the world, compared to 52 per cent with negative views of France (Kull, 2005, 36). In certain quarters, especially on the fringes of American neo-conservatism, the notion of 'British America' was revived, with its implied approval for a new Anglo-American, 'Anglospheric' imperialism (Bennet, 2004). At times a cult of Blair threatened even to rival transatlantic veneration for the memory of Winston Churchill. For Republican Congressman Curt Weldon of Pennsylvania, Blair was 'the Winston Churchill of the 21st century' (*Congressional Record*, 9 April 2003, H3047). Senator John Warner of Virginia foresaw future historians would someday 'parallel the Churchill-Roosevelt era with the Bush-Blair era' (*Congressional Record*, 4 February 2004, S580). It may be imagined that Blair's Republican admirers might have been slightly disconcerted to realise that this was also the British leader whose government presided over the outlawing of foxhunting.

Class, Parent and Child

Two particular subjects clamour for admittance to any discussion of transatlantic perceptions. Both are sources of tension and complexity. These two subjects are social class and the parent-child relationship. In reference to class, the British press often comments on the fascination which Americans supposedly take in the business and troubles of the British royal family. The implication of such stories is that a democratic, monarch-less nation is missing something. Journalist Ben Bradlee reported the interest shown in elite British affairs by his friend, President John Kennedy. America's first Irish Catholic president was apparently deeply fascinated by the 1963 Profumo scandal: 'It combined so many of the things that interested him: low doings in high places, the British nobility, sex and spying'. Seymour Hersh suggests that JFK may also have had more direct, personal reasons for being interested in the scandal (Hersh, 1997, 391). Americans might sometimes show a surprising interest in the upper reaches of British society, but the US has traditionally sought to define itself against a constructed image of European, especially English, society. George Washington, in his 1796 Farewell Address, warned of the dangers of going too far. Americans should avoid 'excessive dislike' of any country (Maidment and Dawson (eds.) 1994, 251) – even Britain. Populist anglophobia may have largely disappeared in the United States, yet Freedland points out that still 'among Americans, Britain is often a byword for non-democracy'. Jim Andrews, campaign manager for the Democrat challenger to Senator Jesse Helms in North Carolina, remarked in 1996: 'Jesse Helms is campaigning for the United States Senate, not the House of Lords.' He might not like it, but in the US he has to face the verdict of the people (Freedland, 1998, 73).

British intellectuals have often been attracted by American class-lessness, not to mention American opportunity and job prospects. In his 1990 travel book, Jonathan Raban described the experience of sailing to the New World in a container vessel: 'the ship, so enormous in Liverpool, so lordly in the Irish Sea, was dwindling into a dot, a cell of dry little British jokes, fine little British caste distinctions and surprisingly formal British manners' (Raban, 1990, 31). Philosopher-politician Bryan Magee, and Member of Parliament and later journalist Matthew Parris, are examples of young Englishmen for whom exposure to the innovative and democratic intellectual life provided by United States higher education proved a liberating experience (Magee, 1997; Parris, 2003). Magee travelled to the US for the first time in 1955 with 'a full set of anti-American prejudices ...: cultural, English, European and left-wing'. He found them all confounded (Magee, 1990). For the young Malcolm Bradbury (1980, 119), American culture provided an escape from the 'constraining class-oriented, provincial embrace' of Britain. Many British intellectuals have no doubt shared the reported reaction of Isaiah Berlin to the US: simultaneously attracted by its democratic vitality and amused by its vulgarity (Ignatieff, 1998, 102). When historian J.H. Plumb first visited America, he spent hours in a 'supermarket just watching' as people loaded up 'carloads of foods' (Pells, 1997, 164).

The parent-child theme is evident in William Bradford's *of Plymouth Plantation*, quoted above. In the character of Alden Pyle in *The Quiet American*, British novelist Graham Greene created a mythic type of American adolescent earnestness. Pyle's character was based on Edward Lansdale in 1950s Vietnam. Greene once wrote of 'the eternal adolescence of the American mind' (Sherry, 1990, 592). For Dennis Brogan, admirer of and commentator on American democracy, American leaders often acted like 'children in world politics', disavowing, in the words of John Adams (US president from 1797 to 1801) 'any notion of cheating anybody' (Brogan, 1959, 21). Parent-child relationships are clearly apparent in the seminal notion of Britain playing 'Greeks' to America's 'Romans' in international politics. In his portrayal of the Glass-Marnham friendship in his novel, *The Innocent* originally published in 1990 and subtitled *The Special Relationship*, Ian McEwan parodied received versions of transatlantic innocence and experience. The notion of American infancy/adolescence is apparent in the following observation by Jonathan Raban regarding the US in the 1980s: 'The great success of Reagan's presidency, it seemed to me, was that he had somehow managed to assure a large number of people that they were actually living in the America of Macy's Thanksgiving Day Parade' (Raban, 1990, 124).

A key text here is D. H. Lawrence's *Studies in Classic American Literature*, written in 1923. For Lawrence, American culture was a culture of rebellion: 'somewhere deep in every American heart lies a rebellion against the old parenthood of Europe. Yet no American feels he has completely escaped its mastery. Hence the slow, smouldering, corrosive obedience to the old master Europe, the unwilling subject, the unremitting opposition.' America's adolescent rebellion has, according to Lawrence (1977, 4), 'given the Yankee his kick'. A character in Lawrence's 1926 novel, *The Plumed Serpent*, saw the new American continent as representing the 'life-breath of materialism' and threatening to 'destroy what the other continents had built up' (Rubin and Rubin, 2004, 47). Interestingly, Alexis de Tocqueville described the US as a country where, in particular American families, paternal authority was in fast retreat (McGiffert (ed.) 1964, 49). The themes of the 'American Adam' and the 'new man', common critical constructs in both American and European discussions of American culture, are clearly apposite here. The idea of American cultural rebellion is a fruitful one, and should not be confused with European disdain for the antics of its adolescent offspring. Yet simple disdain does exist. British journalist Keith Botsford (1990) compared an America which 'has little tolerance of suffering and unhappiness' to a child feeling 'deprived by being denied a sweet'. Such sentiments are a legitimate cause of American resentment. Here is Tom Wolfe in *Bonfire of the Vanities* on Peter Fallow, his sponging Englishman in the Big Apple: 'Like more than one Englishman in New York, he looked upon Americans as hopeless children whom Providence had perversely provided with this great swollen fat fowl of a Continent.' Relieving Americans of their money was simply sporting, 'since they would only squander it in some tasteless and useless fashion' (Wolfe, 1987, 164). Like adolescent rebels the world over, Americans are often seen by Britons as seeking to shock: of veering to extremes of individualism, acquisitiveness, insularity, lack of taste, occasionally of Puritanism, not to mention unreflective responses to communism and Islamic terrorism. When he went to work in the US, Conservative politician George Walden (1999, 220, 222) began 'searching, semi-consciously, as Europeans do, for the essence of the country'. He found 'many essences'. One was provided by a Reaganite denizen of Arizona. Walden records this man's views on foreign relations: 'Can't see no need for Americans to go abroad. Never figured out why we went to Vietnam. Could have nuked them from here.'

British Anti-Americanism

It is incumbent on all who write about 'anti-Americanism' to avoid using the term as a blunt instrument with which to undercut legitimate, policy-specific criticism of the United States. Peter Kilfoyle, former junior defence minister under Tony Blair and critic of British and American policy in Iraq, made a reasonable point about this during Bush's 2003 visit to London: 'No Mr Blair, it is not knee-jerk anti-Americanism which holds sway in the UK. It is the reaction of one old friend to another when the latter is acting wholly unreasonably and unacceptably' (Kilfoyle, 2003). Disentangling legitimate criticism from generalized hostility is very difficult. Yet it is undeniable that generalized, unreflective hostility to the US does exist, and that it was very much in evidence around the time of the Bush visit. As good an effort as any to define 'anti-Americanism' is that attempted by Barry and Joyce Colp Rubin (2004, ix). They contend that anti-Americanism exhibits one or more of the following characteristics: 'antagonism to the United States that is systemic, seeing it as completely and inevitably evil'; any 'view that greatly exaggerates America's shortcomings'; the 'deliberate misrepresentation of the nature or policies of the United States for political purposes'; and 'misrepresentation of American society, policies, or goals which falsely portrays them as ridiculous or malevolent'. Above all, anti-Americanism, however difficult it may be in practice to distinguish it from the kind of criticism offered by Kilfoyle, tends to deny American diversity. There are many Americas; anti-Americans conflate American diversity into a hated or despised unity.

To many American observers, any anti-Americanism in Britain pales in comparison to the hostility to the US supposedly evident in continental Europe. According to Herbert J. Spiro (1988, 124), there has been in Britain, 'virtually no cold war anti-Americanism and less of the policy-specific kind than in major Continental countries, regardless of whether Conservative or Labour governments have been in office'. Despite Samuel Johnson's observation that he was willing to love all mankind, except an American, some of the most celebrated of anti-American statements have come from continental European pens. The German poet Heinrich Heine (1797–1856) was 'afraid of a country where the people chew tobacco, where they play ninepin without a king and spit without a spittoon'. For Georges Duhamel, the legs of American women were 'too beautiful … as if they had come off an assembly line'. In 1984, Nicole Bernheim described Reaganite America in familiar, if unabashed, parent-child terms. The US was 'Europe in its infancy, a country on its way to becoming European, but which is not there yet' (Schulte, 1986, 14; Sorman 1990, 214).

It is important, of course, not to regard particular, and often ill-informed, expressions of cultural condescension as authentically continental European. In Alexis de Tocqueville (1805–59), France, after all, gave us probably the most perceptive of all outside commentators on the United States. Jean Baudrillard's (1988, 79) portrait of America, as the site of a globalizing postmodernist culture of surface and consumption, combined insight with condescension: 'If, for us' wrote Baudrillard, 'society is a carnivorous flower, history for them is an exotic one. Its fragrance is no more convincing than the bouquet of Californian wines'. Rob Kroes (1999, 72) saw European critical constructions of America as incorporating three main dimensions: spatial (American surface 'flatness' versus European verticality and hierarchy), temporal (the lack of an American awareness of the past) and holistic/fragmentary (the absence of cultural cohesion in the US). Continental European anti-Americanism traces its intellectual and philosophical roots to nineteenth century notions of America as the transmitter of shallow, materialist newness: the United States as an imperialist agent of the mind, denying history and infusing the Old World with the vapid amorality of mass society. Such notions may be seen as the negative side of the idea, derived from Hegel and taken over by Leo Strauss and American neo-conservatives, of 'freedom' moving westwards (Ceaser, 2004).

Such notions do not fit all that easily within the more pragmatic, earthbound British tradition. We have, however, already seen the characteristic themes of continental West European anti-Americanism being articulated by a character in D. H. Lawrence's *The Plumed Serpent.* Yet Britain has also long performed the role of 'cultural broker' between the US and continental Europe. The British like to regard themselves as less defensive than other Western Europeans, more assured and more sophisticated in their understanding of, and ability to deal with, American power. John Nott, secretary of state for defence under Prime Minister Margaret Thatcher expressed this view in the following way: 'perhaps the British lack that sense of inferiority – posing as superiority – that seems to dominate so much of the European attitude to the United States' (Nott, 2002b, 70). It is also unquestionably the case that the supposed virulence of continental European, especially French, anti-Americanism has tended to obscure the existence of anti-Americanism in Britain. To many French intellectuals, as Theodore Zeldin (1990, 37) notes, their British counterparts have simply been corrupted by American money and power: 'many British writers ... not only found a good market for their books in the US, but often obtained their first success there'.

Anyone who has lived for any length of time in Britain, certainly anyone who has taught American Studies there, knows that any confidence in the absence of British anti-Americanism is misplaced. British attitudes towards the US often exhibit cultural snobbery, envy, crude stereotyping and resentment at America's power in the world. Such attitudes do not, as we will see demonstrated in public opinion surveys, amount to a rabid hostility. In many ways, they are understandable expressions of group feeling towards an ever-present and powerful 'other'. Many of these attitudes – that, for example, the US is the land both of rampant, destructive individualism and of homogenized sameness – are inherently contradictory. It is absurd, however, to pretend that they do not exist.

At its most superficial, British anti-Americanism consists in rather unreflective, often comic, stereotyping. British commentators frequently write about Americans as creatures from another planet. Julian Critchley, Conservative Member of Parliament for

Aldershot, indulged himself in 1991 in comic speculation about why Americans were quite so gullible: 'could it be the deleterious effects of the hot Californian sun upon the Anglo-Saxon or the inbred nature of American mountain men?' (Critchley, 1991). A key feature of such comment is the implied conclusion that failure to appreciate the joke simply confirms American humourlessness. Due to their exposure to US popular culture and to political reporting on the US, British students tend to approach the study of America in a confident frame of mind, albeit one filled with the familiar stereotypes. Rob Singh (2001, 132) describes the ' "entry-point" student notions about American politics' as follows: 'Americans are religious extremists or bigots, gun enthusiasts, and are not a particularly tolerant people.' African Americans 'are poverty-stricken (celebrities aside), the South remains fundamentally racist and America is being overtaken by Hispanics'. American elections are 'entirely based on personality and looks'. Money determines success and 'the Democrats and Republicans are two right-wing parties with no real differences between them'. Americans are held in this world of popular British distortion and half-truth to be incapable of irony, a notion which survives despite frequent repeats on British TV of 'Sergeant Bilko'. Gore Vidal (1994, 255) responded thus to the irony-deficit charge : 'The British can recognise "irony" only when it is dispensed with an old auntie-ish twinkle … while Americans have yet to discover such a thing. Once we do, the national motto will produce gargantuan laughter from sea to shining sea. *E pluribus unum* indeed!'

Analysis of British anti-Americanism is made difficult by the existence in the UK of unreflective attitudes towards many countries other than the US. In this connection, anti-*Americanism* is given added poignancy by the peculiar power relationship between the two countries after 1945. The British popular press is inclined to present American problems and misfortunes in terms which indicate a degree of satisfaction and 'it serves them right'. As will be discussed later in this chapter, such attitudes were not entirely absent from the British response to the terror attacks of 11 September 2001. It is also clearly the case that expressions of hostility to the US are more socially acceptable than the voicing of similar sentiments towards poorer and less powerful nations and peoples. It is important, though difficult, to distinguish legitimate, policy-specific disagreements from a more deep-seated, negativistic anti-Americanism. For the sake of analysis, let us attempt a typology of British anti-Americanism. The following varieties appear to present themselves: cultural concerns, leftist criticism and nationalism. Each variety embraces genuine and legitimate concerns, but each also has the potential to slide across into unreason.

We have already encountered several examples of anti-American cultural condescension. At its crudest this condescension manifests itself in simple snobbery and rudeness. James Fallows, himself a former Rhodes scholar, commented in 1994 on Bill Clinton's experience as a student at Oxford in the era of the Vietnam War: 'during his time Rhodes scholars were supervised by a warden who viewed most of the scholars as if they'd just come in from eating woodchucks or inbreeding up in the hills' (Greig, 1994). More broadly and excusably, British cultural concerns tend to centre on the putative 'Americanization' of British life. For J. B. Priestley, for example, the 'Americanized' England of mass consumerism 'wasn't really England at all' (Haseler, 1996, 91). Such anxieties are not new. In 1900, the House of Commons debated the supposed effects on national morality of American plays being performed on the London stage. Frank Costigliola (1984a, 39) quotes a London newspaper attacking American films in the 1920s: 'The film is to America what the flag was once to Britain. By its means Uncle Sam may hope some day, if he be not checked in time, to Americanize the world.' By 1990, around 90 per cent of all British cinema box office receipts were for American films. John Lennon once remarked that he had been 'half American' ever since he heard his first Elvis Presley record. A 1997 discussion of 'British cultural identity' pointed to 'the McDonaldisation of Britain', a phenomenon related both to the casualization of work in service industries and to the 'increased importance of standardization and quantity' (Storry and Childs, 1997, 318). This process links, of course, into the debate over the supposed global penetration of American mass culture. Like other aspects of anti-Americanism, protests against British cultural Americanization should not automatically be written off as snobbish and reactive. Yet such protests do often partake of such qualities. Richard Pells argues that, for 'writers, teachers and members of the clergy in Britain, West Germany and Italy, the opposition to "Americanization" was motivated, in large part, by a desire to preserve their position as cultural and moral leaders'. Much Americanization actually is either unnoticed or is, indeed, welcomed by many British people. It should also be remembered that cultural influence is a two-way street. In the 1960s, the Beatles returned to the US market a revived and reworked brand of 'American' music. A similar phenomenon occurred in the 1980s and 1990s in relation to New York's Broadway musicals (Pells, 1997, 238, 319).

There clearly is a class dimension to this. Where residents of Hampstead campaign against siting a McDonalds restaurant there, many working-class Britons welcome the convenience and democracy of fast food. Many upper-class and high-income people in the UK have strong personal or business links to the US. However, Alexander Chancellor's comment rings true. Growing up in 1940s and 1950s Britain, the future editor of the *New Yorker* felt: 'The upper class was generally more anti-American than the working class, because it felt more directly affronted by America's assumption of Britain's former role as a world power.' 'American' comforts like air conditioning and central heating were 'seen as unhealthy and debilitating' (Chancellor, 1999, 4). In 1957, Kenneth Tynan advised anyone attempting to succeed in British cultural life to 'adopt a patronizing attitude to anything popular or American' (Wilford, 2003, 273). There is also a strong generational dimension to British cultural anti-Americanism. The young are keen consumers of American popular culture and American pop music has given the world a means to articulate youthful rebellion. It is impossible to generalize on these issues with any precision. Anti-Americanism in the second half of the twentieth century has been complicated by conflicting emotions of hurt national pride and respect for the Atlantic alliance, by differing perceptions of America's role in Second World War (saviours or Johnny-come-latelies?) and by attitudes towards Europe. However, it is at least worth mentioning that much of Britain's popular press has been more conspicuously intent on Euro – rather than America – bashing. Here is a *Sun* editorial from the early days of the 1990 Gulf crisis: 'Just like old times, isn't it? The Anglo-American partnership, linchpin of victory in the world wars, swings into action again ... our only constant friends and reliable allies in the world are the Yanks. Buddies, we're so glad to be with you again' (*The Sun*, 10 September 1990). Compare this to the weary pessimism of the *Daily Telegraph*, reacting to the 1995 murder of London headmaster Philip Lawrence: 'Given how Britain invariably follows the pattern of America after a decade or so, the recent experience of American teachers shows how dangerous life could yet become' (Freedland, 1998, 12).

The second type of British anti-Americanism emanates clearly from the political left. Leftist anti-Americanism focuses on the imperialist thrust of American foreign policy, on the insidious influence of American intelligence agencies, and on the role of the US as standard bearer for global capitalism. The particular direction of left-wing attack has shifted over the years. It clearly also has varied enormously across the spectrum of reformist, revolutionary, communist and non-communist leftism, although it is far from the case that anti-Americanism has always and invariably gained in strength the further left one travels across the spectrum. In 1957, Aneurin Bevan complained about America's claims to have won World War Two for the cause of freedom. He castigated the US for, in effect, forcing Britain to shoulder 'a crippling burden of arms spending' after 1945 (Bevan, 1957, 65). Forty-one years later, Ken Livingstone, left-wing Labour MP and subsequently mayor of London, wrote that US intelligence had 'managed to place someone sympathetic in virtually every new Labour ministry and achieve an almost complete dominance at the Ministry of Defence' (Livingstone, 1998, 49). Not always unreasonably, nuclear issues have raised extreme passions. Bertrand Russell, philosopher and anti-nuclear arms activist, wrote in 1966 that American soldiers were being sent to Vietnam 'to protect the riches of a few men in the United States'. A veteran visitor to the US and the possessor of great knowledge of things American, Russell had by this time come to hold very extreme views, going so far as to urge Soviet involvement in Vietnam (Hollander, 1992, 374; Monk, 2001, 469).

Several points need to be clarified concerning leftist British anti-Americanism. Firstly, much such sentiment reflects cultural attitudes as well as socialist values. In the early 1950s, for example, E. P. Thompson wrote of the 'American Dream' as 'childish and debased'. Sinclair Lewis's *Babbit* (1922), the story of a culturally retarded, acquisitive house agent, according to Thompson, 'only foreshadows the horrors of today' (Cunliffe, 1986, 25). In fairness, it should be conceded that opposition to American cultural imperialism does not always rest entirely on cultural condescension. It was, after all, Coca-Cola president James Farley who boasted that his product contained the 'essence of capitalism' in every bottle

(Wall, 1991, 113). Second, generalized leftist hostility to the US serves only to obscure and make more difficult the rational criticism of particular American policies. This was the case, for example, in the early 1980s, when the personal unpopularity of President Reagan in leftist and liberal circles distorted perceptions. The British left often found attractive the 'equivalence' doctrine regarding the US and USSR: the, surely always flawed, view that the US was as 'undemocratic' and destructive of freedom as the Soviet Union. With the onset of Reagan's presidency, more people on the British left came to hold Jan Morris's (1983) opinion that 'the greatest threat to the peace of humanity is the United States' (Hollander, 1992, 389). This phenomenon recurred during the presidency of George W. Bush. Third, it must be emphasized that important sections of the British left have been attracted by the democratic and innovative qualities of American society, quite apart from the pragmatic arguments, accepted by post-1945 Labour Party leaderships, for maintaining close American ties Anthony Crosland announced in 1962 his opposition to the view that 'America is run in this crude way by a capitalist power elite'. Compared to Britain, in Crosland's view, America was 'relatively classless, and in some ways a much more democratic country' (Cunliffe, 1986, 21). Although it is misleading to assume that anti-Americanism, as a generalized impulse rather than as policy-specific criticism, automatically gains in strength the further left we travel, it is no surprise that the social democrat-revisionist wing of the Labour Party has tended to see the US classless competition as a model for Britain to follow. For Hugh Gaitskell, Labour Party leader in the very early 1960s, the US represented, as it did for Crosland, the avatar of modernity (Brivati, 1996, 148). By the early 1990s, the idea of US-Soviet 'equivalence' had vanished in the rubble of the vanishing assumptions of the era of the Cold War. The way was open for a new generation of Croslandites and Gaitskellites, incarnated in Tony Blair's New Labour, to revive the notion of America as a model for progressive British political and economic development. Writing in the vanguard of Blairite modernization, Will Hutton argued that there was a 'powerful impulse towards charity and solidarity in US culture' alongside 'competition and the primacy of markets' (Hutton, 1996, 261). President Clinton's Balkans policies in the late 1990s, along with US sponsorship in the same period of economic globalization, did provoke leftist protest in the UK. However, only with the emergence of the intense and febrile opposition to the foreign policies of the administration of President George W. Bush did anti-Americanism regain its hold on large sections of the British left.

Nationalism as an element in British anti-Americanism (our third category) exists across a wide political and cultural spectrum. A sense of hurt national pride emerges, for example, from Tony Benn's diaries. On 1 June 1967, for example, Benn recorded in his diary that Prime Minister Harold Wilson was being received in Washington 'with all the trumpet appropriate for a weak foreign head of state who has to be buttered up so that he can carry the can for American foreign policy' (Benn, 1987, 501). Again, it is important to emphasize that concerns for Britain's dignity and national sovereignty, in the face of the decidedly asymmetrical 'special relationship', do not amount to an insupportable, undiscriminating anti-Americanism. Subsequent chapters will make it clear that such concerns flowed rather naturally from the very structure of Cold War Anglo-American relations. Nationalist anti-Americanism, however, has strong roots in romantic attachments to Britain's imperial past. Julian Amery, long-time representative of imperialist High Tory anti-Americanism, in 1953 condemned the US for undermining European empires: 'European leaders have reluctantly to admit that, if the Soviet Union is the greatest danger to their national and imperial interests, the greatest injuries so far inflicted on them have come from the United States' (Wheen, 1996). Revisionist accounts of the post-1940 'special relationship' blame a combination of poor British leadership, American mischief and the 'European idea' for destroying British greatness (Charmley, 1995). High Tory anti-Americanism was carried into the post-1960 era most conspicuously by Enoch Powell (Conservative, and subsequently Ulster Unionist politician) and Alan Clark, a defence minister under Prime Ministers Thatcher and Major. In January 1991, Clark wrote in his diary in regard to nuclear modernization: 'I see it as most unwelcome that the US should have implied power of veto over our ballistic systems, still further concentration of power in the Washington dung-heap' (Clark, 1993, 394). A notorious piece by Clark published in the *Daily Telegraph* in 1984 portrayed the US military as representing a morally corrupt people addicted to chewing gum and Chesterfields (*Independent* Profile, 1990). If High Tory anti-Americanism has been associated with nationalism, it has also partaken of cultural condescension and dislike of American democracy. Enoch Powell's anti-Americanism, which at times seemed to place him to the left of the Labour Party on defence issues, involved a fear of the American mob. In a 1970 election address, Powell announced: 'The actual policy and administration of the United States has been altered, and altered again, not only by the votes of the electors or the decisions of the Congress, but by the fact or the fear of crowd behaviour' (Powell, 1972, 79).

Our three categories – cultural, leftist, nationalist – do not exhaust the range of British anti-Americanism. There is arguably a pro-European variant, represented in the ambivalent attitudes towards the US characteristic of Prime Minister Edward Heath. Writing in this vein in 1992, pro-Europe Labour MP Giles Radice (1992, 121) observed that, despite the language, the US always appeared more foreign than continental Europe: 'The reason is that one misses the familiar European reference points – the old cities and towns, the medieval churches, the long-settled landscape.' In 1994, Hugo Young wrote a series of pieces in *The Guardian* on the theme of Britain 'sleeping with America when we should be courting Europe'. British anti-Americanism is rarely a virulent phenomenon. The apparently widespread hatred of President George W. Bush, especially in 2002–4, was unusual. British anti-Americanism more normally reflects the complexities and hurt feelings associated with the process whereby children become more powerful than their parents. The British are characteristically eager to find fault with the US, to bring the errant offspring to heel. They also seek approval and validation (witness the huge sales in Britain of Bill Bryson's *Notes from a Small Island*, 1996, an affectionate portrayal of British doggedness and eccentricity). We turn now to examine how these complex attitudes have been revealed in public opinion data.

British Public Opinion : the Cold War Era

The US and UK do have important elements of shared history and a shared well of ideas, yet the US does observe a particular American Creed, defined by Seymour Martin Lipset (1996, 19) in terms of commitments to 'liberty, egalitarianism, individualism, populism and laissez-faire'. As Richard Hofstadter famously put it: 'It has been our fate as a nation not to have ideologies but to be one'

(Huntington, 2005, 47). The case for American exceptionalism has been weakened by its recruitment into nationalist and quasi-imperialist causes. Lipset argues that American exceptionalism is actually a double-edged sword. The American Creed encourages social inequality and high crime, even as it promotes social mobility and voluntarism. What cannot be denied is that, in many ways, America is different. If 'America' is primarily an idea, an ideology or a secular faith, 'Britain' or the 'United Kingdom' are primarily, perhaps exclusively, political and administrative jurisdictions.

Lipset helpfully discusses Anglo-American differences in terms of Canada's position as a country apparently very like the US: 'when Canada is evaluated by reference to the United States, it appears as more elitist, law abiding and statist, but when considering the variations between Canada and Britain, Canada looks more anti-statist, violent and egalitarian' (Lipset, 1996, 33). Surveys undertaken in 1987 indicated that 38 per cent of Americans were prepared to avow support for the 'welfare state', compared to 63 per cent in Britain. Only 28 per cent in the US would support governmental action to reduce inequalities, compared to the British figure again of 63 per cent. While 71 per cent of Americans agreed that 'people like me have a good chance of improving my standard of living', the British figure was 36 per cent (Smith 1989, 61, 66). These surveys, of course, were undertaken in the eighth year of the Conservative Thatcher government, which might have been presumed to have turned Britain towards more individualistic, 'American' attitudes. The 1980s certainly saw a degree of convergence between American and British models of capitalism, both distinguished by flexible labour markets, little in the way of state-led developmentalism, and moves away from universal welfare provision (Gamble, 2003, 104–5). However, US–UK public attitudes to statism, welfare and economic individualism continued to show significant variations.

By the 1990s, one traditional transatlantic difference seemed to be disappearing. Europeans, like Americans, now overwhelmingly identified themselves as middle-class rather than working-class (Lipset, 1996, 252; Featherstone and Ginsberg, 1996, 211–14). However, differences do persist. Typically, around 31 per cent of Americans agree with the proposition that 'what you achieve in life depends largely on your family background'; the British figure is 53 per cent. Americans appear around 10 per cent more likely than

Britons to declare that large income differentials are necessary to maintain economic prosperity (Freedland, 1998, 118, 112). Americans are generally more reluctant to vote than the British, but more likely to participate in local politics. The British seem especially uninterested in electoral politics at either the local or transnational (European) level. Where nearly half of all Americans attend regular church services, only 14 per cent of Britons are regular, weekly attenders (Lipset, 1996, 61). At least two major international surveys in the 1990s suggested that Americans were high among the most religious people in the world, with depth and breadth of religious belief exceeding those of even countries such as Ireland and Poland, much less Britain (Huntington, 2005, 90). Writing in the mid-1990s, Featherstone and Ginsberg concluded that public attitudes in Western Europe were converging, but that transatlantic differences remained. It was not so much that the US and Western Europe were 'growing apart, as that their increasingly close economic relationship is serving to expose, and even magnify, their historic domestic differences' (Featherstone and Ginsberg, 1996, 233). If Britain is the most 'American' of European countries, it still displays 'European' attitudes and characteristics, in the same way, to return to Lipset's earlier point, that Canada displays 'North American' ones.

Opinion polling in Britain does give some support to the idea of shared US–UK culture, or at least to the idea that linguistic ties are a strong bond. A 1990 *Observer/Harris* poll asked respondents to name the country, other than the UK, in which they would like to reside. The winners, in order of preference, were Australia, Canada, the US and New Zealand. Only 6 per cent opted for any continental European country (Denman, 1996, 287). Across the years since 1960, polls – unsurprisingly – show a greater public awareness of Europe's importance to the UK and a decreasing rate of concern for the Commonwealth. Rates of approval for an integrated, federal Europe, however, are not high (Dowds and Young, 1996; Worcester, 1997).

Rasmussen and McCormick, in their 1993 survey of Gallup polling on British attitudes to the US, included the observation: 'at the level of British mass perceptions, the Anglo-American special relationship seems to be largely a myth'. They also noted, however, that the US is consistently regarded 'as the country that would be most trustworthy were Britain involved in a war'. A 1994 Gallup survey revealed 49 per cent of British respondents describing the US as 'very reliable', a figure far ahead of any continental European ally (*The Gallup Poll*, 1995, 104).

A survey of some particularly striking Gallup polls illustrates the complexity of British attitudes. In 1952, 37 per cent of respondents approved of the role the US was playing in the world; 34 per cent disapproved. In 1960, 23 per cent wanted 'closer relations with America', with 31 per cent wanting 'greater independence'; 60 per cent disapproved of 'complete political and economic union with the US', while 19 per cent approved (13 per cent wanted to 'press on right away'). Between 1964 and 1973, Gallup polling tended to focus on attitudes towards the Vietnam War. In 1965, 34 per cent approved 'of American armed action in Vietnam'; 42 per cent disapproved. By 1966, 41 per cent were declaring that the US should 'pull out' of Vietnam. An August 1966 poll, however, found 42 per cent supporting the Labour government's endorsement of US policy in Southeast Asia; 37 per cent said Britain was 'wrong' to support the US. Unsurprisingly, 75 per cent opposed the sending of British troops to Vietnam. Rather extraordinarily, in February 1969, shortly after Richard Nixon had taken over as US president, Lyndon Johnson was named as the fourth 'most admired person' in British public opinion. Enoch Powell topped the list, with Harold Wilson second and Matt Busby (manager of a soccer club) seventh! In January 1973, only 14 per cent of respondents approved US policy in Vietnam, with 65 per cent disapproving. (This poll followed the intense US bombing of December 1972.) In 1975, however, 22 per cent of respondents 'agreed a lot' with the view that the US had broken its promises to South Vietnam; 15 per cent 'disagreed a lot'. This poll was taken shortly after the communist takeover of Saigon in April 1975; a majority was unable to express an opinion on the subject (Wybrow, 1989, 33; *The Gallup International Public Opinion Poll*, 1976, 574–5, 620, 654, 668–9, 882–4, 918–19, 1036–7.)

In 1966, one Gallup survey found 42 per cent agreeing that the 'British way of life' was 'too much influenced by the US'; 44 per cent disagreed. In 1967, 25 per cent saw US–UK relations as 'too close', with 13 per cent viewing them as 'not close enough' (*The Gallup International Public Opinion Poll*, 1976, 918). Rasmussen and McCormick noted evidence of declining confidence in the US during the Vietnam War and immediate post-Vietnam War eras. Poll results have frequently seen fears of *American* action leading to world war lagging only slightly behind fears of Soviet actions. Rasmussen and McCormick (1993, 533) also note, however, that apparently President Jimmy 'Carter brought hope to Britain'. British opinion, at least in recent times, has certainly tended to favour ostensibly peace-promoting Democratic presidents over ostensibly warlike Republicans. A poll in early summer 1977 temporarily reversed the erosion of confidence. Over half the respondents expressed very great or considerable confidence in the US. Confidence soon dropped, however, with further shifts downwards in the Reagan years. The stationing in Western Europe of intermediate range nuclear weapons combined with generally negative assessments of President Reagan, and of the perceived excesses of US anti-communism generally, negatively to influence European attitudes. By 1983, 45 per cent of British Gallup respondents were favouring moves towards West European neutralism (Wybrow, 1989, 130; Godson, 1987; Russett and Deluca, 1983). Around half of respondents to a 1986 poll opposed American use of British bases in that year to launch air strikes on Libya (Wybrow, 1989, 1142). In four 1987 Gallup polls, a higher percentage approved Soviet over US international behaviour. These figures reflected the high levels of popularity in Western Europe of Soviet leader Mikhail Gorbachev. The waning of the Cold War in the later 1980s, however, predictably saw a cooling of British public disapproval of official Washington, if not much sign of generalized national warming towards President Reagan. After a year and a half in the relative doldrums, the Bush Senior administration began to register high approval scores, associated particularly with its reaction to Iraq's 1990 invasion of Kuwait. Surveying data from the 1960–92 era, Rasmussen and McCormick (1993, 527, 524) concluded that 'more Britons consider the US their country's best friend than they do any other country'. Yet, on average, only a tenth of respondents reported that they liked Americans 'a lot'.

Intuition would suggest that Britons are more pro-American than continental Europeans. Figures compiled by Inglehart, from US Information Agency and *Eurobarometer* surveys, again reveal considerable complexity. Inglehart's figures represent the percentage of favourable responses minus unfavourable ones (in West Germany, Britain, Italy and France) to the question: 'Do you have a very good, good, neither good nor bad, bad or very bad opinion of the United States?' In the years between 1960 and 1987, West Germany recorded the most pro-American score in all years except 1972, 1973, 1985 and 1987, when the most pro-American country was Italy. France emerged as the least pro-American in every year except 1981 and 1982, when that role was occupied by Britain (Inglehart, 1994, 394). This accords with other evidence of particular British hostility towards the US in the early Reagan years. Surveys undertaken by the European Commission for the public opinion journal, *Eurobarometer*, tend to reveal the Republic of Ireland (a non-NATO member!) as the most consistently pro-American European country in terms of domestic opinion (Featherstone and Ginsberg, 1996, 226).

The Neo-conservative Moment and 9/11

The terror attacks of 11 September 2001 proved as much a turning point in international history as the Japanese attack on Pearl Harbor some 60 years previously. The ensuing War on Terror, and espe-cially the 2003 invasion of Iraq, exposed transatlantic divisions on a scale that probably surpassed even those of the Vietnam War era. As noted above, sections of European opinion did demonstrate even in their immediate reaction to 9/11 a degree of *schadenfreude*. Some French intellectuals lived up to American, and indeed to British, expectations of them by interpreting 9/11 as a the acting out, in Jean Baudrillard's words, of 'all the world's dream' of destroying 'a power that has become hegemonic' (Rubin and Rubin, 2004, 204). The overwhelming public and elite response in Western Europe, it should be emphasized, was deeply sympathetic. *Le Monde* famously editorialized on 12 September 2001: 'Nous Sommes Tous Americains'. Britain witnessed extensive demonstrations of public sympathy for the 9/11 dead, including of course the significant number of British casualties in the Twin Tower crashes. Yet the weak but insistent undercurrent of *schadenfreude* remained. It surfaced in what developed into a bad tempered and disturbing debate conducted in the pages of the *London Review of Books* during October 2001. Chelsea Clinton, daughter of the former US president and now a postgraduate student at Oxford University, reported: 'Every day at some point I encounter some sort of anti-American feeling' (Rubin and Rubin, 2004, 206). To many who lived through those strange days, the British public mood seemed to embody odd, contradictory impulses: genuine sympathy for the 9/11 victims, fear of an attack on the UK, the feeling that the US would over-react and thus make such an attack more likely. Salman Rushdie wrote about his experiences on the streets of London in February 2002: 'Night after night, I have found myself listening to Londoners' diatribes against the sheer weirdness of the American citizenry. The attacks on America are routinely discounted ("Americans care only about their own dead"). American patriotism, obesity, emotionality, self-centredness: these are the crucial issues' (Crockatt, 2003, 39, 61–2).

From 2002 onwards, global antipathy to the US increased markedly. The reasons for this were complex, but some likely causes included Bush's personal unpopularity and his administration's growing reputation for unilateralism. To many non-Americans, notably but not only in Western Europe, Bush appeared the very model of a parochial and insensitive American leader, hopelessly in hock to big business interests. Even before the Afghanistan and Iraqi wars, the US had pointed itself in a unilateralist direction in its rejection of the Kyoto protocol on greenhouse gas emissions, and non-cooperation over plans to create the International Criminal Court. The further slide in American international popularity was also arguably due to simple resentment at US power and the willingness to use it, to the poor public diplomacy of the first George W. Bush administration, and to particular issues, such as the US treatment of prisoners in Afghanistan, Iraq and Guantanamo. The rise of neo-conservatism, the intellectual movement associated with military primacy, democracy-imposition and confident American power-projection, became the object of intense global interest and opposition. These were all complex issues, but there is no question as to their impact on international opinion. The Pew Global Attitudes survey of 2002 showed deepening hostility to the US, most clearly in the Moslem world, though in 35 out of 42 countries polled more people viewed the US favourably than unfavourably (Schneider, 2003). The world metaphorically voted for John Kerry in 2004 over Bush. A *Globescan* survey of 21 countries reported only India, Poland and the Philippines as believing that the world was safer with Bush's re-election (BBC News, 2005a). The German newspaper *Die Tageszeitung* reflected much Western European opinion by editorializing that it felt 'a chill down the spine' with Bush's election victory (BBC News, 2005b).

British public opinion trailed along behind the Western European trend. Polls tend to show some correlation between pro-Americanism and having actually visited the US. British people do visit the US more than their continental European counterparts (around four million British people travel to the US annually). It should also be remembered that possibly one million UK passport-holders live in the US, with over 250,000 Americans residing in Britain (Garton Ash, 2005, 23). The 2002 Pew polling showed just less than half of British respondents, compared to roughly a third of French and a quarter of Germans holding a favourable view of the US. These figures all represented major drops from polling levels in 2000 (Stokes and McIntosh, 2002). In early 2004, the Pew Center took polls in Western Europe to test perceptions of American trustworthiness following the invasion of Iraq. 58 per cent of Britons declared themselves to have less faith in US trustworthiness as a result of the invasion; this compared to figures of 78 in France and 82 in Germany. Just 51 per cent in the UK were prepared to describe the War on Terror as a 'sincere effort to reduce international terrorism', compared to 35 per cent in France and 29 in Germany (Puchala, 2005, 93). By 2005, 50 per cent of Britons indicated that they saw the US as having a negative global influence, compared to 54 in France (Kull, 2005). To many commentators, the US and Western Europe, despite Blair's bridge-building, seemed to be inhabiting different worlds.

The transatlantic alarms surrounding American foreign policy after 2002 to some degree obscured the degree to which, at least in public opinion terms, the era of the Vietnam War had seen similar effects. Between 1965 and 1972, there was a 23 point drop in British public approval rates of the US. In some respects, British public reactions to the nuclear policies of the first Reagan administration were even more striking. In February 1982, only 47 per cent of Britons were prepared to offer a 'very' or 'somewhat favourable' view of the United States. This compared to a figure of 70 per cent in May 2003, following the overthrow of the Saddam Hussein regime in Iraq. It is also worth noting that Pew polling in 2002 continued to record high (60 per cent plus) levels of Western European admiration for American technology, science and popular culture (Nye, 2004, 36–7, 69).

The early twenty-first century crisis in popular and elite support for the US–UK 'special relationship' – graphically described by the hospital porter quoted in the previous chapter who referred to Britain as 'America's tart' – had some startling features. One of these was the disaffection of the young, usually seen as admirers of at least aspects of American vitality and innovation. School protests and walk-outs in opposition to the Iraq invasion and the November 2003 Bush visit were extraordinary. Generational differences were well captured by Ian McEwan, whose 2005 novel, *Saturday*, was set on 15 February 2003, the day of the huge London anti-war march. In the novel Daisy Perowne debates the Iraq invasion with her father, neurosurgeon Henry Perowne. 'You know very well', she tells Henry, 'these extremists, the Neo-cons, have taken over America. Cheney, Rumsfeld, Wolfowitz. Iraq was always their pet project. ... Why is it that the few people I've met who aren't against this crappy war are all over forty?' (McEwan, 2005, 190–1). Chris Martin, singer with the pop group Coldplay declared at the Brit music awards in February 2003 that 'we are all going to die when George Bush has his way' (KR Washington Bureau, 2003). Books by Michael Moore, the American critic of the war whose work flirted with conspiracy theories concerning the 'true' nature of 9/11, became bestsellers and his film, *Fahrenheit 9/11*, a must-see, in the US as well as in the UK. James Naughtie commented that the Michael Moore vogue was just a symptom of 'a certain discomfort with modern America' now evident in Britain: 'It was more than just the kind of hatred of the Starbucks culture put into words by Michael Moore (who could fill the London Palladium ten times over every night for one of his one-man anti-Bush shows), and it demonstrated that increased closeness in the age of globalization might be an illusion' (Naughtie, 2004, 115–16). The new hostility towards America seemed even to have some potential to damage British social cohesion. If, to some degree, the Iraq War debates pitted young against their seniors, they also revealed gender divisions. After 2000, global polling has fairly consistently shown men to be more sympathetic than women to the goals and operation of American foreign policy (Applebaum, 2005, 39). The upheavals of the early twenty-first century also clearly demonstrated the severely troubling disaffection of a generation of young British Moslems from the traditional assumptions of British governments about the nature and purpose of the 'special relationship'.

3

The House that Jack and Mac Built

With this chapter, we begin a broadly chronological account of US–UK foreign policy relations in the years since Second World War. The immediate post-Second World War period, which has been widely studied and written about elsewhere, is surveyed relatively briefly. The key event of this era was the Suez crisis of 1956, an episode which fixed the US–UK power relationship for the rest of the century The great achievement of President John Kennedy and Prime Minister Harold Macmillan (the Jack and Mac of this chapter's title) was to rebuild the relationship, on the basis of post-Suez realities, but without sacrificing what was advantageous to Washington and to London in their special alliance.

Early Cold War Relations

The Cold War relationship between the US and Britain was established in the wake of World War Two. According to Oliver Franks, British ambassador to Washington between 1948 and 1952, it rested on 'a broad identity of views on the main issues of foreign policy' – Soviet containment and European recovery – together with growing 'habits of working together' (Franks, 1995, 63–4). As John Kennedy said of the entire Atlantic alliance in his 1962 State of the Union address: 'The Atlantic Community grows, not like a volcanic mountain, by one mighty explosion, but like a coral reef, from the accumulating activity of all' (Ryan, 2003, 153). In the immediate post-1945 period, Britain was still more concerned than the Truman administration in Washington over the Soviet threat, and not only in Europe. A significant aspect of the historiographical debate on the origins of the Cold War actually centres on the degree to which Britain actually led the US into a strategy of global containment (Weller, 1998).

There was, however, an initial cooling of wartime closeness. Early efforts by London to establish a partnership in the area of nuclear weapons soon flagged. The so-called 'Groves-Anderson memorandum', produced by US General L. R. Groves and Sir John Anderson, who in 1945 was British cabinet head responsible for nuclear weapons development, declared in November 1945: 'The three Governments, the United States, the United Kingdom, and Canada, will not use atomic weapons against other parties without prior consultation with each other' (Baylis, 1984, 49). Yet Britain's consultative role in the use of atomic weapons against Japan was little more than merely notional. By mid-1946, London and Washington were locked in profound disagreement over these issues of consultation and nuclear partnership. The US cancelled Lend Lease rather rapidly for British preferences, and halted nuclear cooperation. Clear differences emerged over the Middle East. In October 1945, British Foreign Secretary Ernest Bevin informed the British embassy in Washington that the US was allowing its Jewish lobby to distort policy on Palestine, then mandated to Britain: 'To play on racial feeling for the purpose of winning an election is to make a farce of their insistence on free elections in other countries' (Baylis (ed.), 1997, 40). London feared an American cutting loose from Europe and the establishment by Washington of a new regime of economic and security regionalism which effectively excluded Britain from any position of influence.

Despite these problems, the US State Department made the following confidential assessment in April 1946:

> If Soviet Russia is to be denied the hegemony of Europe, the United Kingdom must continue in existence as the principal power in Western Europe economically and militarily. The US should, therefore, explore its relationship with Great Britain and give all feasible political, economic, and if necessary, military support within the framework of the United Nations, to the United Kingdom .... This does not imply a blank check of American support throughout the world for every interest of the British Empire, but only in respect of areas and interests which are in the opinion of the US vital to the

maintenance of the United Kingdom and the British Commonwealth as a great power. (*Foreign Relations of the United States, 1946*, vol. 1, 1170)

Some loans and debt cancellations were extended to London in 1945–6. The policy embodied in the 1946 State Department assessment was by no means entirely in place. But the post-1945 'special relationship' was edging into existence.

Despite his flirtation with the idea of a strong Europe as a balancing force between the US and USSR, the chief architect was Ernest Bevin. He wrote in February 1946 of the need for US–UK armaments integration and for 'an entirely new approach ... that can only be based upon a very close understanding between ourselves and the Americans' (Ovendale 1998, 65). Bevin clashed with his boss, Clement Attlee (Labour prime minister from 1945 to 1951) over this developing relationship and especially over policy towards Greece. With the acceptance by Washington of the anti-Soviet containment doctrine, Bevin floated the idea of a 'Western Union', led by the US and Britain, to contain Soviet power in Europe. Bevin led the European response to the US offer of aid under the Marshall Plan. The *modus vivendi* on nuclear cooperation, agreed in January 1948, gave Britain a rather vague right of consultation in the matter of nuclear use. In February 1949, the foreign secretary oversaw the setting up of a Foreign Office committee, chaired by William Strang, to develop a strategy for Britain's future. The report, which set the course for the subsequent institutionalization of the 'special relationship', argued that Britain's international status depended upon a prioritization of relations with the US.

The US commitment to Europe, encouraged by Bevin, was solidified in the formation of the North Atlantic Treaty Organization (NATO) and in the Berlin blockade (both in 1949). Tensions arose nevertheless: over nuclear policy and general strategy during the Korean War (1950–53), over the war in Indochina, over the recognition of communist China, over policy in the Middle East and over Britain's own nuclear development path. As the US doctrine of containment became globalized, Washington looked to London to promote European integration as well as take its share of anti-communist defence East of Suez. The British official Evelyn Shuckburgh wrote in June 1950 that the Americans were 'of course quite willing to subscribe to the doctrine of continuous close consultation in all matters'. However, Washington had made it 'very clear that the value of this country to the United States, apart from our Commonwealth position and our influence in the Far East and other parts of the world, lay in the leadership which we could give in Europe' (Orde, 1996, 175). Washington was certainly prepared to accept that special relations existed. The State Department policy planning staff reported in November 1951: 'We have, in fact, at the present time a special relationship with the UK which involves consultation between us on a wide range of issues.' The report noted also that 'one of the advantages of partnership is that it can facilitate the shifting of responsibilities to accord with capabilities'. The policy planning staff observed *inter alia* that, in relation to Soviet policy, the UK tended to prioritize 'the narrow objective of reducing tensions', while Washington emphasized strength and the eventual modification of the Soviet system (*Foreign Relations of the United States, 1951*, vol. 4, part 1, 980, 983). Various rows in the early 1950s between London and Washington over the command of NATO forces in Europe revealed continuing tensions; by the mid-1950s, it was clear that Washington would not accept the principle of joint command.

Now Britain was paying a price for the adoption of the policy outlined by Strang in 1949. During 1950, the first year of the Korean War, Britain was spending a larger percentage of its national income on defence than was the USA (7.7 compared to 6.9 per cent). British casualties in the war were second only to the American total. During the Korean War, London was not only concerned to support the American doctrine of globalized anti-communist containment. Malaya and Hong Kong were also being defended against possible North Korean/Chinese aggression. London saw its role in the war also as urging restraint on Washington, especially in regard to the use of nuclear weapons. As Britain struggled to maintain global status – 'forward projection' in the jargon, or, increasingly, 'world-wide' rather than 'world power' – it incurred economic damage. This was not lost on Washington. Anthony Eden (Conservative foreign secretary in Winston Churchill's peacetime government of 1951–5) reported in 1952 that the American leaders were 'polite'. They 'listen to what we have to say, but make (on most issues) their own decisions. Till we can recover our financial and economic independence, this is bound to continue' (Horne, 1988, 347).

Eden's forebodings were justified. The later Truman years saw major rifts, notably in the Middle East, where the US tended to rely excessively on a weakening British power-projection. As British diplomat Roger Makins put it in 1951: 'the Anglo-American partnership is difficult to manage owing to the increasing disparity of power within it' (Hopkins, 2003, 230). It was, however, during the presidency of Dwight Eisenhower (1953–61), that the US–UK relationship suffered its major crisis of modern times. Eisenhower and, to a lesser degree, John Foster Dulles (secretary of state from 1953 to 1959) saw the British relationship as just one relationship among many; they tended to ignore the 'special' status it had begun to acquire during the mid-to-late 1940s. Yet it would be quite wrong to imagine that the Eisenhower administration wished to dismantle close cooperation with Britain. President Eisenhower's dollar-wise military policy, the New Look, put a premium on a sharing of the defence burden with America's close allies. Increasing awareness in the 1950s of the significance of Soviet scientific advances also caused Washington to see the value of technical and research collaboration.

The nationalization of the Suez Canal on 26 July 1956 provoked a strong response from Anthony Eden (British prime minister from 1955 to 1957), who determined not to follow models of appeasement from the 1930s. The Egyptian leader, Abdul Nasser, announced his intention to use canal tolls (the Suez Canal was jointly owned by Britain and France) to fund the construction of the Aswan Dam on the River Nile. London considered a military response more or less immediately, without any real consultation with its allies in the Baghdad Pact. The Pact involved a 1955 agreement between Britain, Turkey, Iraq, Iran and Pakistan. London felt that US support would be forthcoming on account of the nature of the US–UK alliance and of Nasser's connections with Moscow. Israel was recruited to provide a pretext for an Anglo-French invasion. An Israeli attack on Egypt on 29 October was followed by an Anglo-French ultimatum. The British Cabinet approved military action despite the now obvious disapproval of Washington. Worries surfaced in Cabinet lest the action might 'do lasting damage to Anglo-American relations' (Ovendale, 1998, 114). Eden not only misunderstood the dynamics of the 'special relationship'; he also failed to keep the British Treasury, Foreign Office and Ministry of Defence informed of his policy. The results were catastrophic. By

8 November, after intense US pressure, especially economic pressure on sterling, London accepted a ceasefire, and a subsequent troop withdrawal. These events stimulated both anger at Washington's perceived betrayal and an awareness of British weakness. The US embassy in London recorded on 23 November 1956 that 'anti-American feeling' in the UK was 'at a very high pitch'. It also, however, conveyed the common British assumption that 'the US is bound to come to its senses' (Bartlett, 1992, 88). C. F. Cobbold of the Bank of England reported in December 1956 that 'the fundamental trouble' was the overextension of spending commitments (Johnman, 1989, 177). Britain simply could not withstand the kind of economic pressure exerted by Washington during the crisis. The future seemed one in which independence and sovereignty could no longer be assumed.

From Eisenhower's viewpoint, the Suez adventure was misconceived and mistimed. He later regretted the heavy-handedness of his reaction – apparently blocking London's drawing rights on the International Monetary Fund – but saw Eden, despite his former friendship with the British prime minister, as an unreconstructed imperialist. British military action would only increase Soviet influence in the region. Post-colonial nationalism in the Third World needed to be harnessed rather than alienated. Eden had failed to take account not only of the 1956 presidential election, but also of the wider international environment. Britain's action had embarrassed Eisenhower during the election campaign and taken the sting from Western protests when the USSR invaded Hungary in October 1956.

The Suez crisis represented a major break in the development of the 'special relationship'. Yet the crisis actually had very little immediate effect on British strategic thinking (Dockrill, 2002, 25). Its legacy, however, was not only one of distrust and mutual recrimination, but eventually also the perception (stronger in London than in Washington, but not entirely absent from the American capital) that such a rift must not be allowed to recur. The late 1950s saw a process of rebuilding against a background of distrust. A NATO report of December 1956 noted: 'An alliance in which the members ignore each other's interests or engage in political or economic conflict, or harbour suspicions of each other, cannot be effective' (Dickie, 1994, 86).

Some healing did occur before 1960. Duncan Sandys (defence minister in Harold Macmillan's Conservative government of 1957–63) issued a White Paper in 1957, terminating conscription and committing Britain to the doctrine of nuclear deterrence in the context of a revived American alliance. Sandys' White Paper envisaged significant conventional defence cuts, and the surrendering of many imperial commitments. Though a significant turning point in British defence thinking, some of Sandys' assumptions about the credibility of committing the UK to 'massive retaliation' nuclear strategy were dropped in 1962 (Gowing, 1986, 126; Paterson, 1997, 23). During the later Eisenhower period, Macmillan effectively restored US–UK cooperation in the Middle East, now with Britain clearly the junior partner.

In 1957, Harold Macmillan also agreed to the siting of 60 US Thor intermediate-range ballistic missiles in East Anglia. The use of the missiles, which were withdrawn in 1963, was subject to a British veto under a 'dual key ' system. The panic in the Western alliance which followed the Soviet launch of its Sputnik satellite in 1957 drew London and Washington closer. The US offered assistance with development of the British medium- range Blue Streak missile. The Thor missiles were originally intended to plug the gap between the winding down of Britain's V-bomber nuclear force and the coming on stream of Blue Streak some time after 1962. The Fylingdales radar system in Yorkshire was also opened to American use, a decision which was ratified by Macmillan and President John Kennedy in 1960. In July 1958, the US Congress amended the McMahon Act, opening the way to the sharing of more technical nuclear information with London. Upon learning that Eisenhower wished to rescind the Act, Macmillan confided to his diary on 24 October 1957 his delight at 'the end of the McMahon Act – the great prize!' (Macmillan, 1971, 323). The Anglo-American exchange of nuclear secrets benefited both sides, with the US gaining leverage over Britain's nuclear future (Baylis, 2001). A 1958 agreement made it clear that London's access to the information would be preferential. Britain, in John Baylis' words, 'undoubtedly received more than she gave, but her own contribution was far from negligible'. The contribution included Britain's own nuclear and conventional defence research, as well as access for the US to facilities such as those on Christmas Island (Baylis, 1984, 87).

Jack and Mac

A Family Affair

During the Kennedy-Macmillan era (1961–3), the post-Suez rebuilding of Anglo-American relations achieved solidity. The Cold War nuclear relationship was firmly established. No less than all other putative 'golden ages', the era of Jack and Mac is susceptible to revisionist scholarship. The Macmillan-Kennedy era saw significant Anglo-American tensions. One such occasion – the US sale of Hawk missiles to Israel in 1962 in violation of an earlier understanding between London and Washington – provoked Macmillan to inform Kennedy that he could 'hardly find words to express my sense of disgust and despair' (Ashton, 2005, 716). Nigel Ashton notes further that JFK, like Eisenhower before him, did what he could to limit Macmillan's 'scope for independent action on the world stage, particularly in respect of East-West relations' (Ashton, 2005, 722). However, and again as with other supposed 'golden ages', the mythology of the Jack and Mac years acquired its own substantive importance. For future British diplomats, the post-Suez 'special relationship' was the house that Jack and Mac built.

The essence of the Kennedy-Macmillan alliance involved defence, especially nuclear defence, collaboration. Discussion of this, including the Polaris deal, will be postponed until Chapter 7, when we discuss nuclear relations. Nuclear defence defined the Cold War 'special relationship' and deserves to be treated as a distinct issue. The Polaris deal was its cornerstone. Here, some general points about the Jack and Mac years will be made, and attention drawn to two specific episodes: the 1961 Berlin Wall and the 1962 Cuban Missile crises.

Commentators who emphasize the importance of personal leader relations in influencing foreign policy risk not only the charge of sentimentality, but also the danger of confusing form and substance. Macmillan in his memoirs probably exaggerated his intimacy with JFK. The young American president was not above dismissing Macmillan and his foreign secretary, Lord Home, as fuddy-duddies (Lamb, 1995, 313). Arthur Schlesinger, adviser to JFK, noted that Macmillan, the 'languid Edwardian' was sensitive to the danger 'that the brisk young American, nearly a quarter of a century his junior, would consider him a museum piece' (Schlesinger, 1965,

340). Lord Longford recalled Macmillan's comment before meeting the new president: 'How am I ever going to get along with that cocky young Irishman?' (Fisher, 1982, 258). They met for the first time at Key West in Florida in March 1961 to discuss the crisis in Indochina.

There were some tensions between the two leaders, yet there was a genuine cordiality and understanding which lasted until Kennedy's early death. At Key West, Macmillan (1972, 336) 'felt a deep sense of relief ... we seemed immediately to talk as old friends'. Schlesinger (1964, 340) recalled their talk as marking 'the beginning of what became Kennedy's closest relationship with a foreign leader'. Macmillan was impressed by JFK's intelligence and logical, questioning approach. In contrast, Macmillan (1972, 308) described Lyndon Johnson, vice president elect, in 1960 as 'an acute and ruthless politician, but not ... a man of any intellectual power'. The British premier was slightly surprised to find that he was related to the 'cocky Irishman'. Macmillan told George Hutchinson: 'I had a vague recollection of him earlier because his sister had married my – no, my wife's – nephew, Billy Burlington' (Hutchinson, 1980, 104). JFK's elder sister, 'Kick', had married Lady Dorothy Macmillan's nephew, Lord Burlington, later the Marquess of Hartington. Burlington was killed in World War Two and Lady Hartington in a plane crash in 1948. In June 1961 Macmillan was told by Ambassador Harold Caccia that JFK and his circle had a 'rather "raffish" lifestyle'. Macmillan indicated that Kennedy 'looks like being a good friend to me'. JFK had '*some* of the old prejudices (perhaps a little of the Irish tradition) about us – but he lives in the modern world' (Ashton, 2002, 55). The sense of Anglo-American relations being run as a family business was strengthened by the appointment of David Ormsby-Gore (later Lord Harlech) to succeed Caccia as British ambassador to Washington. Ormsby-Gore was also a distant relative of the Kennedys and was appointed after a personal recommendation from JFK. According to Macmillan (1972, 339) Ormsby-Gore 'enjoyed the intimate friend-ship of Kennedy and his family' and 'had access to the White House such as no Ambassador has had before or since'. Theodore Sorensen (1965, 559) recalled JFK as remarking, perhaps with a trace of irony: 'I trust David as I would my own cabinet.'

It may be argued that the JFK – Macmillan – Ormsby-Gore network became especially strong following Kennedy's early foreign policy reversal: the failed Bay of Pigs 1961 invasion of Cuba. Ormsby-Gore's influence is easily detected in JFK's reaction to Dean Acheson's December 1962 remarks about Britain having 'lost an empire' and not yet having 'found a role'. The British ambassador immediately emphasized Acheson's pro-British credentials, while JFK approved a press release: 'U.S.–U.K. relations are not based only on a power calculus, but also on … deep community of purpose and long practice of close cooperation' (Brinkley, 1992, 176–7).

Macmillan saw Kennedy as skilled in detailed crisis-management, but remarked in 1961 that 'on wider issues, he seems rather lost' (Macmillan, 1973, 147). JFK's mixture of strong anti-communist ideology and pragmatism in specific problem-management seems to have caused Macmillan a degree of consternation. During the Jack and Mac years, London was, in very broad terms, concerned to promote the ideas of a degree of demilitarization in Central Europe and of a generalised commitment to coexistence, compromise and détente with Moscow. Macmillan's preference in pursuing these aims, along with British interests generally, was to seek personal contact with JFK, bypassing what he called, in connection with the 1963 Partial Nuclear Test Ban Treaty, 'the State Dept' and 'Pentagon rats' (Ashton, 2002, 10–11, 19). Macmillan pressed the test ban cause in Washington in the face of significant bureaucratic and political opposition, and played an important role in furthering the summit diplomacy which led to the eventual treaty signing. Close diplomatic cooperation was evident in a number of other areas, for example in regard to the threats made towards Kuwait by Iraq in 1961. Macmillan consulted Kennedy closely in 1961–2 over crises in the Congo (the Katanga secession) and in Ghana, where the Nkrumah regime began seriously to abuse human rights. Britain and the US clashed, however, over the issue of whether to recognize a republican regime in Yemen. Britain sought to protect the Aden base by siding with Saudi Arabia over the non-recognition in 1962 of the Sallal regime. Britain withdrew its legation from Yemen.

The limits and importance of the Kennedy-Macmillan friendship were tested during the Berlin Wall and Cuban missile crises, discussed below, as well as in Indochinese, nuclear defence and European integration issues, all discussed in future chapters. One other controversy, however, is worth raising here, before turning to the Berlin Wall crisis. How far do the Jack and Mac years indicate that Washington is happier with a Conservative rather than a Labour government in London? Kennedy certainly did prefer Macmillan's Conservative regime to its Labour rival. JFK, however, was certainly not prepared to allow Macmillan a free hand in exploiting his 1963 visit to London for electoral purposes (Lamb, 1995, 59). (Kennedy visited Macmillan at Birch Grove in Sussex in June 1963, primarily to work on the Nuclear Test Ban treaty.) JFK thought highly of Hugh Gaitskell, though he was a little wary of his successor as Labour leader, Harold Wilson. Kennedy seems to have been genuinely personally fond of Macmillan, but there is no reason to suppose that he would not have cooperated perfectly well with a Labour government, especially one which, like Harold Wilson's 1964 government, claimed to be modernizing Britain (Dobson, 1990a). A Foreign Office survey of elite US opinion in 1962 noted: 'Even the apparent drift of the Labour Party towards neutralism last year was discounted on the grounds that this sort of thing had happened before and that if and when a crisis came Britain would rally at once' (PREM 11 5192).

The 1961 Berlin Wall Crisis

On 5 August 1961 Harold Macmillan wrote to the Queen that he had 'always thought about American Presidents that the great thing is to get them to do what we want'. The prime minister was referring to evidence of the Americans 'getting off their high horse' over Berlin (Macmillan, 1972, 591–2). Macmillan's comment followed considerable disagreement between London and the incoming Kennedy administration over how to respond to Soviet announcements about the imminent signing of a peace treaty with East Germany.

Kennedy was initially keen to demonstrate his commitment to the security of West Berlin by increasing conventional troop commitments. Although JFK, rather surprisingly, failed to mention Berlin in his Inaugural Address, he swiftly instigated a review of Berlin policy. Though London and Washington agreed that NATO should take no initiatives on Berlin, the two capitals differed on the question of how to respond to a peace treaty. Dean Acheson, brought in by Kennedy to participate in the review, wrote that 'a Communist takeover of Berlin' could not be accepted under any circumstances. He advised that Britain would, however, be unlikely to agree to fight for Berlin in advance of such a takeover: 'The United Kingdom would hope something would turn up. It wouldn't' (Gearson, 1998, 164).

In various meetings in the early part of 1961, Macmillan and British diplomats pressed Washington to favour political over military responses. Some success was achieved in persuading Washington that the central issue must be one of access to West Berlin, rather than the peace treaty itself. As John Gearson (1998, 70) writes: Macmillan 'never believed the British people would go to war over the question of who stamped a document'. Yet US military planning (code named LIVEOAK) for a response to a Soviet move on Berlin continued. Lord Home, British foreign secretary, argued that NATO should take seriously Soviet suggestions for an interim period, during which the two Germanys would settle the future of Berlin.

Splits began to appear in Washington. David Bruce, Kennedy's ambassador in London, reported that British public attitudes towards a new European conflict explained Macmillan's opposition to LIVEOAK planning. In July, Macmillan privately described LIVEOAK as 'absurd' (Macmillan, 1972, 389). Llewellyn Thompson, former US ambassador to Moscow, tended to favour the British line (Lamb 1995, 360). Macmillan interpreted these divisions, along with American willingness to negotiate further over nuclear testing, as evidence of British influence. His faith in the continued potency of British diplomacy was reflected in his August letter to the Queen, quoted earlier.

Shortly after this letter was despatched to Buckingham Palace, the flow of refugees from East Germany to West Berlin reached over 2000 a day. Soviet leader Nikita Khrushchev responded by ordering the construction of the wall, which was to divide the city until 1989. Macmillan's diary entries for 19 August 1961 revealed his understanding of Khrushchev's dilemma and his worries about Washington's reactions: 'The flood of refugees had reached such proportions … that they were probably almost compelled to take this course. Partly because the West German elections are going on, and partly because the Americans have got very excited, the situation is tense and may become dangerous.' He resisted JFK's urging to send more troops into Berlin and attributed such American restraint as there was to allied pressure: the 'irony and detachment' of French President Charles de Gaulle and 'our insistence on combining a willingness to negotiate with my declaratory reaffirmation of Allied rights and obligations' (Macmillan, 1972, 392–3).

The remainder of 1961 saw increased tensions over Soviet conduct in Berlin and over nuclear testing. British diplomacy worked both to secure a test ban treaty and, in effect, to achieve American acceptance of the post-August status quo in Berlin. London was also, however, concerned about being seen too obviously as following a policy of appeasement. It was also important to avoid too many public splits with America. London kept a strong commitment to Western access to the divided city. Macmillan continued, however, to press the point that concessions might be made in pursuit of a final settlement. The Federal Republic (West Germany) might publicly recognize the Oder-Neisse line (the Soviet-imposed redrawn boundary between Poland and East Germany). It might renounce its nuclear ambitions. It might even be possible for NATO countries to recognize the German Democratic Republic (East Germany). Such an agenda of possible concessions opened splits between France, Britain, the US and the Federal Republic.

Tensions over Berlin ebbed only in the wake of the Cuban crisis of 1962. The Kennedy administration's acceptance of a physically divided Berlin was not entirely unconnected with Macmillan's influence. British criticism of, and even partial non-cooperation with, LIVEOAK planning also had some effect. Anglo-American tensions remained, for example over JFK's appointment of Lucius Clay, a US general with a confrontationist reputation, as 'adviser' to West Berlin. Macmillan, however, took pride in the way that he had influenced American policy and in the way he felt he had asserted the 'special relationship' over the heads of West Germany and France: 'President Kennedy seemed thoroughly "fed up" with both (West German leader Konrad) Adenauer and de Gaulle', Mac wrote later. His thoughts went back to the 'Greeks and Romans' analogy: 'It is curious how all American statesmen begin by trying to treat Britain as just one of many foreign or NATO countries. They soon find themselves relying on our advice and experience' (Macmillan, 1972, 403).

Macmillan's entire foreign policy, which had more than a hint of the quixotic, is difficult to interpret. He has frequently been accused of weakening the alliance. Like Harold Wilson in the 1960s, he had rather grandiose notions of Britain's role as a mediator between the superpowers. His 1959 visit to Moscow achieved little beyond the annoying of President Eisenhower. John Gearson's study of the Berlin Wall crisis extends little credit to Macmillan. According to

Gearson (1998, 198), Kennedy never accepted Macmillan's 'thesis that as long as he was kept talking, Khrushchev could be deflected from carrying out his threats'. JFK's decision to tolerate the Berlin stalemate was primarily located in his judgement about what was possible, and in his conscious determination to avoid emulating the crisis of July 1914. Yet, by mid-1961, Macmillan had at least managed to restore a degree of influence for Britain which would have been unimaginable during the transatlantic impasse of five years before. The profoundest of all Cold War tests of British influence was to come some 14 months later.

Britain and the Cuban Missile Crisis, 1962

Castro's 1959 revolution in Cuba, his subsequent 'conversion' to communism, the Eisenhower administration's tough reaction, Kennedy's 1961 Bay of Pigs invasion: these events evinced in London much in the way of weary scepticism. In 1960, Macmillan observed the US as 'paralysed and uncertain' in their reaction. Washington had failed to appreciate the extent of anti-American feeling that had been built up in the years of the US-backed dictator Fulgencio Batista: 'what a pity they never understood "colonialism" and "imperialism" till too late'. Macmillan also noted the irony of Washington's pressure on London to retain its colonial relationship with British Guiana in 1962–3 until an anti-communist succession could be assured (Ashton, 2002, 65, 15). Britain continued to trade with the island, despite the 1960 nationalization of Shell Oil. In the view of Bill Marchant, British ambassador to Cuba in the 1950s, Castro would never be a 'good routine, line-toeing communist'. Marchant added that Castro was the kind of chap who was likely to 'have got a good Second', though probably not 'a First Class at Oxbridge' (Scott, 1999, 15).

The degree of British involvement in decisions attending the Cuban missile crisis continues to be a matter of hot dispute. On the one hand, there is the view that London was merely informed of decisions already taken in Washington. Even David Ormsby-Gore, later commented: 'I can't honestly think of anything said from London that changed the US action – it was chiefly reassurance to JFK' (Horne, 1989, 382). Gary Rawnsley concludes that 'Britain's primary function during the crisis seems to have been in leading European and Commonwealth support for the United States' (Rawnsley, 1995, 599).

An opposing view stresses the concern shown by JFK and his advisers for allied opinion. Risse-Knappen (1995, 150) argues that it 'is a widespread myth that the NATO allies suffered from a lack of consultation', at least during the second week of the crisis. All major European allies were notified of Washington's intention to impose a blockade (or 'quarantine') on Cuba. In Risse-Knappen's words, 'certain countries were more equal than others in the eyes of the U.S. administration. Great Britain was in a league of its own'. According to May and Zelikow (eds. 1997, 692), editors of the 'Kennedy tapes' (transcripts of recordings secretly made by JFK in the Oval Office and Cabinet Room), 'Macmillan and Ormsby-Gore became de facto members of Kennedy's Executive Committee.' (The Executive Committee, or ExComm, was the body led by JFK which made key crisis decisions: to impose the quarantine after discovery of Soviet missiles in Cuba; to steer a middle course between air strikes and doing nothing; to finesse the eventual linkage between dismantling of the Soviet missiles and removal of Jupiter missiles from Turkey.) John Dickie stresses that Sir Kenneth Strong, head of the Ministry of Defence Joint Intelligence Bureau, was given privileged access to intelligence on the Soviet missiles possibly as early as 16 October, on the very day that the president himself saw it. For Dickie, and clearly this was the case, 'Macmillan was closer to the evolution of policy than the American Congress' (Dickie, 1994, 1200). John F Kennedy's contact with Ormsby-Gore and Macmillan during the second week seems to have strengthened his determination to find a peaceful solution. British influence is also widely credited in US decisions to reduce the radius of the interception line for the quarantine, to give Moscow more flexibility; in the decision to publish photographs of the missile sites; and the exemption of US forces in Europe from the extreme, and, in the context of Berlin, potentially provocative, DEFCON 3 alert status (Kennedy, 1968, 45; Risse-Knappen, 1995, 156). Intelligence deriving from Oleg Penkovsky, a spy in Soviet defence run jointly by US and British intelligence, certainly influenced Kennedy's understanding of the technical capabilities of the missiles.

It is still extremely difficult to gauge British influence. Qualifications need to be made even to the above examples. For example, Ormsby-Gore recommended the publication of the missile site photographs after they had been released to the London press. The alteration of the quarantine line came after the Soviet order to turn back its surface shipping, and therefore had no substantive effect on the crisis. Penkovsky's intelligence did not touch Washington's ignorance of the missile command arrangements. Judgements on British influence now rest on complex questions of textual interpretation, regarding both the ExComm transcripts and various material, including JFK-Macmillan telephone transcripts. (The transcripts reveal the primitive nature of the technology. Kennedy seems frequently to have failed to press the telephone button which allowed Macmillan to respond to his points (Ashton, 2002, 87)). Much rests on subtle distinctions between 'consulting', 'informing', 'influencing', 'participating' and 'supporting'. To some commentators, the bottle is half-full; to others it is half-empty. Still, some points can be made with confidence.

Although it declined to consult NATO allies in the first week (for fear of being 'hung up' by European objections to some possible courses of action), the ExComm was continually exercised by the issue of allied support. The ExComm transcripts reveal far more stated concern for allied opinion – especially in the context of likely Soviet action over Berlin – than for any domestic political overspill from the crisis. Secretary of State Dean Rusk remarked on 18 October:

> It's one thing for Britain and France to get themselves isolated within the alliance over Suez. But it's quite another thing for the alliance if the United States should get itself in the same position. Because we are the central bone structure of the alliance, I think this is a different kind of a problem that we have to think very hard about. (May and Zelikow, eds, 1997, 128)

Second, there is no question that there was close and privileged consultation with Ormsby-Gore and Macmillan. The US received due support (despite Macmillan's famous comment made when Ambassador David Bruce showed him the photographic evidence of the missiles: 'Now the Americans will realise what we in England have been through for the past many years') (Horne, 1989, 365). Close personal relations are evident from the various transcripts. Yet Macmillan and his ambassador were not entirely uncritical. On 21 October, Ormsby-Gore asked the president 'under what authority they would institute a blockade', and declared: 'Our traditional attitude with regard to freedom of the seas would put us in an awkward position' (PREM 11 3689). On 22 October, Macmillan told Kennedy: 'What worries me, I'll be quite frank with you, [is] having a sort of dragging-on position. If you occupied Cuba, that's one thing. In my long experience we've always found that our weakness has been when we've not acted with sufficient strength to start with' (May and Zelikow, eds, 1997, 284–5).

As the 22 October telephone transcript makes clear, Macmillan initially countenanced an invasion, although he rapidly backtracked and began a search for diplomatic compromises. The Foreign Office view, expressed on 27 October was that 'the Russians acknowledge American nuclear superiority' and would ultimately back down in a direct confrontation over Cuba, despite the 'blow to their prestige' (Scott, 1999, 156). Macmillan was twice asked by JFK on October 25 for his views on the wisdom of invading. The British leader now clearly favoured a deal, though he opposed a direct trade of Cuban missiles for the Jupiter missile deployments in Turkey. Macmillan wrote to Ormsby-Gore on 27 October: 'I could not allow a situation in Europe or in the world to develop which looks like escalating into war without trying some action by calling a conference on my own, or something like that' (PREM 11 3689). However, Macmillan's only substantive suggestion, to immobilize the Thor missiles in Britain as a quid pro quo while negotiations took place on the Cuban missiles, was rejected politely by JFK. The American president also declined Macmillan's offer to travel to Washington. As May and Zelikow put it, by 26 October, JFK seems to have 'become skeptical of the quality of Macmillan's advice' (May and Zelikow, eds, 1997, 692). Macmillan was not party to the secret understanding with Khrushchev over the Jupiters.

The various sources throw important light on British perceptions. London was consistently concerned to maximize its status as an independent US ally within the forum of the United Nations. London opinion generally was uneasy about the legality of American actions, though unprepared, in Macmillan's famous words to the House of Commons, at the 'moment to go into the niceties of international law' (*Parliamentary Debates*, 5th series, vol. 664, 1059 (25 Oct. 1962)). The Cabinet received an opinion from the Lord Chancellor's office that 'the "quarantine" cannot be justified as "pacific blockade" under international law' (CAB 129 111 C (62)).

Important signals emerge also from notes of the JFK-Macmillan telephone conversations taken by Sir Harold Caccia, permanent

Foreign Office under-secretary. According to this source, Kennedy assured Macmillan on 26 October 'that he would not take any drastic action, which presumably means bombardment or invasion, without telling the Prime Minister in advance'. Caccia commented: 'This does not mean that we shall be consulted.' The decision would already have been made prior to 'consultation'. If Britain demurred, 'the President would conclude that when it came to the crunch Britain had wanted to chicken out' (Rawnsley, 1995, 591).

Despite Macmillan's success over DEFCON 3 status for US forces in NATO, the missile crisis raised issues of British control over America's UK bases, and, indeed, over British nuclear forces themselves in acute form. American Polaris submarines were moved out to sea from Holy Loch. A late 1962 Foreign Office report tried to clarify the situation regarding nuclear alert. Evelyn Shuckburgh, FO deputy under-secretary described Macmillan's options in respect of nuclear alert. His understanding was that use of US bases in Britain was 'a matter of joint decision' (under various understandings achieved in the late 1940s, and discussed below in Chapter 7). 'Political consultation' would also take place, however, regarding 'the use of nuclear weapons anywhere in the world':

> The Prime Minister had 24 hours (although publicly we can only admit to 12 hours) in which he could have said that he disapproved of the action contemplated, and advised against it, or that if it were taken he would reserve HMG's position, or even that HMG would publicly oppose the action. The Prime Minister did not say any of these things. (Baylis, ed., 1997, 127)

In January 1963, Ormsby-Gore treated London to his reflections on the crisis. His own role in it had been remarkable: 'a special relationship within the "Special Relationship" ' (Nunnerley, 1972, 39). The British ambassador ran, admittedly without much success, his own campaign to link the future of Cuba with that of Berlin. His review of 1962 suggested that the events of October showed that the US would never write off London's views. Nevertheless, he relayed Washington's insistence 'that the dangers of the nuclear age demand unity of command and decisions at a speed which may preclude wide consultation at the time'. The lesson of the crisis was that Britain's relationship with the US 'is perforce unequal and cannot be static' (FO 371 168405).

Ormsby-Gore's insight was to be borne out by the experience of Anglo-American relations during various 'hot' conflicts between 1962 and the end of the Cold War. The success of British diplomacy after 1962 was to depend upon a combination of nifty opportunism and a fundamental understanding of the asymmetry at the heart of the 'special relationship'. L.V. Scott, author of a full-length study of the British role in the crisis, sees its central diplomatic lesson as the realisation that 'the price of access in Washington was loss of political independence' (Scott, 1999, 185). Sustained access translates into loyalty; it does not even guarantee influence. At the highest levels of superpower confrontation, however, Ormsby-Gore was correct. Washington was not entirely unmindful of London's advice and wishes. However, at the apex of nuclear diplomacy, British influence could only ever be marginal.

Economic Issues and the Premiership of Alec Douglas-Home

Problems with British economic competitiveness and with confidence in sterling strongly affected Anglo-American relations in the early 1960s. At one level, Washington suspected that economic weakness would soon force a contraction in British defence commitments. Perhaps even more worrying for the US was the possible impact of repeated sterling crises on international financial stability. The Bretton Woods congress of 1944 had, in effect, installed the US dollar as the guarantor of international economic exchange, yet sterling remained an important convertible international reserve, whose integrity the US regarded as crucial to the health of the financial system established at Bretton Woods.

During the early 1960s, the question of Britain's economic future began to become inextricably linked to the debate on entry into the European Economic Community. Encouraged by Kennedy, Harold Macmillan formally applied to join the Community in the summer of 1961; ironically, Mac's application was to some extent linked to his doubts, reinforced by the conduct of the Eisenhower administration at the 1960 Paris summit, about American commitment to achieving diplomatic progress in the Cold War (Ashton, 2002, 131). The most obvious source of economic policy tension between London and Washington in the early 1960s, however, involved neither sterling nor European integration. Rather, it raised an area of dispute which was to persist until the closing phases of the Cold War: Britain's economic links with communist regimes, 'trading with the enemy'.

During periods of intense superpower Cold War confrontation, British trade links with communist countries were very strongly resented by Washington. The British view was that trade, at least non-military trade, was a way of easing international tension. London also felt that the US, so comparatively self-sufficient and nondependent on trade, did not appreciate Britain's needs. In March 1961, Sir Patrick Reilly of the British Foreign Office reminded Washington that 'HMG was under very great internal pressure to increase trade with the Soviets' (*Foreign Relations of the US, 1961–63, vol. 9*, 649).

To understand the US view, it is necessary briefly to return to the early days of the Cold War. America's post-1945 economic war on communism dated from April 1948, when the Truman administration promulgated export restrictions on East-West trade. In 1950, a multilateral body (the Coordinating Committee or COCOM) was set up and charged with compiling lists of items which should not be traded to communist countries. Though Eisenhower personally favoured a relaxation of the strict guidelines drawn up in the early 1950s, his presidency saw important Anglo-American clashes over which items should be enlisted. Throughout the 1950s, America's preference was for including non-military items, in order to hit the Soviet economy. The 1951 Battle Act required the executive to curb aid to countries who violated the embargo. In 1957, Britain and France cooperated to destroy the 'China differential': the regime which, since 1952, had applied stricter regulations on trading with communist China than with the USSR.

These disputes continued into the Kennedy years, despite JFK's own willingness to liberalize trade. Shortly before his death in November 1963, Kennedy inaugurated a review of trade with communist countries, designed to take account of the post-Cuban missile crisis easing of tension. The US–UK clashes in COCOM over the Cuban embargo were, nevertheless, severe. In February 1963, Thomas Finletter, Washington's ambassador to NATO, informed Secretary of State Dean Rusk that the UK was giving 'priority to its short range commercial interests over basic interests of Atlantic

Alliance'. He mentioned credits to the Soviet bloc, trade to Cuba, Viscount aircraft sales to China and the sale of wide-diameter pipes for use in the Soviet oil industry. 'If Soviet oil deal consummated,' wrote Finletter, 'UK will have achieved almost perfect score of opposition to us in NATO on all E/W issues' (Dobson, 1988, 608).

The Kennedy era disputes over international listing alarmed Ambassador Ormsby-Gore. He feared that antagonism in this area 'might weaken Anglo-American relations' (FO 371 164567, 27 Feb. 1962). Tension decreased as American attitudes softened after 1962. In 1964, a major US–Soviet grain trade deal was finalized. Nevertheless, British trade with Cuba constituted the major US–UK dispute of the short prime ministership of Conservative Sir Alec Douglas-Home (1963–4). (The former Lord Home became Britain's leader following Macmillan's resignation, in the wake of government scandals, in October 1963.)

Douglas-Home and Lyndon B. Johnson (US president from 1963 to 1969) failed to establish anything approaching a Jack-and-Mac closeness. Douglas-Home's advocacy of 'independence' in the matter of British nuclear deterrence irritated Washington. LBJ also expressed intense anger over the new British leader's attitude to Cuban trade. In February 1964, Johnson reacted strongly to Douglas-Home's refusal unequivocally to cease trading with the renegade Castro. The president treated Walter Heller, his principal economic adviser, to a disquisition on Washington's problem with its close allies:

> everybody just treats us like we all used to treat our mother. They impose on us. We just know that she's sweet and good and wonderful and she is going to be kind to us and she'll always know that we came out of her womb and we belong to her, and every damned one of them talk to me that way. I don't care who it is ... they just screw us to death. (Beschloss, ed., 1997, 243)

A briefing paper prepared for Johnson prior to Douglas-Home's February 1964 visit to Washington seemed to encapsulate the shift that had taken place with the change of leadership personnel in the two capitals. The paper noted that the '*close US–UK association*' was 'the most important single factor in British foreign policy'. The US was simply committed to the 'association' (Bartlett, 1992, 107–8).

US–UK Diplomatic Relations after Jack and Mac

Anglo-American diplomatic relations had resumed a degree of post-Suez business-as-usual even before Jack and Mac assumed their custody of the 'special relationship'. Kennedy and Macmillan succeeded in setting the terms for the future: nuclear and intelligence cooperation, close personal contacts, privileged diplomatic access, a degree of American indulgence towards British global pretension – all set against the background of American superpowerdom, British international shrinkage, and the realisation on all sides that, after Suez, nothing would ever be quite the same. In 1956 the threat of American power had been enough to put British policy into reverse. From Jack and Mac to Tony Blair and George W. Bush, this was not in any sense to be an alliance of equals. We end this chapter with a brief glance forward to two features of the house that Jack and Mac built. There follow short discussions of, firstly, US–UK diplomatic closeness; and, second, the nagging and insistent question of interests. What exactly were the interests, British and American, which were to sustain the post-Suez relationship despite its enormous internal disparity of power?

The history of the 'special relationship' has certainly been distinguished by a degree of elite diplomatic closeness which sets US–UK relations apart from most, if not all, other sets of American bilateral alliances. It is very easy to find witnesses to this putative special intimacy. In 1990, Gregory Treverton, looking forward to a 'special relationship' with no Cold War anchor, wrote that 'bright British diplomats in Washington will continue to be told more by the state department and treasury than those departments regularly tell each other'. Americans 'will continue to feel that Anglo-Saxons can understand each other better than those who do not speak (roughly) the same language'(Treverton, 1990, 710). Nearly 30 years after Kennedy and Macmillan, Treverton still inhabited a world where Anglo-American relations partook of the characteristics of a family affair, if not exactly in the literal Jack and Mac sense, certainly in the sense of an alliance based on close elite cultural sharing. Throughout the Cold War, and after, the British Embassy in Washington was to exploit elite cultural closeness to promote a variety of causes, from Concorde landing rights to the gaining of American support during the Falklands War. Diplomatic closeness manifested itself in relation to the London and

Washington embassies, to the State Department and Foreign Office, to embassies in third countries and to US–UK diplomatic collusion at the United Nations (Wallace, 1975, 153–4). A 1962 Foreign Office report, 'Britain through American Eyes', concluded that 'most Americans regard Britain as the country most like the United States'. The report's implication was that mass and elite diplomatic coincided here (PREM 11 5192, 13 February 1962). In 1970, Lord Gore-Booth, permanent under-secretary at the Foreign Office in the late 1960s, spoke of a 'natural closeness of cooperation', based on 'community of language' and 'seeing things in the way of govern- ment by consent of the governed' (Baylis, ed., 1997, 155). Later in the 1970s, Geoffrey Moorhouse (1977, 35) recorded views of Foreign and Commonwealth Office diplomats that would not have surprised their counterparts in the era of Jack and Mac, or even of Oliver Franks. Moorhouse found a widespread view among British diplomats that Washington, especially the State Department, 'finds it more natural to talk to the FCO than anyone else abroad because American officials know that from the direction of London they'll get an honest answer, an intelligent and considered view'.

It is very difficult to evaluate such views. At one level, there is the familiar desire of British officials to reify and exaggerate Anglo- American cultural closeness. The 1962 Foreign Office report was perhaps guilty of this in its playing on 'common language and literature and sense of kinship', perhaps as a kind of compensation for the recent trauma of Suez. Yet, in other respects, the report was very hard-headed, for example in its view that Americans 'respect money-makers and Russia-haters, and in both ways West Germany has the edge on Britain' (PREM 11 5192). At another level, the US foreign service corps probably has tended, well beyond the era of Jack and Mac, to partake of anglophile attitudes, if not quite to the extent supposed by critics of State Department elitism.

Whatever intangible truths it does convey, the assumption, that a special, culturally-based, intimacy, deriving from the era of Oliver Franks, underpins US–UK diplomatic relations, misses some important points. Most obviously, it neglects the impact of bureau- cratic and international change. By the late 1970s, for example, recruitment patterns for career US diplomats had altered. The view that the entire American foreign service is permanently staffed by Anglophile WASPs is misleading. Accelerating British involvement in the process of European integration, something which President

Kennedy strongly supported, has also tended to reduce the impact of any bilateral Anglo-American cultural closeness. It is also important to appreciate the very different political and decisional contexts in which American and British diplomats operate. As a general rule, the British Foreign Office (after 1968, the Foreign and Commonwealth Office) has worked within a relatively closed elite decisional environment. The State Department, for all its putative elitism, has developed a decentralized structure, suffering, in Zara Steiner's phrase, 'the disadvantages of too much sunlight' (Steiner, 1987, 16). State's decentralization and relative openness is precisely one of the reasons why its powers have tended to be usurped by the White House, an institution somewhat less likely than the State Department to be influenced by generalized, culture-based sentiment. There is also the almost ontological divergence between State, staffed at higher levels by political appointees, and the British Foreign Office, dominated by career people. British diplomats, along with British leaders like Macmillan, are often credited with acute insight into US political processes. Thomas Risse-Knappen (1995, 211) saw the British as 'masters in building transgovernmental coalitions with players inside the US administration'. Yet the reality of British skill should be balanced against a degree of misunderstanding of American ways. Access, within the highly permeable American political structure, may sometimes be confused with influence. A little knowledge, combined with cultural confidence, is a dangerous thing.

Above all, the asymmetry of the US–UK relationship must always be borne in mind. The power dynamics between the two allies were brutally displayed at Suez. Since the days of Jack and Mac, American power, relative to Britain, has actually grown, although American power *over* Britain has ebbed and flowed in line with changes in the international economic and strategic environment. Asymmetry of power was a structural feature of the house that Jack and Mac built, or rebuilt. A striking description of this asymmetry, a vivid counter to the usual diplomatic affirmations of cultural intimacy, was given by former senior British diplomat Sir John Cable in 1994. He wrote of a 'culture of dependence' affecting the British embassy in Washington. Even more revealingly, this former head of the Foreign and Commonwealth Office planning staff noted: 'Known American wishes tend to bring an element of precensorship to the process of decision-making in London' (Cable, 1994, 112).

Given this asymmetry, it is appropriate to end this chapter by briefly indicating the underlying interests which undergirded the Cold War 'special relationship', the relationship that Jack and Mac rescued from the mangle of Suez. At its centre, of course, was the 'common fate' that Dean Acheson had mentioned in 1952. The logic of anti-Sovietism certainly bound the allies together for around 40 years. Beyond this, it is a little easier to discern British than to discover American interests. On the British side, there was the familiar desire to maintain global influence on the cheap, to enjoy privileged access to sanctums of power, to retain American support for British presence on the UN Security Council, possibly to increase Britain's leverage in Europe, and so on. Some of these desires no doubt led London into counter-productive and unrealistic policy postures, but it is not in question that they existed.

On the American side, it is frequently pointed out that world (even 'free world') leadership is a lonely business, and that US diplomats and leaders welcome a reliable, culturally familiar, friend. British military, basing and intelligence capabilities were very valuable to the US. It is also worth noting, however, that the 'special relationship', at least as refashioned by Kennedy and Macmillan, did not involve all that much in the way of American commitment. Intelligence sharing; a generous financial deal on nuclear weapons; military cooperation; privileged, though still limited, consultation and access; absolutely no blanket guarantee of support in all eventualities (that, after all, was the lesson of Suez): Washington could certainly live for the foreseeable future with these aspects of its alliance with London. According to a 1968 State Department report, Britain also provided the US with 'diplomatic reports from capitals where it has no representation'.. In the nuclear field, it made 'contributions to weapons technology ... independent analyses of new weapons design, and the use of Christmas Island as a base for certain atmospheric tests'. To a declining extent, the US could also benefit from diplomatic and other openings associated with British imperial and global history (Colman, 2003, 132: State Department Research Memorandum, 'What Now for Britain?', 7 February 1968). In some respects, and in compensation for its global decline, British weakness actually increased British reliability. After all, London no longer had anything to gain in trying to rival the US. As an unthreatening, yet still credible and (regionally, if not in any independent sense globally) influential ally, Britain augmented American Cold War 'soft power' (Elie, 2005). According to Joseph Nye, 'soft power' involves 'the ability to shape the preferences of others'. A country's 'soft power' rests on three resources: 'its culture (in places where it is attractive to others), its political values (when it lives up them at home and abroad), and its foreign policies (when they are seen as legitimate and having moral authority)' (Nye, 2004, 11). At least when it worked smoothly, the US–UK relationship after 1960, the house that Jack and Mac built, served to enhance the appeal of American global authority. The British side of the 'special relationship' bargain depended upon London's ability to be both a reliable and an internationally credible ally: in other words a reliable and credible contributor to American 'soft power'.

4

Lyndon Johnson to Jimmy Carter

The presidencies of Lyndon Johnson, Richard Nixon, Gerald Ford and Jimmy Carter saw major tensions and irritants in the 'special relationship'. In contrast to Jack and Mac, these tensions were exacerbated by problematical leader relations, notably between President Johnson and Harold Wilson and between President Nixon and Edward Heath. The Vietnam War, British economic difficulties and British military cuts dominated the early part of this period. Yet the institutions of the 'special relationship' persisted, even enjoying something of a revival in the last two years of Jimmy Carter's presidency.

The British Labour Government, 1964–1970

Wilson, Johnson and the Limits of Cooperation

Harold Wilson's own background was on the left of the Labour Party. He had subscribed to the Keep Left group's 1951 manifesto, *One Way Only*, which was severely critical of US policy. In the debates of the early 1960s, however, over unilateral nuclear disarmament, Wilson had emerged as a compromiser. The 1960 Labour Party conference voted for unilateral nuclear disarmament, causing the party leader Hugh Gaitskell to denounce the Campaign for Nuclear Disarmament as 'pacifists, unilateralists and fellow travellers' (Morgan, 1990, 183). Gaitskell campaigned successfully for a reversal of the unilateralist resolution in 1961. At one level, he was able to exploit tensions between the left's anti-nuclearism and its anti-Americanism. In 1960, for example, he argued that unilateralism 'would mean sheltering behind the United States deterrent and there is no morality in that' (Jones, 1997, 110). The logical conclusion of the unilateralist position lay in neutralism, which did not command a viable political constituency. By the time Wilson became shadow foreign secretary in 1961 – certainly by the time he became premier in 1964 – he was essentially himself a pro-American modernizer, a partaker of the spirit of Kennedy's Camelot. By the mid-1960s, following the Cuban missile crisis and the 1963 Partial Test Ban Treaty (and also linked to splits in CND), the issue of unilateralism had ceased to trouble the Labour leadership (Keohane, 1993, 22–3).

To Lyndon Johnson, Harold Wilson's Labour Party indeed was a modernizing force, free of the stuffed-shirt elitism of the Conservatives under Alec Douglas-Home. The Kennedy administration admittedly had formed some negative views of Wilson. Ed Murrow of the US Information Agency advised National Security adviser McGeorge Bundy that Wilson was 'devious as a garter snake'. In 1963, CIA Director John McCone actually made a formal approach to Harold Macmillan regarding allegations that Wilson was working for Moscow (Ashton, 2002, 24). The Johnson White House, however, did not become alarmed at the election of a socialist government in London in 1964, this despite the continuing efforts of elements in the CIA and British intelligence to smear Wilson as a 'Soviet asset' (Dorrill and Ramsay, 1991; Ramsay, 1993). As Henry Kissinger later wrote, Harold Wilson (prime minister from 1964 to 1970; and from 1974 to 1976) represented a 'generation of Labour Party leaders which was emotionally closer to the United States than were many leaders of the Conservative party' (Kissinger, 1979, 92). Johnson's outbursts of temper, especially relating to Vietnam, are well-known. His famous description of Wilson as a 'little creep camping on my doorstep' may be apocryphal, but does have a ring of authenticity. Johnson was widely quoted in 1967 as warning Wilson: 'Every time you get in trouble in Parliament you run over here with your shirt-tail hanging out. I'm not going to allow it this time' (Hitchens, 1993). Wilson's tone towards LBJ did sometimes border on the sycophantic. In 1965, for example, the British prime minister agonized over whether to send a letter of congratulation to Washington in connection with LBJ's progress on black civil rights. Wilson received Foreign Office advice to the effect that Washington was 'hypersensitive to any suggestion that third parties might be offering advice'. Yet Wilson's letter was sent (FO 371 179611, R. M. K. Slater, 16 March 1965). A Johnson aide in 1967 told his boss that Wilson wanted to offer an excuse for meeting Robert Kennedy, by then an open opponent of the president. Wilson 'wanted to be sure you understood the circumstances. He felt he could not say no to the Senator's request' (NSF: Name File: Bator, box 1, 26 Jan. 1967). Yet both David Bruce and Barbara Castle reported a genuinely friendly mutual respect between Wilson and Johnson (Castle, 1984, 147; Bruce Oral History, LBJ Library, 8). This complex combination of respect and irritation, of occasional British sycophancy and American temper, of subtle acceptance of the unequal power relationship, seemed paradigmatic of the entire Anglo-American partnership.

As with the Kennedy-Macmillan era, some important elements of Anglo-American relations in the mid-to-late 1960s will be treated in the thematic chapters which follow our chronological survey. The debate over Britain's deterrent, American plans for the Multilateral Nuclear Force, Britain's policy towards the Vietnam War and the developing impact of European integration will all be covered in subsequent chapters. What must be emphasized here, however, is how strongly Britain's parlous economic condition came to dominate the transatlantic relationship in these years.

The two topics dealt with in detail in this chapter, the 1967 British currency devaluation and the debate over UK defence commitments, reveal the extent to which economic troubles were now driving Britain's relationship with the US. The difficulties of this period should not, however, be exaggerated. Close cooperation between the two governments did continue. Sir Trevor Lloyd-Hughes, a Downing Street press secretary during the Wilson years, has even asserted that Wilson raised with President Johnson the possibility of Britain one day becoming the fifty-first American state. According to Lloyd-Hughes, discussions took place on those lines in 1966 and 1967, following the French veto over Britain's entry into the Common Market. If true, the episode may also have reflected Wilson's disillusionment over Commonwealth criticisms of his handling of the Rhodesian question. We may speculate that any request for federal union was disingenuous, designed to enhance Johnson's opinion of the Labour leader. The US president was, of course, keen to see Britain firmly committed to Europe, acting as a counter to

French anti-Americanism (*The Independent on Sunday*, 24 January 1999).

Britain benefited in American eyes from being contrasted with anti-Americanism and political upheavals in France. The US and Great Britain cooperated in a successful operation to exclude leftists from office when Britain Guiana gained its independence. On the Rhodesian question, where Ian Smith had made a unilateral declaration of independence in 1965 to preserve white rule, the US was generally supportive of sanctions. According to Wilson, Africanists at the State Department pressed on Johnson 'the need to keep on close terms with black Africa' (Wilson, 1971, 187). Yet there were tensions with the US over sanctions, especially oil sanctions. British Ambassador to the US, Patrick Dean reported in 1966 that American officials 'without any hint of blackmail' were connecting Rhodesian sanctions to the continuation of British shipping links to North Vietnam (FO 371 185002, 10 Feb. 1966).

The issue of Rhodesia was discussed during a January 1967 National Security Council meeting in Washington. Secretary of State Dean Rusk declared that Rhodesia was 'first a UK problem, then a UN problem, and only then is it a US problem'. According to Rusk, the US 'must get UK Prime Minister Wilson talking to Smith and exert our influence behind the scenes'. US Ambassador to the UN Arthur Goldberg described US policy as torn between pressure from the 'Rhodesian lobby' in the US and what he called 'domestic racial difficulties'. Goldberg continued: 'We have been talking to US Negro leaders trying to convince them that we are not pulling UK chestnuts out of the fire as they believe.' President Johnson drew out some of America's problems in supporting the British line:

> What are the British going to do if Rhodesia won't give in, and economic sanctions won't work, primarily because South Africa won't comply with them? A blockade would not be effective and there is no way to stop South African oil from going to Rhodesia. The British would be hurt if South Africa moves against them. We can't prevent South Africa from giving aid to Rhodesia ...
>
> How are we going to work out of this black/white African problem: (a) without drifting into a situation involving the use of force; (b) upholding the UN; (c) maintaining our good relations with the UK; (d) avoiding a showdown with South Africa; and (e) retaining our

influence in black Africa? (NSC Meetings File, box 2, 'Summary Notes of 567th NSC Meeting, January 25, 1967').

Harold Wilson and Devaluation

The Wilson government's failure to devalue the pound before November 1967 has frequently been ascribed to American pressure. The US, in Perry Anderson's phrase, 'regarded sterling as an out-work of the dollar' (Anderson, 1992, 170). Washington, fearing exposure of the dollar if Britain devalued, encouraged London to maintain sterling at a damagingly high rate. Several commentators have held that some kind of deal or (in Ben Pimlott's phrase) 'secret agreement' was made by the early summer of 1965: the US would lead a multilateral rescue for the sinking pound and extend loans to Britain. In return, Wilson would abandon 'socialist' policies of high public spending, accept deflation, retain overseas military commitments and offer at least rhetorical support for the US in Vietnam (Pimlott, 1993, 386; Ponting, 1989, chs 3, 13; Wrigley, 1993, 128). Edward Short, Wilson's chief whip, even alleged that a 'deal' was done before the 1964 general election: the US would make substantial loans available to support sterling if the new Labour government undertook not to devalue (Short, 1989, 117; Ziegler, 1993, 191).

We shall return to the question of 'deals' after reviewing the background to the 1967 devaluation. The documentary record, both in Britain and the US, makes it clear that Washington did indeed fear that a collapsed and devalued pound would endanger not only the dollar but the entire world financial system. Reviewing American policy in 1965, British Ambassador to Washington Patrick Dean described President Johnson as 'acutely conscious of the internal politics of economic problems, but ... less at home in their international aspects'. At heart, LBJ, 'a remote and difficult man', was 'a nationalist in economic matters'. US policy in 1965 had, according to Dean, 'been one of support for sterling and sympathy for United Kingdom economic difficulties':

Even if the United States balance of payments deficit is eliminated, the United States Administration will wish to keep its close touch with the sterling problem since it recognizes its common interests with sterling as a reserve currency, although it regards sterling as a junior partner. It also recognizes the political importance of a stable pound sterling in relation to the United Kingdom's defence effort.

In trade and monetary issues, wrote Dean, Washington saw 'the same pattern of a measure of common interest with the United Kingdom, of French intransigence, and of the hope of German support' (FCO 371 185019, 14 Jan. 1966).

On the American side, Treasury Secretary Joseph Fowler gave his opinion to President Johnson in July 1966 that a sinking pound would have 'very serious consequences for the United States, its entire foreign policy and the continued stability of the free world financial system' (NSF: CF: UK, box 209, 14 July 1966). In 1965, George Ball argued in favour of large loans to support the pound: 'if we let the British go to the wall, they will not only devalue, but devalue big' (NSF: CF: UK, box 215, 'British Sterling Crisis'). Multilateral rescues for the pound, backed by US money, were organized in 1964, 1965 and 1966. Johnson's advisers differed on the question of how long Britain could hold out. The chief optimist was Walter Heller, of the Council of Economic Advisers. In June 1965, Heller opined that Britain could avoid devaluation with US loans: 'the pessimism had [*sic*] been overdone' (NSF: CF: UK, box 207, O. Eckerstein to G. Ackley, 11 June 1965). A month later, Ambassador David Bruce warned of an 'almost terrifying run on the pound, with presently incalculable consequences' (NSF: CF: UK, box 207, 26 July 1965). Yet, even as late as September 1967, Heller was maintaining that, with 'US help over the rough spots', devaluation could still be avoided (NSF: CF: UK, boxes 211, 212, Heller to Johnson, 9 September 1967).

Throughout the period 1965–7, US policy makers debated the merits of unilateral versus multilateral rescues, as well as the extent to which aid could be made conditional. In July 1965, Bruce feared that Washington was backing itself into a situation where the US would be 'faced with the alternatives of British devaluation or full support of the pound by ourselves' (NSF: CF: UK: box 207, 26 July 1965). Any absolute commitment to back sterling, even in a multilateral setting, might simply embolden Wilson. If the pound would be supported in any event, he might increase public spending and withdraw from global military commitments. A high-level policy group decided to tell Wilson during the summer 1965 sterling crisis that devaluation was 'unthinkable and cannot be permitted'

(NSF: CF: UK, box 215, Ackley to Johnson, 29 July 1965). Council of Economic Advisers chairman Gardner Ackley was sceptical:

> the *UK has to make its own decision* as to whether the costs are worth it. If they hold back because *we*.ask them to, or demand it, it's not going to work ... If we say its unthinkable, the end of the world, we'll get hung up with a unilateral rescue. (NSF: CF: UK, box 215, Ackley to M. Bundy, 29 July 1965)

The sterling crisis of November 1967 provoked frantic transatlantic negotiations. Chancellor James Callaghan informed Washington on 10 November that 'we are getting to the end of the period when we can afford to carry on [*sic*] a hand-to-mouth basis month by month'. The 'time for long-term decisions' was 'very close at hand' (Ponting, 1989, 291). One of the ironies of the situation was that, to many leading London actors in this drama, Britain's plight had been aggravated by the inflationary impact of LBJ's Vietnam policy. In early 1966, J.L.N. O'Loughlin of the Foreign Office reported: 'I do not see how the Great Society and Vietnam can be paid for without serious strain' (FO 271 185018, 13 Jan. 1966).

Wilson's account of the devaluation crisis has him taking the final decision to devalue as, in effect, an assertion of national sovereignty: 'We rejected any idea of relying on an international package with, almost certainly, intolerable accompanying domestic measures'. Despite evidence on 15 November that Washington was further 'stiffening' against devaluation, 'this was not backed by anything in the nature of a cheque-book' (Wilson, 1971, 454–5). The US brought pressures to ease the conditions for an International Monetary Fund (IMF) rescue; it would not act unilaterally and unconditionally. On 18 November, Wilson announced a 14.3 per cent devaluation. US Treasury Under-secretary Frederick Deming reported to Johnson from London: 'Situation in London was black; nobody wanted to see the pound go, but in the end they could not see any feasible alternative' (NSF: CF: UK, boxes 211, 212, 'Notes on President's Meeting', 19 Nov. 1967). Federal Reserve chief Martin reflected the sense of crisis: 'It is the dollar to which the whole world is looking ... We must show the world ... that we can keep the dollar sound ... if we are not to go the way of the UK' (Cabinet Papers, box 11, Minutes of Cabinet Meeting Nov. 20, 1967).

Without any question, American pressure – and support for sterling – was an important factor in Britain's postponement of devaluation until late 1967. In a sense, there was a 'deal' involving, as Alan Dobson (1990b, 250) has put it, 'an inextricable intertwining of economic and defence matters'. Some Johnson advisers did not shy away from using the word 'deal', and rumours of a secret agreement were rife in London. Foreign Secretary George Brown felt that Wilson had sold his soul to Johnson (Castle, 1984, 41, 147; Crossman, 1975, 574; Goodman, 1979, 492–3; King, 1972, 78), yet leading protagonists, notably James Callaghan and David Bruce, later keenly denied that there was any 'deal'. It certainly never attained any formal status, remaining rather at the level of shared understandings within a well defined power relationship. It should also not be forgotten that the Wilson government did not *want* to devalue. According to Callaghan, Wilson felt that devaluation probably would be a consequence of joining the European Community, but that it should be postponed as long as possible. Callaghan himself believed 'that our sustained work in improving Britain's industrial structure combined with a substantial increase in exports should suffice to see us through with an unchanged parity' (Callaghan, 1981, 210). American pressure must take its place alongside other factors which delayed the devaluation. These factors include self-deception and a belief that devaluation would undermine national prestige and open the door to global financial chaos.

Conventional Defence Commitments

Washington was especially preoccupied in the mid-1960s with the prospects for retention of British military commitments in the Far East. The Wilson government's support for US-led anti-communism in the region was compromised not only by economic troubles at home, but also by Wilson's determination to keep Britain out of the conflict in Vietnam. London's preference was for arms sales, rhetorical backing and intelligence cooperation over actual military support. These preferences were evident both in Vietnam and in Indonesia, where London offered support after 1965 to the anti-communist generals' purges. Thousands of Indonesian oppositionists, real or imagined, were killed in this period. London was content to supply arms and intelligence. The Wilson governments also deprioritized the conflict in Borneo, a territory claimed by Indonesia, to avoid, as the British ambassador in Jakarta put it, 'biting the Generals in the rear' (Curtis, 1998, 29).

For all of London's good offices, there was no substitute in Washington's view for actual military presence. Wilson's military commitment to East of Suez was taken initially at face value. By mid–1965, however, LBJ and his advisers were having doubts. To some extent, US concern about the British military presence East of Suez was bound up with the Vietnam War. In American eyes, however, it went to the heart of anti-communist burden sharing and had implications for the US guarantee to Europe. At the end of 1965, Secretary of State Dean Rusk advised LBJ, that in many Far East regions, 'the UK can perform security functions that no other nation can take over' (NSF: CF: UK, box 206, Rusk to Johnson, 'Visit of PM Wilson', undated). Defence Secretary Denis Healey summed up Australian as well as American pressure to remain in the Far East in November 1965: 'It is one thing to think that we should not get out of Singapore merely to save money; it is another for them to imply that we ought to stay there (and could stay there) regardless of the practical and political difficulties which will mount up against us if current trends continue' (Dockrill, 2002, 133). From Washington's perspective, Wilson was in constant need of reminding that the UK flag should be 'nailed to our mast' in the Far East (NSF: CF: UK, box 215, M. Bundy to Johnson, 16 Dec. 1965). The message was even reinforced by Republican Richard Nixon when he visited London in March, 1967 (PREM 13 1904). As Washington focused on the defence review of 1965–7, consideration was given as to how directly Britain could be either cajoled or entreated to keep its global commitments. George Ball, in a July 1965 telephone conversation with Francis Bator indicated the connection between East of Suez and US backing for the pound: 'we could not afford to do big bail out .... they will threaten us on the defense line' (Papers of G. Ball, telecom, 27 July 1965). He told Treasury Secretary Fowler: 'the President could say to Wilson that obviously we are coming to your rescue on condition that they are not going to pull back from their present commitments' (Papers of G. Ball, box 1, telecom, 29 July 1965). In February 1967, Washington offered a deal: funding of the sterling balances and the setting up of a joint sterling-dollar area for currency protection if Britain continued its Far East commitments. Wilson's refusal reflected a combination of prime ministerial determination to bite the post-imperial bullet, assertion of national sovereignty and a commitment to a European future.

As late as July 1966, Wilson was assuring LBJ that 'the UK will not shirk its East of Suez responsibilities' (NSF: CF: UK, box 216, Bator to Johnson, 29 July 1966). In June 1967, LBJ told the British leader that Far East cutbacks would provoke a 'chain reaction … a reaction which could extend to the American troops in Germany'. Secretary of State Rusk enquired if 'the British policy of reductions East of Suez was to please the Europeans'; he proclaimed his failure to understand why London 'felt compelled to try to decide now the defence posture which they should maintain in the mid-1970s' (PREM 13 1904). Wilson raised the possibility of deploying Polaris submarines in the Pacific.

The London debates over the East of Suez retreat were dilatory, partly because of American pressure but also because, as Saki Dockrill has shown, 'there never seemed to be an ideal time for Britain to withdraw' (Dockrill, 2002, 214). The Malayan/ Indonesian conflict, the Vietnam War, London's desire not to be seen to be cutting commitments in the panic of one of the periodic sterling crises, the politics of military and bureaucratic resistance, encouraged by Washington: all these factors, and several others, delayed the british grasp of the nettle. The *Supplementary Statement on Defence* of July 1967, however, announced major cuts. The seal was set by the Cabinet in January 1968 when Wilson himself deserted what Cabinet diarist Richard Crossman called the 'right-wing junta of George Brown, Denis Healey and Michael Stewart reinforced by Jim Callaghan'. Roy Jenkins, appointed Chancellor of the Exchequer in November 1967, emerged as a key opponent of the East of Suez 'Great Britain addicts'. By cutting commitments in the Far East and also cancelling purchase of the American F–111 aircraft, Wilson was now 'breaking through the status barrier' (Crossman, 1976, 639).

The 1967–8 defence cuts provoked a sense of outrage in Washington, and stoked the resentment felt at Britain's failure to supply troops to Vietnam. Various pressures continued, but by February 1968 Secretary of State Dean Rusk was only able to advise LBJ to 'reiterate our distress at the UK's accelerated withdrawal from Southeast Asia and the Persian Gulf' (Diary Backup, box 90, Rusk to Johnson, 3 February 1967). The annual review for

1967, submitted by Ambassador Patrick Dean, reflected a weary sadness that British presence East of Suez seemed likely to be confined to Hong Kong: 'subsequent Administrations will be liable to consult with us less and take us less into their confidence about areas of the world from which we are consciously opting out' (Annual Review 1967, '1967 Foreign Office Annual Reviews'). In regard to Europe, President Johnson was able to broker a deal, in April 1967, which deflected British threats to withdraw from Germany by offering American money to offset London's German expenditures.

Despite this success, the American verdict on the Wilson defence commitment contractions was clear. 'Tantamount to a British withdrawal from world affairs': this was how LBJ responded to the January 1968 announcement that East of Suez forces would now depart by 1972. Wilson assured the American leader that the UK had simply 'come to terms with our role in the world' (*Foreign Relations of the United States, 1964–1968*, vol. 12, 608, 612). US Defense Secretary Clark Clifford announced at a 1968 National Security Council meeting that a new era in Anglo-American relations had begun. It was one in which Britain 'cannot afford the cost of an adequate defence effort' (NSC Meetings File, box 2, Summary Notes of 587th NSC Meeting, 5 June 1968). Ambassador Patrick Dean recorded the American reaction as one of 'sadness at the passing of an era rather than of indignation' (Dockrill, 2002, 226). The State Department report of 1968, quoted towards the end of the previous chapter, had set great stock on the fact that both US and UK were 'world powers', and identified this as 'a distinguishing characteristic of the special relationship'. The report referred to 'what has been called the "strategic value of residual empire" ', from which flowed 'an unrivalled network of bases and other military facilities that served US foreign policy global interests' (Colman, 2003, 132–3). The East of Suez drawback did not destroy the 'special relationship', but clearly compromised what were, for Washington, some very attractive aspects of it.

A major goal of the Wilson years was to manage the transition to a more affordable defence and diplomatic posture for Britain, without sacrificing the 'special relationship'. London feared both an American decoupling from Europe and a new US-West German alliance. To the Wilson team, German economic success and changing troop configurations in NATO raised the prospect that Bonn might replace London as America's favourite ally. Foreign Secretary Patrick Gordon Walker noted in 1964: 'We must at all costs avoid a US alliance with Germany over our heads' (Pearce, ed., 1991, 299). As events turned out, the intertwined issues of defence commitments, the Vietnam War and the value of the pound dominated Anglo-American relations after 1964. The period saw an adjustment to British status, now defined by Foreign Secretary Michael Stewart as a 'major power of the second rank'. Where post-1945 commentators had echoed Winston Churchill in speaking of Britain's three circles of influence (the Commonwealth, the US and Europe), it was now common to assert that the first two of these two circles were closing. As early as 1966, Patrick Dean was reporting diplomatic anxieties that Britain's seriousness as a world power was being eroded. He commented: 'if mini-skirts instead of the Beefeaters get the headlines for a while, I do not think we should be too upset' (FO 371 185002, 19 July 1966).

From Johnson to Nixon

By the time of the 1968 US presidential election, London could claim a significant role (within NATO's Nuclear Planning Corps) in the negotiations which led to the 1968 nuclear anti-proliferation treaty with over one hundred countries, including the USSR. Yet the treaty really was something of a last hurrah for Britain's place at the diplomatic top table. Ironically, the treaty was even interpreted by some developing nations as tending to invalidate the special US–UK nuclear partnership. The strains on Anglo-American international diplomatic cooperation at the close of the Johnson presidency were evident in Patrick Dean's 1968 report of 'some uneasiness on the part of America about where British foreign policy may be going in terms of relations between the United Kingdom and the USSR' (Bennett and Hamilton, eds, 1997, 28 (2 March 1968)). When Richard Nixon (US president from 1969 to 1974) briefly visited RAF Mildenhall in August 1969, strategic arms limitation talks (SALT) were in process without any significant British input. Nixon told Wilson that 'there was a limit to the amount of bilateral consultation in which they could engage'. Wilson offered to smooth the way for the SALT talks by trying to assuage 'deep European anxieties'. Wilson's own record of the meeting represented a strangely sad meditation on the possibilities for enhancing British influence in a world without global UK commitments: 'precisely because we were a nuclear power ... we could be helpful to the Americans both in helping to indicate to them the more sensitive points which they should seek to meet in advance'. Nixon, continued Wilson, 'no more regards us as a super Power than we do ourselves'. Yet, he 'does not regard us as a poor relation; he is essentially lonely carrying out the great responsibilities and wants to share them at any rate in analysis and prognosis before taking the decisions he has to take' (PREM 13 3009).

Nixon and National Security Adviser Henry Kissinger repeatedly emphasized their commitment to special US–UK relations. They even developed a good working relationship with John Freeman, the former *New Statesman* editor who Wilson appointed as Ambassador to Washington in apparent expectation of a Democratic victory in the 1968 presidential election (Kissinger, 1979, 94–6). (Freeman had described Nixon in the *New Statesman* as a 'man of no principle'). Nixon and Kissinger certainly valued the role which could be played by British diplomacy. Michael Palliser recorded the president's view that 'all over the world' Britain 'had diplomats of very high quality ... It would always be useful to him to have two opinions on some of these questions' (PREM 13 3008). Nixon was prepared to observe the formalities of the 'special relationship' and indeed showed every sign of enthusiasm for them. Nixon was also happy to treat Wilson as a bridge to Europe, underlining the US nuclear commitment to European defence during a February 1969 visit to London: 'The credibility of the United States nuclear deterrent must be maintained not only in the eyes of the Russians, but also in Europe, where it was doubted in some quarters that the President of the United States would risk all-out nuclear attack on his own country by using nuclear weapons to block or halt an attack on Europe' (PREM 13 2097).

Both Wilson and Nixon found the personal side of their relationship difficult. On the evening of 25 February 1968, Wilson arranged for Nixon to attend an impromptu Cabinet meeting. The prime minister later offered a characteristically Pooterish gloss on what was probably a rather grisly occasion: 'Nixon, wrote Wilson, 'still recalled it a year later as the highlight, unexpected and unplanned though it was, of his tour' (Wilson, 1971, 621). Kissinger reported that Wilson's suggestion that he and Nixon move to first name terms was met by a 'fish-eyed stare' from the US leader (Kissinger, 1979,

92). The final Wilson-Nixon meeting took place in Washington in January 1970, with the agenda covering East/West relations, Vietnam, Rhodesia, trade, the Middle East, Greece, the Nigerian civil war and European integration. On the latter point, a high level Downing Street meeting on 12 January concluded that the current US administration was, not as committed to our European venture as President Kennedy had been' (PREM 13 3545). Wilson was reassured about Europe – both in terms of the US defence commitment and of Washington's support for integration – during the Washington meeting. In respect of Nigeria, Kissinger recalled that 'Wilson influenced Nixon's policy to a degree and curbed our interventionist impulses' (Kissinger, 1979, 417).

Edward Heath's Conservative Government, 1970–74

It is tempting to portray the Heath years as witnessing a clear redefinition of Anglo-American relations: a transmogrification of the 'special relationship' into what Heath (1998, 472) and President Nixon in 1971 called 'the natural relationship'. (Heath later wrote that the 'natural relationship', based on common history, was something 'which nobody could take away from us'. The 'special relationship', by contrast, could 'be broken at a moment's notice by either partner'). This relationship, so it can be argued, bore the mark both of Heath's own reservations about US power, and of the conscious distancing of London from Washington which he saw as necessary to ease Britain into the European Community. Heath assured the French president, Georges Pompidou, that Britain would not be a 'Trojan horse', acting for the US in Europe (Hurd, 1979, ch. 5; Lundestad, 1998, 104; Young, 1996). Many commentators assumed that the 'natural relationship' would affirm Britain's acceptance of its position as, in Heath's words, 'a medium power of the first rank' (*US News and World Report*, 21 Dec. 1970, 25). It would also involve the articulation of British foreign relations within a multilateral, European context.

Edward Heath's personal orientation towards the US was far more idiosyncratic and ambivalent than that of any other post-1945 British leader. Henry Kissinger wrote later that 'of all British leaders, Heath was the most indifferent to the American connection and perhaps even to Americans individually'. President Nixon welcomed Heath's 1970 victory over Labour, but developed, again in Kissinger's words, an attitude towards him 'like that of a jilted lover' (Kissinger, 1982, 141). Nevertheless, the notion of a sharp Anglo-American transition in the Heath years can be overstated. The 1970–74 Conservative government was, at one level, merely dealing with strains and pressures inherited from the 1960s. Heath's own attitudes were also complex and do not entirely justify Nixon and Kissinger's impression of him in 1971 as 'a more benign British version of De Gaulle' (Kissinger, 1979, 965).

Some interesting sidelights on elite British diplomatic views at this time emerge from a Foreign and Commonwealth Office report, prepared shortly before Heath's first prime ministerial meeting with Nixon. Entitled 'Anglo/United States Special Relations' and dated 23 September 1970, the report discerned recently 'an American tendency to down-grade us, often subconsciously'. To some degree, matters had actually improved since Nixon's accession. The new president 'did not conceal his pleasure in private conversation at the Conservative victory last June'. Major US–UK differences were seen to revolve around defence burden-sharing, the possible rise of American trade protectionism, and also over the emergent troubles in Northern Ireland. The report exuded the idea of a relationship at the crossroads: 'our European policies will bring us into conflict with some American commercial interests, and after our entry into Europe, the special links between the United Kingdom and the United States are bound generally to become less and less "exclusive" ' (FCO 7 1810).

Washington was initially heartened by the new London regime's decision to keep a small Far East military presence. A Five Power Pact was negotiated with Australia, New Zealand, Singapore and Malaysia in the early days of the Conservative government. At the October 1970 meeting between Heath and Nixon at Chequers, the US leader welcomed the apparent rethinking over East of Suez. On Rhodesia, Heath insisted that London would not yield to pressure from 'Black Africa'. Nixon observed awkwardly that 'the position of the United States government' on Rhodesia was 'complicated by the substantial Black element in the population'. Generally, the UK could help with America's 'lonely position' (FCO 7 1811). US–UK cooperation developed over joint use of the Diego Garcia base in the Indian Ocean. The removal of native people from the island was part of this understanding, originally conceived in 1965;

uncomfortable details about Anglo-American conduct regarding local Chagossians were aired in relation to a London high court decision of 2000, which recognized their right of return. The removal of the Chagossian people from the island of Diego Garcia was achieved by the early 1970s through a mixture of trickery and coercion (Curtis, 2003, 414–431).

Yet, at least from the point of view of maintaining global commitments, as Lord Carrington (defence secretary from 1970 to 1974) later described them, these moves did not amount to a great deal. The Five Power Pact 'wasn't a major defence treaty'. Regarding East of Suez, there was 'no question of completely putting the clock back' despite the protests made by the Conservatives in opposition (Carrington, 1988, 218–19). The new government tacitly accepted the point made by Laurence Martin in 1969: 'Not even as a way to curry favour with the United States does neglect of Europe and concentration upon Asia recommend itself' (Martin, 1969, 20). The British decision to withdraw from the Middle East (announced in March 1971) occasioned less resentment in Washington, who now looked to the Shah of Iran as a reliable guarantor of US interests in the Gulf region.

Edward Heath, the 'jilter' of President Nixon, was the least likely of British leaders to wish to curry favour in Washington. According to Raymond Seitz (1998, 317), his personal relationship with Nixon 'ended in mutual contempt'. At the December 1971 Bermuda conference, Heath spoke passionately about the need for European defence integration. In the late 1960s, he had floated the idea of a 'nuclear force based on the existing British and French forces which could be held in trusteeship' (Campbell, 1993, 341). For Heath, the 'special relationship' tag was misleading. It implied a 'two-member club': 'Even in World War II this was not the case' (*US News and World Report*, 21 Dec. 1970, 24). So concerned was Prime Minister Heath to conduct UK–US relations within a European framework that he instructed his officials to avoid private consultations with their US counterparts. When Kissinger met British Cabinet Secretary Burke Trend in the summer of 1973, the former felt that for 'the sake of an abstract doctrine of European unity ... something that had been nurtured for a generation was being given up'. Trend 'came as close to showing his distress as the code of discipline of the British Civil Service and his sense of honour permitted' (Kissinger, 1982, 191–2).

Heath certainly lacked the instinctive pro-Americanism of other British prime ministers. Later in his long parliamentary career, he made no bones about his dissatisfaction with the defence relationship with the US. Asked in 1990 about Whitehall's attitude towards nuclear sharing and Anglo-American defence links, Heath replied: 'I think it gratifies their ego. We have an enormous staff in Washington, which I tried to get dramatically reduced and it ought to be reduced (not the Embassy staff but all the rest of the military and so on).' Commenting on the 'special relationship' in the context of the 1971 Indo-Pakistan war, Heath declared: 'What they wanted from the special relationship was to land Britain in it as well' (Hennessy and Anstey, eds, 1990, 17, 25). Heath felt in 1971 that America's tilt towards Pakistan was injudicious, serving merely to move India closer to the USSR. Both during and after his premiership, Heath was openly contemptuous of the Nixon-Kissinger idea of a 'Year for Europe' in 1973, writing in his 1998 memoirs that it was equivalent to 'my standing between the lions in Trafalgar Square and announcing that we were embarking on a year to save America!' (Heath, 1998, 493).

Unsurprisingly, the Indo-Pakistan war was not the only occasion of US–UK tension between 1970 and 1974. Economic relations and the role of the dollar were one such area. In a *Foreign Affairs* piece, written before his accession to power, Heath described the global monetary system forged at Bretton Woods in 1944 as depending 'upon a continued US deficit which in turn means a flow of real resources to the richest country in the world'. Under 'the dollar system', the world was 'forced to march in step' with the US (Heath, 1969–70, 45). Nixon's August 1971 suspension of dollar convertibility, effectively terminating the Bretton Woods system, was actually provoked by a British request that the US Treasury should convert three billion dollars into gold. The end of Bretton Woods opened new opportunities for Britain, but London's immediate reaction was to protest the lack of consultation (*The Economist*, 21 August 1971, 3). Tensions between Washington and London were also exacerbated by the degree to which the Nixon administration, though still generally favouring European integration, was becoming apprehensive about the economic competition which could be mounted by an enlarged European community (Lundestad, 1998, 101–4).

Rifts between Europe and the US over the American commitment to NATO were exacerbated by Nixon's insistence that the cost of keeping troops in Europe be kept to a level commensurate, in balance of payment terms, with stationing them in the US. In 1972, the head of the UK delegation to NATO noted a lessening in America's commitment to Europe and 'evidence of an increasing tendency for the Americans to deal bilaterally with the Russians over the heads of the Europeans'. The debate over NATO 'burden sharing' became entwined with that over superpower détente. On the one hand, détente held out the prospect of European demilitarization, allowing defence spending cuts; on the other, it raised fears of an American 'decoupling' from the continent in negotiations with the USSR from which allies were excluded. Heath was clear that 'American troops' could not 'effectively be replaced by Europeans in the foreseeable future' (*US News and World Report*, 21 December 1970, 25), yet inevitably his interest in a European defence identity was read in Washington as a bluff which might some day be called. George F. Kennan echoed elite US opinion in 1974 when he wrote that Western Europe was unwilling rather than unable to provide its own conventional defence (Kennan, 1974). For his part, Heath seems to have come to the view that Nixon and Kissinger were playing off European capitals, one against the other, in a policy designed to establish a clientistic European foreign policy (Hill and Lord, 1996, 308).

The Middle Eastern, Yom Kippur, war of October 1973 occasioned a major dispute between the transatlantic allies. Throughout the war, London and Paris concurred in the view that Israel, sure of US support, was guilty of intransigence regarding the land acquired in 1967. Heath's conduct in 1973 contrasted significantly with Wilson's toeing of America's line six years earlier. On the first day of the 1973 war (6 October), Britain and France refused support to an American-sponsored UN ceasefire resolution, which recognized the post-1967 borders. The French and British leaderships blamed Washington and Israel for the threat to oil flows. According to Kissinger's account, all the NATO allies (except Holland, Portugal and, for a time, West Germany) 'banned our overflight of their territories' for purposes of re-equipping Israel. Later, Kissinger 'complained to Sir Alec Douglas-Home that the Soviet Union had been freer to use NATO airspace than the United States'. Again, in the US secretary of state's memory, Heath did not formally refuse access to the British bases in Cyprus; rather, 'it had been made plain that we should not ask' (Kissinger, 1982, 708–9).

From London's viewpoint, the nuclear alert, which came 19 days after the start of the 1973 war was unnecessary and unilateralist. London was unimpressed by the quality of American readings of Soviet intentions, and speculated about the sureness of Nixon's conduct of policy against the background of the Watergate crisis. The British ambassador, Lord Cromer, was the first allied representative to be informed (personally by Kissinger at 1.03 a.m. on 25 October, half an hour after the alert had technically started). Foreign Secretary Douglas-Home, generally a strong Kissinger supporter, criticized the alert and personally intervened with Soviet Foreign Minister Andrei Gromyko in an attempt to 'repair some of the damage'. Yet Home defended the US, however uncomfortably, in the House of Commons: 'the Americans must be allowed to alert their forces the world over, just as we might in certain circumstances'. Even as the Foreign and Commonwealth Office protested to Washington about the lack of prior consultation, Home was telling the House that 'British interests in an emergency are safeguarded by the agreed arrangements for consultation' (*Parliamentary Debates,*5th series, vol. 863, 969, 7 Nov. 1973).

Douglas-Home, as foreign secretary in Heath's government, consciously saw himself as working to save the 'special relationship': not only in the context of the 1973 alert, but also in the face of the Europeanized drift of UK foreign policy under Heath. The prime minister himself, it must be emphasized, showed, in the words of Hill and Lord (1996, 307), 'no desire to rock the Anglo-American boat. except on his own priority of the construction of Europe'. The nuclear special relationship remained intact, with schemes for Anglo-French nuclear collaboration foundering on the rocks of France's absence from the integrated NATO structure. Reactivation of the Western European Union, the European defence identity within NATO which had originally been established in the early Cold War era, had to wait until the mid-1980s (Carrington, 1988, 221). Encouragement of a separate European voice in NATO also conflicted with traditional British desires to strengthen the American commitment. Heath supported the US line in Vietnam, condemning Enoch Powell's remarks on London's subservience to Washington (Gilmour and Garnett, 1998, 230–1). At the diplomatic level, Kissinger worked closely with Lord Cromer and Burke Trend. Cromer reportedly responded thus to the news of the 1973 alert: 'Why tell us, Henry? Tell your friends, the Russians.' Thomas

Brimelow, FCO deputy under-secretary, was even recruited by Kissinger to draft arms control agreements with Moscow (Dickie, 1994, 151). This involved him as a more intimate party to the diplomacy of détente than either the US Congress or William Rogers, Nixon's first secretary of state!

From the Mid-1970s to the Election of Ronald Reagan

Wilson, Callaghan and Ford: 1974–77

Both Harold Wilson (as prime minister in the years 1974–6) and his Labour Party successor, James Callaghan (1976–9) were concerned to repair the fences which they saw Heath as having damaged. In March 1974, Callaghan, speaking as the new foreign secretary under Wilson, condemned 'the view that Europe will emerge only out of a process of struggle against America' (Baylis, ed., 1997, 187). Henry Kissinger saw the Labour team as having 'a more subtle view of the requirements of European unity' than its predecessor. He noted Callaghan's early promise to have 'an end put to the mutual needling' (Kissinger, 1982, 933).

Both as foreign secretary and as prime minister, Callaghan developed noticeably warm personal relations with Gerald Ford (US president from 1974 to 1977) and, especially, with Kissinger, who served as secretary of state in the Ford administration. According to Callaghan's biographer, Kissinger 'came to regard Callaghan as … a wise old bird', as 'friendly and unstuffy' (Morgan, 1997, 441). In March 1975, the US secretary of state actually took a special flight to Cardiff to see Callaghan being granted the freedom of that city. Kissinger was also apparently charmed by the slightly louche flair of Tony Crosland, who served Callaghan in the post of foreign secretary. Crosland involved Kissinger in a complex game whereby points were awarded for social gaffes at public functions (Kissinger, 1999, 977).

The Wilson team of 1974–6 made further defence cuts, including the proposed withdrawal of all British naval vessels from the Mediterranean. Also to be cancelled was the Simonstown naval agreement with South Africa. (The agreement, which allowed Royal Navy access to bases to safeguard the Cape route, had been strengthened and utilized by the Heath government.) Barbara Castle reported (20 November 1974) Wilson's remarks in Cabinet in November 1974 that Washington had taken the news on Simonstown 'very calmly', though deemed it 'the limit of what is tolerable' (Castle, 1984, 227).

On nuclear policy, Wilson resisted the pressure coming from Labour Party grassroots to rupture the American connection. His secret continuation of the Chevaline nuclear programme was clearly contrary to the letter and spirit of the manifesto on which he was elected in 1974.

The severest test of US–UK cooperation between 1974 and 1976 came in relation to the overthrow of the Makarios regime in Cyprus. The military junta in Athens set up a puppet leader in July 1974 and proclaimed the union of Cyprus with Greece. Foreign Secretary Callaghan looked to Washington to press moderation on Athens in the face of a likely Turkish invasion of the island. He was disappointed. Even when Turkey invaded on 20 July, the US prevaricated and resisted London's calls for an Anglo-American military response, coordinated by the UN. Kissinger's policy – 'neutrality in favour of the Turks' (Morgan, 1997, 446) – reflected his concern for the role of Turkey in NATO and for opinion in the Middle East. The US Congress was opposed to any American intervention (it imposed an arms embargo on the Turks later in the year). Moreover, 'in the last three weeks of Nixon's Presidency we were in no position to make credible threats' (Kissinger, 1982, 1191).

The collapse of the Athens junta defused the crisis, and presaged the division of Cyprus into Greek and Turkish sectors. Wilson was prepared to accept Kissinger's 'regret that the United States had been so ineffective' (Wilson, 1979, 63). For Callaghan, however, Turkey had been encouraged by Washington to profit from aggression; Britain had been cast adrift, left by Washington with the options of accepting Turkey's action or embarking on 'a second Suez' (Callaghan, 1981, 356). Callaghan himself later spoke of the US, in effect, stopping the UK from going to war against Turkey. The US was certainly concerned about the possibility of the Makarios regime drifting towards communism. Of particular concern to Washington was the security of secret defence and intelligence facilities on the island in the face not only of the uncertainties associated with Makarios, but also of British defence cuts. The US not only failed to act against Turkey, but conspicuously neglected to attempt to head off the coup against Makarios. Plans for the partition of Cyprus appeared to have been considered in Washington since the mid-1960s. Spying facilities, some capable of monitoring Soviet nuclear tests, continued to be used by the US in the north of the island, following the Turkish invasion and partition (O'Malley and Craig, 1999).

Despite bitterness over Cyprus, relations between London and the Ford administration were close. Barbara Castle (1984, 305) noted in February 1975 that Wilson 'could not resist a touch of the old self-satisfaction' when talking in Cabinet about the way he was being treated by the new president. Callaghan and Wilson took a visible role in the evolving diplomacy of détente. A case can even be made for British leadership in some areas. Callaghan stood at the fore of diplomatic initiatives to protect Portugal from Soviet influence following the 1974 revolution in that country. In August 1975, Wilson bluntly informed Soviet leader Leonid Brezhnev that: 'One test of détente was the position of Portugal.' His remark came during negotiations relating to the Conference on Security and Cooperation in Europe (CSCE). London was a late convert to the Soviet proposal of a European security conference, yet the Wilson government of 1974–6 played an important role in the CSCE process and in the achievement of its Final Act in August 1975. Proposals for force reductions in Europe were acceptable to the US in the context of post-Vietnam War retrenchment. The broadening of the CSCE agenda to include Soviet human rights also helped mollify domestic American critics of the Nixon version of détente. As it developed, the CSCE process provided London with a coordinating role, a link between Washington and a nascent integrated West European diplomacy. Many British diplomats were sceptical about the negotiations. As the Final Act was signed, Sir J. Killick, former British ambassador in Moscow, wrote that it remained to be seen if the Cold War was 'over, or has only taken new shape'. Sir T. Garvey, Killick's successor in Moscow, told Callaghan in September 1975: ' "Security in Europe" has meant for the Soviet Government the consolidation and perpetuation of the new territorial and political order in Eastern Europe established by Soviet arms, diplomacy and skulduggery ... in the years following 1944.' Sir P. Ramsbotham informed Callaghan from Washington in March 1976 that the USSR was now clearly emerging 'as a Super Power'. There could be no return to the 'over-optimistic Nixonian version of détente'. Detente itself was to collapse in the years following the

1979 Soviet invasion of Afghanistan. However, from London's viewpoint, important diplomatic precedents had been set by Britain's conspicuous role of transatlantic linkage during the CSCE talks (Bennett and Hamilton (eds) 1997, 463, 447, 475; Bennett and Hamilton (eds) 2001, 446–7).

Kissinger's efforts in 1976 to intervene in the Rhodesian impasse raised some diplomatic hackles in London. Kissinger's initiative, tied inevitably to the shifting superpower competition in Africa, involved the creation of an interim administration, with black involvement and guaranteed by Britain and South Africa. With US-backed forces in Angola in disarray, the US initiative rested upon Ian Smith's putative need for American backing against a 'communist' invasion. Callaghan told Kissinger that Britain could 'not be tarred with the South African brush, especially with a Commonwealth conference coming along in London in 1977' (Morgan, 1997, 452–3, 595–6). The Americans' initiative folded in the face of Pretoria's ambivalence and Ian Smith's refusal to countenance the goal of majority rule. South African leader B.J. Vorster was not pre-pared to pressure the Smith regime into accepting the principle of majority rule. Kissinger's pressure on Smith secured a commitment only to majority rule that was 'responsible'. During this abortive initiative, Kissinger effectively made several unilateral reinterpreta-tions of the British position on Rhodesia (Windrich, 1978, 26).

During the Ford years, Wilson presented himself to Washington as a guide to the complexities of the Middle East: 'broadly pro-Israel' and prepared to resist pro-Arabism at the FCO, but with important Arab connections (Wilson, 1979, 165). Callaghan's role, however, was more substantial, and seems to have amounted to more than the one of 'sympathetic listener' (Callaghan, 1981, 490) claimed in his memoirs. Carter certainly actively sought Callaghan's advice over Israel, and in January 1978 the British premier seems to have played a substantive part in influencing Washington's policy. Following a visit to Cairo, the British leader made proposals regarding human rights guarantees on the West Bank and the need to include Jordan in the negotiations (Morgan, 1997, 808). Nonetheless, following the Camp David peace accords, Callaghan denied Washington's request that Britain should guarantee to sell North Sea oil to Israel in the event of future regional disruption (Dickie, 1994, 165).

Callaghan was, in his own words, 'a strong advocate of Anglo-American cooperation when crises developed'. As events in Cyprus demonstrated, this tended to translate into a tendency to seek American help when Britain faced international problems. Callaghan was not only disappointed over Cyprus. Still acting as foreign secretary in the Wilson government, he gained little sympathy from Washington in regard to the increasingly dangerous fishing dispute with Iceland (the 'Cod War'). Following a December 1975 collision between an Icelandic gun boat and a British frigate, Callaghan complained directly to Henry Kissinger. The secretary of state merely responded with a stoic comment from Bismarck: 'The weak are strong because they are reckless. The strong are weak because they have scruples.' Presumably Callaghan was intended to interpret the comment as being of relevance to Cold Wars as well as to Cod Wars. Yet Callaghan, of course, remained a sturdy Atlanticist. He was especially determined never to expose Britain 'to the kind of differences with the United States which existed at the time of the Suez invasion and which had resulted in a terrible setback for British arms and influence' (Callaghan, 1981, 341, 385).

In Callaghan's conduct both at the Foreign Office and as premier, and despite the various rifts with Washington, we can detect a clear aspiration to the role of Atlantic intermediary: explainer of America's ways to Europe and of Europe's ways to America. This role had been desired by Wilson, but rejected by Heath. Callaghan consciously put himself forward as a defuser of potential US-European misunderstandings on the intertwined issues of disarmament and détente (Lane, 2004, 163). As developed by Callaghan, however, the role of Atlantic intermediary raised some acute difficulties. At one level, there was the problem of being taken for granted by the US. With Britain following a clear 'Atlantic intermediary' strategy, Washington might be tempted to concentrate its favours and attention either on France (NATO bad boy) or, more likely, on West Germany (key to NATO modernization and security, and probable leader of an integrated Europe). Even more damaging was the simple issue of Britain's credibility in Europe. Roy Jenkins, who served as president of the European Commission between 1977 and 1981, ridiculed the Atlantic intermediary role as transforming Britain into 'a sort of enlarged Iceland', remote from centres of power in Europe (Jenkins, 1991, 462).

On issues of nuclear defence, the huge cost increases in the Chevaline system strengthened the case for an alternative. As we shall see in more detail in Chapter 7, the post-1976 Callaghan years put Britain firmly on the path to the acquisition of a new (American) nuclear system, Trident. To many in the Labour Party, the Wilson-Callaghan attitude towards nuclear defence exemplified their abject deference to the United States. Nuclear subservience, for those on the party's left, compounded a fundamental economic dependence. In this connection, the defining episode of the 1970s was the 1976 International Monetary Fund crisis. To a generation of leftist critics of the Labour leadership, the crisis was to typify the internal weakness of the British brand of Atlanticist, parliamentary socialism.

The 1976 IMF Crisis

The sterling devaluation of 1967 did not mark the end of British monetary troubles. The 1976 crisis stimulated huge resentment among Labour's supporters at the power of international capitalism in general, and America's role in particular. As Chancellor of the Exchequer Denis Healey turned back from Heathrow airport at the height of the September crisis, he was – in his own words – 'close to demoralisation' (Healey, 1989, 429). Most of the policy shifts – spending cuts, cash limits on spending, money supply targeting, and abandoning the commitment to full employment – were actually already well in train before 1976 (Ludlam, 1992). As Jim Tomlinson (2004, 61) writes, 'it is inaccurate to see the IMF as the major instigator of Labour's policies'; these policies grew from the fractious party debates about economic options, and from the dictates of perceived necessity. However, the symbolic and psychological importance of the crisis is not in doubt. According to Kathleen Burk and Alec Cairncross (1992, xi), the crisis 'was a watershed in postwar economic policy in which the postwar consensus on how the economy should be managed broke down'. The government would now clearly prioritize the battle against inflation. For Tony Benn, 'the victory of world bankers in the IMF over a Labour Cabinet clearly marked the beginning of what has subsequently come to be known as "Thatcherism" ' (Benn, 1989, xii).

For most Labour leaders, and indeed for most Labour supporters, the real villains were the international markets rather than the US. To Prime Minister Callaghan (1981, 428) the 'markets behaved with all the restraint of a screaming crowd of schoolgirls at a rock concert'. The September crisis was, however, precipitated by a row with Washington. The Ford administration did not see its job as being to underwrite the spending policies of Callaghan's government. When the US arranged a standby credit with central banks in June, it attached strings to the two billion dollars which Washington contributed: the credit would have to be repaid within six months. The US knew that Britain would very likely have to go to the IMF before the year's end, and to accept the IMF's inflationary conditions. Edwin Yeo, American undersecretary for monetary affairs, later noted: 'Our role was to persuade the British that the game was over. They had run out of string.' Along with Treasury Secretary William Simon and Federal Reserve head Arthur Burns, Yeo saw the opportunity to force Britain to take 'responsible' action: 'We feared that if a country like Britain blew up, defaulted on its loans, introduced foreign exchange controls and froze convertibility, we could have a real depression' (Burk and Cairncross, 1992, 37; Fay and Young, 1978).

Callaghan deeply resented both the six month limit of June 1976 and the wider strategy of Yeo, Burns and Simon. He appealed directly to President Ford to loosen the IMF's deflationary strings and to provide a safety net for the overseas sterling balances. He received support from US labour leader George Meany, who urged Ford to 'place our strength and resources in the balance on the side of Britain'. In Callaghan's view, however, he was being undermined, not only by the US Treasury and Federal Reserve, but also by 'orthodox' economists in his own Treasury, and by 'a prominent front-bench' Tory who 'was in Washington trying to influence the Administration very strongly against the Labour Government' (Callaghan, 429–31). British resentment was increased by the feeling that, since 1974 and in contravention of shared understandings, the US had already deflated its economy so as, in Denis Healey's words, 'to reduce their deficits at our expense'. Now, felt Healey, Johannes Witteveen, IMF managing director, was being pushed by the US Treasury to impose deflationary conditions on any loans. Neither Germany nor the US was prepared to help with the sterling balances safety net in advance of an IMF deal (Healey, 1989, 431).

In Washington, the crisis was viewed as potentially threatening to international stability. Later interviews revealed fears that leftists in Labour's Cabinet, led by Energy Secretary Tony Benn, might succeed in turning policy towards protectionism, radical investment and compulsory planning agreements. Foreign Secretary Tony

Crosland argued that the protectionist threat could be used as a lever against IMF strings. Ford's National Secretary Adviser Brent Scowcroft reportedly viewed the threat of Britain cutting loose from global free trade as 'the greatest single threat to the Western world' (Burk and Cairncross, 1992, 77).

The key players in London, of course, were Healey and Callaghan. Neither was prepared to follow either Benn's radical, or Crosland's leverage, strategy. Some efforts were made to exploit the Ford administration's preoccupation with the 1976 presidential election. However, Callaghan was successfully pressured by William Simon and by visiting IMF teams. After momentous Cabinet debates – at one time Benn circulated minutes of the 1931 Cabinet meeting which had split Labour – a package was accepted. Healey sent a 'letter of intent' to the IMF before a loan was made. Spending cuts of one billion pounds for 1977/8 and one and a half billion for 1978/9 were promised. When Healey announced the cuts to the House of Commons on 15 December, his reception among Labour MPs was intensely hostile. However, as his deputy Joel Barnett recorded, the 'response from William Simon, the US Treasury Secretary was good' (Barnett, 1982, 110).

Carter, Callaghan and Thatcher: 1977–80

Callaghan developed a cordial personal relationship with the Democrat Jimmy Carter, who became US president in 1977. Although the Foreign Office initially judged it unlikely that the new president 'was more likely to change style than substance' (Bennett and Hamilton (eds.) 2001, 463), Carter took important steps towards injecting human rights concerns into US foreign policy. He became a relatively popular figure in the UK. The new American leader's visit to his distant family roots in Newcastle upon Tyne and Durham in 1977 was an extraordinary success. It illustrated how ties of lineage could still enliven the 'special relationship'. The British ambassador to Washington, Peter Jay (Callaghan's son-in-law), drew close to the Carter team. He aspired almost to the role of a latter-day David Ormsby-Gore, and soon became the Carter administration's greatest champion in the London press (Jay, 1980). The Carter-Callaghan relationship, however, was probably not as close as that between Callaghan and Kissinger. For Callaghan, Carter was a 'gentle and good man' (Callaghan, 1981, 483). David

Owen, Callaghan's second foreign secretary, offered a different perspective on Carter: 'He combines a fundamental decency and good Baptist values with a mean, competitive streak' (Owen, 1992, 319). Carter himself was impressed by Callaghan. The 1979 Conservative electoral victory was regarded with disappointment in Washington. Again, it was clear that Washington did not automatically favour Tory control in Downing Street. White House staffer Jim Rentscher tellingly suggested that Carter should personally congratulate Margaret Thatcher, the new British leader, to 'help counter some of the distorted speculation that we were hoping for a Labor win and "troubled" by the idea of the Tories taking over' (WHCF: Subject File: Countries 167 (executive), box CO-64, 4 May 1979).

The conclusion of a major civil air agreement in 1977 augured well for the Carter-Callaghan relationship. The renegotiation of the 1946 Bermuda Air Service Agreements represented a significant British advance. Secretary of State for Trade Edmund Dell observed that 'Britain secured more of its objectives than a cool assessment of the relative strength of the two contenders made possible'. The UK acquired six new American entry points for its airlines. Alan Dobson has attributed British success in 'Bermuda 2' partly to President Carter's desire to avoid further embarrassment to Callaghan, following the 1976 IMF crisis. The US may also have seen agreement with London as a test for the development of a new, deregulated and multilateral, regime in air transport (Dobson, 1991a; 1995b).

The Rhodesian ball passed to the Carter administration in 1977. Tony Benn's diary entry of 31 March indicated his own approval of Carter's stance, as well as suspicion of David Owen, who took over as foreign secretary from Anthony Crosland in 1977:

> On the United Nations, David reported that the Carter administration was producing what he called 'alarming resolutions' on South Africa, including a suggestion that Britain might actually be asked to introduce economic sanctions against South Africa, which would be impossible because of our economic interests there. It appears we now have a Labour Government on the right of an American Government. (Benn, 1991, 101)

Owen's view on Rhodesia was that 'Kissinger's belated involvement in Southern Africa' had demonstrated 'that US power was crucial'.

He cooperated with US Secretary of State Cyrus Vance on the settlement plan presented in September 1977. This plan unravelled in its turn over the question of the role of Robert Mugabe's leftist Patriotic Front in transitional arrangements, pending elections. In March 1978, Ian Smith arranged an 'internal settlement', which excluded Robert Mugabe. During this period, US and British negotiators worked in partnership. For example, on 6 October 1978, Ambassador Jay and Secretary of State Cyrus Vance met Smith and Ndabaningi Sithole (one of the parties to the 'internal settlement') to urge the view that the March settlement, if unchanged, would produce all-out civil war. US influence over Rhodesia was complicated by clashes with Congress (notably the 'Rhodesia lobby' led by Senator Jesse Helms of North Carolina) over sanctions. Jimmy Carter arranged a meeting with Bishop Abel Muzorewa in July 1979, following pressure from Helms. Muzorewa, another party to the 'internal settlement', became prime minister of 'Zimbabwe-Rhodesia' in April 1979. By this time, Anglo-American diplomacy had made considerable headway, with the US at one stage holding out the prospect of the provision of considerable development funds for a settled Rhodesia-Zimbabwe (Lane, 2004, 166).

Callaghan consciously sought common US and continental European ground on issues of détente. He supported the early Carter administration's commitment to human rights issues and to preserving détente. According to Roy Jenkins, European leaders saw Callaghan as 'too attached to the unesteemed President Carter' (Jenkins, 1991, 462), yet Callaghan continued to promote a strong British role in arms control negotiations taking place outside the Strategic Arms Limitation (SALT II) process. He received private American assurances that any SALT II agreement would not disbar future nuclear transfers to Britain. Callaghan led, however reluctantly, NATO's ambivalent acceptance of US plans to deploy in Europe the Enhanced Radiation Weapon or 'neutron bomb'. Described in the European press as the ultimate capitalist weapon, the ERW was apparently capable of killing people while leaving property untouched. Carter's eventual decision to cancel no doubt caused Callaghan a mixture of embarrassment and relief.

The Carter administration's stance towards the Soviet Union began to harden considerably after the summer of 1978. This movement towards more traditional anti-communist policies was associated with the bureaucratic rise of National Security Adviser Zbigniew

Brzezinski, with continued Soviet internal human rights violations, with changing US domestic political configurations and with evidence of increasing Soviet influence in the developing world. It was certainly not in any way attributable to British influence. In this changing environment, Callaghan found himself in the familiar role of moderator of American anti-communist zeal. NATO's 'twin track' decision to press ahead with cruise and Pershing II nuclear missile deployment in Western Europe, while keeping the door open to arms control negotiations, suited Callaghan's agenda. It provided scope for his role as Atlantic intermediary, while reaffirming the US commitment to Europe in the wake of the ERW cancellation. At the Guadeloupe summit (January 1979), Callaghan achieved American confirmation of the 'twin track' approach and an understanding on Trident.

Callaghan's return from Guadeloupe to a Britain suffering public sector strikes – and especially the pinning to him of the 'Crisis? What crisis?' tag – set the stage for the Thatcher general election victory in May 1979. Detailed assessment of the Thatcher years will be postponed until the next chapter. Prime Minister Thatcher did not establish any special personal closeness with the Carter administration in 1979–80, yet, as Carter noted in his memoirs, she proved herself Washington's surest European ally in relation both to the US hostage crisis in Iran and to the revived anti-Sovietism of Carter's final year (Carter, 1982, 304).

During 1979–80, London repositioned itself as a staunch American supporter in the evolving 'second' Cold War. A compromise settlement was also finally achieved over Rhodesia. The settlement bore the imprint of the pragmatism of Lord (Peter) Carrington (British foreign secretary from 1979 to 1982) rather than Thatcherite confrontation. When Thatcher was first elected, it was presumed in Washington that she would support the Rhodesian 'internal settlement' and the regime of Bishop Muzorewa. Washington was pleasantly surprised to find that, in the words of Carter's national security adviser, 'she was gradually persuaded by a small group in the British Foreign Office' that only 'an all-parties solution' would hold (Brzezinski, 1983, 142). The US did not participate directly in the Lancaster House conference which led to the settlement. Secretary of State Cyrus Vance recalled that Thatcher and Carrington had a 'quite different conception' of America's role in the negotiations, compared to Callaghan and Owen. Yet the US, at the very least, provided support for the final settlement, including an undertaking to seek economic aid from Congress for an independent Zimbabwe. Robert Mugabe took over as prime minister of the country in April 1980. Vance also made it clear to Carrington that, as Carter's secretary of state put it, 'British decisions on Rhodesia would affect Britain's relations with us' (Vance, 1983, 295, 297).

5
Reagan and George H. W. Bush

In this chapter we consider the extraordinary, and perhaps surprisingly complex, relationship between President Reagan and Margaret Thatcher. We follow the Anglo-American theme through the international crises of the early 1980s, the winding down of the Cold War and the early establishment, under President George Bush Senior, of a new order of US–UK relations in utterly changed international conditions.

Margaret and Ronnie

Reagan, Thatcher and the Cold War

The warmth of the friendship between Ronald Reagan (US president from 1981 to 1989) and Prime Minister Margaret Thatcher was intense, and unprecedented in recent history. Margaret Thatcher was not above making privately disparaging remarks about Reagan's grasp of issues: 'There's nothing there' was apparently her private verdict on the Presidential mental apparatus (Campbell, 2004, 262). Their relationship, however, was alive and highly charged. According to Hugo Young, 'gained its particular timbre from their personal contact, founded on ideological sympathy and supported by a mutual male-female empathy of utmost innocence but considerable power' (Young, 1990, 561). To Thatcher, the US–UK relationship was not only 'natural' and 'special'; it was 'extraordinary' and 'very, very special'. She instructed the Conservative Party conference in 1981: 'Had it not been for the magnanimity of the

United States, Europe would not be free today' (Campbell, 2003, 260). Her implication was that, under her leadership, Britain would not endorse the ingratitude of continental Europeans. By 1991 she was calling the US–UK relationship 'the greatest alliance in the defence of liberty and justice the world has ever known' (Hames, 1994, 114, 128). Moreover, Ronald Reagan was 'the American dream in action' (Thatcher, 1993, 157).

Margaret Thatcher was President Reagan's first official visitor in the White House. Ronald Reagan's admiration and personal fondness for the British leader were palpable. Unintimidated by her grasp of policy detail, Reagan was consistently reassured by her reiteration of conservative verities. As John Campbell has put it: 'Out of his depth with most foreign leaders, Reagan knew where he was with Mrs Thatcher, if only because she spoke his language: he understood her, liked her, admired her and therefore trusted her' (Campbell, 2003, 261). He also – somewhat unusually for an American leader of Irish descent – admired Britain and its aristocratic history. According to his wife, Reagan's study was 'covered with photographs of family, friends and members of the British royal family' (Reagan, 1989, 250). For Ronald Reagan, Margaret Thatcher was the leader who set to to apply American remedies to a country which had become demoralized and impoverished by an excess of socialism. In his memoirs he described the Anglo-American alliance as the firmest during his presidency (Reagan, 1990, 357).

The most important test of US–UK relations in the Reagan-Thatcher era occurred over the 1982 Falklands War. This conflict will be examined in detail in Chapter 8, when we consider wartime relations between the allies. The 1983 Grenadan invasion and the 1986 Libyan bombing (both discussed later in this chapter) also raised important questions about the limits and nature of US–UK cooperation. The 'special relationship' during the 1980s was not without its strains and tensions. Despite this, it is important to emphasise that the achievement both of American approval and of a new international partnership with the US were key goals for Thatcher. When new ideas were floated by ministers, they seemed almost always to emanate from the US (Balen, 1994, 156). In 1991, Norman Fowler recalled the desire of his colleagues in the Thatcher years to reverse America's view that Britain had 'gone downhill to the point that we had become an irrelevance' (Fowler, 1991, 150).

Even those ministers not especially closely identified with Thatcherism routinely praised the qualities of Americans. According to Michael Heseltine, defence secretary from 1983 to 1986: 'As a people we are, I fear, less generous than they' (Heseltine, 1987, 278).

In some policy areas, the Thatcher government operated as little more than an enthusiastic anti-communist client of the US. In 1984, Thatcher announced her support for the American 'aim to promote peaceful change, democracy and economic development' in Central America (Curtis, 1998, 13). British involvement in the Central American conflicts of the 1980s was complex; the private security firm KMS seems to have trained some of the rightist Nicaraguan *contra* forces, even at times directly aiding their operations (Curtis, 1998, 13; Curtis, 2003, 108). Thatcher enthusiastically backed the war against the Sandinistas in Nicaragua, regularly siding with the US in international fora. London's clandestine role in following the US lead by arming Saddam Hussein's regime in Iraq in the 1980s has been clearly demonstrated (Phythian, 1997a). Iraq received US aid as a counter to the Islamicist regime in Iran. Following Reagan's election, Britain helped the US effort in Afghanistan: in this case by cooperating in training programmes for Islamicist guerrillas opposed to the pro-Soviet regime in Kabul. Cooley (1999) sees post-1982 support on Afghanistan as a direct quid pro quo for US aid during the Falklands War. By 1986 MI6 was supplying the Afghan mojahidin Islamists with 'blowpipe' shoulder-launched missiles. British policy on Afghanistan after 1982 certainly seemed to contrast with earlier initiatives offered by London. In 1980 and 1981, Foreign Secretary Peter Carrington had offered various proposals involving Afghan neutralization. The recent origins of Al Qaeda, of course, are now conventionally traced to the 1980s mojahidin campaigns in Afghanistan.

Elsewhere, Chester Crocker, assistant secretary of state for African affairs, looked confidently to London for support over 'constructive engagement' policies for South Africa. According to Crocker (1992, 460), 'Thatcher's tough stance against indiscriminate punishment of South Africa brought special influence to bear in Pretoria when our own clout with the South Africans plummeted after the 1986 fiasco over sanctions'; that is, after Congress had imposed sanctions on South Africa over Reagan's veto. Joint US–UK military action outside Europe also resumed. Royal naval patrols were revived in the Gulf of Oman in the early 1980s. The

UK participated to a small extent in the Lebanon multinational force of 1982–4. British minesweepers were despatched to the Persian Gulf in 1987, during the later stages of the Iran–Iraq war.

Yet the Thatcher government was not merely engaged in what Denis Healey (1989, 450) called 'supine acquiescence' regarding Washington. Labour's own flirtation with neutralism in the early 1980s actually left a lot of foreign policy centre ground for the Conservatives to occupy. The degree to which Labour, if elected in 1983 would have actually followed a non-nuclear, neutralist path outside NATO is, of course, open to question (Jones, 1997, 190–3). Thatcher also tended to find some of her more extreme pro-American positions undermined by the Foreign and Commonwealth Office. The FCO and its ministerial heads (Lord Carrington, 1979–82, Francis Pym, 1982–3, Geoffrey Howe, 1983–9 and Douglas Hurd, 1989–95) were significantly more accommodationist and more Europeanist than Margaret Thatcher. Howe (1995, 688) later described his problems with Downing Street in the following terms: 'My real wickedness may … have lain not so much in a tendency too often to agree with foreigners (although that was serious enough) as in a growing disposition not to agree often enough with the Prime Minister.' As Tim Hames (1994, 136) writes, the leader's 'instinct to support the United States was often watered down in practice by the Foreign Office'.

Thatcher's pro-Americanism was also compromised to some degree by her own interpretation and development of Callaghan's 'Atlantic intermediary' role. Whatever Thatcher's personal feelings, any real revival of the 'special relationship' was bound to involve some kind of role for Britain as a credible broker between US and European interests. Again, whatever the leader's inner voices might tell her, Britain was a European power, and was bound at least to some degree to bring European perspectives to bear. Britain's Middle East policy during the 1980s, for example, involved attempts at coordination with European Community initiatives in the region (P. Sharp, 1999, 138). It should also never be forgotten that it was Thatcher's government which secured passage of the 1985 Single European Act. To the extent also that she sought to soften Reagan's confrontational anti-communism before 1985, she was also able to play on Washington's anxieties about anti-Americanism and disarmament movements in Europe.

By the time Reagan became president in 1981, Thatcher had both demonstrated her flexibility in connection with the Rhodesian settlement, and proved herself to be Washington's surest ally in relation to the crises of Jimmy Carter's final year in office. She did not join her European colleagues in seeking to resist the renewed anti-Sovietism of the Carter administration after 1979. Thatcher's unrivalled access to the new president presented new opportunities, and permitted some degree of boldness. She protested the cancellation of the Siberian pipeline project in 1981, telling Secretary Haig that it 'affronted the Europeans to be asked to make enormous sacrifices while the United States made none'. The cancellation broke existing contracts and raised severe questions about the extraterritoriality of US law. A compromise, which allowed the pipeline to proceed, was achieved in 1982. Thatcher was also willingly recruited by the State Department in various battles with the Pentagon, notably in keeping intact the negotiating side of NATO's 'twin track' strategy, affirmed at Guadeloupe in 1979, and in ameliorating the severity of sanctions imposed following the setting up of martial law in Poland in late 1981. She supported the US attachment to the arms levels agreed in the unratified SALT II treaty of 1978 and concurred in American views on the exclusion of the French and British deterrents from the superpower arms counting. (The US respected the SALT II levels until 1986.) Thatcher also leapt precipitously into intra-administration quarrels over Africa, backing the 'Marxist' Filimo regime in Mozambique.

By far the greatest success of Margaret Thatcher in promoting European perspectives related to 'Star Wars', the Strategic Defense Initiative for laser-based anti-missile defence, announced by Reagan in March 1983. Britain's pre-1982 position on arms control had, as just indicated, been supportive of the NATO negotiating track. Thatcher, however, originally opposed the 'zero option'. Presented to the Soviets at Geneva in 1981, the option would have swapped non-deployment of the cruise and Pershings in Europe for elimination of the SS-20s. The Pentagon won the day in Washington battles over the 'zero option' and Thatcher was forced to concur. She accepted Weinberger's view that Moscow was bound to reject the offer (as indeed it did, though Gorbachev was to accept it in 1986). Thatcher's main concern in the 'zero option' debate was the tying of America to Europe (Smith, 1990, 57–8; Clarke, 1985). Her fears in this respect were heightened by moves in Congress, culminating in the 1984 Nunn amendment, to apply cost conditions to the US troop presence in Europe. Even more alarming, however, was Reagan's

SDI speech. The prospect, however remote, of the US being able to shelter under its own defensive umbrella, at arm's length from Europe, raised immediate anxieties. As Geoffrey Howe (1995, 389) put it: 'Was the President not opening the way to the very notion we all feared, of Fortress America?' Moreover, if the Soviets followed the US into the 'SDI club', British nuclear weapons would be 'rendered ineffective and thus obsolete'. 'Star Wars' also appeared to breach the 1972 Anti-Ballistic Missile Treaty. For Thatcher, although she came to see the point of SDI (and claims not to have been surprised by the 1983 speech), SDI was initially redolent of Reagan's unrealistic hankering after 'a nuclear weapon-free world' (Thatcher, 1993, 473). Europe would be exposed to the Soviets' conventional military superiority.

Thatcher declined to follow France into outright opposition to SDI. On 21 December 1984 she declared that it was important to remember that the Soviet Union had put up the first defensive satellite over Moscow. It was 'advisable that the United States should carry on with their own research in these very, very important spheres' (Campbell, 2004, 288). A day or so later at Camp David, however, she secured from Reagan a written commitment to nuclear deterrence doctrines, to treaty obligations, to the achievement of an East-West nuclear balance and to continuing negotiations. Playing on the doubts about SDI deployment of administration figures such as Secretary of State George Shultz, the Thatcher team effectively 'bounced' Reagan into affirming the US commitment to nuclear deterrence and to Europe. A statement to this effect, drafted by British foreign policy adviser Charles Powell, was drafted over lunch at Camp David and presented to Reagan as a *fait accompli* (Campbell, 2004, 290). Although the US refused Heseltine's request to guarantee the UK at least one billion dollars in SDI research contracts, Thatcher's strategy achieved significant promises for research money for Britain (Weinberger, 1990, 220). The 1986 Reykjavik summit, where Reagan came close to bargaining away nuclear weapons altogether, elicited a repetition performance of Thatcher's personal diplomacy. Aghast at the 'whole system of nuclear deterrence which had kept the peace for forty years' being endangered without consultation, she once again pinned Reagan down at Camp David. Not least among Thatcher's worries was the prospect of Britain being effectively forced to abandon Trident. In November 1986, he signed up to nuclear deterrence and strategic nuclear modernization (Thatcher, 1993, 473). As John Campbell has argued, however, Reagan's post-Reykjavik declarations did not represent an unalloyed triumph for London. Thatcher was prevailed upon to endorse the prospect of halving strategic weapons holdings by 2001 and, quite contrary to her expressed wishes, making large reductions in intermediate nuclear weaponry (Campbell, 2004, 295).

In fact, Thatcher remained very marginal to the personal super-power diplomacy which was winding down the Cold War. In the early days of Gorbachev's leadership of the USSR, she had acted as something of a sponsor of the exciting new Soviet decision-maker in Washington. She was briefed about Gorbachev by Oleg Gordievsky, the former KGB head in London whose 1985 defection did so much to revive the reputation of British intelligence at this time. According to David Mellor, sometime minister of state at the FCO, she 'took to Gorbachev and did her best to sell him' (G. Urban, 1996, 11). Foreign policy adviser Percy Cradock recalled Thatcher's 'formidable powers of self-identification and advocacy' being enlisted on Gorbachev's behalf (Cradock, 1997, 101). However, her attempts to establish herself as a US-Soviet go-between after 1985 were no more successful than parallel efforts regarding Middle Eastern diplomacy. The SDI and post-Reykjavik Camp David undertakings represented the apogee of Thatcher's role as privileged Atlantic intermediary. She could not exercise a veto, nor secure lasting guarantees from Washington. As Geoffrey Howe (1995, 392) pointed out in March 1985, the Camp David undertakings did not really answer European objections to SDI ('there would be no advantage in creating a new Maginot Line ... in space'). Yet she could, occasionally, and when rifts appeared in Washington – as they so often did in the Reagan years – assert an Anglicized version of Europe's interests. The post-1986 arms control dynamic, over which London had little control, had the potential of undermining Thatcher's preferred policy on nuclear weapons. London's concurrence in what Paul Sharp calls 'zero rhetoric' raised the possibility of the disappearance of Britain's nuclear arsenal. Defence Secretary George Younger recognized this in a House of Commons address in December 1986. Thatcher set her policy preferences, however, within a European context. When the Intermediate Nuclear Forces treaty was signed in 1987, she immediately declared not only that 'we must keep a few American atomic weapons in Europe' but that she would 'never give up' Britain's 'independent nuclear deterrent and neither will France' (Sharp, 1999, 136). From the viewpoint of European leaders, her access to Reagan was potentially useful; but, even more than with Callaghan, her pro-Americanism damaged her credibility. Her immediate reaction (softened by Heseltine and Howe) to the mid-1980s reactivation of the Western European Union was to condemn it as 'some new Parisian counter to NATO' (Howe, 1995, 386). Also damaging to Thatcher in this respect was her defence of Reagan in the context of the Iran-*contra* scandal, which broke around the time Reagan was making his post-Reykjavik undertakings in 1986. (Reagan's White House had sold arms to Iran in return for hostage releases – directly contravening promises made alongside London about the folly of dealing with terrorists – and illegally routed proceeds to rightist rebels in Nicaragua.) Jerry Bremer of the State Department joked that Thatcher should be told that, since the IRA 'does not conduct terrorism against Americans, we … are making some token arms shipments to them' (Shultz, 1993, 821–2). Her defence of Reagan over Iran-*contra* on US television earned her the applause, conveyed by telephone, of Reagan's Cabinet (Smith, 1990, 213).

Despite the 1981 defence review, British defence spending during the Thatcher years was well above the European average, as a percentage of GDP. The Falklands War, and British willingness to support the US militarily outside the NATO area, went against the grain of the era of defence thinking inaugurated by the Sandys White Paper of 1957. Above all, the Thatcher government committed itself to an expansive defence identity by concluding, in 1982, the purchase of the Trident nuclear system.

The Trident deal will be examined further in Chapter 7. For the remainder of this chapter's discussion of the Thatcher-Reagan years, we will concentrate on two important economic disputes, and on the Grenadan and Libyan episodes.

Economic Disputes: the Siberian Pipeline and Westland

Washington's cancellation of the Siberian pipeline project was taken in direct response to the imposition, in December 1980, of martial law in Poland. As the Carter years melded into the Reagan era, the possibility of a Soviet invasion of Poland figured prominently in Western calculations. The pipeline was designed to bring Soviet gas to Western Europe. Designed to extend almost

3000 miles, it involved several Western European private companies in its construction. The main bureaucratic proponent of cancellation was US Assistant Defense Secretary Richard Perle, famously dubbed by Denis Healey 'the prince of darkness'. Perle was a proclaimed admirer of Margaret Thatcher and the advocate of a 'squeeze' strategy on the USSR. The pipeline cancellation was also designed to prevent any new French or German dependence on Soviet energy supplies. From Washington's viewpoint, it may have been felt that London's opposition would be muted, owing to British access to North Sea energy supplies.

Thatcher was actually far from unsympathetic to Perle's 'squeeze' on Moscow. She had strongly supported the sanctions imposed by the Carter administration following the 1979 Soviet invasion of Afghanistan. These included some contract cancellations, tightening of terms for technology transfers and abandonment of Anglo-Soviet credit agreements. However, the pipeline issue raised a range of objections.

Thatcher told Secretary of State Al Haig 'that the French and the Germans were never going to abandon their contracts' for the pipeline: She drew attention to 'a certain lack of symmetry' in Washington's response to the Polish crisis: US grain sales were not to be affected by the embargo (Thatcher, 1993, 255). America's sanctions policy of 1980–82 was actually far less damaging to immediate American economic interests than Carter's action had been in 1979. Thatcher was clearly worried about the impact on British jobs. John Brown Engineering had contracts worth more than one hundred million pounds. She especially resented the extraterritoriality of Washington's June 1981 announcement that the embargo on gas and oil technology transfers would apply to the foreign subsidiaries of US companies and to foreign companies making components under licence. The announcement was provoked by the failure of the Western allies to agree a sanctions strategy at the Bonn NATO summit of June 1982. Four days later, Thatcher was in Washington, denouncing the policy of extraterritoriality to Haig and Vice President Bush. Lord Cockfield, trade secretary, told the House of Lords that the government condemned an 'unacceptable extension of American extraterritorial jurisdiction in a way which is repugnant in international law' (Smith, 1990, 102). The Thatcher government's nationalism and respect for free trade was conflicting with its pro-Americanism. Its protests exposed divisions within the

Reagan administration, which was also seeking to reconcile anti-communism with US market interests. Under the 1982 compromise engineered by Haig's successor, George Shultz, contracts were honoured.

The Siberian pipeline dispute saw Britain, however reluctantly or improbably, presenting a 'Europeanist' perspective to Washington. The attendant tensions were reflected throughout British political and economic life in the 1980s. The UK seemed to be at a cross-roads, often mired in contradiction and uncertainty over future paths. Even for Margaret Thatcher, in her Bruges address of 1988, Britain's future was 'in Europe as part of the Community'. Thatcher's nationalism clashed both with her pro-Americanism and with her intellectual realization that Britain must have some kind of European future. As with other Britons at the time, she exhibited, in Sir Anthony Parsons' words, 'an inclination to turn with relief from the high-flown notions of Euro-idealists to the cosy pragmatism and cultural familiarity of Anglo-American relations' (Parsons, 1989, 162). Nowhere were these various tensions reflected more clearly during the 1980s than in the Westland helicopter affair of 1986.

Towards the end of 1985, the small Yeovil-based Westland helicopter company announced its immediate need for more capital. At a Cabinet economic strategy committee meeting in December, Margaret Thatcher and Industry Secretary Leon Brittan decided that the company board and shareholders should decide on Westland's future. Though Westland was Britain's only remaining manufacturer of military helicopters, Thatcher and Brittan held that no great defence or industrial issues were at stake. The most likely solution, closer relations with the US Sikorsky company, with which Westland was already linked, would be acceptable. If the Sikorsky deal went ahead, arrangements to buy European antitank helicopters would be cancelled in favour of Sikorsky's Black Hawk helicopter. At this December meeting, Defence Secretary Michael Heseltine argued that Sikorsky's acquisition of Westland would damage both the British defence industry and the future harmonization of European defence procurement. He demanded, unsuccessfully, that the issue be put before the full Cabinet.

Heseltine soon emerged as a leading proponent of a joint British-French-German-Italian counter-bid. He argued that British defence and industrial interests would be damaged if Westland technology passed to Sikorsky, a subsidiary of the US defence giant, United

Technologies. Similar fears were revived later in 1986 when the government announced that it intended to scrap the Nimrod early-warning aircraft in favour of the American AWACS plane from Boeing.

The ensuing public row, replete with leaked letters from Downing Street and accusations of lying at the highest levels, raised serious constitutional issues. Both Brittan and Heseltine left the government. From the viewpoint of Anglo-American relations, the affair exposed divisions between 'nationalist', 'Europeanist' and 'Americanist' positions. Heseltine variously espoused both the 'nationalist' and 'Europeanist' position. 'Europeanists' felt that a Sikorsky takeover of Westland might endanger defence collaboration in projects like Eurofighter. The prime minister in this instance presented herself as the leading 'Americanist'. She received a telephone call from President Reagan on 25 January 1986, assuring her that she had a friend 'out here in the colonies'. She deplored 'the fuel which had been poured on the flames of anti-Americanism'. In her memoirs, she detected such anti-Americanism on the left, among 'the more fanatical European federalists' and 'on the far right' – notably 'Enoch Powell with whom I so often agreed on other matters' (Howe, 1995, 459–75; Thatcher, 1993, 435–7).

A storm in a Somerset teapot which nearly brought down a government, the Westland affair ended in a Sikorsky take-over. The issues raised did not subside. Reviewing the efforts of Senator Sam Nunn, Senate Armed Services Committee chairman, to achieve greater intra-NATO collaboration, Grayling and Langdon wrote in 1988:

> The Nunn amendment projects have provided a means of improving NATO-wide collaboration but they have also – like the Westland affair – served to highlight the dilemma that faces Europe. The American armed forces are by far the biggest single market for defence systems, but despite the moves towards the two-way street in arms supply that Sam Nunn has so enthusiastically endorsed, there is little prospect of the Americans buying a complete, major defence system, such as the Eurofighter, from its allies. (Grayling and Langdon, 1988, 167–8)

To many European governments during the Cold War, the familiar American argument that the US might lose European sources of arms in wartime seemed inadequate. Resentment was caused by the reluctance of the US to pass project leadership on important NATO military developments on to the allies.

Almost immediately after the Westland affair, announcements about the future of British Leyland sparked opposition to possible American domination of, especially, domestic passenger-car production (*The Economist*, 8 February 1986). In the long run, ownership in this area passed to Germany. In 1987, it was also revealed that British contracts connected to Reagan's Strategic Defence Initiative were falling below expectations.

Grenada, 1983 and Libya, 1986

As we shall see in Chapter 8, the Falklands conflict in 1982 involved an extended debate in Washington about whether, and how strongly, to support Britain against Argentina, another US ally. The debate was decisively resolved in favour of the pro-London lobby, led by Defense Secretary Caspar Weinberger. The two military episodes considered in this section, the Grenada invasion of 1983 and the Libyan bombing of 1986, must be seen, in terms of Anglo-American relations, as having been deeply affected by the Falklands conflict. In the case of Grenada, the US acted without significant regard for British sensitivities; one view in Washington was that, following the Falklands, Britain was unlikely to protest any American activism in the Western hemisphere. British cooperation in the Libyan bombing represented, at least at one level, a *quid pro quo* for help in the 1982 conflict.

On 25 October 1983, the US launched an invasion of the tiny Caribbean island of Grenada, an independent member of the British Commonwealth. Maurice Bishop's leftist/nationalist New Jewel Movement had ruled the island since 1979, drawing Grenada into the ambit of Cuba. Immediately preceding the October invasion, Bishop was murdered by a New Jewel faction under General Hudson Austin. Reagan described the invasion as a 'rescue mission' aimed at American students on the island. After three days of intense action against New Jewel and Cuban forces, a 'democratic' administration was installed under British Governor General Paul Scoon. The invasion was linked by Washington to an invitation issued to the US by the Organisation of East Caribbean States (OECS). Imputed motives for the invasion ranged from a desire to send messages to Havana (and to leftist movements elsewhere, notably in Nicaragua), to a concern to take firm action following the massacre (on 23 October) of 241 US military personnel in Lebanon. (Margaret Thatcher, 1993, 330, later wrote: 'What precisely happened in Washington, I still do not know, but I find it hard to believe that outrage at the Beirut bombing had nothing to do with it.')

The Grenada invasion caused intense embarrassment for Prime Minister Thatcher and her foreign secretary, Geoffrey Howe. The threat of American invasion had been mooted since Bishop's murder on 19 October. On 21 October, the State Department undertook to keep Britain informed of US intentions. On 22 October, Thatcher received a report of a National Security Council meeting which considered the OECS request for intervention; the US would keep the invasion option open, but would be sure to consult London.

On 23 October, meetings took place at the British Embassy in Washington concerning an imminent invasion. Ambassador Oliver Wright made it clear that Britain was opposed to an invasion. As US Secretary of State George Shultz later noted of these discussions: 'Margaret Thatcher preferred economic and political pressure' (Shultz, 1993, 331). Foreign Secretary Howe assured the House of Commons on 24 October that an invasion was unlikely. The same evening saw two messages from Reagan to Thatcher: one conveying that the US was considering a direct response to the OECS request; the second confirming that the invasion would proceed. A British reply was sent at 12.30 A.M.:

> This action will be seen as intervention by a western country in the internal affairs of a small independent country, however unattractive its regime. I ask you to consider this in the context of our wider East-West relations and of the fact that we will be having in the next few days to present to our Parliament and people the siting of Cruise missiles in this country. (Thatcher, 1993, 331)

Thatcher and Howe now had the job of explaining to the Commons 'how it had happened that a member of the Commonwealth had been invaded by our closest ally' (Thatcher,1993, 331–2). As Geoffrey Howe (1995, 331) later recalled: 'The truth is that the government had been humiliated by having its views so plainly disregarded in Washington.' The Commons debate on Grenada of 26 October widened into an examination of the 'special relationship' across a range of issues. Denis Healey, Howe's Labour shadow, urged the prime minister to get 'off her knees' before Reagan, and join other American allies in protesting US policy in Central America and the Caribbean. David Steel, speaking for the Liberal Party, referred to a remark attributed to George Shultz 'that the United States does not always have to agree with Britain'. According to Steel, this 'has a corollary ... Britain does not always have to agree with the United States'. Enoch Powell, now sitting for South Down, attributed the invasion to the American delusion 'that it is within the power of any nation, let alone the United States, to create what it calls freedom and democracy by external military force'. An embarrassed Howe attempted to combine scepticism about the invasion with a generalized defence of Reagan's anti-communism (*Parliamentary Debates*, 6th series, vol. 47, 295, 306, 307, 332).

Thatcher was less capable of restraining her exasperation. Her foreign policy advisers George Urban and Hugh Thomas even feared that she would adopt a 'softer' approach to Soviet relations (in Urban's phrase 'more as pique than as an expression of considered policy ... on the rebound from Grenada') (G. Urban, 1996, 64–5). Within a few days of the invasion, she was condemning, on the BBC World Service, the use of force 'to walk into independent sovereign territories' (Howe, 1995, 332). When a House of Commons Select Committee investigated the matter, it condemned London's 'somewhat lethargic approach' in the pre-invasion period (House of Commons Select Committee on Foreign Affairs 1984, para. 41). Howe came to the view that British sensibilities were sacrificed in the bureaucratic battle between state and defence departments. According to Howe (1995, 334), George Shultz was concerned to keep the Pentagon (which tended to resist the invasion) in ignorance: 'British *amour propre* was only an incidental victim of his determination to outwit the Pentagon.'

On the American side, apologies were scarce on the ground. On 26 October, Shultz couched his opinion in very stark terms: the islands were 'no longer British colonies ... The Caribbean is our neighborhood' (*Washington Post*, 26 October 1983). The situation was made even more difficult when US Information Agency Director and close Reagan friend, Charles Wick, declared that Thatcher had not supported the invasion because she was a woman (Speakes, 1988, 159)! Shultz's memoirs accused Thatcher of forgetting the help given by the US in the Falklands (Shultz, 1993, 340).

In the *Washington Post* (28 October 1983), Edwin Yoder scoffed at 'the worry over the fine points of constitutionality when, in fact, Sir Paul Scoon had been under house arrest and perhaps in mortal danger'.

Even domestic opponents of the invasion were not conspicuously bothered about the failure to consult London. Senator Charles Mathias of Maryland, for example, objected to the fact that Margaret Thatcher *had* been consulted, while the Senate majority leader and House speaker had not (*Washington Post*, 27 October 1983). When Reagan phoned Downing Street on 26 October, he said that the next time he came to visit he would be sure to throw his hat in first (Thatcher, 1993, 332; Young, 1990, 347).

Whether or not the request was preceded by Reagan's hat is uncertain. However, on 8 April 1986, London received an American request to use US air bases in Britain for the bombing of Libya. The request came three days after a bomb in a Berlin nightclub had killed one and injured 60 US servicemen. American intelligence had traced the bombing to General Gaddafi's regime in Libya. The tone of the request was more than a little imperious, with an answer being sought by noon on the following day. According to Hugo Young (1990, 475), not only was Reagan informing rather than consulting, he was asking the British leader to renounce her earlier, publicly expressed, opposition to retaliatory strikes which were difficult to justify under international law. Reagan's message conceded that US carrier-based aircraft, stationed off the North African coast, could be used. But F-111 bombers, based in Britain, could mount a far more accurate, and less risky, operation. Thatcher's reply was evasive, and raised a range of questions, later enumerated in Foreign Secretary Howe's memoirs: 'What targets? What would be the public justification? Won't this start a cycle of revenge? What about Western hostages?' (Howe, 1995, 504, 506). Reagan's reply indicated, in Thatcher's words, that he 'was clearly determined to go ahead' (Thatcher, 1993, 444). By 13 April, Howe, Thatcher and Defence Secretary George Younger, who had previously voiced his reservations on Scottish radio, had discussed their doubts with Reagan's envoy, Vernon Walters. The White House was told that US aircraft could use the bases to further America's right to self-defence under Article 51 of the UN Charter, against specific targets kdemonstrably involved in the conduct or support of terrorism.

The Foreign Office feared attacks on British embassies in the Middle East if clear backing were given to the US action. In the

Cabinet, only Lord Hailsham seemed unequivocally to back the US position (Renwick, 1996, 250–1). For Thatcher, however, and even for the more cautious Howe, British interests lay ultimately in backing Washington. The attack took place on the night of 14 April. The 16 F111s hit only some of the specific targets agreed with London, striking also civilian targets and the French embassy in Tripoli. British support contrasted strongly with the attitude of the other European allies. As Secretary Shultz put it on 14 April: 'with respect to our allies, we have a variety of responses' (*New York Times*, 15 April 1986). Requests to overfly France and Spain were rejected, and the F-11 is circled around and flew through the Gibraltar straits.

If it was difficult to sell the Thatcher-Howe line in Cabinet, the ensuing House of Commons debate revived the embarrassment, albeit in different form, associated with the Grenada invasion. For the prime minister and foreign secretary, the US was exercising its Article 51 rights. Thatcher reminded the House that the UK had also suffered from Gaddafi's excesses: 'The House will recall the murder of WPC Fletcher in St James's Square.' Moreover, there was 'no doubt ... of the Libyan Government's direct and continuing support for the Provisional IRA, in the form of money and weapons'. In response, Labour leader Neil Kinnock quoted Sir Anthony Parsons' description of the raid as a 'kind of vigilantism'. David Steel accused the .prime minister of 'writing a blank cheque for President Reagan'. Former Labour leader Michael Foot argued that, if Article 51 was a justification for America's action, Thatcher should have urged Reagan to take the matter to the UN Secretary Council. For Enoch Powell, the episode demonstrated 'how flimsy would be our protection against the use of bases on British soil for the launching of nuclear operations'. Former Conservative prime minister Heath asserted that, in 1973, he had had the courage to deny the US the use of British bases in Cyprus during the Yom Kippur War. For Heath, Article 51 manifestly did not justify the raid. It was as if Britain was using the 'self-defence' argument to support the bombing of 'IRA camps on the west coast of Ireland'. Tony Benn, now left-wing Labour MP for Chesterfield, accused Howe and Thatcher of envying 'the Americans for being able to engage in the sort of gunboat diplomacy that is now beyond our resources'. He interpreted Thatcher's support for the raid as the price for US help in the Falklands: 'they told us the position of the

Belgrano'. The decision to give permission to fly the F-111s derived from the unpublished agreements of 1951 pertaining to US bases in the UK. Benn continued:

> I want to know what would have happened if the Prime Minister had refused? Is there a provision that when there is an overriding American national interest British agreement is not required? I do not know. If the Americans had used the bases without our consent, what would have happened?

Several MPs argued that the US action was illegal, and that the alternative of economic sanctions had not been properly explored (*Parliamentary Debates*, 6th series, vol. 95, 729, 732, 733, 890, 891, 905, 906).

In the US, the administration played down the split in NATO. It was left to Henry Kissinger to express the view that the Atlantic alliance was now a one-way street, with only the UK willing to back America in a proper manner (*New York Times*, 16 April 1986). The perceived decline in Libyan-sponsored terrorism eased the situation, although the 17 April kidnapping of British journalist John McCarthy in Beirut boded ill for the wider situation in the Middle East. Polls in Britain showed widespread disapproval of Thatcher's support for the raid (Dickie, 1994, 193).

However, American gratitude to London was expressed in the Senate ratification (on 17 July) of an extradition treaty, easing the deportation of Irish republican terrorists. Ratification was strongly backed by the Reagan administration. On 31 July, the UK abstained in a UN Security Council vote on the international Court of Justice ruling against US policy in Nicaragua. Geoffrey Howe (1995, 508) records that, although he was now positively reconciled to his public position over the Libyan raid, he was 'disconcerted by the strange sequence of events':

> first, Britain supports US action against Libyan terrorism; second, US supports Britain in action against Irish terrorism; third, Britain condones US-sponsored 'terrorism' against Nicaragua. This was yet another occasion on which Margaret insisted on carrying the 'special' relationship one bridge too far.

To George Urban (1996, 95), the relationship was now 'becoming one-sided to the point of embarrassment'.

Bush, Thatcher and the Cold War's End

Reagan's departure from the White House in 1989 represented an end to the personal, idiosyncratic, often unpredictable and instinctual style of leadership, which had characterized US foreign policy since 1981. Relaxed to the point of abdicating authority, emotional to the point of governing by instinct and feeling, Reagan's style was not that of his successor, George Bush (president from 1989 to 1993). The later Reagan years saw major developments in the winding down of the Cold War. They were also years which saw, especially in relation to the Iran-*contra* scandal, a calling into question of Reagan's control of his administration. When visiting Washington in 1989, Margaret Thatcher discerned that President George H.W. Bush 'felt the need to distance himself from his predecessor'. This involved, according to Thatcher (1993, 783) 'turning his back fairly publicly on the special position I had enjoyed in the Reagan Administration'.

During the presidency of George Bush Senior, the US was presented, in the words of Michael Mandelbaum (1990–91, 5), with 'the greatest geopolitical windfall in the history of American foreign policy'. The events of 1989 to 1992, from the fall of the Berlin Wall to the extinction of the Soviet Union, surprised both Washington and London. The new administration turned its attention to managing the transition to a new order, both avoiding triumphalism – 'dancing on the Berlin Wall' – and remaining true to its underlying doctrines of strategic conservatism. American allies in general – not just London – performed the role of spectator as the world was transformed.

Thatcher and the elder Bush shared a sceptical caution about the break-up of the Soviet empire. However, in 1989, Mikhail Gorbachev interceded with London to protest the degree to which the optimistic dynamic of the late Reagan era was being stalled by the new Washington regime. These anxieties were conveyed by London to Washington, although Thatcher continued to counsel that Gorbachev might fail to shift Soviet vested interest (Baker, 1995, 87; Thatcher, 1993, 786). Developing London attitudes were also shaped both by a cooling in personal relations at the top and by fears of the 'special relationship' being buried amid new US-German accords. Thatcher saw Bush as consciously distancing himself from her, as a way of drawing a line under the Reagan era. In September

1989, President Bush gave a television interview to David Frost. Bush was asked which country he regarded as America's closest ally in Europe. He referred to the 'special relationship', but added: 'I don't think we should have to choose up [*sic*] between friends' (Smith, 1990, 256). Secretary of State James Baker was accused of briefing against the British leader, portraying her as a Cold War dinosaur and Germanophobe. Margaret Thatcher (1993, 768, 783) saw herself as confronting 'an Administration which saw Germany as its main European partner'. In more measured tones, Foreign Secretary Geoffrey Howe recalled 'a real conviction on the part of US policymakers that relations with Europe could not sensibly be dependent on the compatibilities of Anglo-Saxon instinct'. The UK 'was only one of five medium-sized European nations, and by no means the most successful – or influential in continental politics'. On 31 May 1989, President Bush referred publicly in Mainz to the 'partnership in leadership' between the US and Germany (Howe, 1995, 559–60). Gregory Treverton wrote in 1990 that, increasingly, 'America will see Europe through the prism of Germany' (Treverton, 1990, 708).

Between 1989 and 1993, US–UK tensions revolved around the issues of short-range nuclear force (SNF) modernization, NATO's future, German reunification, and Bosnia. London's desire for SNF modernization conflicted with Bonn's keenness to negotiate with the Soviets over SNF levels, regardless of modernization. Chancellor Kohl told James Baker: 'Mrs Thatcher is rid of *her* missiles' (the intermediate range weapons which formed the basis of the 1987 INF treaty). Washington forced through a compromise, 'a judgement of Solomon', in Howe's words, 'with little, if any, consultation' in May 1989. The modernization promise was kept technically intact, but new proposals on conventional force reductions seemed to call into question the rationale for any new generation of tactical nuclear weapons. According to Baker, the US 'would negotiate down, we wouldn't by implication allow total elimination of SNF'. While Margaret Thatcher claimed a victory, Howe noted that the compromise seemed to point towards a new German-American closeness (Howe, 1995, 565).

The end of the Cold War stimulated a major debate over the future of NATO, and especially about the American commitment to Europe. At one level, the debate concentrated on issues of 'architecture': the various organizational structures which sought to reconcile the 'European defence identity' with continued American leadership (Cornish, 1996). The Western European Union, revived in the late 1980s, was generally seen as a natural bridge between NATO and the European Community. Beyond 'architectural' issues, fundamental questions raised themselves. Designed to contain Soviet power, did NATO have any purpose now that the USSR had ceased to exist? How strong was America's commitment in the new era? Could Europe ever muster a credible defence identity? Did Europe *need* the US?

Among sections of American opinion, the existential rationale for NATO was questioned. In 1995, neoconservative writer Irving Kristol called NATO an 'organization without a mission, a relic of the Cold War' (*Wall Street Journal*, 6 February 1995). For Republican Congressman John Lander of Georgia, 'NATO expired in 1989' (*Congressional Quarterly Weekly Report*, 3 February 1996). This questioning of NATO's purpose to some degree grew out of prior anxieties about 'burden sharing', and about the way Europeans tended to exploit American internationalism for their own ends. By 1989, significant cuts in America's military commitment had already been made. By 1995, the official total of US troops in Europe was 139 200, with planned reduction to 100,000 (Heuser, 1996, 67). From the European viewpoint, doubts about the US commitment extended beyond 'burden sharing' issues, to perceptions of isolationism and American decline. Surveys of US public opinion in the early 1990s revealed signs that the national mood was 'homeward bound', although a substantial majority certainly favoured remaining in NATO. Neo-isolationist or 'America First' movements seemed to be emerging in both Democratic and Republican parties. Perceptions were also strong, despite America's Cold War triumph, of a secular US decline, precipitated by imperial over-extension and domestic insecurities. Christopher Coker wrote in 1992 that it was 'ironic to find Britain still intent on maintaining the special relationship, clinging to a power whose only reassuring thought is that it might prolong its own decline as skilfully as the British did' (Coker, 1992, 413).

The post-Cold War debates on the future of NATO, on the European defence identity, and on relations generally between the US and an integrated Europe, will be taken up in more detail in Chapter 9. The Transatlantic Declaration, negotiated by US Secretary of State James Baker and promulgated in November 1990, represented Washington's attempt to accommodate and manage evolving European integration. Margaret Thatcher was horrified at Bush's suggestion that 'the events of our time call for a continued, and perhaps intensified, effort by the Twelve to integrate' (Sharp, 1999, 209). The Bush Senior administration, much to London's relief, did, however, retain a strong commitment to US leadership of NATO.

Britain's view in this period was that America's commitment to European defence should be encouraged wherever possible, and that new rationales for NATO, whether the 'pre-containment' of Russia, or 'out-of-area' peacekeeping, be developed. Senior Downing Street adviser Charles Powell (who served both Thatcher and her successor, John Major, as chief foreign policy aide) wrote in February 1992: 'The special relationship with the United States will remain vital in the years ahead. We shall need to work harder to retain it' (Williams and Schaub, 1995, 193). Part of this hard work would, following Powell's line, involve a resistance to any tendency of George H. W. Bush's New World Order to develop into indiscriminate multilateralism. America must be made aware that Britain was, and would remain, its most staunch ally. The Gulf conflict provided a unique opportunity to demonstrate this. Britain remained keen to keep the lid on 'Europeanist' military developments. In 1992, Defence Secretary Malcolm Rifkind achieved a compromise whereby 'Eurocorps' forces would be included among 'the forces available to' the Western European Union, but only – at least according to Rifkind – in situations 'when NATO chose not to be engaged, for instance in humanitarian operations' (Cornish, 1997, 40).

Central to NATO's prospects, of course, was the future of Germany. As a front-line state during the Cold War, West Germany had been forced to balance its desire for détente with the USSR with a fundamental security dependency upon the US. The termination of the Cold War threw future German intentions into confusion (hence, no doubt, Bush's concern to promote the new US-German axis). As Vivekanandan (1991, 421) wrote: 'Germany did not choose to foster ties to the United States in the postwar period; this arrangement was thrust upon Germany.' Here indeed was another new rationale for NATO. The organization might develop as an institution whereby the US could broker and contain post-Cold War 'renationalization' in Europe, preventing a return to destructive nationalism (Art, 1996). British perceptions of such a role for

NATO and the US were encouraged by the prospect, and then achievement, of German reunification.

British writer John Dickie (1994, 208) described Margaret Thatcher's resistance to German reunification as 'the most serious misjudgement of her career in international politics'. It put Britain on the sidelines of the momentous reconstruction taking place in Europe, leaving, in George Urban's words, 'some of Britain's allies and many of the prime minister's supporters exasperated' (Urban, 1996, 100). Thatcher's most frequently stated concern was the need to foster democracy in East Germany before reunification, a consideration linked to historical memories of a greater Germany. Writing in 1993, she observed: 'East German political immaturity has affected the whole country in the form of a revived (though containable) neo-Nazi and xenophobic sentiment.' In her view, 'premature' reunification simply served to encourage at least three unwelcome developments: 'the rush to European federalism as a way of tying down Gulliver', 'the emergence of a strengthened Franco-German alliance to push for deeper integration', and 'the gradual withdrawal of the US from Europe on the assumption that a German-led federal Europe will be both stable and capable of looking after its own defence' (Thatcher, 1993, 814). She was also concerned, in 1989 and 1990, to protect Gorbachev's position in Russia. Her attempts to mount an Anglo-French resistance foundered on the pragmatic acceptance by President Mitterrand that, given the determination in Washington, swift reunification was inevitable. The US plan, the 'two-plus-four' mechanism, devised by Robert Zoellick of the State Department, proved unstoppable, especially when Gorbachev showed himself prepared to live with a united Germany in NATO. (The plan involved determination by the two Germanies of their futures, followed by subsequent agreements with the US, USSR, UK and France: the victorious powers of World War Two. Gorbachev's acceptance of the outcome flowed from his desire to pass 'tests' devised by the West, and was eased by the payment of money by Bonn to cover the relocation of Soviet forces.) As the dynamic unfolded, British attitudes appeared increasingly irrelevant. Douglas Hurd tried rather desperately to finesse his boss's recalcitrance, describing Thatcher in January 1990 as 'a reluctant unifier: Not against, but reluctant' (J.A. Baker, 1995, 199; Zelikow and Rice, 1995).

George H. W. Bush and John Major

The transfer of prime ministerial authority from Margaret Thatcher to John Major (Conservative prime minister from 1990 to 1997) coincided with the onset of the Gulf War against Iraq. For Thatcher, the Gulf crisis and war represented a deeply symbolic reassertion of the 'special relationship'. To Major, the Gulf War also 'vividly' illustrated the vitality of Anglo-American relations. Major wrote in 1999 of the 'unique rapport between Britain and the United States' and of a relationship where 'confidences are shared as a matter of course'. Major sensed this intimacy in his first Gulf crisis meeting with President Bush in December 1990: 'There was no hesitation. No unease. No holding back. No probing to find out the other's position' (Major, 1999, 496, 225).

The 1991 Gulf War will be examined in more detail in Chapter 8. At the time British-American cooperation tended to be regarded as much as a last gasp of the 'special relationship' as a confident reassertion of it under changed international geopolitical conditions. However, there is no doubting the good personal and working relations between Major and Bush. A dispute over the British plan for Kurdish 'safe havens' in March 1991 was swiftly resolved.

Major's understanding of US–UK relations was not unlike that of James Callaghan and other upholders of the 'Atlantic intermediary' role. According to Major, 'We straddled the divide between the United States and Europe.' The US did not want 'a fifty-first state', but rather a strong ally in Europe (Major, 1999, 578). The increasingly European context of British political and economic decision making was illustrated in sterling's 'Black Wednesday' (16 September 1992) fall-out from the European exchange rate mechanism (ERM). London's agony was increased by Federal Reserve Bank decisions in Washington. The Fed's lowering of interest rates caused a transfer of investment from the dollar to the Deutschmark, with disastrous effects for a pound whose value was tied to the German currency. However, Britain's 1992 exit from the ERM was conducted primarily in the context of intra-European, rather than Anglo-American, relations. The structures of British economic policy had shifted considerably since the crises of 1967 and 1976.

Niggling disputes, for example the continuing problem of Vietnamese refugees entering Hong Kong, continued to affect US–UK relations in the Bush-Major period. The principal area of tension, however, was policy towards Yugoslavian disintegration. The limitations of various initiatives regarding NATO and US-European Community 'architecture' (including James Baker's 1990 Transatlantic Declaration) were exposed in the failure of *any* US and/or European agency to lessen the agony occurring in the former Yugoslavia. Washington regarded the ethnic warfare in the Balkans as a European problem. It was prepared, in April 1992, to follow the EC (primarily German) lead in recognizing Slovenia, Croatia and Bosnia-Herzegovina as independent states. (Britain had initially followed the US in pressing for the preservation of Yugoslavian territorial integrity.) Faced by public and congressional lack of enthusiasm, and unwilling to take a gamble on the impact on Russia of an American intervention, the Bush administration remained aloof. As James Baker (1995, 636) later put it, the conflict 'seemed to be one the EC could manage' and 'unlike in the Persian Gulf, our vital national interests were not at stake'. Washington remained in the background as EC mediation, coordinated by Lord Carrington in 1991–2, foundered. Even the involvement of former Secretary of State Cyrus Vance, working with former British Foreign Secretary David Owen to produce a complex partition plan, failed to bring forth any decisive American activism. Thatcher, now an ex-leader, condemned the US detachment as a failure of nerve. Major organized a conference in London in 1992, in the forlorn hope of clarifying and implementing a concerted European policy on the war. Extraordinarily 'in one of those rare but not unheard-of diplomatic cock-ups' (Major, 1999, 536), the Russians were initially not invited. In December 1992, London managed to deflect a four-point US plan, which included banning military flights over Bosnia-Herzegovina and lifting the UN arms embargo on the Bosnian Muslims. According to Major, 'the US military did not know *how* to enforce the flight ban' and British troops, deployed in Bosnia in November 1992, 'were very vulnerable to the threatened retaliation of the Bosnian Serbs' (Major, 1999, 538). Secretary of State Baker later gave a frank summation of America's attitude, referring to 'an undercurrent in Washington, often felt but seldom spoken, that it was time to make the Europeans step up to the plate and show that they could act as a unified power. Yugoslavia was as good a test as any' (Baker, 1995, 637). Major's ability or willingness to have Britain 'step up to the plate' was slight. Peter Hall, British ambassador to Yugoslavia, told him bluntly in 1992 that 'these people ... like going around cutting each other's heads off' (Seldon, 1997, 306).

British military capabilities for the post-Cold War era were outlined in Defence Secretary Tom King's 'Options for Change' review of 1990, which foresaw cuts of around one-fifth in the defence budget. Britain was still committed to purchasing Trident nuclear submarines and to retaining three aircraft carriers, yet force totals were reduced from 316, 700 in 1989 to 236,900 in 1995 (this figure put Britain well below Italy and France, and slightly above Spain (Heuser, 1996, 67)). The 1993 defence review involved some reprieves for particular regiments and sectors, but essentially continued the line of 'Options for Change'. Major did not respond positively to a service chiefs' deputation, led by chief of Defence Staff Peter Harding, who argued in October 1993 for a reversal of cuts. British defence policy in the 1990s envisaged no threat of Cold War proportions, despite recognizing that risks in some areas of the world had increased. The distinction between 'in area' and 'out-of-area' defence planning was also dropped at this time.

The 'Special Relationship' Beyond the Cold War

As indicated in Chapter 1, the end of the Cold War was accompanied by an outbreak of 'end of the affair' literature. Numerous commentators put forward the view that the 'special relationship' could not survive the global transformations which occurred during the presidency of George H. W. Bush. The arguments may be summarised as follows. The 'special relationship', though benefiting from cultural closeness, was rooted primarily in military and intelligence cooperation. Its root was in interests, not sentiment nor even shared outlook. Its rationale was the transatlantic 'common fate'. With the Cold War's end, the US commitment to Europe, much less to the UK, was in question. The commitment, as Beatrice Heuser put it in 1993, was a product of the 'existential struggle with Soviet communism' and of the recognition, deriving ultimately from World War I, that US security was linked to European stability (Heuser, 1993, 248). In the new, post-Cold War order, the commitment was in doubt. Neo-isolationism and a foreign policy oriented to Asia rather than to Europe were clear options for the American future.

More narrowly, if the US wanted a European interlocutor in the future it would surely look to Berlin, not to London. The rationale for US military bases in the UK seemed largely to have disappeared.

A flavour of this 'end of the affair' literature may be gleaned from the British journalism of the period. According to Neal Ascherson, the myth of the 'special relationship' was now well and truly dead. 'What survives is a dependence and a buried resentment about that dependence, both still difficult to admit or discuss' (Ascherson, 1993). For Adrian Hamilton, John Major, in his assumption that Britain had any special influence in Washington, was 'clutching at something that has already slipped through his fingers' (Hamilton, 1994). Hugo Young poured scorn on the fantasy that London was 'at the head of Washington's transatlantic concerns'. Such a delusion 'would have been hard to credit even in the palmy days of Thatcher', much less in the post-Cold War era (Young, 1994). *The Independent* editorialized on the Clinton presidency on January 22, 1994 that 'the arrival of a Democratic president' had made explicit what 'was perhaps obscured by the warmth of Margaret Thatcher's friendship with Ronald Reagan: Britain seems not to figure large in American minds. Canada, Mexico and Germany probably matter more'.

And yet, the 'special relationship', defined in terms of military and intelligence cooperation, together with a plausible claim to privileged access, even to a degree of influence, in Washington, did survive. It will be argued below that the main reason for this was Blair's personal reaction to 9/11 and to the foreign policy of President George Bush Junior. However, it is certainly the case that, even by the end of the Clinton years, the US–UK relationship was in healthier shape than most commentators saw likely from the perspective of the early 1990s. To some extent, as throughout its history, the relationship had been rescued by personal friendship: in this case, between Blair and Clinton. More fundamentally, however, there clearly were forces operating in the post-1989 to hold the two old allies together, just as there were certainly forces operating to pull them apart. Let us take a moment, before taking up the story of US–UK relations under President Clinton, to indicate the nature of these forces.

The most obvious force keeping the alliance afloat in the choppy post-Cold War waters was simply inertia. Habits of cooperation, bureaucratic contact and (especially) defence and intelligence

personnel interweaving, sustained US–UK closeness in these difficult years. Inertia alone could hardly be expected to maintain the
'special relationship' indefinitely, but its short term effect should
not be neglected. Similarly, even in the good times, the 'special relationship' had been kept alive to some degree by a combination of
American public politeness – the reluctance of US leaders, unless
horribly provoked, to cut the rhetorical knot tying London with
Washington – and British puffing-up of its transatlantic intimacies.
After 1989, London continued to talk up US–UK 'special relations', partly to bolster brittle egos, partly to sustain the case for
Britain's global influence, partly to shame Washington into recipro-
catory acknowledgement, partly to emphasize that Britain was not
merely a European power. The resilience of the 'special relationship', however unfashionable it may be to argue this, also had
something to do with shared culture, particularly but not entirely at
the elite level. At its most fundamental, the survival, even in a somewhat attenuated and changed form of the 'special relationship' into
the post-1989 era, of the 'special relationship' was linked to
interests (Dumbrell, 2004).

As noted at the end of Chapter 3, the mutual interests underpin-
ning the house that Jack and Mac built were fairly straightforward.
They consisted, in summary, of British aspirations to wield influence on the cheap, of Britain's need for help with anti-Soviet
defence, of American 'hard power' designs on British bases, and
'soft power' gains from the presence of a reliable and credible ally.
The end of the Cold War had certainly removed the binding of the
'common fate'. However, although thereby weakened, the alliance
still, with the very important exception of US military bases in the
UK, answered these interests. Privileged access, a lever to use in
European arguments, possible economic benefits: it is not difficult
to understand the continued attractions of 'special relations' for
London, especially in the pre-9/11 era when the price of the alliance
appeared less expensive than it later became. From the American
side, there is no question that, with the end of the Cold War, the UK
alliance declined in importance, along with the strategic value of
US air bases. However, the 'soft power' payoffs of the alliance continued (Elie, 2005). Again, from Washington's viewpoint, the
'price' of the alliance after 1989 – the price, if you will, of enhanced
'soft power' – was not very high. After the Cold War, particularly if
the world was indeed to enjoy the benefits of some species of

'democratic peace', the alliance was likely to cost far less in dollars than during the Cold War, and unlikely to involve the US in military action to protect its ally. Bolstered by inertia and culture, these benefits were just about enough to keep the relationship alive in the period between the Cold War's end and 9/11.

6
After the Cold War: Clinton and George W. Bush

The revival of close US–UK foreign policy was primarily a feature of the international reaction to the terror attacks of 11 September 2001. Before describing and accounting for the alliance between the Blair and George W. Bush governments, this chapter will review Anglo-American experiences under Bill Clinton, a president whose impact on the UK, notably in connection with the Irish policy described in Chapter 10, eventually belied the view that, in the post-Cold War era, the two old allies would go their separate ways. Clinton was knowledgeable and well informed about Britain. Of post-1960 presidents, only Kennedy could be regarded as his equal in this respect. Clinton, the former Rhodes scholar told the Oxford paper, *The Mertonian*, before his election that Americans often failed to understand British 'underlying toughness … I liked England. I was a real Anglophile when I was there'. His own back-ground in rural Arkansas, of course, was the very opposite of that normally associated with American anglophilia. The younger Bush, who lacked Clinton's close knowledge, was, ironically, from an elite background much more associated with enthusiasm for England (if not for the wider UK). Yet, Clinton was also a president who had experienced condescending anti-Americanism while at Oxford. His aide George Stephanopoulos, also a Rhodes scholar, described how 'the English behaved when they passed you on the street.' The American 'Rhodies' called it 'bird in the tree': 'the moment the English spotted you coming they would suddenly turn their atten-tion to a bird in the tree' (Greig, 1994). Above all, Clinton was the first US president who came to power in the post-Cold War era. His presidency was to be a test of the alliance in untried conditions.

Clinton and Major

Personal Relations and Balkan Politics

Elected in 1992 primarily on a platform of domestic renewal, Bill Clinton, despite his Oxford background, did not appear a president likely to encourage notions of a 'special relationship' with London. In the post-Cold War mid-1990s, the very phrase became almost a diplomatic joke, and was informally banned within Britain's Washington embassy. US Ambassador Raymond Seitz (1998, 322) recalled a visit made by John Major to Washington in early 1993 to meet the new American leader:

> Just before the Prime Minister arrived at the White House, Clinton was sitting with a few aides in the Oval Office. 'Don't forget to say "special relationship" when the press comes in,' one of them joked – a little like 'don't forget to put out the cat'. 'Oh, yes,' Clinton said, 'How could I forget? The "special relationship"!' And he threw his head back and laughed.

The new administration's plan to promote the inclusion of Germany and Japan as permanent members of the UN Security Council raised British hackles. Action was taken to terminate favoured British access to nuclear testing facilities in the Nevada desert. In his first year in office, Clinton was also widely seen as favouring a 'Pacificization' of US foreign policy: partly as a response to the need to reconsider priorities with the end of the Cold War, partly as a way of tying the US into the Asian economic 'miracle'. Even in 1997, a year after the crash of the Asian economies, Defence Secretary William Cohen repeated to Asian business leaders the received wisdom of the early 1990s: 'The Mediterranean is the ocean of the past. The Atlantic is the ocean of the present. And the Pacific is the ocean of the future' (Cheney, 1998, 156.) Between 1990 and 1995, US troop levels in Europe declined by around two-thirds; by the mid-1990s, the Asian and European troop commitments were roughly on a par.

Against this background, tensions appeared between London and Washington over a series of issues: over the settlement of Vietnamese boat people in Hong Kong, over the sanctions policy in Iraq and over tactics to be adopted in relation to the nuclear development policy in North Korea. The US air attack on Iraq of 27 June 1993 was unilateral, with no prior consultation with London. Especially in its early phase, the Clinton-Major relationship 'stayed', according to Raymond Seitz (1998, 322), on a 'grin-and-bear-it basis'. Clinton staffers, notably George Stephanopoulos, found it hard to forgive Downing Street for extending help to the Bush cause in the 1992 presidential election. In his memoirs, Major dismissed this as 'a staffers' feud' (Major, 1999, 498.) Press stories appeared about Clinton's own ambivalence towards the UK, deriving from the anti-American cultural snobbery he had encountered at Oxford University. For John Major (1999, 499), Clinton was too concerned with 'appeasing opinion at home'. He was also, at least in the early days of his presidency, 'alarmingly underbriefed'. The Clinton–Major relationship did recover somewhat from its shaky start, despite London's irritation at US interventions in the politics of Northern Ireland. Clinton certainly came to appreciate that Major did not come from a financially or socially privileged Tory background, and became more willing to make conventional remarks about 'specialness'. In a joint press conference in February 1994 with John Major, Clinton acknowledged that the US–UK relationship was 'special to me personally and is special to the United States' (*Public Papers of the Presidents ... 1994, vol. 1*, 1995, 196). Visiting Britain as part of the fiftieth anniversary of D-Day, Clinton offered an emotional account of wartime transatlantic friendship: 'At every level, Yanks and Brits worked together like family' (*Public Papers of the Presidents ... 1994, vol. 1*, 1995, 1024). Yet, to many of Clinton's team, British Conservative politicians appeared conceited and condescending. Secretary of Labour Robert Reich, for example, later described Chancellor Ken Clarke as extolling the free market 'with such pomposity that I have to restrain myself from causing an international incident by telling him what I think' (*The Observer*, 1 June 1997).

In relation to NATO, Major sought to exploit the Gulf War revival in Anglo-American cooperation, and the weakness of European defence coordination in the conflict, to deflect a strengthening of the 'European pillar'. Ironically, this stance seemed to put Britain at odds with the thrust of US policy towards Europe as it developed after 1993 (Chapter 9 will take up these issues in more detail). Clinton's 1994 launch of the NATO Partnership for Peace proposal, designed to alleviate Russian fears of the alliance, signalled a new European activism. Washington now presented itself as keen on all aspects of European integration, including defence. Opposition to the 'Eurocorps' idea was dropped after a 1994 agreement (in line with Rifkind's understanding of 1992) that NATO would have first call on all units for 'in area' missions. The US supported the new European Combined Joint Task Forces, designed for 'out-of-area' missions, as 'separable not separate from NATO'. NATO was to 'remain the bedrock of security in Europe' (*Public Papers of the Presidents ... 1994, vol. 1*, 1995, 2144). Administration officials also began to talk up the importance of Europe to the US, especially in relation to transatlantic free trade and the 1995 'New Transatlantic Agenda'.

Over policy towards the former Yugoslavia, the US–UK dialogue at times almost ceased to exist. John Major (1999, 497) recalled the issue as a 'running sore' between London and Washington. At one level, the European partners to the alliance were internally divided. To quote Wayne Bert (1997, 218–19): 'lacking a track record of providing direction for the alliance in foreign affairs, and still unsure whether their identity was primarily European or primarily national, they were not in a position to provide the leadership that the US would not'. Writing of his Bosnian experience David Owen (1995, 367) concluded that the European Union 'does not know how to exercise power'. NATO was also in disarray, with its 'crisis manager' role, accepted at the 1991 North Atlantic Council meeting in Rome, in tatters. According to Lawrence Kaplan (1996, 30), 'Europeans and Americans had not been so divided since the Suez debacle of 1956.' The European priority was to support a neutral UN humanitarian presence in a civil war, pending a peace agreement. Washington was much more concerned to condemn Serb aggression, and to protect the Bosnian Muslims – but without committing ground troops. At the beginning of the Clinton presidency, Britain was still urging a US troop commitment to implement the Vance-Owen ten-way division of Bosnia. In February 1993, Major was informed that Washington regarded the plan as unacceptable in its recognition of ethnic cleansing. Washington's preference for anti-Serb air strikes, combined with the lifting of the arms embargo on Bosnian Muslims, was opposed by London as endangering the two thousand or so British forces engaged in UN operations in the region: this despite Major's public assurance that he was 'not remotely concerned' about US air action endangering British troops (*Public Papers of the Presidents ... 1994, vol. 1*, 1995, 196). Neither the limited NATO air strikes of February 1994 nor the US attempts – supported by the UK, Spain and France – to create Muslim 'safe havens', could disguise the powerlessness of both the EU and NATO. The Bosnian Serbs felt able to spurn the 1994 'contact group' proposed solutions without fear of concerted action. The 'contact group', which offered various partitionist 'solutions', consisted of the US, Britain, Russia, Germany and France. Its very existence testified to US impatience with the EU. US involvement in the 'contact group' set the stage for a new American activism, and the Dayton Agreement of 1995.

Writing in 2005, Christopher Meyer recalled the European-American tensions over Balkan policy at this time as deriving from a combination of the fact that, far from settling the Balkan question, the EU could 'barely boil an egg', while Washington could 'not desist from back-seat driving, so infuriating to the Europeans' (Meyer, 2005, 98). Clinton's post–1994 activism, implemented principally through the diplomacy of Richard Holbrooke, had many causes, not least the threats made by the Republican Congress to take over direction of his failed Bosnian policy. The more direct involvement by Washington, which was generally welcomed by London, was nonetheless rooted in the view that it made no sense to continue excoriating Europe for failing to provide the leadership of which it was incapable. (The US took advantage also of the Croatian anti-Serb offensive of the summer of 1995.) Under the Dayton peace terms, some 60,000 NATO troops would be committed to the state of Bosnia-Herzegovina, split into the Bosnian Serb Republic and the Bosnian and Croat Federation. John Major organized a Dayton implementation conference in London in December 1995. The British contribution to the NATO force was the second largest, following the US. Despite such efforts, the Bosnian crisis of 1991–5 yielded little evidence of any special understandings between London and Washington.

The difficult and prickly Clinton–Major relationship, as we have seen, never degenerated into outright hostility. The US president apparently later expressed awareness of his own insensitivity towards Britain in relation to the 1993–4 Bosnian initiatives. Major also subsequently informed Clinton that the government at Westminster would probably have fallen if London had accepted the 1993 plan (Hyland, 1999, 143.) London supported Washington over policy towards Russia and cooperated in US-Swedish initiatives to secure the exit of Russian troops from the Baltic states (Walker, 1996, 277). Clinton certainly did not kill the 'special relationship'. Rather, he recognized implicitly the removal of its geopolitical foundation, leaving the way open for a future US leader to conduct the funeral rites.

Hong Kong

In general, the Major years saw British influence on the US increasingly set within a European framework. However, there was at least one outstanding issue, the future of Hongk Kong, where unilateral British policy still intersected with US security interests. In order briefly to explore this, we need to return to the early 1980s. When Geoffrey Howe took over from Francis Pym as foreign secretary in 1983, he found the problem of Hong Kong's future at the top of his 'pending' pile. Like Rhodesia and the Falklands, it was 'a problem left over from history' (Howe, 1995, 261). Britain's 90-year lease was due to expire on 30 June 1997. The lease applied to 92 per cent of the territory. Britain's 'freehold' title to Hong Kong Island and Kowloon was contested by Beijing. Margaret Thatcher defined her negotiating aim as 'to exchange sovereignty over the island of Hong Kong in return for continued British administration of the entire Colony and well into the future' (Thatcher, 1993, 259). Such a position did not prove tenable and, in 1984, London and Beijing reached agreement. A Joint Declaration was issued and negotiators began to write a Basic Law, eventually produced in 1990. Hong Kong as a whole would revert to China in 1997, but would retain its economic, legal and social institutions for at least 50 years after 1997. Beijing would control security and foreign relations.

The US role in the negotiations leading to the Joint Declaration was not apparently an important one. Pressure may have been applied on Britain to compromise over the 'freehold' territory, but the agreement was achieved with sufficient speed to avoid any public leaking of this. The decade before 1984 had not seen a high degree of tension on Hong Kong's border with China. The US benefited from British communications interception facilities on the colony. The influx of Indochinese refugees also implicated the US in Hong Kong's affairs. However, Washington's role was low-key. Following the Joint Declaration, Hong Kong's future became an issue in American domestic politics. The 1984 Republican Party platform called for 'self-determination' for the colony. Burt Levin, US consul general, gave assurances that America would regard Hong Kong after 1997 as a trading entity separate from China. The US led the move to accept the Joint Declaration within the United Nations (Tucker, 1994, 219).

The 1989 Tiananmen Square massacre in Beijing, followed by the anti-democracy crackdown, ignited fears about the viability of China's promises. Various resolutions were introduced into the US Congress, calling on Washington to monitor – even guarantee – the transition in Hong Kong. A largely symbolic measure was passed in August 1992, requiring the White House to report to Congress on human rights conditions and guarantees in Hong Kong. Human rights campaigner Martin Lee Chu-ming told a House committee that 'Britain's handover of 5.5 million Hong Kong people to China may be likened to the handover of 5.5 million Jewish people to Nazi Germany during World War II' (Tucker, 1994, 219). American anxiety in this period was linked to the close economic ties between the US and Hong Kong. The colony had over 20,000 US residents, operated as regional headquarters for many US corporations, and was a significant trading partner for the US. Margaret Thatcher (1993, 495) later recalled that 'we were ... brought under strong pressure immediately to accelerate the process of democratization in Hong Kong'.

The George H.W. Bush administration was not prepared to go out on a diplomatic limb to aid the cause of human rights in Hong Kong. Relations with Beijing were swiftly restored following the 1989 massacre. Nevertheless, the arrival in the colony of Governor Christopher Patten in 1992 marked a new British commitment, backed by the US, to pre-handover democratization. In 1996, the State Department applauded the Legislative Council elections as 'fair, open' and resulting 'in the most representative and democratic legislative body in Hong Kong's history' (Tucker, 1997, 220). Patten was eager to stiffen the White House's stance on democratization and human rights. He encouraged the American Chamber of Commerce in Hong Kong, along with various bodies in the US, from local bar associations to Supreme Court judges, to pressurize Clinton. His tactic was to persuade the Clinton administration that the renewal of 'most favoured nation' trading status for China could be exploited as a bargaining chip. In 1994, with Patten at his side, Clinton told the press that 'the democracy initative in Hong Kong is a good thing'. He continued: 'I hope it doesn't offend anybody, but how can the United States be against democracy?' (Dimbleby, 1997, 192–3; Patten, 1999, 111).

The problem for Patten was twofold. On the one hand, Beijing interpreted any attempt openly to include the US in the democratization process as an 'internationalization' of the dispute, and potentially destructive of the Declaration. On the other, Clinton's hopes not to 'offend anybody' betrayed a pragmatism which was to govern future presidential policy towards China. The annual debate on 'most favoured nation' status during the mid-to-late 1990s saw the White House consistently arguing for renewal, regardless of the situation in Hong Kong. Beijing's declaration of intent to abolish the Legislative Council was predictably greeted by greater hostility among 'containers' of China in Congress than by 'integrators' of China in the administration. In 1996, Martin Lee condemned the US failure 'to speak out' and warned of Hong Kong going 'down the drain like Tibet' (Tucker, 1997, 228).

The 30 June 1997 handover was accompanied by a flurry of legislative activity. A law, passed in March 1997, authorized the president to withhold trade privileges if Chinese promises were not kept. Democratic Congressman E.F. Hilliard of Alabama described this as 'our way of saying if you value your relationship with the United States, then respect the rights and liberties of the people of Hong Kong' (*Congressional Quarterly Weekly Report*, 16 March 1997, 658). During the following year, Hong Kong undertook Legislative Council elections under rules redrawn to placate Beijing.

Clinton and Blair

The election of Tony Blair's Labour government in 1997 brought into power a group of British politicians who admired both Clinton and recent developments in the Democratic Party. The post-1997 Anglo-American closeness was partly attributable to Blair's positive welcoming of US activism in Ireland. It was even more closely linked to good personal relations, and to the degree to which Clinton's political and policy centrism provided a model for New Labour. The process of remodelling had deep roots, but the particular influence of Clinton began to be seen during John Smith's brief tenure (1992–4) as leader. Just as Clinton had won back the 'Reagan Democrats', so Labour must reclaim those skilled workers who had supported Margaret Thatcher. Blair and future chancellor Gordon Brown visited Clinton's transition team in January 1993, and were exposed directly to the 'modernizing' ideas of the Democratic Leadership Council. The Blair-Brown visit (organized by Jonathan Powell, then of the British embassy in Washington, later Blair's chief of staff) was rightly seen by New Labour critics as of prime symbolic importance. Clare Short condemned the 'secret, infiltrating so-called modernisers of the Labour Party' who 'have been creating myths about why Clinton won, in order to try and reshape the Labour Party in the way they want it to go' (Rentoul, 1997, 283–4).

Personal friendship clearly existed between Clinton and Blair, even evoking memories of Reagan and Thatcher. The closeness was apparently based on a shared earnestness and generational identity. The new Labour government in London declared its concern to develop an ethical foreign policy; it also consciously sought, following the difficult Major years, to align itself with the international outlook of the second Clinton administration (Hodder-Williams, 2000). At a 1997 Washington press conference, Blair referred to 'the type of different agenda that I think a different generation of politicians is reaching towards' (*Public Papers of the Presidents ... 1997, vol. 1*, 1998, 677). Key Clinton personnel conspicuously acknowledged the aura of Blair's Britain and 'cool Britannia'. Upon his appointment as US ambassador to London in 1997, Philip Lader declared: 'I see the response to the tragic loss of Princess Diana, and the personal excitement that is palpable about the UK economy and in the thriving arts and film world, as a tremendous energy that is consistent with the view that life can be embraced in many dimensions'. Lader, a close Clinton friend and organizer of the 'Renaissance weekends', succeeded Admiral William Crowe, who in turn had followed Raymond Seitz (*The Times Magazine*, 4 October 1997, 12).

Many of Blair's early policies and attitudes appeared to reveal a preference for American rather than European models. Several Labour modernizers, notably Philip Gould, had worked on Clinton's

1992 campaign. Stanley Greenberg, a Clinton pollster, advised Gould in 1995: 'reassure ... voters again and again by visibly restraining the influence of the unions' (Macintyre, 1999, 321; Gould, 1998, ch. 5). Themes from the Clinton campaign, along with the Little Rock open-plan war room, were transferred to Labour's 1997 effort. Gould later described a 1990 Greenberg article as Labour's 'defining text' (*The Economist*, 20 September 1999; Greenberg, 1990). During visits to the UK during the Major years, Clinton outlined policy themes which were to resurface in New Labour's war on 'social exclusion'. The US president announced in 1994 that Britain had enjoyed 'a quite impressive run of growth'. The problem, however, was that too many people were 'isolated': 'either isolated in geographic areas where there has been disinvestment' or isolated 'because they don't have sufficient skills to compete in a global economy' (*Public Papers of the Presidents ... 1994, vol. 1*, 1995, 1023). At the joint Blair-Clinton press conference in Washington, held less than four weeks after his election, the new British prime minister enthused: 'Bill said something then just a moment ago that I think is very, very important, that the progressive parties of today are the parties of fiscal responsibility and prudence.' Clinton invoked the Anglo-American 'unique partnership' (*Public Papers of the Presidents ... 1997, vol. 1*, 1998, 679, 673). 'Third Way' international policy conferences, involving Clinton, Blair and other centre left leaders like Germany's Gerhard Schroeder and Fernando Henrique Cardoso of Brazil, were a feature of the 1990s. The US connections of key Blair advisers like Ed Balls and David Miliband were strong. Journalist Larry Elliott commented after three weeks of Blair's government: 'Almost every idea floated since the election – operational independence for the Bank of England, a beefed-up Securities and Investment Board, Welfare to Work, hit-squads in schools, an elected mayor for London – has its origins on the other side of the Atlantic' (*The Guardian*, 26 May 1997).

Blair's personal support for Clinton remained intact as the president approached, and eventually suffered, impeachment. When Tony and Cherie Blair came to Washington on a state visit in February 1998, with the Whitewater and Lewinsky scandals in full spate, they were (as Clinton wrote recalled in his memoirs) 'a sight for sore eyes for both Hillary and me' (Clinton, 2005, 778). London remained a staunch foreign policy ally, despite clear indications of a revived unilateralism in post-1995 US international behaviour. Not all such behaviour was promoted primarily by the Republican Congress. The 1996 Helms-Burton Act, with its threat of extraterritorial penalty for British firms trading with Cuba, clearly was; however, the 1998 anti-terrorist strikes on Sudan and Afghanistan were Clinton-led unilateral actions, and caused embarrassment in London.

The Blair–Clinton outlook on European development was more harmonious and coordinated than that of Clinton-Major. At the joint press conference in May 1997, Blair announced that he and Clinton had agreed 'that Britain does not need to choose between being strong in Europe and being close to the United States'. Rather, 'by being strong in Europe we will further strengthen our relationships with the US'. Clinton repeated his vision of a Europe 'that is undivided, democratic, and at peace for the first time in its history' (*Public Papers of the Presidents ... 1997, vol. 1*, 1998, 672). President Clinton expressed a wish to see 'the old Cold War alliance which was designed to confront the Soviet Union' developing 'into a new Euro-Atlantic alliance security system which includes Russia' (Walker, 1999, 28).

The Blair government's support for US policy towards Iraq led Britain to near-war in February, 1998, and to participation in air bombardment of Iraq in December of the same year. The US–UK air assault lasted four days and involved the launching of some 400 cruise missiles. As the sole active supporter of the US in December, London was isolated from France and other European allies who had joined the 1990–91 Gulf coalition. Blair's support for Washington opened the way for familiar charges of British obsequiousness. Journalist Alan Watkins wrote about the February 1998 threats to Iraq in the following terms: 'Mr Clinton's attraction for Mr Blair is that it allows him to cavort on the international stage, now getting into aeroplanes, now getting out of them, appearing before us as a person of consequence and power' (*Independent on Sunday*, 8 February 1998). Tony Benn, now leading Labour's Old Left, commented that Britain was 'so weak we have to ride piggyback on top of an American military superpower' (*Parliamentary Debates*, daily edition, 322 no. 16, 17 December 1998, 1129). The December action, however, was overwhelmingly supported in Parliament, though less convincingly in the country.

In March 1999, Britain commenced the air bombardment of the Kosovo province of Serbia, and of targets within Serbia/Yugoslavia itself. The action, a joint NATO operation, was a response to 'ethnic cleansing' by Serb police and paramilitaries of Kosovo Albanians. In the early part of 1999, London strongly backed the US position. At the unsuccessful Rambouillet conference of February 1999, Britain stood firmly behind the US view that NATO should be the dominant player in resolving the problems of Kosovo. The Rambouillet process was later criticised for making unrealistic demands. Although London and Washington stood publicly together, Kosovo diplomacy did expose an Anglo-American tension which was described in the diaries of Liberal Democrat leader Paddy Ashdown. According to Ashdown, Blair told him on February 22: 'We can't bomb Milosevic if he accepts the Rambouillet deal but the KLA (Kosovo Liberation Army) don't. That is our firm view. But the Americans seem to think otherwise'. This disagreement was 'putting a lot of political pressure on the relationship' (Ashdown, 2002, 407). London's support for a domi-nant NATO role conflicted not only with Russian claims, but also with the efforts of the continental Western Europeans to promote a 'European solution' (Weller, 1999, 212). Coming so soon after the St Malo summit, which countenanced 'autonomous' European mil-itary action, the US–UK position indicated the limits to both coun-tries' commitment to European Security and Defence Identity (ESDI). As the conflict erupted, Blair again faced accusations of being Clinton's poodle. In a House of Commons debate held to coincide with the start of the air war, Tony Benn expressed his regret 'that we take our orders from Washington' (*Parliamentary Debates*, daily edition, 328 no. 62, 25 March 1999, 566).

In the ensuing weeks, the British prime minister became an increasingly enthusiastic advocate of actual land invasion. Foreign Secretary Robin Cook became an ally of US Secretary of State Madeleine Albright in her efforts to persuade Defence Secretary William Cohen and Clinton himself of the virtues of using ground troops. Blair consistently promoted the view that NATO should indeed transform itself into an offensive, peace-imposing organiza-tion. On 22 April he delivered what was to become a famous address to the Economic Club of Chicago on what he called the 'new doctrine of international community', rooted in humanitarian intervention. Ambassador Christopher Meyer recalled the speech as utterly blind-siding the British Foreign Office. The prime minister was greeted by calls of 'Blair for President' (Meyer, 2005, 104). One American commentator Paul Starobin (1999, 1312) even coined the phrase, 'Blair Doctrine', to describe the US-led 'liberal hawkism': the willingness to intervene militarily for clearly stated moral purposes. At times, Blair's enthusiasm seemed to run well ahead of that of the American president. By May 1999, the two leaders were reported to be at odds over the advisability of sending troops into a hostile environment. Newspaper reports indicated Clinton's annoyance at Blair's resolution. According to this analysis, British toughness, rooted in Blair's public and parliamentary support, needlessly exposed Clinton's ambivalence: the comparative domestic weakness of the American president, connected to factors ranging from the 'Vietnam syndrome', through the Lewinsky affair, to congressional hostility to a NATO invasion (Cornwell, 1999). Blair's personal phone calls to and from Clinton became heated. The British leader at one point evidently feared a separate US deal with Milosevic (Seldon, 2004, 402). Blair apparently made private references to the possibility of Kosovo becoming his Suez. Clinton aides complained about Blair's 'god thing' (Kampfner, 2003, 48–9). General Wesley Clark, NATO Supreme Allied Commander in Europe (SACEUR), attempted to edge Washington towards possible ground commitment. A combination of US and, crucially, Russian pressure caused Milosevic to back down and withdraw troops from Kosovo. Blair's role was nevertheless important. Shortly after the public rift with Blair, Clinton replied to a press inquiry about ground troops with the insistence that the US 'will not take any option off the table' (*The Independent on Sunday*, 23 May 1999).

The June commitment of NATO troops followed the climbdown by Yugoslavian President Milosevic, and was achieved without huge bloodshed. As the occupation began, new Anglo-American military tensions emerged. According to contemporary reports, these involved the actual refusal by General Michael Jackson (the British ground commander in Kosovo) to obey orders given by Wesley Clark. At issue was the precipitate entry of Russian troops at the airport of Pristina, Kosovo's capital, on 12 June. US force leaders were angry that Jackson had apparently allowed the Russians to believe that this action would not be resisted. Clark ordered a French-British airborne assault to intercept the Russian move. Jackson refused, declaring that he would not be responsible for starting World War Three. Jackson was backed by London, while Washington swiftly withdrew support from Clark. It was swiftly announced that Wesley Clark would be quitting his post as SACEUR earlier than anticipated (W.K. Clark, 2001, 394–9).

The Kosovo campaign saw a degree of US–UK tension, and the disorganized air campaign certainly demonstrated to Washington the operational attractions of unilateralism. Nonetheless, despite difficulties along the way, war had again brought London and Washington closer. From Blair's viewpoint, Kosovo demonstrated the potency of the 'Atlantic bridge' and of the US–UK alliance. As Anthony Seldon (2004, 407) puts it, 'Clinton's equivocations gave him a mistrust of the ability of the US to reach the right conclusions without him'. Later in 1999, British Defence Secretary George Robertson, a close ally of US Defence Secretary William Cohen, took over as NATO secretary-general. The following year witnessed the deployment of around 1,300 British troops in another (at least initially) non-UN sanctioned operation: this time to protect British personnel and defence of the elected regime in Sierra Leone. Neatly reversing traditional roles, the US supported Britain against charges of neo-colonialism (Bellamy and Williams, 2005, 181).

The Anglo-American convergences over military issues contrasted with a range of non-military disputes. The 1998 arrest, pending extradition, in London of former Chilean dictator Augusto Pinochet posed diplomatic problems for the US (Hawthorn, 1999). In August 1999, it became clear that in 1998 American lobbying had been a factor in the decision to resume the building of gas-fired power stations. US Commerce Secretary William Daley had intervened directly in the interests of US-owned utility companies, threatening international court action (*The Guardian*, 13 August 1999). In 1999, Britain and the US also lined up on opposite sides in various EU-US trade disputes, involving bananas, beef and biotechnology (Granville, 1999). Such disputes had their comic side, especially when viewed against the background of the dramas being played out in Kosovo, yet they threatened jobs, global trade flows and the authority of the World Trade Organization. They also illustrated the degree to which US–UK relations were now being mediated through transnational institutions.

Blair and the George W. Bush Foreign Policy

Tony Blair's friendship with Bill Clinton did not prevent him from striking up a good relationship with the younger Bush. Anxious to avoid the mistakes made by Major in 1992, Downing Street had put out positive feelers to the 2000 Bush campaign team. The new transatlantic couple caused considerable consternation in Britain. The British Embassy in Washington counselled Downing Street against underestimating Bush (Seldon, 2004, 607). Journalist Peter Stodhard (2003, 40) mused: 'How was it possible that Tony Blair could switch so quickly to a close relationship with George Bush, a Texan conservative with whom he shared almost nothing in his life and barely a single belief about how a country should be taxed and run?' Blair and Bush certainly had Christian beliefs in common, though the former's high Anglicanism, shading into Roman Catholicism, was a long way from the latter's evangelical creed. The two leaders worked well together, for example in the international diplomacy involving the short, intensely dangerous, nuclear stand-off between India and Pakistan in 2002. Blair declared his liking for 'George's directness' (Stodhard, 2003, 70). After his first meeting with the new president, Blair reported, in a phrase which seemed to imply a degree of distancing from the experience under Clinton: 'he just tells you what he thinks' (Halper and Clarke, 2004, 132).

With the interesting and important exception of Northern Ireland, George W. Bush oriented his initial approach to foreign policy in terms of ABC: 'anything but Clinton'. Where Clinton had sought to work the world morally, the new approach would be 'humble'. It would also, as several key Bush advisers indicated early on, be based on a deliberately tough calculation of American interests.

The foreign policy of the first George W. Bush administration divides naturally into pre- and post-9/11 phases. The first nine months of 2001 were already distinguished by transatlantic bad temper. Bush's 'Americanist' foreign policy, though portrayed as a departure from Clinton, in some respects actually grew rather naturally from the late 1990s. Forced to react to the Republican takeover of Congress and buoyed up by the manifest acceleration in US relative international power, Clinton had already shown a degree of disregard for multilateralism. The Kosovo campaign was waged without UN sanction. The attacks on Sudan and Afghanistan were unilateral. America also, in the later Clinton years, rejected international agreements on land mines and child soldiers, as well as on the International Criminal Court. (Clinton had a 'deathbed conversion' to the ICC in his very last hours in the White House).

Transatlantic rifts deepened in the early part of 2001. With the anchor of anti-Soviet defence removed, the US–Western European alliance seemed to be floundering amid economic rivalries, the rise of American unilateralism and mutual suspicion. US administration spokesmen criticised European integration as an attempt to sideline America and undermine NATO. *The Economist* (9 June 2001) summed up prevailing administration attitudes towards Western Europe as follows: 'The American stereotype is of a Europe that is economically scelerotic, psychologically neurotic and addicted to spirit-sapping welfare schemes and a freedom-infringing state'. Policy disagreements included the continued rejection of international agreements: the ICC, the Kyoto protocol on greenhouse gas emissions, the land mine and biological weapons ban, and international agreements on biodiversity and the regulation of genetically modified foods. The US policy of going ahead with anti-missile defence, including the abrogation of the 1972 Anti-Ballistic Missile Treaty (ABMT), further raised European hackles. Western European leaders became exasperated by the neo-conservatives and offensive realists in the administration. Foreign Secretary Jack Straw reportedly described John Bolton, undersecretary of state and vocal proponent of 'Americanism' in foreign policy as a 'nightmare' (Kampfner, 2003, 97). Only Secretary of State Colin Powell was held by much Western European opinion to be genuinely committed to multilateral cooperation. Bush's first trip to Europe in June 2001 rather pointedly, at least in the opinion of British commentators, did not include a visit to the UK. Rather than recognizing the UK as a bridge to Europe, Bush arrived first in Spain, Europe's bridge to Latin America. The trip did little to ease tensions and tempers. Bush was reported as concluding that new ideas in Europe were coming only from the East (*US News and World Report*, 25 June 2001, 24).

The Blair government's response to these difficulties was, broadly, to reaffirm the 'Atlantic bridge' role, but also to recognise that these really were problematic times for the transatlantic partnership. A 2005 analysis of US–UK relations, prepared by the Congressional Research Service (CRS), described Blair's notion of the 'transatlantic bridge' as 'essentially an extension of long-standing British foreign policy'. The CRS study saw London as concluding that 'Britain might cease to matter to Washington if London were perceived as being a fringe player' in the wider Europe (Archik, 2005, 8). London was happy to take a more Europeanist line and to criticise Washington on the economic and climate change disputes. Blair faced significant opposition from within his own party to the prospect of being asked for British assistance in respect of the anti-missile programme. Foreign Office minister Peter Hain publicly criticised the programme in early 2001. Liberal Democrat foreign affairs spokesman Shirley Williams called on Blair to oppose the unilateral drift of US policy which threatened the 'fragile network of multilateral arms agreements and arms control mechanisms that have helped to keep peace between nuclear powers for 50 years' (Williams, 2001). The tough US line on European defence integration severely embarrassed Blair, whose position was consistently that NATO remained at the heart of Europe's security. By the middle of 2001, Washington had actually rowed back from some of its unilateralist positions. An offer was made to share anti-missile technology, for example, and negotiations over North Korea's nuclear programme were resumed. Some journalists traced Washington's acceptance of the joint NATO-Russia council to Blair's influence (Young, 2002b). In an extraordinarily poignant interview, published in *Time* magazine on 10 September 2001, Colin Powell declared: 'You can't be unilateralist. The world is too complicated'.

The terror attacks of 11 September 2001, the 'gate of fire' which, as UN Secretary General Kofi Annan put it, ushered the world into the new century, transformed the international environment (Shawcross, 2003, 11). US foreign policy became organized around the War on Terror, military budgets skyrocketed and talk of American disengagement, or even neo-isolationism disappeared. The unilateral thrust of the pre-9/11 foreign policy remained and was refashioned in a world divided rhetorically between friends of freedom and friends of terror. Neo-conservatism, a set of ideas associated with second tier administration figures like Paul Wolfowitz and Douglas Feith, and emphasizing the use of US military primacy to promote democratic goals, became newly influential, especially in relation to policy in the Middle East. The offensive against Afghanistan gave way to war preparations against

Iraq, with US policy towards the latter, in the words of Michael Clarke (2004, 38) 'effectively on tramlines'.

The Blair government's reaction to these events was, by turns, dynamic, inspired and reckless. The British leader was immediately prominent in expressing sympathy and support for the new anti-terror international coalition. To quote Timothy Garton Ash (2005, 49): 'All the Churchillian bells rang'. Blair delivered a memo to Washington, outlining an appropriate and measured response, emphasizing multilateralism, intelligence sharing but certainly not ruling out military action. Blair's diplomatic skills in this immediate post-attack period were extraordinary. Within days, the personal diplomacy side of the 'special relationship' was revitalized. Blair became favourite foreign leader in Washington, rivalled only by cooperative leaders of 'front line' Moslem states. He operated as a species of international pro-American ambassador, would-be multilateralizer and explainer of the Bush response to 9/11. Shortly before the conflict in Afghanistan the *Wall Street Journal* described Blair as America's 'chief foreign ambassador to members of the emerging coalition' against terrorism (Curtis, 2003, 113).

The reasoning behind Blair's reaction to Bush's reaction to 9/11 was complex. Let us try to break it down into its component parts. Firstly, there was the question of the 'Atlantic bridge'. However doomed it was to failure – German leader Gerhard Schroeder summed up the general Western European view by declaring that traffic on the bridge seemed to move in just one direction (Riddell, 2003, 142) – Blair unquestionably saw his role in this period as an encourager of transatlantic mutuality. Secondly, there was the familiar accommodation to American power, allied to a 'Greeks and Romans' view of how to use and enhance British influence. According to former Foreign Secretary Robin Cook (2003, 116), he told the Cabinet in March 2002 that London 'must steer close to America'. Jack Straw, who replaced Cook at the Foreign Office after the 2001 election, told *The Observer*, in an interview published on 6 November 2003, that 'there isn't anything that can be done about the fact' of American international power. The priority for the UK was to 'relate to America in the most constructive way possible ... to ensure that this power is used for the better'. For Blair, standing aside and criticising Bush from the sidelines was both irresponsible and also, as he put it in 2002, 'the biggest impulse to unilateralism there could be' (Pond, 2005, 48). Alan

Milburn, Blair supporter in the Cabinet, told *The Guardian* on 26 March 2005 that British policy had been based on 'the reality of the way the world is', with 'one superpower'. Blair sought to channel that power: towards multilateralism and a broadening of its agenda, to include issues such as the Israeli-Palestinian peace process and even poverty in Africa.

Lastly, there is the question of Blair's own beliefs, not just concerning American power and British obligations under the 'special relationship', but also his core beliefs about international change and world order. Time and time again, Blair told audiences that 9/11 had transformed the world and that the world needed to change its psychology. In a sense, however, Blair's own psychology had not changed. To Blair and to many others of his generation, international failure in regard to the genocide in Rwanda and to the Balkan horrors of the early 1990s stimulated a new kind of post-Cold War liberal, interventionist internationalism. The Balkans-oriented 'liberal hawkism' outlined in his 1999 Chicago speech – the view that older notions of sovereignty and deterrence needed to be qualified in the light of humanitarian imperatives – was simply updated to fit the world after 9/11. Some commentators, notably William Shawcross (2003, 51), have labelled Blair as the British neo-con. Extracts from the 1999 Chicago speech found their way into a 2004 collection edited by Irwin Stelzer and entitled *Neoconservatism*. In a 2002 interview, Blair came close to declaring his 'international community doctrine' the thread that bound together London and Washington, under both the Clinton and the George W. Bush administrations. 'This', declared Blair, 'is a Republican administration with a certain view, so they will couch what they do in terms of US national interest'. However, the 'doctrine of international community is just enlightened self-interest, so whatever the different rhetorical perspectives you come to the same point' (Goodhart, 2002, 17). Blair's muscular Christian 'liberal hawkism' was actually some way from US neo-conservatism, with its proto-messianic commitment to American primacy and its suspicion of multilateralism. Nevertheless, there was at least some degree of convergence.

By early October 2001, Britain was involved in the air bombardment of Afghanistan. Blair disappointed the hopes of some emerging critics of the War on Terror by implying that other countries besides Afghanistan could be attacked: 'We are in this for the long haul. Even when al-Qaeda is dealt with, the job is not over'

(Kampfner, 2003, 130–31). As in the case of Kosovo, tensions between London and Washington did quite swiftly emerge. Blair was apparently making little progress in broadening the US agenda beyond military responses to 9/11. At a joint press conference in Washington between Blair and Bush on November 7, the US leader told journalists that America had 'no better friend in the world' than the UK. However, he also insisted that terrorism would be conquered 'peace or no peace in the Middle East'. Secretary of Defense Donald Rumsfeld emphasized that Washington would call all the shots: 'The coalition must not determine the mission' (Seldon, 2004, 508–9). George Robertson, the Labour politician who had now become NATO chief, was effectively rebuffed by the US military heads, who had no wish to repeat the confusion of the Kosovo campaign. The conflict in Afghanistan was directed almost entirely from Washington, with US forces working through the surrogate Afghan Northern Alliance against the Taliban. British commando and special forces did play an important role, particularly from early 2002. However, near-public rows broke out between London and Washington over post-war reconstruction, with the US resisting talk of 'nation-building' and keeping cooperation with the 17-nation International Security Assistance Force, a body which included Britain, to a minimum. By the end of 2001, Labour Party, and general British public opinion, was becoming uneasy about London's role in the War on Terror. What exactly was this influence which Britain was supposed to be enjoying over Washington? By early 2002, with British citizens among those held by the US without trial at Camp X-ray at Guantanamo in Cuba, any such influence was very difficult to discern. By this time, Blair was also effectively isolated from the mainstream of Western European governmental opinion. Although Paris carefully declined entirely to separate itself from the War on Terror – France actually flew more air sorties against the Taliban in Afghanistan than did the RAF (MacShane, 2006) – French President Jacques Chirac's view of the Afghan War became increasingly apocalyptic. He told Blair in November 2001 that 'a mosque will be bombed during Ramadan' and that humanitarian abuses by US forces were already occurring (Riddell, 2003, 167).

By early 2002, the sniping of a French president had developed into a major transatlantic rift. Western European public opinion, including British opinion, began to turn unmistakably against the

Bush administration in Washington. Blair offered a nervous defence of American unilateralism, declaring in 2002: 'because of America's special position, people tend to exaggerate the extent to which the US is saying we don't care what the rest of the world thinks' (Goodhart, 2002, 17). Hugo Young (2002a) commented that 'instead of being Europe's voice in America and America's in Europe', Britain now ran the risk 'of having a small voice, and smaller audience, in either place'

Among Western European elites, Bush's 2002 State of the Union address, wherein he identified Iraq, Iran and North Korea as an 'axis of evil', and Deputy Defence Secretary Paul Wolfowitz's remarks at a major security conference in Munich (February 2002), seem to have been major turning points. At the Munich conference, Wolfowitz informed NATO defence ministers that the US was looking to work through 'coalitions of the willing', as much as through the traditional transatlantic defence alliance. In March 2003, *Financial Times* columnist Philip Stevens accused the US of having carried out, over the previous year, the 'wilful destruction of the international security system' (Pond, 2005, 34, 47). The German election campaign later in 2002 saw both left and right candidates promising degrees of neutralism in the event of a war in Iraq. From Washington's viewpoint, the Western European allies, with the partial exception of the UK, were living in a world of illusion; believing themselves somehow immune from the threat of terrorism, and either congenitally unable to shoulder a responsible security burden, or hankering after some absurd idea of acting as a 'balancer' to the United States. London was probably now more isolated from other Western European capitals than at any time in the previous half century.

Iraq and After

Tony Blair's predicament in 2001–3 rapidly reached the proportions appropriate to Jacobean tragedy. In April 2002, he was apparently informed in no uncertain terms at the Bush ranch in Crawford, Texas, that policy was set for the invasion of Iraq. His subsequent conduct, knowing that invasion was all but inevitable, but acting as if the anti-terror coalition might be prepared to go one more mile for peace, exposed him to the accusation of bad faith. It may be argued that decisions, even the Bush administration's decision to invade Iraq, are never irrevocable. Christopher Meyer, former UK ambassador to the US, has argued that London was actually unduly pessimistic about the likelihood of war, and that Blair thereby missed the chance to exercise leverage over the US. He told *The Observer* (16 November 2003) that Blair had made a forlorn personal appeal to Bush to delay the war in January 2003. Meyer also held that Blair and Bush acted in good faith, never conspiring to 'mislead their publics as to their true, bellicose intentions' (Meyer, 2005, 283). The record of the American policy 'tramlines' over Iraq – together with the sheer unlikelihood of US troops being withdrawn once despatched to the Iraqi border – does, however, seem compelling.

The American goal was regime change *per se*. Evidence, or rather the lack of it, regarding the existence either of Iraqi weapons of mass destruction or of any connection between Baghdad and 9/11, was secondary. Blair's own priorities were to support America, to push Washington away from unilateralism and, if at all possible, to bring British and Western European opinion behind Washington. For Blair, as noted above, the cause was right, even if relations with some Washington hawks (notably Vice President Richard Cheney) were strained, and even if he were not even to be protected from public embarrassment at Washington's hands. The treatment of NATO during the Afghanistan conflict in late 2001 was a sign of things to come. The announcement, as war in Iraq loomed, of the imposition of US tariffs on British steel imports was one particularly miserable moment. Trade Secretary Patricia Hewitt's denunciation of the steel tariffs as being 'in clear disregard of international opinion' was not without its ironies, given the situation regarding Iraq (Curtis, 2003, 115). Donald Rumsfeld's attacks on European defence proposals that were being sponsored by Blair, compounded the agony (Hastings, 2003).

Determined on his version of the 'Greeks and Romans' strategy, Blair announced at the Labour Party conference in October 2001: 'The starving, the wretched, the dispossessed, the ignorant, they are our causes too' (Seldon, 2004, 500). He set himself the task of communicating more clearly than Washington that the War on Terror was not a 'crusade' against Islam. Seeking to broaden and soften the American agenda, Blair opened himself to the charge of being taken for granted by Washington. The resulting pain was well captured in

David Hare's play, *Stuff Happens*. At one stage in Hare's play, Blair declares: 'With the Americans there's only one rule. The earlier you join, the more influence you have.' Hare also put the following brutal gloss on the 'special relationship' in the mouth of Vice President Dick Cheney: 'When the cat shit gets bigger than the cat, get rid of the cat' (Hare, 2004, 88, 104).

Hare's play captured more than the opposition of the British literary intelligentsia to Blair's support for the Bush White House. It unquestionably reflected the sentiments of important sections of liberal and leftist opinion in Britain, sections of which now inclined to conspiracy theory in regard to the War on Terror. Among top Labour Party figures, the opinions of Michael Meacher, Blair's environment minister between 1997 and 2003, illustrated the extraordinary attitudinal context in which Blair was now operating. In a remarkable piece in *The Guardian*, Meacher rehearsed the post-9/11 conspiracy views of Michael Moore and some of the wilder internet sites. Why had Osama bin Laden not been captured in 2002? Why was not 'a single fighter plane scrambled to investigate from the US Andrews airforce base, just 10 miles from Washington DC, until after the third plane (on 9/11) had hit the Pentagon?' Meacher concluded: 'the "global war on terror" has the hallmarks of a political myth propagated to pave the way for a wholly different agenda – the US goal of world hegemony, built around securing by force command over the oil supplies required to drive the whole project'. Britain's role under Blair, according to Meacher, was to provide 'collusion in this myth' (Meacher, 2003).

Meacher's argument took him to the far shores of political conspiracy-mongering. By 2002–3, however, one did not have to travel down that road to appreciate the gap between London's hopes for the alliance, and Washington's understanding of it. In the real world of international diplomacy, David Manning (close Blair adviser and Christopher Meyer's successor as British ambassador to Washington) outlined these hopes, even as he accepted the limited nature of British influence, as follows: 'At the best of times, Britain's influence on the US is limited. But the only way we exercise that influence is by attaching ourselves firmly to them and avoiding public criticism wherever possible' (Kampfner, 2003, 117). The Iraq War will be discussed in more detail in a subsequent chapter. Christopher Meyer, however, argued very plausibly in 2004 that, rather than maximizing London's influence, Blair's strategy led to Britain being taken for granted. Washington, Meyer told Anthony Seldon (2004, 572), 'had a working hypothesis from September 2001 onwards that we had committed ourselves fully to whatever they were going to do, whether we in London thought we had or not. It was in their bloodstream'.

With the British die firmly cast over Iraq, Blair did begin to pressure Bush, notably at their war meeting at Hillsborough Castle in Northern Ireland in April 2003, on the need to work more through the United Nations and to re-engage with the Israeli-Palestinian peace process. A few concessions were made, notably regarding the release from Guantanamo of some British detainees. Their press stories of maltreatment and of UK–US collusion in their interrogation further embarrassed London. Following Bush's 2004 re-election, there was a manifest switch in Washington towards a more emollient public approach to foreign policy, despite the departure of Colin Powell and the retention of Donald Rumsfeld. Nicholas Burns, the new undersecretary at the State Department for political affairs spoke at Chatham House in London about the 'renewed spirit of purpose, compromise, and unity in transatlantic relations' (Burns, 2005). The switch to greater concern for public diplomacy was no doubt encouraged by London, but also clearly embodied a simple recognition of the damage done to American international alliances during the first term.

During 2004–5, Blair's government sought, to the degree made possible by the continuing conflict in Iraq, to distance itself from some of the more controversial statements emanating from Washington. In August 2005, the Foreign Office issued a briefing in direct response to veiled American threats to take military action against Iran. 'We do not', declared a Foreign Office spokesman, 'think there are any circumstances where military action would be justified against Iran' (*The Sunday Times*, 14 August 2005). Also, during 2004, Blair began to push publicly for US aid to Africa to be increased, and progress to be made on the agenda, worked out by Chancellor Gordon Brown on international debt relief for very poor countries. At one level, London's Africa initiatives were an attempt to leave behind the bad memories of Iraq and to exercise a degree of emotional blackmail on Washington. Muted, though public, rows broke out over the agenda for the G8 summit in Gleneagles, Scotland, scheduled for July 2005. Press reports indicated US unhappiness about accepting the need for concerted action on global warming and about Brown's plan for an international finance facility for Africa, to allow governments to spend future aid money in advance. The public unpopularity of the Bush administration ensured that the president's quite reasonable insistence that US aid to Africa had already greatly increased under his watch fell on deaf ears. A fierce disagreement apparently occurred between Brown and new Secretary of State Condoleezza Rice over British lobbying for Africa at the Foreign Office in February 2005. Environment minister Margaret Beckett declared that Blair had 'a choice of siding with Europe as he assumes the EU presidency (in mid-2005) or with an increasingly isolated US president' (*The Guardian*, 1 July 2005). On environmental issues, London certainly did now stand on the 'European' side, though not, it scarcely needs recording, on wider international security agendas.

Blair and Brown's efforts at the G8 summit in Scotland (July 2005) brought a degree of response from the US, although the public announcements associated with the summit were rather lost in the attention given to the London terrorist bombings of 7 July 2005. By this time, the Blair government had been re-elected on a respectable, if significantly reduced, parliamentary majority. Iraq and the Bush-Blair links unquestionably damaged Labour in, the campaign, although the only major anti-war party, the Liberal Democrats, failed to make breakthrough gains. Yet more transatlantic tensions emerged in late 2005 over the practice of 'extraordinary rendition', the putative transporting, possibly via British airports, of War on Terror prisoners by the CIA to secret destinations. Foreign Secretary Jack Straw was publicly obliged to deny knowledge of any such flights.

The Blair–Bush relationship rather cruelly exposed the limits of British influence over American policy. From one angle, it must be admitted that expectations of moving the first term Bush team were always rather unrealistic. From another, public and press hopes of 'cashing in' the support for the invasion in terms of increased aid to Africa, or altered attitudes towards climate change, betrayed both an exaggerated sense of Britain's importance to the US, and an ignorance of the American politics of separated powers, wherein the US Congress holds the purse-strings and the US Senate ratifies treaties. From early 2003 onwards, however, a clear pattern did seem to emerge: Blair's efforts to promote multilateralism, movement on the Israeli-Palestinian 'road map', a greater role for the UN in Iraq, or whatever was the cause of the moment, would appear to be making headway, but in the longer run simply could not overcome opposition from influential conservatives in Washington. Asked in 2002 about the degree of influence he enjoyed in Washington, Blair was coy: 'I never like to talk about it that way – it either looks as if you are some sort of supplicant for the ear of the president or you're boasting about your position' (Goodhart, 2002, 17). However, American diplomat and think-tanker Richard Haass told Anthony Seldon, in relation to US policy towards the UN: 'The cold fact is that this was an area which demonstrated the limits of British influence' (Seldon, 2004, 621). The point could be made that the French strategy of opposition also had little policy impact. Denis MacShane, sometime Europe minister in the Blair government, argued in 2006 that Downing Street's influence could be detected in the American decision to rejoin UNESCO, 'which used to be more loathed by American conservatives than the Soviet Union', and also in 'the current developments in Israel' (MacShane, 2006). The 2005 Israeli exit from Gaza was no doubt, at one level at least, a response to US pressure. Blair's influence on Washington may have been a factor here, but hardly a decisive one. Even in the wake of the British commitment to Iraq, it was indeed very difficult to identify what exactly *were* the areas of British influence.

7
Nuclear Defence and Intelligence Cooperation

With this chapter, we begin a series of thematic investigations into the structures and development of US–UK relations: into nuclear and intelligence cooperation here, and, in subsequent chapters, into the experience of war, the impact of European integration, and the politics of Ireland.

During the Cold War, at least following the repeal of the McMahon Act in 1958, the UK enjoyed privileged access to nuclear information from the United States. This, along with the intimate intermeshing of US and British intelligence under the UKUSA agreement of 1947, formed the essence and beating heart of the Cold War 'special relationship'.

From Britain's viewpoint, nuclear attachment to the US had some obvious benefits. It seemed to ease Macmillan's 'problem of being poor and powerful at the same time' (J.W. Young, 1997, 174). Linking up with the US, at least insofar as such linkage could be presented as partnership rather than simple dependence, might allow Britain a great-power-by-proxy status. Yet there were drawbacks. Some of these were relatively minor: for example, the problems deriving from having to accommodate large numbers of American servicemen on British soil. Others were more serious. Too close a nuclear attachment to the US might endanger British sovereignty, actually erode the UK's 'great power' status and involve dangerous gambles on the future American commitment to Europe. This last consideration was recalled by Clement Attlee when he described the secret decision made by an ad hoc Cabinet group in 1947 to develop a British atomic bomb:

> We had to hold up our position vis-à-vis the Americans. We couldn't allow ourselves to be wholly in their hands, and their position wasn't

awfully clear always. At that time we had to bear in mind that there was always the possibility of their withdrawing and becoming isolationists once again. (Baylis, 1984, 33)

Ernest Bevin, Attlee's foreign secretary, wanted a nuclear bomb 'with a bloody Union Jack on it' (Morgan, 1990, 54).

From Washington's point of view, Britain was a valuable nuclear ally and an important site for American bases. Britain, however, in the US view was also too inclined to seek shelter with Uncle Sam as a way of avoiding the costs of an adequate conventional defence. Washington was continually concerned to impress upon London that nuclear power did not obviate the need to assume a large burden of conventional defence spending. This was true whether the US adhered to a doctrine of 'massive retaliation' or 'flexible response'. 'Massive retaliation' was the doctrine advocated by President Eisenhower and Secretary of State John Foster Dulles. It involved, in Dulles' words, 'a great capacity to retaliate, instantly, by means and at places of our choosing' (Paterson, 1997, 18–19). 'Flexible response' was introduced by US Defense Secretary Robert McNamara in the early 1960s and put more emphasis still on the need for European powers to achieve adequate conventional counters to Soviet aggression. By the early 1960s, Washington clearly appreciated the need rationally to integrate not only conventional but also nuclear forces (in the Multinational Nuclear Force). In this context, London's preoccupation with sovereignty, independence and a seat at international top tables provoked annoyance.

We begin our survey of nuclear and intelligence cooperation with the focal issue of the British deterrent.

Britain's Deterrent

As noted above, the original decision to develop an independent deterrent was taken against the background of perceived isolationist and anti-British sentiment in Washington, especially in the US Congress. London proceeded with the independent deterrent despite pressure from the Truman Administration in 1949 to drop these plans in return for enhanced cooperation and even 'a supply of bombs to Britain "on call" ' (Baylis, 1984, 44). At the Blair House meeting of July 1949, leading congressional figures continued to oppose nuclear sharing and attacked Britain's status as a dependent and costly ally to the US.

Britain's pre-1960 nuclear weapons were credibly described as 'independent'. Faced with the exclusionary McMahon Act, the Attlee, Churchill and Eden governments developed a British nuclear programme of considerable scale. Plutonium was made at Windscale in Cumbria and a uranium enrichment plant opened at Capenhurst, near Chester. In 1954, British chiefs of staff decided to support the development of an 'independent' hydrogen bomb, as 'it would be dangerous if the United States were to retain their present monopoly since we would be denied any right to influence her policy in the use of this weapon' (Ovendale, ed., 1994, 104). A simple British atomic bomb had been exploded in 1952. Under Operational Grapple, a series of megaton bomb tests took place on Christmas Island in 1957. A hydrogen – certainly an enhanced fission – bomb was ready by 1958.

Britain was now the only country, other than the US and USSR, to have tested megaton bombs. Randolph Churchill boasted to the US Chamber of Commerce in London in 1958: 'Britain can knock down twelve cities in the region of Stalingrad and Moscow from bases in Britain and another dozen in the Crimea from bases in Cyprus. We did not have that power at the time of Suez. We are a major power again' (Paterson, 1997, 19). The son of Britain's prime minister in World War Two was engaging in characteristic nationalist bluster. The development of Britain's H-bomb actually ended the 'independent' phase of British nuclear history. London had greatly resented the McMahon Act, but its very existence had set the conditions for an independent UK nuclear path. Its repeal, and the nuclear information sharing agreed in 1958, established Britain as a privileged but dependent nuclear partner.

As part of the 1962 Polaris deal and the Trident deal of 1980–82 (both described in more detail below), the UK bought in virtually fully developed nuclear technology from the US. The Polaris submarine missiles were manufactured by Lockheed in the US. The warheads were constructed in Britain, following closely an American design. After 1958, Britain also imported highly enriched uranium and tritium, essential as fuel for nuclear explosions. After 1976, tritium began to be produced at a plant in Scotland. Britain's contribution to America's Cold War nuclear stock was in the form of exported plutonium, from both civil and military reactors in the

UK. In 1963, Britain gained access to underground nuclear testing sites in Nevada. In relation to the 1980 Trident deal, about half of British expenditure related to components actually purchased in the US. These included the entire missile delivery and re-entry systems, certain components related to the warheads and some essential submarine design. Trident in service remained dependent on highly enriched uranium from the US, on missile components and servicing at King's Bay (Georgia), as well as periodic testing in Nevada.

Spokesmen for British defence policy regularly proclaimed the independence of the deterrent. John Nott in his memoirs, for example, insisted: 'we are truly independent; the Americans hold no veto over us' (Nott, 2002a, 218). However, except perhaps in purely formal/legal terms, this was not an 'independent' deterrent. Beyond issues of production and servicing, leftist and nationalist critics in the UK focused also on Britain's operational dependence on the US. Clearly, a British leader could, in concert with the chiefs of staff, have ordered missiles to be fired. Polaris or Trident submarine commanders would have obeyed, presumably without interference from the US. However, as Malcolm Chalmers argued in 1984, 'That Britain's nuclear weapons could be used "cold" in normal peacetime conditions is ... so implausible as to be of marginal interest.' The crucial question was one of British independence (notably in target selection, communications and guidance) during extreme crisis or war:

> Britain's nuclear forces form part of the nuclear forces available to NATO's SACEUR (Supreme Allied Commander, Europe), who is a US General. As such, they are assigned targets by a Joint Strategic Target Planning Staff ... based at Omaha, Nebraska. Though precise details are unknown, British forces appear to form an integral part of the US plan for all-out nuclear war – its Single Integrated Operational Plan. ... As part of SLOP, they would be used as part of a NATO nuclear war, limited or otherwise.

Severe doubts were raised also about the integrity both of British communications links and of missile guidance technology. Chalmers went on to express the near inexpressible: 'the faintest possibility of a British nuclear strike against the Soviet Union without US permission is likely to make British installations prime targets for nuclear strikes by *both* superpowers' (Chalmers, 1984, 30–3).

The persistence with an independent deterrent was closely allied to questions of prestige. For Alec Douglas-Home, Britain's deterrent was the 'ticket of admission' to a 'seat at the top table' (Freedman, 1980, 88). By the mid-1960s, British leaders tended to claim status more as a result of special nuclear partnership with the US, rather than as a consequence of possessing 'independent' nuclear weapons. However, Britain still clearly had a deterrent which was not fully integrated into America's arsenal, though dependent on the US in several ways. As such, the independent deterrent often received the worst of all worlds. It was attacked as unnecessary by the US itself, as well as by critics across the spectrum of British opinion. On the pro-American right, the retention of the deterrent was difficult to defend, particularly insofar as it implied 'mistrust' of the US (Pierre, 1972, 251). The nationalist right, never a force in Britain to equal that in France, looked to some kind of Gaullist solution: an end to American bases and development of a genuinely independent deterrent along the lines envisaged for the *force de frappe* in France. Sometime Conservative minister Enoch Powell argued that 'Britain became conceptually and morally a satellite of the United States ... once it relied on the United States for its own nuclear deterrent' (Grayling and Langdon, 1988, 42). 'Exposure' of the British deterrent as an extremely dependent one also enabled disarmers to appropriate nationalism and equate unilateral disarmament with a revolt against American imperialism. More generally, throughout the later Cold War, a significant body of elite opinion in Britain held the independent deterrent to be a sham and a waste. As maverick defence chief Field Marshal Lord Carver remarked: 'I don't believe that whether or not Britain keeps an independent nuclear force makes much difference to anybody else. If the French want to waste their money on these things let them' (Ramsbotham (ed.) 1987, 180).

US Bases

Seven months after the election of Margaret Thatcher's Conservative government, Tony Benn, former Labour minister, asked in his diary (13 December 1979):

does the British Government have a veto on the use of American nuclear weapons from British bases? I've always assumed there was a veto ... Have the American Government got the power to use these [cruise] missiles from our bases without the explicit consent of the British Prime Minister? (Benn, 1991, 564–5)

At the time of Benn's diary entry there were about 30,000 American service personnel and civilians, excluding dependants, in Britain (Duke, 1987, 138–63; 1989, 304). From Washington's viewpoint, the British bases represented a valuable part of America's forward defence, and a vital air force and logistics centre in case of war. The precise purpose of the bases varied somewhat over the years. In the early 1960s, US Strategic Air Command maintained 'reflex' forces of mainly B-47 bombers. By the mid-1960s, with greater reliance on long-range missiles, Washington's need for strategic manned nuclear bomber facilities in Britain decreased. Air Force cuts were compensated, however, by increased US naval presence (mainly in association with nuclear submarines) and by the relocations associated with General de Gaulle's expulsion of the American military from France in 1966. Under Operation Frelock (the code name for the relocations), Air Force numbers in the UK again increased, and the US Army gained a significant presence in Britain for the first time.

Washington's view of the bases shifted somewhat in the later years of the Vietnam War. Concern grew about the European allies failing to shoulder their share of the defence burden. Senator Mike Mansfield's resolutions in Congress, prescribing troop withdrawals from Europe, provided an annual focus for American resentments. Some British leaders began in the late 1960s and early 1970s to grow anxious about the prospects of a post-Vietnam War US neo-isolationism (Williams, 1985). With the faltering, and eventual collapse, of superpower détente in the later 1970s, however, the bases acquired new purposes and new notoriety in the UK. By 1978, US 3rd Tactical Air Force bases at Upper Heyford, Lakenheath and Bentwaters constituted around 40 per cent of the US air commitment to NATO. Significant increases in F-111 aircraft deployment occurred between 1978 and 1982.

In 1979, James Callaghan's Labour government agreed to the siting of 96 intermediate-range cruise missiles, designed to counter Soviet SS-20s in Britain. The agreement was made in the context of NATO force modernization, and of undertakings by Washington to work first for a negotiated removal of the SS-20s. The cruise missiles (designed to be launched from the ground, but also capable of being carried by the F-111s) were deployed in 1983 at Greenham Common and Molesworth bases. The missiles provoked fears of a 'limited' nuclear war in Europe, and ignited a major public protest in Britain – part of a European revival of disarmament activism. Cruise missiles in Britain (along with the SS-20s and Pershing Its in West Germany) were eliminated under the terms of the 1987 Intermediate Nuclear Forces treaty. Following the 1987 treaty, however, the Thatcher government approved the basing of 50 more F-111 bombers, especially designed to deliver nuclear weapons, in Britain by 1990.

The waning of the Cold War in the later 1980s removed the impetus behind British protest at US military activity in Europe. However, the anti-cruise protests of the early 1980s were certainly the strongest expressions of hostility to American bases since the Aldermaston disarmament marches of 1957–61. Following the decline of the Campaign for Nuclear Disarmament (CND) fortunes in the early 1960s, occasional incidents associated with the bases had always threatened to provoke public resentment. For example, US sailors rioted in Dunoon in 1973. The 1952 Visiting Forces Act, under which American service personnel were removed from the jurisdiction of the British courts, also provoked intermittent public disquiet. Following a 1979 incident in Cornwall, for example, a US court martial fined a marine, who had killed a local man in a car crash, the sum of one dollar (Duncan Campbell, 1984, 302). In general, the US military kept a disciplined and low profile, making contributions to local economies. In terms of benefit to the British exchequer, however, such factors need to be set against the money expended by the Ministry of Defence in purchasing new land for the rent-free bases. Public unease also occasionally surfaced concerning the extent to which the bases increased the risk of Britain being the target of a Soviet nuclear attack. The 1983 Defence Estimates took the unusual step of addressing such fears directly, arguing: 'So far from putting the United Kingdom at greater risk, the presence here of United States forces is a vital element in ensuring that war does not break out' (Duncan Campbell, 1984, 299, 302–3).

Benn's 1979 question hovered over all these considerations. How much control *did* the British government have over the bases? In October 1951, Prime Minister Attlee reached an understanding with President Truman over the bases. This understanding, drafted by British Ambassador to Washington Oliver Franks, was reaffirmed by Churchill and Truman in 1952. As Harold Macmillan told the House of Commons in 1957, it asserted that 'the use of bases in an emergency was accepted to be a matter for joint decision by the two Governments in the light of the circumstances prevailing at the time' (Baylis, 1984, 41). Clearly, the US was committed to consultation, if only at the level of personal understandings. In December 1963, Prime Minister Alec Douglas-Home contacted the new American president, Lyndon Johnson, regarding 'the understandings which have existed between former Presidents and Prime Ministers about the use of nuclear weapons'. He referred Johnson to 'the requirement for joint decision by the President and Prime Minister on the use of force equipped with United States nuclear weapons operating from bases in the United Kingdom, or from British territorial waters'. According to Home, previous British leaders had also received 'a general assurance about consultation, if possible, before using nuclear weapons anywhere in the world'. Johnson was requested to confirm these 'personal assurances' as 'remaining fully valid' (PREM 11 5199 (20 Dec. 1963)).

All this, of course, begged further questions. What was the status of 'personal assurances'? What if time pressures made meaningful consultation (even regarding operations from UK bases or territorial waters) impossible? What if, following consultation, Washington and London disagreed? These issues were raised also in the context of the (conventional) 1986 Libyan air raid, discussed in the previous chapter. Would the US *ever* use the bases without consent, either in respect of conventional or nuclear forces?

Answers to these questions lay ultimately in Washington's claim to supreme sovereignty over its forward defence. Robert McNamara, defence secretary to Presidents Kennedy and Johnson, stated in 1983: 'I doubt very much that there was any understanding that Britain had a veto' (Duncan Campbell, 1984, 310). Henry Kissinger wrote frankly about the events of 24/25 October 1973, when US forces worldwide were put on nuclear alert: 'to be frank, we could not have accepted a judgement different from our own' (Kissinger, 1982, 713).

London, of course, had some power in these matters. Non-cooperation by the British authorities, for example regarding the clearing of air space, would have complicated the situation for Washington. In October 1973, shortly before the nuclear alert, Prime Minister Edward Heath actually denied US planes the use of

RAF facilities on Cyprus during the Middle Eastern war. In the case of nuclear missiles, there was also the precedent set by the Thor missiles in 1958–63 of a 'dual key' operating system. (The integrity of even this system has been called into question, but it did at least set up the physical possibility of a British veto over use.) The 'dual key' precedent was mooted, but rejected, in the case of the cruise missiles deployed at Greenham Common in October 1983. The cost of the 'dual key' was estimated at one billion pounds. In February 1983, Prime Minister Thatcher told journalists: 'A joint decision on the use of the bases would of course be dual control. Got it?' Like an elephant wading through butter, President Reagan subsequently came to Thatcher's aid during a television interview: 'I don't think either one of us will do anything independent of the other ... er ... this constitutes a sort of veto doesn't it?' (Ovendale (ed.) 1994, 166).

Intelligence

As was evident during the Falklands conflict described in the following chapter, Cold War Anglo-American intelligence cooperation was extremely close. The 1947 UKUSA agreement formally tied together the signals intelligence (SIGINT) organizations of Britain, the US, Canada, Australia and New Zealand. The 1947 agreement assigned parts of the globe to different national SIGINT bodies. Britain's Government Communications Headquarters (GCHQ) in Cheltenham undertook responsibility for much of Eastern Europe, the USSR east of the Ural mountains, and for Africa. Signals and communications cooperation between GCHQ and America's National Security Agency (NSA) was an important feature of the Cold War. The NSA had a major presence at Cheltenham, operating in conditions of extreme secrecy. (The local newspaper in Cheltenham was for years prevented from publishing the names of the GCHQ football team in local match reports (Aldrich, 2002, 143)). There were also American SIGINT facilities at Menwith Hill in Yorkshire and at RAF Chicksands. In addition, the Central Intelligence Agency (CIA) maintained close links with its British counterparts and mounted operations from the American embassy in Grosvenor Square. Defence intelligence was coordinated via the British Defence Staff, numbering up to two hundred in Washington, and American equivalents in Whitehall. America's

National Reconnaissance Office, the communication satellite spying agency whose bureaucratic existence was only officially acknowledged in 1994, and Defense Intelligence Agency also had presences in the UK. Richard Aldrich (1998, 337) has argued that the fragmented specialization of intelligence structures strengthened Cold War Anglo-American cooperation, with compartmentalized coordination remaining untouched by either security failures or wider policy disagreements.

The closeness of US-British intelligence was demonstrated on many occasions during the Cold War. As Richelson and Ball (1990, 301) commented :

> The UKUSA security and intelligence community, with more than a quarter of a million full-time personnel and a total budget of 16–18 billion [US dollars], constitutes one of the largest bureaucracies in the world. As such, it not only wields enormous political power and influence, but also exhibits most of the typical attributes of large bureaucratic organizations, including a tendency to define and pursue bureaucratic political objectives which are not necessarily in complete concordance with the national interests of the five UKUSA countries themselves.

The 1968 State Department report, 'What Now for Britain?', commented: 'In the intelligence field, as in the field of nuclear weaponry, the UK gets more than it gives, but what it gives is not insubstantial'. The two intelligence services involved themselves in 'swapping of estimates' and 'the preparation of joint estimates'; on 'some areas and subjects, each nation is dependent for its intelligence mainly on the other' (Colman, 2003, 132). In July 1969, GCHQ Director Sir Leonard Hooper informed NSA Director 'Pat' Carter that 'I have often felt closer to you than to most of my own staff' (Richelson and Ball, 1990, 305). The NSA and GCHQ cooperated in lobbying their respective governments for resources. GCHQ worked with the NSA to intercept communications between US anti-war activists in the Vietnam War era. British intelligence encouraged CIA infiltration of British trades unions and supported a disguised CIA propaganda agency, Forum World Features, in London. When the Iranian revolution of 1979 deprived the US of facilities used to monitor Soviet arms deployments, Washington fell back on U-2 spy flights from Cyprus and Wethersfield in Essex (Duke, 1987, 169).

There were tensions in the intelligence partnership. US agencies typically made up about 90 per cent of the total UKUSA budget. On the British side, there was a desire to make the most of the special relations. The early Cold War history and reputation of British intelligence was naturally severely compromised by the 'Cambridge spies' and the experience of Soviet penetration. However, MI6 in particular developed an institutional memory which celebrated the professionalism and ability of British intelligence to contribute in a decisive manner to America's conduct of world affairs. The Penkovsky defection of 1960 was thus remembered in London as enabling President Kennedy to call the Soviet bluff during the 1962 Cuban missile crisis (Naughtie, 2004, 167). London continued to secure important defections, such as that of Oleg Lyalin, a leading agent connected to the planning of sabotage programmes, in 1970. Periodic British successes raised the UK intelligence profile in Washington and presumably eased transatlantic tension. British intelligence, however, also tended to feel, and to resent the fact, that the US was too powerful to be a genuine partner. One GCHQ officer interviewed by Mark Urban in the mid-1990s recalled: 'The requirements from our friends across the water often had to be met first under the special relationship. They were quite clearly the Big Brother.' Martin Morland, former chief of assessments on the Joint Intelligence Committee (the British coordinating body, whose weekly meetings were regularly attended by CIA representatives), described the situation in the Reagan-Thatcher era as follows:

> Everything is meant to be completely shared, but even then the Americans were gradually holding back a bit. It didn't happen on the central area of the Soviet Bloc, but more where they had particular interests, like Cuba, or where commercial matters were concerned. (M. Urban, 1996, 59–60)

On the American side, there were inevitably some concerns about the loyalty of the British intelligence services, and also an occasional feeling that Britain was a small country that was asking too much. William Odom (National Security Council staffer under Jimmy Carter and NSA director between 1985 and 1989) told Mark Urban: 'It's a very uneven relationship, to put it mildly ... the name of the British game is to show up with one card and expect to call the shots.' Stansfield Turner, CIA head in the late 1970s, simply refused to share sensitive satellite imagery with London (M. Urban, 1996, 28, 59–60). As already noted, however, US–UK intelligence linkages were strengthened in the wake of the 1979 Iranian revolution and were sometimes extraordinarily close in the campaigns which followed the Soviet invasion of Afghanistan (Grasselli, 1996). Generally US and British intelligence services complemented one another, with the US making use of British facilities in countries and areas (notably China, Hong Kong and Cyprus) where cover for American operations was difficult.

The post-Cold War era raised the possibility of special intelligence relations being severed. Unsurprisingly, the desire of UK intelligence to maintain its special links outweighed any resentful desire to be rid of its overbearing 'partner'. In the post-Cold War years, Washington continued to use GCHQ as a kind of 'default' facility for its own signals intelligence, and continued to support it financially. London has little desire to pool intelligence with its European allies. It gains prestige and policy salience from the US connection, even at the cost of risking involvement in expensive policy failures. The 9/11 attacks unquestionably reinforced special intelligence relations. Immediately after the terrorist assaults, a special aircraft ferried to Washington the top UK intelligence chiefs: Richard Dearlove of MI6, Eliza Manningham-Buller of MI5 and Francis Richards from GCHQ (Meyer, 2005, 188). A source interviewed by James Naughtie (2004, 166) described Central Intelligence Agency influence on the London intelligence agenda around the time of the 2003 Iraqi invasion: 'Every morning a huge pipe opens up in Whitehall and the stuff from the agency just pours out'.

The US–UK intelligence interlinkages in the run-up to the Iraq war were many and deep. The accusation that Saddam Hussein had attempted to obtain 'yellowcake' uranium oxide from Niger to help develop nuclear weapons first appeared openly in the British Iraq dossier of September 2002. It was soon taken up by Washington. Former US Ambassador Joseph Wilson was sent to investigate, thus setting in train a course of events that would culminate (following Wilson's finding that there was no basis in the claim) in the 'outing' of Wilson's wife, Valerie Plame, as a CIA operative, and subsequently in a major scandal that would dog Bush's second term. From the point of view of US–UK intelligence operations, the Wilson/Plame affair was significant in at least two ways. The limits to transatlantic partnership were indicated by Washington's apparent inability to see the need to share Wilson's findings in Niger with London (Sharp, 2004, 67). The affair also pointed up the tension between the CIA on the one hand, and the Pentagon and White House (especially Vice President Cheney's office) on the other. British intelligence found itself stranded amid American bureaucratic rivalries, with the (highly politicized) Office of Special Plans in the Pentagon regularly outflanking the CIA. The notorious claim that Saddam could prepare and use WMD in 45 minutes emanated from an exile group – Iyad Allawi's Iraqi National Accord – which both the CIA and MI6 considered superior to the Pentagon's favourite, Ahmed Chalabi's Iraqi National Congress, On the US side, elementary intelligence blunders were made: the over-eager acceptance of evidence concerning weapons of mass destruction from competing groups of exiles and from unreliable sources – notably the source codenamed 'Curveball' – in Iraq itself. Despite the best efforts of professional British intelligence, the contagion, exacerbated by CIA-Pentagon antagonisms, spread across the Atlantic. The situation was worsened by Blair's own personal and apparently increasingly unshakeable conviction that Saddam did have WMD. Far from using its intelligence professionalism to correct American errors, London's politicized handling of complex and ambiguous Iraqi intelligence replicated and reinforced them.

Polaris to Trident: Technology and the Development of the Cold War Nuclear Alliance

Skybolt and Polaris

Despite the post-Suez healing process, important tensions remained at the beginning of the 1960s. Washington fretted about British economic weaknesses preventing London from sustaining commitments, particularly East of Suez. The 1957 Sandys White Paper was indeed a sign of things to come. The status and feasibility of Britain's own deterrent were being called into question. The cost and spread of technical developments made these problems more acute. The British long-range Blue Streak missile programme was actually recognized in 1960 to be outdated even before it was deployed.

At this stage, London came to see the benefits of acquiring the US Skybolt missile, which could also be used in conjunction with

Britain's ageing V-bomber fleet. Capable of being launched hundreds of miles from target, Skybolt was seen as protecting the bombers from ground-to-air defences. Skybolt was also seen in London as compatible with the objective of maintaining a credible independent deterrent. Yet when Macmillan (at Camp David in March 1960) acquired a commitment on Skybolt from Eisenhower, the missile had not been fully developed, or even purchased by the Pentagon! Macmillan was informally assured that, in the event of Skybolt proving unsatisfactory, (submarine-based) Polaris missiles would be made available. The problem was that, in 1960, the Royal Navy had neither the will nor the facilities to deploy Polaris. Washington was also reluctant to allow London access to Polaris in the context of an independent, British – rather than a multilateral NATO – nuclear force. Macmillan staked all on Skybolt, and rapidly achieved cancellation of Blue Streak. The Holy Loch facilities on Scotland's West coast were opened up to American Polaris submarines – in Macmillan's words (following a visit to Washington in May 1960 by Defence Minister Harold Watkinson) – 'more or less in return for Skybolt' (Macmillan 1973, 254). Macmillan assured the House of Commons in November 1960 that 'no decision to use these missiles will ever be taken without the fullest possible previous consultation' (*Parliamentary Debates*, 5th series, vol. 629, 38).

By the end of 1962, Washington, now represented in these matters by President Kennedy's Defense Secretary Robert McNamara, had concluded that Skybolt development was too expensive and uncertain, and that the US should concentrate on Polaris and Minuteman. McNamara later described Skybolt as 'an absolute pile of junk' (Hennessy and Anstey, eds, 1990, 11.) The decision to cancel Skybolt was not only communicated to London in an insensitive fashion, but appeared to affirm what many observers took as the lesson of the 1962 Cuban missile crisis: that Washington was uninterested in substantive consultation. McNamara met British Defence Minister Peter Thorneycroft in what George Ball, adviser to JFK, called a 'foregone disaster'. The US was variously accused of wishing 'to put Britain out of the nuclear club' and 'threatening cancellation to force the British to fulfil their troop quota in Western Europe'. The Nassau summit (in the Bahamas, December 1962) was, according to Ball, 'one of the worst prepared ... in modern times' (Ball, 1982, 264–5). 'Never before,' comments historian Kenneth Morgan, 'had Britain's subservience been so explicit'

(Morgan, 1990, 216). Paradoxically, Macmillan's case rested on the assertion (used later, also with some success, by Harold Wilson in his Vietnam War dealings with President Johnson) that Britain was more use to Washington as an ally than as a satellite. Loss of Britain's status as a credible, independent ally could not benefit the US. In raising the stakes at Nassau, to the status of a fundamental debate about Britain's 'great power' and 'nuclear club' status, Macmillan was, in effect, calling the bluff of those Kennedy advisers who wished to terminate the nuclear special relationship. In a sense, Macmillan was deliberately exacerbating, even distorting, the crisis. Air Chief Marshal Sir George Mills always insisted that the Americans had given consistent warning that Skybolt might be abandoned (Baylis, 1984, 101.) Macmillan wanted Polaris, which the Royal Navy was now ready to receive. Still committed to an 'independent' British deterrent, Macmillan was following a very high-risk strategy. As Solly Zuckerman, government scientific adviser, later noted Macmillan 'had no technical fall-back position when we went to Nassau. Having abandoned Blue Streak, itself based on an American model, we were unlikely to embark on another "stationary" ballistic missile' (Zuckerman, 1988, 265). If Britain seriously wanted to go it alone, it would have had to rely on V-bombers and free-falling bombs. Yet in public Macmillan assured everyone that a deal could be made 'with our transatlantic chums' (Evans, 1981, 234).

Macmillan's chums were reluctant to cut a bilateral deal with London that might upset Paris and provoke a French veto of British membership of the European Community. Despite this, Britain emerged with, as John Dickie (1994, 124) later put it, 'almost the bargain of the century': Britain would be allowed to purchase Polaris on very favourable terms, with only a rather ambiguous indication that this new British nuclear capability was to be set in a multilateral context. Kennedy did manage to extract from Macmillan a promise to discuss the American project for a NATO multilateral nuclear force (MLF). However, in his annual review of Anglo-American relations for 1962, David Ormsby-Gore (British ambassador to Washington) concluded that 'the outcome of the Nassau meeting was a compromise which no other ally could have achieved' (FO 371 16405, 1 January 1963).

George Ball, who counselled against the deal, recalled that JFK wished to strengthen Macmillan's domestic electoral hand. He feared an incoming Labour government might come out squarely against British entry into Europe. France, led by General de Gaulle, would certainly object to the Polaris deal. But, so Kennedy reasoned, de Gaulle might well veto Britain's entry application in any case. 'Moreover, our nuclear arrangements were unquestionably reciprocal; Britain had agreed to make Holy Loch available for our Polaris submarines and had let us establish our missile warning station at Fylingdale' (Ball, 1982, 267). Kennedy attempted to strengthen the deal's multilateral dimension by extending the offer to Paris. He was swiftly rebuffed by de Gaulle, who saw the offer as an attempt to impose US domination. For the time being, British pretensions to independent nuclear status were to be indulged by Washington. London was also able, primarily through Macmillan's urging of the issue onto Kennedy's agenda, to raise its international nuclear policy profile in connection with the 1963 Partial Nuclear Test Ban treaty negotiation.

The Skybolt/Polaris episode provoked a high level debate about the status of Anglo-American relations. To Richard Neustadt, adviser to the Kennedy and Johnson administrations on alliance issues, the psychology of 1962 was a virtual replay of Suez. Images of mutual friendship were rapidly, and unrealistically, replaced by conceptions 'of the other side as possibly or surely false to the friendship' (Neustadt, 1970, 136). Alec Douglas-Home, foreign secretary to Macmillan, recorded that the events of 1962–3 revealed JFK's knowledge 'that a country with a record such as we had, could not … hand over our defence to another power, however friendly' (Thorpe, 1996, 251).

The Multilateral Nuclear Force

The Polaris deal, despite the promise made by Macmillan at Nassau. represented meagre progress for pre-existing plans for a multilateral nuclear force in Europe. John Kennedy, never himself an unequivocal MLF advocate, announced in Canada, in May 1961, his support for a European nuclear force ultimately under American control. Behind the MLF proposals were calculations of economic and strategic rationality, emphasized by McNamara, and a desire to contain Germany's nuclear ambitions. During the early 1960s, a strong pro-MLF bureaucratic coalition emerged in Washington. On the British side, a split developed between the Foreign Office and the Ministry of Defence. With military opinion generally hostile to the MLF, diplomatic opinion came to see the virtues of a modified MLF. Thorneycroft presented a series of proposals in December 1963, designed to mitigate the degree of integration envisaged by MLF enthusiasts in Washington. Britain was also concerned that Polaris should remain outside the new arrangements, that new weapons costs be kept down, and that any prospect of US control being relinquished to multilateral leadership be abandoned. As Paul Y. Hammond (1992, 119) has put it: 'For peculiar domestic political reasons – they trust Europeans less than Americans – the British wanted a guarantee that the US veto would never be given up.' British concern to retain US control over use of nuclear weapons in this MLF context allied London with congressional guardians of American control in the Joint Committee on Atomic Energy (Middeke, 2000; Middeke, 2001).

Following John Kennedy's death in November 1963, the Johnson administration in Washington revived pressure for the MLF, developing a plan for a Polaris-armed surface fleet, manned by mixed-nationality crews. Central to the American strategy was Defense Secretary McNamara's hostility to the independent European deterrents. President Johnson's briefing book for a visit to Washington by Wilson at the end of 1965 noted: 'The essence of our position is to encourage the British in any action which "lowers the status" of their "independent" deterrent' (NSF: CF: UK, box 5, vol. 17 (16 December 1965)).

In his dealings with Johnson, Wilson insisted that the central problem with the MLF was not the compromising of British independence, but the issue of German participation. He told LBJ that the Soviets would never believe that German nuclear ambitions could be contained within the MLF (Wilson, 1971, 49). Wilson's counter to the MLF was the Atlantic Nuclear Force (ANF): a proposal under which British and US nuclear submarines would be loosely linked into NATO. Wilson's and Healey's hostility to the MLF was palpable. Defence Secretary Denis Healey later called it a 'military monstrosity' and blamed Macmillan for even accepting a degree of commitment to it at Nassau (Healey, 1989, 304). Naval and air lobbies in Britain also resented the MLF, seeing it as destructive of their special relations with the American military. Under the ANF proposal, British strategic nuclear weapons would be committed to the new force. Britain, the US and France (if France wished to join) would exercise a veto over use of any part of the force.

In effect, the ANF proposal, which President Johnson accepted in late 1964, scuppered the MLF. Franz-Josef Strauss of the West German Christian Democratic Union famously described the ANF as 'the only fleet that had not been created that torpedoed another fleet that hadn't sailed' (Ziegler, 1993, 209). By the end of 1964, some of LBJ's close advisers were coming to the view that the MLF train was running out of steam and of prospective passengers. McGeorge Bundy felt the 'costs of success would be prohibitive'. These costs included 'A deeply reluctant and unpersuaded Great Britain', as well as a 'protracted and difficult congressional struggle in which we would be largely deprived of the one decisive argument – that this arrangement is what our major European partners really want' (Memo, Bundy to Rusk, McNamara and Ball, 25 November 1964, 'McGeorge Bundy, 10/1 – 12/31/64' folder, box 2, memos to the President). Following Wilson's December 1964 visit to Washington, the status of both the MLF and ANF became one of bureaucratic purgatory. The understandings reached at the meeting, like Macmillan's original acceptance of multilateralism at Nassau, were open to various interpretations. According to Denis Healey, 'Within a year the ANF had also sunk without trace, because nobody wanted it' (Healey, 1989, 305).

Wilson and Healey certainly viewed the ANF as a way to destroy the MLF, and their success spoke well of British ability to work the circuits of Washington's top defence bureaucracy. Yet, at one level, the ANF had to be a serious proposal in its own right. As a British proposal and as a force with a large British input, the ANF would have been a most promising arena for exercising British influence. It exemplified the point made by Patrick Gordon Walker (foreign secretary from 1964 to 1965) in his private 'thoughts on foreign policy' of August 1964: 'If we are dependent upon the US for ultimate nuclear protection, we must so arrange our relations with the US that our share in the pattern of US alliance is as indispensable as we can make it.' Gordon Walker expressed here a major British fear of the post-1960 era: that West Germany might come to replace the UK as America's foremost ally. The fear was exacerbated by evidence of German economic success, and by changing troop configurations in NATO. The foreign secretary noted: 'We must at all costs avoid a US alliance with Germany over our heads' (Pearce, ed., 1991, 299).

Wilson was able to present the ANF as a redemption of his promise to renegotiate the Nassau agreement, while retaining Polaris. The ANF was also far less expensive for London than the MLF. Evidence of continuing British interest in the ANF comes from a memorandum submitted to the Cabinet in March 1965 by Michael Stewart (foreign secretary from 1965 to 1966 and from 1968 to 1970). Stewart emphasized that 'the mixed-manned element of the ANF should consist of existing or already planned weapons systems'. Britain's 'first choice' would be existing Minuteman missiles on United States soil (CAB 129/130 C(65) 48)!

Nuclear Issues, 1964–79

We saw in Chapter 4 how, during the Wilson years of the 1960s, economic troubles came to dominate British defence policy. The US might oppose the 'great power' symbol of the independent deterrent, but it fervently favoured another: British military presence East of Suez. Britain's post-1967 Far East military evacuation created strains which reverberated throughout the defence relationship.

Wilson's own attitude to the independent deterrent was equivocal. The Polaris deal had been criticized by Labour in opposition as increasing Britain's dependence on the US. While in opposition, Wilson had told McNamara that the independent deterrent was 'highly electoral' and 'had an emotional appeal to the man in the pub' (Ziegler, 1993, 208). Labour's 1964 election manifesto had promised 'renegotiation' of the Nassau agreement. There was little, if any, American pressure to keep Polaris. McNamara indicated there would be no 'ill-feeling' if the deal were cancelled, though he also reported 'mixed feelings' in Washington about the UK dropping out of 'the future deterrence business' (Priest, 2005, 362). In the event, Wilson, apparently convinced of Polaris's value for money, advanced the view that the Polaris programme was (in Wilson's words) 'well past the point of no return', despite Healey's advice to the effect that cancellation was still feasible (Healey, 1989, 302). In the first days of the new government, the Cabinet Defence Committee also decided that there was to be no 'suggestion of a go-it-alone British nuclear war' (H. Wilson, 1971, 40).

Wilson acknowledged the dependent status of the Polaris technology, at least partly as a response to leftist critics of the 'independent' deterrent. He consistently set Britain's bomb within a NATO alliance context, and avoided difficult questions about the strategic rationale. In 1966, he declared: 'For the first time the British Government has had the guts to admit that independence in the ability to wage war as a separate national undertaking is a thing of the past' (*The Times*, 16 June 1966; Freedman, 1980, 30). Yet to Washington, still pushing for the MLF, Wilson was determined to cling on to nuclear guarantors of 'great power' status. Johnson was advised by aides in July 1966: 'The nuclear deterrent is the most important of the great power symbols still in British possession. Although Wilson is committed to give it up, he has so far shown no disposition to do so' (Ziegler, 1993, 210).

US–UK defence tensions were eased to some degree in these years by the good personal relations between Healey and his American counterpart, Robert McNamara. Richard Crossman (1976, 647) viewed Healey as playing the 'role of the young McNamara'. Others saw Healey's management techniques as 'an undesirable something we caught from the United States' ('Witness Seminar' 1993, 626 (Sir F. Cooper)). Healey was even able to exploit McNamara's December 1967 resignation, primarily over Vietnam War issues, to consolidate his own eminence in NATO's Nuclear Planning Group. The adoption of 'flexible response' by NATO in 1967 represented a success for London's policy of compromise within the Nuclear Planning Group. McNamara had argued that a conventional Soviet attack in Europe should always be met conventionally; Bonn held to former notions of nuclear 'massive retaliation'. The 1967 compromise allowed for possible early allied use of tactical nuclear weapons. The same year saw further important adjustments within NATO, with London again offering constructive compromise over 'offset' payments (for troops stationed in Germany) and generally over achieving a doctrinal balance between security and new negotiating postures. In February 1967, ironically as the first elements of Britain's Polaris fleet were awaiting actual deployment, LBJ broached the possibility of strategic arms negotiations with Moscow.

Britain's entry into the European Economic Community raised again the issue of possible future European defence integration. However, as noted in Chapter 4, the years of the Heath government (1970–74) witnessed no significant moves in that direction. Heath sounded out Richard Nixon in 1970 on the subject of an Anglo-French nuclear deterrent. The American president promised London 'a great deal of running room on this', although Henry Kissinger indicated 'the risks which the President would be taking with American public opinion if he appeared to be lending his authority to any project of this kind' (Heath, 1998, 488). Anglo-French nuclear pooling would have run foul of the 1958 agreement with the US, and was opposed by the British Ministry of Defence (Carrington, 1988, 221). France showed little inclination to abandon its nuclear independence, the *force de frappe*.

The main nuclear policy issue for Britain in the 1970s related, not to integrated European defence, but to Polaris modernization and replacement. The first operational, Polaris-equipped submarine was not launched until 1968, by which time the US was moving to the Poseidon system. Edward Heath had been ambivalent over the original Polaris deal, fearing for the effects on Anglo-French relations. He had accepted, however, that it was a unique 'opportunity to replace our aging deterrent with a proven successor, for which the Americans had borne all the costs of research and development' (Heath, 1998, 227). Again, in the early 1970s, there seemed no practical alternative but to look to the United States.

Improvement, and possible eventual replacement of Polaris, had been considered by Wilson's 1964–70 government. Research co-operation began with the Americans on what was, in effect, a Polaris upgrade: Project Chevaline. British interest in Project Chevaline derived from a 1969 study undertaken into nuclear upgrading by (then) Navy Secretary David Owen (Lane, 2004, 160). This refinement of Polaris was designed to circumvent and deceive new Russian anti-ballistic missile deployments. Heath and Defence Secretary Lord Carrington considered buying a fifth Polaris submarine and also reviewed the option of purchasing the US Poseidon submarine nuclear system. They decided that Chevaline could best cope with the anticipated future problems of Polaris. In 1972, Heath's government approved the production of the Chevaline warhead. (The Chevaline system involved a manoeuvrable space vehicle aimed at a single target; it was not a fully fledged Multiple Independently-Targetable Re-entry Vehicle System (MITRVS) aimed at different targets.) That the Chevaline decision took place in the year when the US and USSR signed the Anti-Ballistic Missile Treaty was ironic. The ABM treaty appeared to remove the improved Russian anti-missile defences which Chevaline was designed to evade. Though there clearly was little coordination between London and Washington over the ABM-Chevaline link, Heath's 1972 decision did seem to answer the immediate need to do something about Polaris replacement.

Heath and Carrington expected Chevaline to be deployed in 1981. It was not, in fact, until 1981 that the House of Commons was even informed of the existence of the project. By then costs had exceeded one billion pounds. Wilson's post-1974 government concealed the escalating costs by concealing them in the defence maintenance budget (Dockrill, 1988, 107; Baylis and Stoddart, 2003).

The Labour governments of the 1970s sought a broker role between Europe and the US over nuclear détente with the Soviet Union. James Callaghan, as noted in Chapter 4, extracted an important undertaking from the US that any deal forthcoming from the strategic arms control talks with the USSR (SALT II) would not include a prohibition on future nuclear transfers to the UK. NATO's 'twin track' decision of 1979, to press ahead with (intermediate range) cruise and Pershing II missile programmes, while keeping the door open to arms control negotiations, also suited Callaghan's agenda. It provided scope for his role as Atlantic intermediary, while reaffirming the US commitment to Europe in the wake of the 'neutron bomb' cancellation. In the early part of 1979, the British Cabinet decided to follow a course designed to boost the Atlantic intermediary role. Polaris would be included in any forthcoming SALT III negotiations, 'preferably representing all the European members of NATO' (Healey, 1989, 455). At the Guadeloupe summit (January, 1979) Callaghan achieved both American confirmation of the 'twin track' approach and an understanding on what was to be the eventual replacement for Polaris: the Trident system.

Nuclear policy in the Callaghan years was the preserve of an elite Cabinet group: Defence Secretary Fred Mulley, Chancellor Healey, Foreign Secretary Owen and the prime minister. The deputy prime minister, Michael Foot, refused to compromise his disarmament beliefs and declined to be involved. In Owen's words, 'all nuclear matters' were 'slipped through the Labour Party, avoiding discussion'. The huge cost increases in the Chevaline system strengthened the case for an alternative. Owen argued that 'we were playing out of our league and that we need to look at a cut-price deterrent' (Owen, 1992, 380–81). In public, Labour defence spokesmen denied that any decision on Polaris replacement was imminent. To Callaghan's Nuclear Defence Policy group, it seemed politically impossible to acknowledge that Trident, an American system costing perhaps around ten billion dollars, was being seriously considered contrary to manifesto commitments.

Trident

Shortly before Callaghan left for Guadeloupe in 1979, to meet the leaders of France, West Germany and the US, he was presented with a scientific report from the Defence Ministry recommending Trident. The Duff-Mason report argued that Trident was technically superior to all alternatives, that adoption of a US system would minimize technical risks, and that the allies would accept conventional British force reductions if Trident were deployed. David Owen (1992, 382) argued that Britain was in danger of playing 'out of our league'. However, President Carter was compliant about Trident at Guadeloupe, seeing no problem with the technology transfer and offering talks to work out costs. Memories of Jack and Mac in 1962 were stirred. As well as his good personal relationship with Carter, Callaghan was able to exploit the growing anti-Sovietism in Washington, associated with the bureaucratic rise of National Security Adviser Zbigniew Brzezinski. The UK leader's return to a Britain suffering public sector strikes ironically set the stage for his disastrous 1979 general election campaign. When Callaghan departed Downing Street in May 1979, he left Carter's written undertaking on Trident for Margaret Thatcher (Callaghan, 1981, 557).

Trident negotiations in the pre-1981 period were complicated by the US Senate debate over ratification of the SALT II treaty, and by the Carter administration's reaction to the Soviet invasion of Afghanistan. The British decision for Trident was made in December 1979, with Thatcher negotiating terms with US Defense Secretary Harold Brown in June 1980. As ever in the history of US–UK nuclear relations, negotiations were conducted in secret without any broad consultation with the British Cabinet. John Nott later recalled on one Thursday morning at the regular meeting of the full Cabinet' (when Nott was Trade Secretary, before his move to Defence) that 'a decision had been taken in conjunction with the Americans to modernise the deterrent with the introduction of Trident' (Nott, 2002a, 216). The terms were broadly similar to the Polaris deal, though with a British undertaking to accept the funding of Rapier Air Defence Systems at US bases in the UK, and extension of American presence on the island of Diego Garcia (Boren, 1994; Thatcher, 1993, 246).

The Reagan administration's decision to upgrade the original Trident system (the C4 system, with separately targeted multiple nuclear warheads) caused the June 1980 deal to unravel. Reagan's decision, and the anticipated cost of the new, D5, system stimulated a major Cabinet debate about the price and rationale of Britain's deterrent. Yet Margaret Thatcher (1993, 247) remained 'utterly determined' to replace Polaris and to do so in the context of the nuclear special relationship. Exploiting Reagan's good opinion of her, the prime minister negotiated a deal for the D5 on more generous terms than the C4. Research and development costs in excess of 116 million dollars were effectively waived. It was, according to Defence Secretary John Nott, 'a bargain', though he could not offer anything approaching an accurate figure on costs (P. Sharp, 1999, 128). Privately, Nott was concerned by reports that Polaris needed an upgrade costing around 300 million pounds 'if it was to remain credible to the Soviets'. He recalled: 'by reshuffling cash flow we were able to fit Trident 11 into the programme and also upgrade Polaris' (Nott, 2002a, 219).

Critics of the D5 system suggested that it involved excessive and unnecessary destructive capacity. The original Trident D5 delivery system could carry 14 warheads, compared to three on Polaris and eight on the C4. Larger submarines would also be needed. As eventually deployed, the Trident fleet consisted of four submarines carrying as many as 48 nuclear warheads. Certainly, the 1982 deal did revive the transatlantic nuclear relationship, and was correctly again compared to Polaris in 1962. The US kept its undertaking not to include Trident in any bilateral arms deal made with Moscow. Yet the case against Trident was not simply that it involved expensive overkill. There were all the old questions of sovereignty and independence. Denis Healey raised these in blunt form in 1987: 'If we continue with the Trident programme, we risk crippling our expenditure on conventional forces for no real military advantage and with some serious political disadvantage, which can be summed up as a period of prolonged and humilating dependence on the United States (Ovendale (ed.) 1994, 182–3).

As plans for the Trident system evolved in later Cold War and immediate post-Cold war years, it appeared that the Trident fleet would operate at roughly half its potential warhead capacity.

The UK Tridents are deployed in four Vanguard submarines; in 1999 it was announced that each of these submarines would carry up to 48 warheads. There have been occasional attempts to present Trident as the flagship for a newly integrated European nuclear defence. Labour's manifesto for the 1987 general election, the last British general election held under Cold War conditions, actually declared it 'time to end the nuclear pretence' (Labour Party, 1987, 15). By the time the Blair government was elected 10 years later, the 'nuclear pretence' was accepted by the Labour leadership, despite the drastically changed international conditions. The pretence of nuclear independence was underlined, however, by reported Royal Navy estimates to the effect that the Trident fleet could only operate for around 18 months following any withdrawal of US technical support. Following Trident deployment, the US was (and is) kept continually informed about the fleet's whereabouts; missile firing without data supplied from US sources would be extremely difficult, if not practically impossible (Plesch, 2005).

Defence Relations Beyond the Cold War

As has already been noted at several points, US–UK defence and intelligence collaboration survived the disappearance of the integrating Soviet threat and was conspicuously revived and resuscitated following the 9/11 terror attacks. The Congressional Research Service conveniently summarised the defence interlinkages in 2005. By 2005, the United Kingdom still hosted about 11,000 American military personnel, together with around one hundred civilians. Though not at Cold War levels, this US presence in the UK involved substantial indirect financial support, primarily in the form of waived taxes and free accommodation. The UK continued, from the 1980s into the new century, to support and participate in the US Ballistic Missile Defence programme. Mutual US–UK governmental defence sales for fiscal year 2004 totalled 479 million dollars. The figure for US–UK commercial sales, via defence contractors, was considerably higher. The CRS study estimated it at averaging two billion dollars annually (US to UK) and one billion (UK to US). Major joint defence projects in 2005–6 included the Joint Strike Fighter and British technical involvement in the Patriot Advanced Capability missile and Predator unmanned aerial vehicle.

The US Department of Defense during 2005 became UK defence contractor, BAE Systems' biggest customer, replacing the UK ministry of defence. In the US itself, BAE Systems actually employed in 2005 some 45,000 people (Archik, 2005, 19–20).

The post-Cold War defence relationship, unsurprisingly, was and is not without its difficulties. The tensions associated with the post-9/11 Washington foreign policy need no further emphasis. Another layer of tension derives from the Blair government's orientation to defence integration in Europe, and will be discussed in a later chapter. Following the 2003 invasion of Iraq, much comment also attached to the difference between US and British war-fighting culture: the former oriented more towards aggressive 'force protection' and big operations, the latter towards low-intensity, low-aggression peace support. There also remained the formidable problem of negative interopability: the mismatch between relatively high and relatively low levels of military technological sophistication, seen, for example, in the areas of airborne-targeting systems and general electronic reconnaissance and surveillance.

Another major source of tension, identified in the 2005 CRS study, relates to US market and technology access. From Britain's perspective, both the administration and the US Congress became excessively sensitive about defence technology transfer following 9/11, especially in regard to International Traffic in Arms Regulations (ITAR). Possible re-export from the UK of defence technology to China (in possible contravention of the arms embargo imposed following the Tiananmen Square repression in 1989) has been a major American worry. British defence firms continued to press for ITAR waivers, citing intimate British support for US defence objectives and for the War on Terror. It should also be emphasized that these market and technology access disputes did not prevent the BAE Systems growth in America, nor its acquisition of the US defence firm, United Defense Industries, in 2005 (Archik, 2005, 20).

The post-Cold War US–UK nuclear relationship centred on the issue of Trident renewal. During the Major government years, there were attempts to develop sub-strategic roles for Trident. The ending of the Cold War also led to substantial reductions in UK tactical nuclear weapons holdings. The Trident system inherited by the Blair government in 1997, however, was still one with a strategic role (whatever the change in international conditions since the 1980s), a continuing dependency on US technology, and a limited shelf life.

(The current system is probably due for replacement some time between 2020 and 2025). Part of the nuclear problem facing the Labour government on its election in 1997 derived from the gap between the slow pace of nuclear system deployment and the fast pace of defence technology research. Trident renewal became an issue for the Blair government even before Trident actually became fully operational. Clearly, both Trident and the Trident renewal debate do operate in a defence context that is much more Europeanized than that envisaged by Margaret Thatcher and John Nott in 1982. Yet US domination of defence technology research and production is as strong, or stronger, than ever. It is difficult to image how Trident renewal can escape the contradiction identified by Denis Healey in 1987: 'We need Trident only if we cannot rely on the United States in a crisis, but if we cannot rely on the United States in a crisis, can we rely on the United States to provide us with Trident?' (Ovendale (ed.) 1994, 182).

From one perspective, the Trident deal was a good one for Britain. However, Washington's switch to the D5 system rather cruelly exposed the one-way dependency at the crux of the nuclear 'special relationship'. As a result of the move to D5 technology, Britain acquired a system which was both more expensive than intended and really beyond UK needs. From a post-Cold War perspective, the debate over Trident renewal reignited these concerns. The Ministry of Defence quickly set itself against the view that 9/11 somehow made Trident replacement irrelevant. Defence Secretary John Reid attacked the view in September 2005 that 'just because a new threat of international terrorism has arisen the old threats will necessarily go' (Wintour and Kettle, 2005). One major concern, of course, remains that of money. There are various possibilities for Trident renewal, including multi-role submarines (able to fire nuclear and non-nuclear missiles) and adaptation of the Royal Navy's Astute subs. Any replacement, however, seems almost certainly to be both very expensive – twenty billion dollars is a common guess – and once again part of a deal involving dependence on American technology. Shortly before his death in 2005, former Foreign Secretary Robin Cook wrote that Trident replacement, or even upgrade, would be 'against Britain's national interests' and 'against our international obligations' (*The Independent*, 27 November 2005). To other critics of US foreign policy (Plesch, 2004), the oncoming obsolescence of Trident seemed a fine opportunity to uncouple Britain from the whole post-1962 tradition of nuclear dependency on the United States.

8

War: Vietnam, the Falklands and Iraq

The 'special relationship', according to Alex Danchev (1998, 160), has 'waxed fat on war'. This generalization applies most certainly to World War Two, during which the 'special relationship' was actually invented. It applies also to the Cold War, when the US–UK relationship was framed and defined so much in terms of security cooperation against a clear and common enemy. At least in one possible line of argument, the most controversial of all allied military cooperative efforts – the 2003 invasion of, and subsequent conflict in, Iraq – revived a flagging relationship.

Some words of caution about wartime cooperation do, however, need to be entered. The notion of the 'special relationship' evokes images of the UK and the US – 'our foremost ally', in John Major's account of the Gulf War (Major, 1999, 226) – standing shoulder to shoulder when the chips are down. Military and intelligence cooperation, combined with sentimental and ideological attachment, would seem to point in that same direction. However, what stands out from the material presented in this chapter is that, actually, neither side could automatically count on the support of its putatively close ally. British involvement in the 2003 Iraq invasion was not 'inevitable', but was largely a product of Tony Blair's personal commitment to, at least a version of, the Washington policy towards Iraq.

The Vietnam War was the severest military trial for the US during the era of the Cold War. Its domestic and international repercussions were intensely damaging to American power, confidence and purpose. The US fought in Vietnam alongside soldiers from South Vietnam, South Korea, the Philippines, Australia, New Zealand and Thailand. Britain refused to commit troops, on occasion even condemned American tactics, and continued a controversial (if small) commercial relationship with North Vietnam. London's cool and complex response to American involvement in Vietnam pushed the 'special relationship' to its limits.

The importance of the Vietnam War to the US was matched by the importance of the Falklands conflict to Britain. During the 1982 conflict, the tables were turned. Britain, not the US, needed help: diplomatic, informational and logistical, rather than psychological and symbolic, as had largely been the case with the US in Vietnam. Again, it was clear that the 'foremost ally' would not necessarily and automatically come to Britain's aid. Eventually, of course, the US chose not to exact 'revenge' for London's failure to commit troops to Vietnam.

Examination of the Vietnam and Falklands conflicts presents as much evidence of tensions in the Cold War relationship as of the sturdiness of a 'special relationship' forged in, and thriving on, war. The explanation lies in the detailed circumstances of the two wars. Both conflicts, of course, were conventional rather than nuclear confrontations. Issues of nuclear cooperation did not arise. The two wars revealed a considerable gap between policy preferences in the two capitals. To many in Britain, the Vietnam War represented an insensitive and unnecessary application of anti-communist global containment theory. To many in America, the Falklands War represented an insensitive and unnecessary expression of Britain's imperial past.

It is rather ironic that of these first three major conflicts of the post-1960 era, the one that proved least difficult for the 'special relationship' was the Gulf War of 1991. The 1991 war against Iraq took place in post-Cold War geopolitical conditions. London certainly saw the Gulf crisis and war as a test of the 'special relationship' under these new conditions. At least at first sight, the close US–UK cooperation of 1990–91 appeared to confound those who proclaimed that the 'special relationship' would end with the termination of the Cold War. The 2003 Iraq conflict again severely tried the view that the old military alliance would not survive either the removal of the Soviet threat or the intensification of European defence and foreign policy integration.

Vietnam

By 1960, a considerable degree of mutual Anglo-American mistrust and irritation had accumulated in relation to the future of Indochina.

By the early 1950s, the US was already funding a major part of the French military effort against the communist/nationalist forces of the Vietminh in Vietnam. The imminent collapse of the French at Dien Bien Phu in April-May 1954 ignited a major debate in Washington about how to respond to the threat of communism in South East Asia. President Eisenhower and Secretary of State John Foster Dulles, under congressional pressure, requested British backing for and assistance in American intervention. Prime Minister Winston Churchill and Foreign Secretary Anthony Eden felt (according to the latter) that US involvement 'might well bring the world to the verge of a major war' (Eden, 1960, 105). It has been suggested that Eisenhower's request was more than a little disingenuous (Billings-Yun, 1977, 377). However, Eden's rebuttal certainly infuriated Dulles. London did, however, consent to joining the new security organization, the South East Asia Security Organization (SEATO) set up by Washington (Boyle, 2005, 50). To the British, the Americans seemed to be fighting a lost cause in Vietnam, as well as threatening to unite the forces of nationalism in the Third World. Eden, in particular, was annoyed by American insouciance about India's interest in the future of Indochina (Warner, 1988).

The Macmillan era saw considerable British involvement with the Kennedy policy in Vietnam. The British Advisory Mission Vietnam (BRIAM), headed by Robert Thompson, generally encouraged the JFK administration's commitment to the government of Ngo Dinh Diem in South Vietnam (Busch, 2003). The Foreign Office in London presented a variety of concerns: notably, hopes for US aid to counter Indonesian president Sukarno's 'crush Malaysia' policy, and worries about the consequences of possible US military intervention in Laos. Wedged between North Vietnam and the People's Republic of China, Laos had come to be regarded by the Eisenhower administration as the pivotal point of the region's future. Macmillan himself wrote in December 1960: 'If Laos goes, what chance is there for South East Asia ...?' (Horne, 1989, 291). British caution over Laos played some part in JFK's decision to avoid confrontation and promote 'neutralization' in Laos. This decision in turn opened the way for communist exploitation of the Ho Chi Minh trail, the supply line through Laos and Cambodia which underpinned the anti-American effort during the Vietnam War. In September 1961, Macmillan complained to the Queen that Britain faced the risk of 'being asked' by the Americans to intervene in Indochina, even as the Berlin situation worsened in Europe (Horne, 1989, 418). As late as April 1963, Foreign Secretary Alec Douglas-Home was telling the British Cabinet that, if northern Laos fell 'under Sino-Soviet influence', the US 'might feel obliged to intervene in the south and to take additional measures to support Thailand' (CAB 12837, 26th Conclusion, 25 April 1963).

The majority of historiographical and journalistic interest in the subject of Britain and the Vietnam War has focused on Harold Wilson's 1964–70 governments. Less obviously Atlanticist than Hugh Gaitskell, his predecessor as Labour leader, Wilson was forced to play a complex and difficult hand with regard to Vietnam. He managed to avoid open commitment of British troops to Vietnam, despite intense pressure from the Johnson administration, especially in the period 1965–6. Debate about Wilson's policy on Vietnam centres around three overlapping areas: the extent to which Britain *did* aid the US in Vietnam in the 1960s; the mediation initiatives and the various ways in which Wilson was able to avoid committing troops; and the putative existence of a 'deal', whereby Britain would extend limited support for US action in Vietnam in return for US loans to rescue the sinking pound.

Wilson, along with his foreign secretaries (Patrick Gordon Walker, Michael Stewart and George Brown), was generally willing to express generalized verbal support for the US effort in Vietnam. Rhetorical backing for the US ignited strong protest on the Labour backbenches and at conference. Wilson publicly presented himself as a restraining influence on the US and in May-June 1966 he, along with Defence Minister Denis Healey, 'dissociated' Britain from the US bombing of Hanoi and Haiphong. Wilson and Healey also declared that arms sales to the US and Australia for use in Vietnam would be suspended. In November 1967, Foreign Secretary George Brown recommended to Cabinet the continuation of 'our present policy of committed detachment'. He concluded: 'Uncritical alignment behind the Americans would be an act of folly' (CAB 129, 134, 151, 154, 15 Nov. 1967). British diplomatic opinion tended to bring into play a version of the 'Greeks and Romans' paradigm. Patrick Dean, UK ambassador in Washington saw LBJ as believing rather naively that 'what is good for Americans is good for everyone else'. Efforts by Hanoi to reunify Vietnam clearly were not reducible simply to Chinese expansionism; this, however, was 'too sophisticated an analysis for the average American' (FCO 371 185003, 20 May 1966).

What did Britain contribute beyond words and 'committed detachment'? London supplied 2.4 million dollars in economic aid to South Vietnam given between 1968 and 1971 (Larsen and Collins, 1975, 167–8). British help also included intelligence assistance, notably via Hong Kong, and arms sales. Washington was aware that, as the CIA put it in December 1964, BRIAM had 'played a variety of useful functions'. Johnson initially looked for a modest increase in the commitment, probably to a token force of around one hundred. London managed to avoid any such open commitment, though it did respond early on to Secretary of State Dean Rusk's request that Britain be less reluctant to show the flag in Vietnam. Patrick Gordon Walker acknowledged (December 1964) that UK medical and training assistance for South Vietnamese forces 'would in fact step up the British commitment' (Ellis, 2004, 29–31). Arms sales were frequently disguised. In June 1965, Patrick Dean, British ambassador to Washington, told Rusk that 'the UK was naturally happy to sell the bombs but preferred that in the future it not be said that they were to be used in Vietnam' (NSF: Country File: UK, box 208, 'memo of conversation': Dean Rusk, 22 June 1965.) London was happy to provide advice on counter-insurgency, and it seems likely that some elite special forces were covertly assigned to assist the US in Vietnam (Campbell, 1984, 142; Hannah, 1987, 165).

Despite all this, Wilson resisted Johnson's requests for open commitment of even a symbolic 'platoon of bagpipers' or Gurkhas. LBJ himself seems to have stepped back from enforcing what some of his advisers in 1965 and 1966 were calling 'the Hessian option': the putative ability of Washington to force the commitment of British troops as the price for loans to support the pound. White House staffer McGeorge Bundy wanted Johnson to indicate directly 'that a British Brigade in Vietnam would be worth a billion dollars at the moment of truth for Sterling' (NSF: Country File: UK, box 215/16, Bundy to Johnson, 28 July 1965).

Wilson was able to muster various arguments as a means of resisting Washington's pressure to commit troops. He pleaded poverty, and, with decreasing credibility, argued that Britain was shouldering its share of the anti-communist burden in Malaysia. However, his main case rested on London's supposed utility to the Americans as an 'honest broker' or mediator. Especially since Britain was still co-chairman, with the USSR, of the Geneva Conference, responsible for Vietnam's partition, Wilson maintained that London should not become openly involved. The Foreign Office appears to have become convinced, surprisingly early, that an outright defeat of communists in South Vietnam was unlikely, and that the US would at some point welcome Britain's offer to be a credible .mediator. Only four months after taking office, on 21 March 1964, President Johnson complained to Defense Secretary Robert McNamara about British (and French) defeatism: 'Why do they want the Commies to take over all of Southeast Asia?' (Beschloss, ed. 1997, 293). In October 1964, J. E. Cable, South-East Asian chief at the British Foreign Office, commented for Foreign Secretary Gordon Walker's benefit: 'In the long run the Americans may well be defeated not by their own shortcomings or by the abilities of the Vietcong, but simply by the specifically Vietnamese brand of oriental behaviour and thinking' (Steininger, 1997, 241). In March 1965, Gordon Walker's successor, Michael Stewart, informed Wilson: 'The fact is that the Americans cannot win and cannot yet see any way of getting off the hook which will not damage their position internationally' (Steininger, 1997, 258). On 4 March 1965, the Cabinet decided that policy for the foreseeable future would concentrate on persuading Washington of the case for British mediation, and for an international conference (CAB 128 39, 4 March 1965).

Washington was prepared, to a degree and rather unenthusiastically, to indulge Wilson in his mediation ambitions. London ventured various mediation initiatives in the mid-1960s, culminating in the near farcical 'Phase A/Phase B' plan of February 1967. White House staffer Benjamin Read prepared in August 1965 a list of British mediation efforts. Read dealt with a series of suggestions that Britain might reconvene the Geneva Conference, with Patrick Gordon Walker's attempts to contact Hanoi, with the 'stillborn' Commonwealth mission and Harold Davies mission (both in 1965). Read's tone was one of slightly irritated tolerance (NSF: Country File: Vietnam: folder 'Negotiating Initiatives in Vietnam', boxes 196/197, Read to M. Bundy, 2 Aug. 1965). The 'Phase A/Phase B' plan grew out of pre-existing contacts, via various intermediaries, of which London was only one, between Hanoi and Washington. It involved a complex formula whereby North Vietnam would secretly agree to cease infiltration into the South in response to an indefinite US bombing halt, and then move to negotiations. The plan was presented to Soviet leader Alexei Kosygin during his February trip to London. At one point, LBJ's envoy, Chester Cooper, secreted himself in a Chequers attic in order to brief British leaders without Kosygin's knowledge. The collapse of 'Phase A/Phase B' was linked to a shift in Washington, following heavy North Vietnamese troop movements. The hardening of LBJ's position was also linked to his personal rivalry with Robert Kennedy (*Foreign Relations of the United States, 1964–1968*: vol. 5 (2002), 122). Johnson had a blazing row with Kennedy on 6 February 1967, while Kosygin was in London. It was not simply, as some early accounts suggested, merely a bureaucratic mix-up over the wording of the proposed agreement.

Clearly, also, London was taking too much on itself and was not in command of the full facts pertaining to other Washington-Hanoi contacts. Even Foreign Secretary George Brown (1971, 146) later acknowledged: 'We were too anxious to be intermediaries.' The presumption that Kosygin could command events in Hanoi was also naive. Chester Cooper later reported to LBJ's senior foreign policy adviser, Walt Rostow that 'Wilson was confronted not with a failure of communications on our part, but bad faith on the part of Hanoi (or of Kosygin …)' (NSF: Country File: Vietnam, box 256, folder, 'SUNFLOWER vol. 1', Cooper to Rostow, April 1967). Wilson blamed Walt Rostow for sabotaging the 'deal' in Washington. According to a 'personal minute' from Wilson to Brown, Rostow 'was largely responsible for the misunderstandings' (FCO 15 633, 6 March 1967). D.F. Murray of the Foreign Office advised in March that it 'would be best to accept that a breakdown in communications did occur, but also to accept that we shall probably never know exactly what considerations were being applied in Washington' (FCO 15 633, 6 March 1967). Brown advised Wilson to let sleeping dogs lie. He warned against raising the issue of Rostow's role in the affair with President Johnson: 'better not to run the risks of unnecessarily irritating L.B.J.' (FCO 15 633, 14 March 1967) (Dumbrell and Ellis, 2003).

Washington's coolness was at least one factor in the failure of the mediations between the US and Hanoi and/or its big power sponsors. However, Wilson's general argument, that the UK is 'more useful to you, as well as to the world as an Ally rather than a satellite' (NSF: Country File: UK, box 209, F. Bator to Johnson) was appreciated and understood in Washington. The US did not want to be seen to be, in the 1965 words of George Ball, adviser to LBJ, 'making Hessians [mercenaries] out of their soldiers' (*Papers of George Ball,* box 1, telecon (Fowler-Ball) 29 July 1965). Wilson also, as Ball further remarked, had considerable 'bargaining power ... if he is pushed into a corner' (*Papers of George Ball*, box 1, telecon (Solomon-Ball) 27 July 1965). The last thing that the US wished of Britain in 1965 or 1966 was a major devaluation of the pound, followed by a precipitate withdrawal of troops from Asia and the Pacific. As for British troops East of Suez, the Vietnam War made it even more urgent, in Washington's eyes, that Britain accept its part in the Asian theatre.

The idea that Wilson signed on to some kind of explicit 'deal' with Johnson over Vietnam has a rich and colourful provenance. The London *Evening Standard* even reported on 3 March 1964 that Wilson, then opposition leader, had proposed to hand the Royal Navy over to the US! According to commentators such as Clive Ponting, Wilson agreed to support US policy in Vietnam (and to postpone devaluation of the pound) in return for American loans. However, British policy on Vietnam was inevitably the product of complex calculations about the way criticism of or support for the US would affect other areas of policy: Rhodesia, support for the pound, US backing for Britain in Malaysia, and so on. Yet Anglo-American agreements, deals or shared understandings within a well defined power relationship – in the final reckoning, the precise term matters little – did shape British policy, primarily economic policy. On Vietnam, Wilson, by playing well his restricted hand, was still able to keep British troops away from the conflict.

The 1967–70 period saw a general cooling in Anglo-American relations, in which Britain's failure to commit troops played a significant part. London had a minor supporting role in the diplomacy which followed Johnson's 31 March 1968 withdrawal from the presidential election and offer of peace negotiations. On May 20, for example, Foreign Secretary Michael Stewart discussed his forthcoming trip to Moscow with David Bruce. Stewart recorded in his diary: 'We agree that in Moscow I should point out that U.S. want a real (but not necessarily admitted) *quid pro quo* for complete cessation of bombing, in the form of proper observance of the Demilitarised Zone, and reduction of N. Vietnam's use of Laos as a supply route' (Young, ed., 2005, 503–4). At his 1968 retirement party at the State Department, however, Dean Rusk upbraided British journalist Louis Heren: 'All we needed was one regiment. The Black Watch would have done. Just one regiment, but you wouldn't. Well, don't expect us to save you again. They can invade Sussex, and we wouldn't do a damned thing about it' (Heren, 1970, 231). Rusk's bitterness contrasted with the commonly expressed British view that Wilson had kowtowed to Johnson.

Domestic criticism of Wilson was not confined to the Labour left. Enoch Powell alleged in 1966 that Wilson had a clandestine, cowardly plan to commit British forces to do America's dirty work in Vietnam (Shepherd, 1997, 306). As leader of the Conservative opposition, however, Edward Heath tended to criticize Wilson, not for his obsequiousness towards Washington, but for supporting the policy but trying frequently to dissociate himself from the policy's implementation (Ellis, 2004, 173). As prime minister, Heath continued to back Washington, although there was now no question of committing troops. Henry Kissinger (1979, 425) later recalled Heath during the Nixon years arguing 'vigorously that an American withdrawal from Vietnam under conditions interpreted as a collapse of the American will might unleash a new round of Soviet aggression in Europe'. Throughout the war's final stages, Heath continued to offer stout defences of American action, even, in June 1972, praising Nixon's 'unparalleled restraint' (*Parliamentary Debates*, 5th series, vol. 838, 1253, 13 June 1972). In November 1970, Heath told Senator Charles Percy, on a visit to London, that the 'US Government's policy of Vietnamisation and at the same time giving the North Vietnamese "an occasional bloody nose" was right'. He even 'admired' the way that the Cambodian invasion had been handled (PREM 15 212).

A close study of Anglo-American relations during the Vietnam War reveals a complex set of perceptions affecting the conduct of the allies. President Johnson and his close staffers were both aware of Wilson's difficulties in supporting America on Vietnam and intermittently annoyed at his equivocations. Johnson does not seem to have taken at all seriously the rumours, associated with elements in the CIA, that Wilson was a 'Soviet asset'. LBJ received reports from Richard Neustadt (occasional London functionary to the JFK and LBJ administrations) and ambassador David Bruce that Wilson was dependable and pro-American (Dumbrell, 1996, 213). David Klein reported to McGeorge Bundy in March 1965: 'The firmest public support from *any* government on our policy in Vietnam has come from the British. This, despite the fact that Vietnam is a difficult issue for any British Government, and especially a Labor

Government' (NSF: Country File: UK, box 207, Klein to McG. Bundy, 23 March 1965).

Johnson's annoyance with Wilson nonetheless sometimes erupted into bursts of intense telephonic anger, some recorded by Wilson himself in his memoirs. British economic links with North Vietnam were a constant source of irritation. On occasion, notably in March 1965, LBJ went so far as, in effect, to dictate Wilson's House of Commons remarks on Vietnam. The job of mediating between London and Washington fell to David Bruce, who considered the business of telling a foreign head how to address his own parliament 'a tasteless proceeding' (Lankford, 1996, 331). Bruce, who had his own personal doubts about the war, had no illusions about Wilson's willingness to commit troops. He advised Washington that there was little prospect of overt UK troop commitment. Bruce kept the British leadership informed on developments in Vietnam, and took a close role in the 'Phase A/Phase B' mediation plan of February 1967. By this time, Bruce was at times almost a prisoner in the embassy in Grosvenor Square: 'Genocide Square' to the anti-war protesters, who besieged the building. Yet Bruce continued to advise Washington of Britain's essential stability. In June 1968, for example, he described British opinion as beset by 'disappointment, discouragement and disillusion', rather than anger. Any 'explosion like that across the Channel' was unlikely (incoming calls to Dept. of State, 5 June 1968, NSF: NSC Meetings File, vols 3–5, folder, 'Current issues affecting US/UK relations'). Generally, Washington was inclined to see public opinion in the UK as defeatist over communist 'aggression', rather than either sympathetic to it or criitical of US actions in the Third World. Walt Rostow told President Johnson in July 1966 that the British had 'an attitude of mind which, in effect, prefers that we take losses' rather than risk 'sharp confrontation' (Diary Backup, box 41, Rostow to Johnson, 28 July 1966).

The Falklands War

Although initially viewed in some Washington circles as the stuff of comic opera, Argentina's invasion of the Falkland (or Malvinas) Islands on 2 April 1982 created immediate and profound dilemmas for the US. In the words of David Gombert, a member of US

Secretary of State Alexander Haig's Falklands mediation team: 'Important American interests were on a collision course with one another: on the one hand, the Anglo-American special partnership and the principle of non-aggression, on the other, our Latin American relationships and our ability to maintain peace and tranquillity in this hemisphere' (Gombert, 1985, 110). Jeane Kirkpatrick, US representative at the UN and leader of the 'Latin Americanist' tendency in Washington during the crisis, later recalled: 'Britain and Argentina had a stake in the Falklands, but in many ways the United States had the largest stake of all' (Beck, 1988, 14).

The breakdown of Anglo-Argentinian talks in February had precipitated a tense interlude, in which Britain had appealed for American assistance. Haig promised British Foreign Secretary Lord Carrington that the US would take a constructive line (Carrington, 1988, 72). British concern mounted about apparent American equidistance between the British and Argentinian positions, and especially about the reportedly 'Latin Americanist' orientation of Assistant Secretary Thomas Enders. The landings on South Georgia on 19 March provoked new efforts to swing Washington against Argentina. On 31 March, intelligence reports were received to the effect that a full invasion was on imminent. As Robert Renwick (1996, 227), then political counsellor at the British Embassy in Washington, later wrote, Haig insisted that the US 'would have a greater chance of influencing Argentine behaviour if they appeared not to favour one side or the other'. President Reagan telephoned an apparently drunken General Galtieri (the Argentinian leader) on 1 April, only to be told, in effect, that the invasion was going ahead.

The invasion triggered the despatch of the British task force and also Carrington's resignation. Washington was torn in different directions: some, notably Secretary of Defense Caspar Weinberger, urging support for Britain and the rule of law; others (notably Kirkpatrick) arguing that Argentina had legitimate claims to Falklands sovereignty, and that US anti-communist interests lay in conciliating Latin American opinion. British Ambassador Nicholas Henderson (1994, 449–50) recorded in his diary on 4 April a conversation with Haig's deputy, Walter Stoessel: 'He seemed immensely detached. I suppose that's the impression British diplomats gave a century ago when we were a great power and some lesser country sought our support.' For his part, Weinberger offered virtually immediate military assistance to the UK. The defense secretary established a Pentagon committee on 5 April, chaired by Dov Zakheim, to remove bureaucratic obstacles in the way of aiding Britain. Assistance flowed freely, with the UK receiving everything requested. Admiral Henry Leach, First Sea Lord, later wrote that the American military 'went further than politicians would have permitted had they known in time' (Richardson, 1996, 123). Military aid to Argentina, already largely suspended owing to congressional inhibitions relating to the junta's appalling human rights record, quickly disappeared. Unsurprisingly, Buenos Aires soon moved to question American 'neutrality'. At a National Security Council meeting on 7 April, Haig and Weinberger argued that mediation was worth attempting, but that, if it failed, the US should back Britain. Reagan approved Haig's mediation plans, declaring that their credibility depended on the appearance of US neutrality.

In essence, the US mediation position involved the assertion of neutrality over the issue of Falklands sovereignty, although not over the clearly illegal invasion. Haig's early mediation position involved the introduction of a multinational peacekeeping force, Argentine withdrawal and negotiations on sovereignty and the island's future. Renwick later identified his fundamental difficulty: 'the British were prepared to talk only without pre-conditions and when Argentina's forces had left the islands. Argentina was not prepared to withdraw its forces ... until it was assured that the question of sovereignty would be settled – in its favour' (Renwick, 1996, 227). In intense and complex diplomacy, Haig developed various positions on an interim administration for the Falklands, with Argentina's flag flying alongside the Union Jack. The London negotiations with Haig were difficult. Some senior UK officials like Defence Secretary John Nott resented the very notion of American 'mediation'. On April 12, Nott and Thatcher succeeded in persuading Haig to drop the idea of UK forces withdrawing 4,000 miles to Ascension Island and Argentinian troops merely to their mainland (Nott, 2002a, 288, 292). British Foreign Secretary Francis Pym recommended accepting Haig's plan prior to the 25 April reoccupation by British forces of South Georgia. Margaret Thatcher opposed terms which did not embody a return to the conditions of the pre-invasion British administration. The buck was passed to Argentina, who rejected proposals which did not guarantee its position on sovereignty. London became increasingly wedded publicly to the view that the islanders' wishes (in effect, to remain under British administration) must be 'paramount'.

On 28 April, the US Senate passed a resolution stating that the US 'cannot stand neutral' and must help Britain 'achieve full withdrawal of Argentine forces'. The only dissenting voice was Republican Senator Jesse Helms of North Carolina, who warned that support for Britain would destroy the Latin American 'coalition we must have if we are to prevent a communist takeover of Central America' (*Congressional Quarterly Weekly Report*, 1 May 1982, 1014). Pro-British forces in Congress were led by Democratic Senator Joe Biden of Delaware, who told Henderson: 'Don't mind all this crap about self-determination, we're with you because you're British' (Richardson, 1996, 202). On 30 April, President Reagan announced a formal end to American 'neutrality'. He blamed Buenos Aires for the failure of mediation and declared the US would give the UK material support. Economic sanctions were to be directed at Argentina.

With sea and air bombardment of Argentine forces commencing on 1 May, Haig encouraged the Peruvian government to present proposals which moved slightly more towards Argentina's position. The sinking of the Argentine ship, *Belgrano*, on 2 May, provoked calls for a ceasefire. The notion that the sinking of the *Belgrano* was part of London's campaign to undermine the Haig peace initiatives has been raised frequently, but lacks any documentary basis. Following the loss of the British destroyer, *Sheffield* (3 May), London reluctantly agreed to yet more proposals, based on the concept of an interim administration. The American pressure on London to accept mediation on terms – to quote John Nott – 'which would have been seen as a surrender by political, press and public opinion in the United Kingdom', was intense (Nott, 2002a, 291). Again, the various proposals were rejected by Galtieri and the junta. On 17 May, Margaret Thatcher, acknowledging that 'we could not afford to alienate the United States', accepted the idea of a United Nations administrator for the Falklands. Against the direct advice of Jeane Kirkpatrick, Buenos Aires effectively rebuffed UN mediation. Following the 21 May landings, Haig's efforts became geared towards avoiding an Argentinian humiliation and towards pressing on London the virtues of magnanimity. During a late night telephone conversation on 31 May, the last of several such difficult exchanges, PM Thatcher convinced Reagan that she could not be expected 'to snatch diplomatic defeat from the jaws of military victory'. Reagan was asked how he would feel if Alaska were invaded (Thatcher, 1993, 230–31; Parsons, 1983)! On 4 June, the US joined Britain, represented at the UN by Anthony Parsons, in vetoing a UN Security Council call for an immediate ceasefire. After casting the vote, Kirkpatrick announced that the US really intended to abstain. Her extraordinary announcement reflected a change of heart by Haig, whose desire to communicate this to London caused a delay in changing instructions to the US delegation to the UN.

The Argentine surrender of 14 June prompted open cheering in the White House Operations Room. As the battlefield noise subsided, it became difficult to evaluate the impact of American assistance to Britain. US sensitivity to Latin American opinion encouraged coyness on Washington's part, while London was all too keen to accept undiluted glory. John Nott later downplayed the significance of Washington's help. For Nott (2002a, 291), America was almost indecently keen to save Galtieri's face, with only France giving unqualified assistance. British bitterness about Washington's concern to mitigate Galtieri's plight is amply recorded in Lawrence Freedman's official history of the conflict (Freedman, 2005). Despite this, US support – facilities on Ascension Island, material supplies, Sidewinder air-to-air missiles, Stinger anti-aircraft systems; above all, satellite and other intelligence cooperation – was important. The spectacle of the American superpower tilting towards London must have had a deleterious effect on Argentinian purpose and morale. The US contribution to the British victory was enhanced by the intermeshing of Anglo-American defence and, particularly, intelligence systems. As Assistant Secretary Eagleburger later put it: 'You were so much in our intelligence breeches anyway that, had we decided to turn it off, we would have had to send every Brit home from Washington to accomplish it' (Smith, 1990, 84).

As in the case of the Vietnam War, the Falklands conflict raised fundamental questions about the nature and purpose of the transatlantic alliance. Was the US *bound* to come over to Britain's side? John Campbell (2004, 142) has argued that neither the 'special relationship' nor Reagan's undoubted regard for Britain and its conservative leader actually determined the outcome. He credits the Foreign and Commonwealth Office, an institution regularly disparaged by Thatcher and the Thatcherites, for swinging elite US opinion in Britain's direction. The 'exercise in old-fashioned diplomacy' by Anthony Parsons and Nicholas Henderson clearly had a impact.

Factors other than Britain's status as an old ally also had sig. cance: the need for British help in Europe (especially regarding t. Pershing II and cruise missile deployments); America's commitment to international law; the insouciance, as perceived in London if not always in Washington, of the USSR, especially when it refused Argentina's request to veto UN Resolution 502; and, surely at least to some degree, the friendship between Reagan and Thatcher. While John Nott saw Reagan as severely compromised by his passionate commitment to Latin American anti-communism, there was, at least according to Weinberger (1990, 146), never any doubt that the president's heart was with Britain. When Al Haig arrived in London on 8 April, he 'assured the prime minister, in so many words, that there would be no repetition of Suez, in which the United States had coerced Britain and France into retreating from a military expedition in 1956' (Haig, 1984, 273; Henderson, 1994, 444; Nott, 2002, 286–96).

Memories of Suez attended the entire Falklands episode. For Thatcher, 'British foreign policy had been one long retreat' since 1956, and 1982 was the year to turn around. Nicholas Henderson drew less comforting lessons: 'The Falklands crisis touched on certain American nerves that had proved sensitive at Suez: a recessive feeling about colonialism: concern that the British were expecting the United States eventually to pick up the cheque: worry about the Russians: and the fear that what Britain was doing would rally other countries in the area against Western interests' (Henderson, 1987, 87). Clearly, the US *could* have used economic and other pressure, as at Suez, to force an effective retreat, however unlikely it was that the US would actively support Buenos Aires. What had changed since 1956? Louise Richardson suggests that the Vietnam War had encouraged US 'appreciation of the complexities of the exercise of power' (Richardson, 1996, 203). The US could now sympathize with other countries who were accused of neo-colonialism and was not (in the Falklands case) inclined to any narrow interpretation of the 1823 Monroe Doctrine's opposition to European military operations in the western hemisphere. In a sense, London was able in 1982, as it failed in 1956, to 'entrap' the US into following policies which, at least arguably, contradicted core American interests. In any such analysis, the crucial element in 1982 was indeed the British campaign, led by Henderson, to cast the crisis in terms of international law, to emphasize the differences, especially in terms of international law and UN Resolution 502, with Suez and to woo US public, congressional and executive branch opinion.

Henderson himself was anxious to keep London from simply assuming that US support was inevitable. Given the events of 1956, it is perhaps surprising that such assumptions were ever made. However, Margaret Thatcher had certain private assurances, and relied on Reagan's friendship, believing 'that the US has a duty to support us' (Henderson, 1994, 469). In fact, the US risked quite a lot in becoming 'entrapped' by Britain. Haig never accepted that the Soviet Union was unconcerned about the Falklands issue. Henderson later testified: 'Certainly Haig said to me almost every time he saw me that one of the things that worried him ... whatever the outcome, or particularly if there was a prolonged conflict, was the increase in Soviet influence' (Richardson, 1996, 190). Argentina was a useful ally, especially in relation to US covert operations in Central and Latin America. Certainly it can be argued that the South American dictatorships had nowhere else to go – but, again, the same point could be made about Britain. The fall of the Argentinian junta could well produce conditions conducive to the progress of anti-American leftism (in the Argentinian context, a possible revival of leftist Peronism, if not of Argentine communism). The short-term damage done to US-Latin American relations, by Haig's 30 April announcement of support for Britain, also swiftly became evident. On 9 May, a Venezuelan embassy spokesman was quoted as follows: 'The United States chose to side with its stepmother and not with its little brother.' Mario Hildago from the Costa Rican embassy attacked Haig as having 'completely destroyed' the hemispheric defence principles of the Organisation of American States. Within the OAS, only the Anglophile Caribbean islands supported the US line. A Brazilian commentator, Dorritt Harazim, argued that it was now evident that the US had 'first' and 'second class allies' (*Washington Post*, 9 May 1982, A15, D2). Thomas Enders and Jeane Kirkpatrick both later held that America's Falklands decision set hemispheric relations back many years (Richardson, 1996, 157–9).

From Britain's viewpoint, of course, the US was doing no more than its international and alliance duty. Indeed, Washington was to be severely criticized for its early neutrality and for actually encouraging the invasion in the first instance. Sir Michael Palliser, adviser to the War Cabinet, later told Louise Richardson (1996, 133): 'Haig would have been happy with any settlement, including one which

gave Argentina everything.' As for inadvertent encouragement of
the invasion, it has been argued that excessive American closeness
to the junta bred the expectation that the US would support the
invasion. Jeane Kirkpatrick later admitted that she had, without
realizing it, been sounded out by Buenos Aires on this subject
(Richardson, 114–15). Margaret Thatcher (1993, 176) felt that 'a
wildly exaggerated idea of their importance to the United States'
had emboldened the Argentinians to invade. General Miguel Mallea
Gil, Argentine military attaché in Washington, certainly did relay
the view that US support would be forthcoming. There is also the
argument, taken up by Labour MP Tam Dalyell, that US General
Vernon Walters had encouraged the invasion by floating the idea of
a joint US-Argentine missile base in the South Atlantic. Certainly,
stories to this effect appeared in Buenos Aires newspapers in early
1982 (*Washington Post*, 9 April 1982, A 19). Perhaps a more vigorous
US reaction to the South Georgia landings might have fended off
the invasion. Against these arguments, Haig (1984, 296) has pointed
out that the Argentinians *were* warned not to invade, and were
cognizant of the close Anglo-American intelligence and defence
cooperation. Thomas Enders also rapidly denied the story about
the US seeking a joint military base with Argentina (Richardson,
1996, 115). After Haig's 30 April announcement, Argentine sources
began to suggest that the junta had always expected US opposition.
A Buenos Aires 'political source' was quoted in the *Washington
Post* on 9 May, for example, saying that Haig had been simply
'giving the same arguments that we have been hearing from the
British for 17 years'. Galtieri's handling of the pre-invasion phone
calls from Reagan, the first two of which were refused, certainly suggests he accepted America's disapproval. Nevertheless, the junta also
remembered Suez and doubtless drew their own lessons therefrom.
Galtieri, as even Haig (1984, 275) admitted, expected *some* kind of
'quid pro quo for Argentinian support for the United States in the
Southern Hemisphere'.

Haig's mediation split opinion in London. The British, however,
did have the secretary of state's reassurance that there would be no
repetition of 1956, as well as the concrete evidence of Pentagon
support. As Henderson (1987, 90) recalled, the idea that there was
no scope at all for mediation was absurd: 'nobody involved in the
decision [to send the task force] thought at the time that it would be
bound to lead to war'. Henderson and UN ambassador Anthony

Parsons, aided by foreign secretary Pym, consistently urged London to keep options open, and above all, to ensure the retention of American goodwill. The 'war party' (led by Margaret Thatcher) undertook to rely on Argentinian intransigence, rather than risk snubbing Haig. On no fewer than three occasions (just before the 30 April announcement, following the loss of the *Sheffield* on 4 May and immediately prior to the 21 May landings), Buenos Aires obliged. A more flexible attitude on the part of the junta would have put London in an extraordinarily difficult position. Admiral Terence Lewin later testified, *apropos* the Haig proposals of 27 April, that the 'War Cabinet had with great reluctance agreed' that Haig put them to Galtieri. They 'would indeed ... have been very difficult for the War Cabinet or the British Government of all parties to accept' (Dillon, 1989, 145.) Former chancellor of the exchequer Nigel Lawson (1992, 127) reasoned that 'had the Galtieri junta accepted the British proposal of 20 May to place the islands under the indefinite jurisdiction of the United Nations, it is possible that the recall of the Task Force would have commanded a majority in Cabinet'. For Henderson (1987, 107), Haig's (and Peru's) mediation was valuable to the British cause. As the task force sailed south, 'there was a need for something to fill the diplomatic vacuum'. Without Haig, 'Argentine intransigence would not have been exposed, and without this exposure the American decision to give Britain support would probably not have come when it did or have been so categorical'. In her memoirs, Thatcher (1993, 188) adopted a tellingly different tone: America's pre-30 April stance was 'fundamentally misguided'. Yet, 'in practice, the Haig negotiations, which flowed from all this, almost certainly worked in our favour, by precluding for a time even less helpful diplomatic intervention from other directions, including the UN'.

At one level, the question – was the US *bound* to support Britain? – can only be answered with reference to the near-textbook 'bureaucratic politics' configurations engendered in Washington by the crisis. The Argentine invasion immediately set bureaucratic actors off in different directions. At the State Department, Europeanists clashed with Latin Americanists. UN Ambassador Kirkpatrick interpreted the crisis in line with her own version of neo-conservative anti-communist realism. At one stage, she remarked to British journalist Geoffrey Smith (1990, 81): 'I do wish you people would look more at the map.' Several National Security Council staffers saw the conflict as essentially a dispute over oil drilling rights (Haig, 1984, 268). The Pentagon not only followed Weinberger's pro-London stance, but also respected the logic of its close relationship with the British military. Some sections of Pentagon opinion inclined to the view that Britain would lose without American help. Haig, however, floated above his department's inner conflicts. Having recently suffered important bureaucratic defeats, he embarked on a classic piece of entrepreneurship. As Hedrick Smith reminded *New York Times* readers (15 April 1982, A14), Haig was concerned to set down a bureaucratic marker and to make the Falklands 'his' issue. The Reagan administration, of course, was no stranger to chronic 'bureaucratic politics'. In the Falklands case, however, it was adjudicated, and in the classic manner, by the president himself (Weinberger, 1990, 146).

Within a month of the invasion, the US was able to make a clear and public declaration of support for Britain. The weight of elite, public and congressional opinion was important in influencing Reagan's adjudication, as no doubt was his personal regard for Margaret Thatcher. Nevertheless, even leaving aside Kirkpatrick's Latin Americanist case, it is important to note that not all strands of American opinion pointed to unalloyed sympathy for London's cause. Haig (1984, 296) later pointed to Britain's psychological need, in the Falklands context, for 'legends and traditions' in the 'afterglow of empire'. Some commentators criticized the expenditure of American effort in such an apparently insignificant arena. Must America do *everything*? A *New York Times* editorial of 15 April urged Haig to 'stay home'. Others interpreted the war as an example of Britain's residual imperial overstretch, with important lessons for the US. In the *Washington Post* (9 April 1982, A19), George Will expressed his hope that the crisis would draw America's attention to the following adage: 'that when your political will and military assets are perceived to be insufficient to sustain your commitments and pretenses, other nations begin acting rudely'.

[The Falklands conflict was a war waged between a parliamentary democracy and a military dictatorship. Communism, anti-communism and the Cold War were, at least on first inspection, secondary issues. Yet it was a conflict fought at a critical juncture of the Cold War. American anti-communism cut both ways. Washington feared leftist advances in Argentina if the junta fell in Buenos Aires, even as it wished to back its Cold War ally in London. The diplomatic, intelligence and military structures of the Cold War 'special relationship' pulled Washington towards London.

The final two major conflicts to be discussed in this chapter occurred in an entirely different international environment.

Gulf Crisis and War, 1990–91

To Margaret Thatcher (1993, 769), the 1991 Gulf War represented the post-Cold War reassertion of the 'special relationship': 'Suddenly a Britain with armed forces which had the skills, and a government which had the resolve, to fight alongside America, seemed to be the real European "partner in leadership".' Some other memoirs from this period offer a significantly different view. For James Baker (1995, 381), for example, the British and French contributions to the conflict were bracketed together. Both countries 'had a long and checkered history in the Middle East', and both 'saw in this crisis an opportunity to emphasise their heritage as global powers'. With the end of the main communist rival, 'America's status as the pre-eminent superpower was magnified'. The result was that *everyone* 'wanted to get closer to the United States'. For US Ambassador Raymond Seitz (1998, 326), Anglo-American cooperation in the Gulf was 'the last hurrah of the old regime'. John Dickie (1994, 232) saw the conflict as marking the 'end of the [Anglo-American] affair'. He noted that, precisely as the allies were going to war, in January 1991, plans 'were drawn up for 79 of the American bases in Europe – including 13 in England – to be drastically scaled down or closed'. The British role 'as a standard-bearer in Europe for the Americans was clearly coming to an end'.

Prior to 1990, the US and the UK were prepared to arm Saddam Hussein's largely secularist regime in Iraq as a counter to militant Islamicism in the region (Phythian, 1997a). Britain became closely involved in the unravelling of this policy, firstly in relation to the arrest and execution (in March 1990) of London-based journalist Farzad Bazoft. Secondly, also in March 1990, British customs authorities seized, and later intercepted abroad, engineering parts apparently destined for an Iraqi 'supergun'. A joint US–UK customs team confiscated possible nuclear triggering material, bound for Iraq, at Heathrow airport. Prior to the 'supergun' seizures, British authorities had ignored at least 11 tip-offs about military exports to Iraq (Hiro, 1992, 75).

Margaret Thatcher's presence in the US at the time of Iraq's invasion of Kuwait (2 August 1990) gave her a fortuitously privileged opportunity to influence American policy. At a prearranged meeting in Aspen, Colorado, immediately following the invasion, she advised Bush to resist stoutly the violation of international law. The US president announced to the press: 'Prime Minister Thatcher and I are looking at it on exactly the same wavelength' (Freedman and Karsh, 1994, 73). The legend has grown that it was the British leader who strengthened the presidential resolve; no doubt this interpretation strains the evidence. However, General Colin Powell (1995, 467) was impressed by Thatcher's contribution, and felt that Bush would have been influenced by her Falklands experience. According to Powell, Bush's 5 August 1990 comment to journalists – 'This will not stand' – 'had a Thatcherite ring'. Thatcher had been able to assure Bush almost immediately not only of British, but also, following a call to President Mitterrand, of French military support. Anglo-American diplomatic cooperation was put to work at the UN, despite disagreements between Thatcher and Secretary Baker over whether military action required a separate United Nations resolution. Thatcher preferred to rely on Kuwait's right to seek defensive aid under Article 51 of the UN Charter. The Gulf War was eventually waged under a separate resolution of 29 November, which set the 15 January 1991 deadline for Iraqi withdrawal. On 26 August, Thatcher first used the phrase, 'no time to go wobbly', which was taken up with amusement in Washington, and which served in journalistic memory to symbolize her contribution (Renwick, 1996, 262).

Between August 1990 and her departure from government on 22 November 1990, Margaret Thatcher took every opportunity to demonstrate British enthusiasm for the operation, and to press the case – as in the Falklands crisis – for a military solution. European allies were excoriated for their feebleness, and various negotiating initiatives, including that of former leader Edward Heath, treated with cold derision. Heath (1998, 654–6, 669) later clashed personally with James Baker over the latter's supposedly lukewarm attempts to promote the cause of diplomacy. At Margaret Thatcher's final Cabinet, on the day of her resignation, it was decided to increase the British military presence to divisional levels. The accession of John Major brought no obvious change of direction. Bush's personal relations with Major were far less fraught than with the Iron Lady, who had supposedly stiffened his resolve at Aspen. The retention in Downing Street of Charles Powell, Thatcher's chief foreign policy adviser, also fostered continuity. The British and American commanders, British General Sir Peter de la Billière and US General Norman Schwarzkopf, established close working relations, albeit with the clear understanding that (in de la Billière's words) 'America was running the show' (de la Billière, 1992, 50; Schwarzkopf, 1992, 297).

British public support for the use of force was actually stronger than similar support in the US. The bulk of pro-war British opinion also saw an important goal as the overthrow of Saddam, rather than merely the liberation of Kuwait (Freedman and Karsh, 1992, 347; Mueller, 1994). At Westminster, the Labour opposition argued that sanctions against Iraq should be given time to work. However, there was never any great doubt that the Labour leadership would support the use of force if and when it was used. The House of Commons war debate of 15 January 1991 was less acrimonious than the equivalent debate in the US Congress. The vote at Westminster was 534–57 in favour of using force to enforce the deadline. By comparison, the US Senate voted 57–42, and the House of Representatives 250–183, to back President Bush's request for authority to go to (undeclared) war. In London, Labour leader Neil Kinnock dismissed doubts raised by some in his party:

> All of us could draw up a supportable, desirable agenda for addressing the atrocities committed by dictators all over this planet. But we know very well that what we have to do now is to address the one posing the most direct threat to the stability of the region and the peace of the world.

Labour MP Andrew Faulds described US policy as in thrall to 'the 3 to 4 per cent of the population that makes up the Zionist lobby which dictates America's middle eastern policies'. Former Defence Secretary Denis Healey foresaw 'an appalling loss of life', which might cause the US to retreat into isolationism, leaving the UK 'beached offshore on the edge of Europe having lost its relationship with the Europeans'. Edward Heath urged the US to persevere with diplomacy, and clearly to set a date for a Middle Eastern peace conference. Conservative MP Ian Gilmour accused the US of consistently, despite its Gulf pronouncements, rewarding aggression, not least by selling arms to Saddam in the 1980s (*Parliamentary Debates*, 6th Series, vol. 183, 15 Jan. 1991, 745, 781, 772, 780).

Britain's contribution to the Gulf coalition was second only to that of the US. Over 30,000 British military personnel, around one-quarter of the entire British army, saw Gulf service. The Royal Air Force flew around 5 per cent of Gulf combat missions. The 22nd Special Air Service Regiment was operating in Iraq prior to the start of the air campaign, while the Delta force (the elite commando unit of the US Joint Special Operations Command) remained in North Carolina. In contrast to previous wars, Americans were struck by the informality of British military discipline, and by the fact that many British soldiers were wearing the *shermagh* or Arab headdress (Atkinson 1994, 400). Anglo-American harmony was marred by the deaths of 9 British soldiers in 'friendly fire', and especially by the subsequent refusal of the Pentagon to explain or cooperate publicly in investigations. In the last hours of the war, Major General Rupert Smith, a British divisional commander, managed to have his orders altered so as to avoid close proximity to American forces (Atkinson, 1994, 464).

The decision to end fighting after just four days of ground war, rather than press on to oust Saddam, was taken by Washington without consulting allies. British Foreign Secretary Douglas Hurd, who apparently considered arguing the point, was told that the operation was complete and that the 'slaughter' should not continue (Freedman and Karsh, 1992, 405). Margaret Thatcher, now of course out of power, made no secret of her opposition to the decision. Prime Minister Major turned to the development of a 'safe havens' plan for the Northern Iraqi Kurds – a plan which, despite initial US opposition, Bush coopted on 16 April 1991.

For Major, the 'safe havens' episode illustrated that London did have an important persuasive power in Washington. The Gulf War 'reinforced the United States as the foremost military power in the world'. The US had acted effectively alongside Britain, its surest European ally, in a region where both countries had 'significant economic interests' (Major, 1999, 243–6). Whether such cooperation would be replicated in other post-Cold War arenas was another question. What seemed very likely, at least by the mid-1990s, was that such cooperation was increasingly likely to be filtered through the institutions of European integration. Any such expectation was to be confounded.

Iraq, 2003

The Balkans interventions of the later 1990s revealed the new complexity of the US-UK-EU relationship. However, when the really big test came in 2003, London was firmly located on America's side of the Atlantic. Let us take a look at the development of US–UK policy towards the invasion of Iraq.

Saddam Hussein's evasions of United Nations weapons inspections led to Anglo-American air attacks in the Clinton-Blair era. The actual invasion of Iraq had been advocated in US rightist Republican circles from at least the mid-1990s, and was certainly the subject of Pentagon contingency planning well before 9/11. The prospect of an Iraqi invasion was raised in National Security Council meetings held immediately after 9/11. At this time, British influence was squarely directed against invading any country, such as Iraq, which could not credibly be shown to have been involved in the September 2001 attacks. President Bush's January 2002 State of the Union address promised that America 'will not wait on events'. In April 2002, the month when Bush appears to have informed Tony Blair of American intentions towards Saddam, the US president began publicly to advocate regime change in Baghdad (Woodward, 2003, 60, 330–3). By this time, the UK was intensely active in Operation Southern Focus, a major bombing campaign, ostensibly linked to the Iraqi 'no fly zone' policy adopted in the South of the country following the 1991 war, but widely interpreted as at least a possible preparation for invasion (Sharp, 2004, 62).

A Joint Intelligence Committee report submitted to Blair in early 2002 showed little if any evidence of weapons of mass destruction (WMD) being developed following the exit of UN inspectors from Iraq in 1998, though Saddam's failure to cooperate, of course, made firm judgements impossible. Important contacts developed between Tony Blair's foreign policy adviser David Manning and US National Security Adviser Condoleezza Rice, as well as between Foreign Secretary Jack Straw and Secretary of State Colin Powell. Each set of contacts was used by London to attempt to ease, or at least multilateralize, the drive to action. By the Summer of 2002, Blair began to emphasize the need to take the issue of Iraq and WMD to the United Nations, as 'a way of dealing with the matter rather than a means of avoiding it' (Wintour and Kettle, 2003). The prime minister's case for war, failing full and unambiguous cooperation with the UN inspection regime, rested on various arguments: for example that Baghdad's prior use of chemical weapons had already violated international norms; and that the old policy of 'keeping Saddam in his box' had collapsed with the departure of the UN inspectors in 1998 (Keohane, 2005, 66). In September, London published a dossier, suggesting that Baghdad's WMD amounted to a 'current and serious' threat to UK security. This dossier contained the first public charge that Baghdad had sought to buy 'yellowcake' uranium oxide from Niger, as well as Blair's claim in the preface that some Iraqi destructive weapons could be ready for use in 45 minutes. As indicated in the previous chapter, a similarly angled CIA estimate was released by Washington shortly after. In November, the US, aided by Britain, finally achieved unanimous passage of UN Security Council Resolution 1441, calling on Iraqi inspection compliance on pain of serious consequences. With US and British forces now deploying in friendly Gulf states, the Iraqis readmitted UN inspectors and began a new round of the 'cat and mouse' evasion and semi-cooperation which culminated in the invasion of March 2003.

The road to war was beset by confusion, tragedy and farce. Former Foreign Secretary Robin Cook reported Blair's response to Cabinet doubts about the degree to which the September dossier actually justified war: 'To carry on being engaged with the US is vital. The voices on both left and right who want to pull Europe and the US apart would have disastrous consequence if they succeeded' (Cook, 2003, 213). Another dossier – 'a real Horlicks' in Jack Straw's phrase (Sharp, 2004, 64) – was released in February 2003. By this time, Blair's priority was to shove Washington in the direction of a second resolution, explicitly endorsing an invasion. His influence was certainly one factor in pushing Washington in that direction, although it should be remembered that US public opinion was also in favour of as much UN sanction and multilateral risk-sharing as was compatible with the perceived needs of US national security. In the event, Washington did press for a second resolution, though without great zeal or enthusiasm (Daalder and Lindsay, 2003, 144). Downing Street's inclination to blame French intransigence for the failure was never entirely convincing. Ambassador Christopher Meyer recalled French diplomats confiding to him privately that the word, 'never' was indeed unknown in international diplomacy (Meyer, 2005, 281). When British Defence Secretary Geoff Hoon informed Donald Rumsfeld that failure to secure another resolution might make British involvement in the invasion politically impossible, the American defence chief made a speech to the effect that London's assistance was not needed anyway (Seldon, 2004, 593). Robin Cook wrote on February 25 that 'Tony's attempt to wrap himself in the UN flag is fatally hobbled by his inability to say that the UN will have the last word' (Cook, 2003, 311). By this time, few people believed that anything could possibly prevent an American invasion, with or without the support of any other nation or international organisation. The House of Commons vote for war on 18 March 2003 was actually something of a victory for Blair, with 'only' a minority of 139 Labour MPs voting in opposition. Blair emphasized Britain's duty to back the US, but the House of Commons victory was widely attributed to a combination of playing the 'French card' (citing President Chirac's putative intransigence) and an appeal to Labour members that they must act, as Jack Straw put it, 'to keep this government in business' (Wintour and Kettle, 2003). The government's majority, of course, rested also on the support of Conservative Members, though by no means all Tories backed Blair. Former Conservative minister John Gummer declared on 26 February ''There is no member of Parliament who does not know that this is war by timetable, and the timetable was laid down before the United States had any intention of going to the United Nations' (Keohane, 2005, 68). Tory MP Boris Johnson mused that perhaps 'America should be encouraged to go around making appropriate adjustments to the geopolitical scene'. However, it 'would help if someone started to make' the case for war 'honestly' (Johnson, 2003, 365).

British forces had seized the Southern Shia city of Basra and its surrounds by early April, shortly before US forces entered Baghdad. The US infantry was stretched, by a combination of Rumsfeld's tactical reliance on light force and the temporary non-availability, following the Turkish refusal to cooperate, of the US division originally due to enter Iraq from the North. British help was therefore of more than merely propagandistic value. The example of British involvement in both the ground and air war was also widely credited with encouraging other countries to participate (Seldon, 2004, 598). Following the initial toppling of Saddam's regime, British forces continued to be deployed in the Basra region, where their tactics contrasted with the strong 'force protection' stance of American forces operating in regions more closely identified with the accelerating insurgency. The developing conflict appeared to demonstrate the greater British prioritization of 'Information Operations' (IO) (essentially development of strategies designed to secure good civilian-military relations). IO in US military jargon tended to be a 'low-density skill set', with a paucity of resources. In the South of Iraq, however, British tactics seemed to do little to prevent substantial Iran-oriented militia infiltration of the new domestic security forces. Some US commentators also made the point that when, in 2005, the Black Watch was temporarily redeployed closer to Baghdad, these British forces adopted much more of a 'force protection' stance. The post-invasion handling of the emerging anti-coalition insurgency in Iraq seemed to show little concern for British preferences. London was widely reported to have lacked confidence in post-invasion US administrator of Iraq, Paul Bremer, and to have advised against the rapid disbanding of Iraqi security forces (Hastings, 2003). By the end of 2005, there were approximately one hundred British combat deaths.

The various post-invasion inquiries, leaks and memoirs tended to reinforce the view that Blair had acted primarily to place Britain in a position in which to influence the United States, rather than as a result of clear evidence pointing to Iraqi possession of weapons of mass destruction. The Hutton (2004) inquiry into Downing Street's handling of intelligence – especially in connection with the charge of having 'sexed up' information on WMD, aired on BBC radio in May 2003, and later linked to the suicide of government scientist David Kelly – cleared the government of the charge of deliberate deception. Blair did, however, unquestionably present complex and often compromised intelligence in a disconcertingly confident manner. The subsequent Butler (2004) inquiry criticised the closed style of decision-making favoured by Blair, with not even Cabinet members being given regular briefings. It also indicated that, although there was no deliberate attempt on the government's part to deceive, it should have been made much clearer that the various dossier conclusions about WMD were based on vague and highly challengeable intelligence. The memoirs of Clare Short (minister for overseas development), who resigned from the Cabinet in protest at the lack of a UN mandate for the post-invasion occupation, constituted an attack on Blair's presidentialism and on New Labour's lack 'of respect for the truth', only for 'the danger of being caught out'. According to Short, the decision to support the invasion reflected Blair's 'hubristic pleasure in being the only world leader who could deal as an equal with the president of the US' (Short, 2004, 181, 272)

Both Bush and Blair had good reason to distrust Saddam's promises on WMD, but certainly had no reliable intelligence on the matter. While Saddam had certainly brought down certain destruction on his own head, the invasion was reckless, not least in the lack of preparation for a post-Saddam order in Iraq. Blair's closeness to Washington and his knowledge of American regime change objectives left him open to charges of bad faith. A leaked briefing paper, circulated to Blair, Hoon, Straw, MI6 chief Richard Dearlove and others on 23 July 2002, warned that Britain was already on board in an American drive to invade Iraq. Dearlove apparently referred to policy and intelligence now being 'fixed' around the certainty of American military action. London needed to 'create the conditions' to make regime change legal. In Blair's defence, however, it seems likely that Washington was not yet assuming that Britain would actually send forces: 'US plans assume, as a minimum, the use of British bases in Cyprus and Diego Garcia' (Meyer, 2005, 283; *The Sunday Times*, 1 May 2005). Further leaked documents on the run-up to war appeared in 2005. One showed the sharp increase in US–UK bombing of Iraq in mid-2002, despite both the insistence in London and Washington that peaceful resolution was still possible, and also despite Foreign and Commonwealth Office worries about their legality (Freedland, 2005).

Blair's decisions over the war are explicable, as indicated previously, primarily in terms of his own personal beliefs about the logic of the 'special relationship' and in terms of the convergence between his own liberal internationalism and the priorities of American neo-conservatives. The structures and generalized expectations of the 'special relationship' inclined London towards supporting the invasion, but did not determine Blair's choices. The prime ministerial decisions, moreover, were made with little reference to any institutionalized, bureaucratic foreign policy and defence channels. 1960s parallels are instructive. Harold Wilson, after all, resisted huge American pressure to commit troops to Vietnam, and actually in a context where the US enjoyed far greater power over Britain's economy than was the case in 2003. As in the 1960s, there was sympathy and understanding in Washington for a Labour leader's domestic political predicament. Rumsfeld, however disingenuously, did offer Blair a public way out of his dilemma in early March. Blair's decision was not indefensible, given the record of Saddam's evasions and crimes. In more prosaic terms, it should also be recalled that Blair went on to win another general election victory in 2005. In terms of the transatlantic balance sheet, however, it is difficult to see what concessions and policy shifts were extricated from Washington as a price of his support. Far from revealing the inherently determined nature of the US–UK war-making partnership, the Iraqi invasion may come to be seen by future British leaders, despite the 2005 election win, as a warning against excessive loyalty to American war agendas.

9

Britain, the United States and European Integration

American attitudes towards European integration have generally been positive. British reluctance to play a full and active part in an integrated Europe has been viewed in Washington as atavistic and unhelpful. For their part, British leaders have often seen the virtues of greater integration. The prospect of a splendidly isolated Britain, shut off from Europe and seeking desperately an economic home under the wing of Uncle Sam, is hardly an attractive one. The fact remains, however, that the 'special relationship' – especially British understandings of that relationship – has been a powerful force militating against enthusiastic Europeanism in the UK. However much Washington has proclaimed the contrary, the view persists that, somehow, Britain can choose between an Atlanticist and a Europeanized future.

As will become apparent in this chapter, European integration poses numerous and complex problems for US–UK relations. At one level, there is the long-standing American impatience with Britain's reluctant Europeanism. At another, there is the increasing extent to which, after 1973, Anglo-American relations have been conducted in the context of integrated European institutions: primarily economic, but also diplomatic, political and even military. American attitudes towards this new context become increasingly ambivalent. By the 1990s, Washington was seeking to balance its support for integration with accelerating anxiety about possible dangers posed by galloping integration. At the end of this chapter, and in the final chapter of this book, we will consider some of these implications of post-Cold War European integration.

This chapter is mainly concerned, however, with the history of European unity, as it has affected Anglo-American relations, since 1960. Britain's political elites have tended to look eastwards for prosperity, and westwards for security. Bargains with Europe over prosperity, and with the US over security, have both compromised British sovereignty. The US-UK side of the US-UK-European triangle, however, is not entirely dominated by security issues. Britain has long had substantial economic links with the US and, as noted in an earlier chapter, partakes of what Andrew Gamble (2003) calls 'the Anglo-American model of capitalism'. This chapter begins with an assessment of US–UK economic relations, and then proceeds to a consideration of Britain's post-1960 role in Europe and its implications for the 'special relationship'.

Asymmetry and Interdependence

Two features of the US–UK economic relationship cannot fail to strike the most casual observer: asymmetry and the increasing Europeanization of British economic priorities. In the era of the Cold War, Britain was but one economic actor in the liberal economic order set up by the United States after the Second World War. Between the era of the Vietnam War and the early 1990s, intense speculation focused on evidence for American decline. However, by the turn of the century, with the former USSR in economic turmoil and East Asia in crisis, the US basked in prosperity. Between 1990 and 1998, consumer buying power in the US rose some 23 per cent. The Clinton administration paraded its success in fiscal deficit reduction. 'All business' productivity rates for the mid-1990s revealed a 15 per cent US lead over Germany and France, a 42 per cent lead over Japan and a 27 per cent lead over Britain (Dent 1997, 138). To British financial journalist Hamish McRae, the UK appeared 'a subcontractor to the great American growth machine' (*The Independent*, 22 July 1999). Doubts remained over aspects of the American economic outlook, especially regarding education, savings levels and capital market structure. However, the US position at the century's end was one of extraordinary power, and constituted an effective rebuttal to notions of inevitable decline. Above all, the US remained able, as it really had been ever since the late 1940s, to dictate the terms of much international economic activity. As Stephen Gill wrote in 1988: 'the sheer size and weight of the US within the international system substantially affects the psychological, cultural, economic and political conditions under which others must operate, not just their policy responses' (Gill, 1988, 5). America's undisputed lead in information technology innovation underscored this view of US economic hegemony. The era of President Bush's War on Terror was punctuated by fears of sluggish performance rooted in a series of long-term difficulties: low savings levels; record current account deficits; oil price rises; political and economic uncertainty associated with turbulence in the Middle East. Economic resilience remained a feature of the US economy in the middle years of the first decade of the new century. *The Economist* (10 December 2005, 54) noted: 'someone plainly forgot to tell the economy that it was in trouble'.

Set against this, Britain appeared an economic dwarf, operating within a European context. By the early 1980s, it was clear that economic growth in the UK had trailed behind that in other major capitalist countries for over a century. Relative decline became particularly intense after 1945. Between 1960 and 1973, the average annual growth rate in the US was 4 per cent, compared to 3.2 per cent in Britain. The same figures for the economically troubled period of 1974–83 were 1.8 and 1.1; and for 1984–94, 2.9 and 2.4. Underlining Britain's move to Europe, the proportion of UK exports going to European Union countries grew from below 30 per cent in 1970 to over 50 per cent in 1994 (Harrington, 1996).

Other statistical indicators, however, paint a slightly more complex picture. The UK share of world trade remained fairly constant, at around 5.3 per cent, between the mid-1970s and mid-1990s. Reflecting the continued importance of home demand in stimulating the American economy, the US share rose from 11.8 to only 12.4 per cent (Johnes and Taylor, 1996, 31). Throughout the post-1960 era, despite increasing British Europeanization, the US and UK remained substantial trade partners. In 1955, 7.1 per cent of UK exports went to America; in 1994, the figure was 12.4 per cent. In 1955, 10.9 per cent of imports came from the US; by 1994, the figure had risen to 11.8 (Green, 1996, 357). Throughout the post-1960 period, around 10 per cent of British industry has been owned by US corporations. By the late 1980s, it was estimated that American firms paid around 13 per cent of the British workers' pay bill (Grayling and Langdon, 1988, 174). In 1992, some 624 US-owned manufacturing firms operated in Britain (compared to 838 in 1983). They employed 47.8 per cent of Britons working in the foreign-owned manufacturing sector (Sawyer, 1996, 234). Throughout the 1990s, there was more American investment in the UK than in the entire Asia-Pacific region. British investment in the US accelerated hugely after the lifting of exchange controls in 1979. By 1986, UK investment in the US stood at 51.4 billion dollars, twice as much as the figure for Japan. By century's end, the UK remained the leading foreign investor in the US (Burns, 1997, 27). British financial institutions also held significant proportions of America's international debt.

The familiarity of most British people with Microsoft computer technology and with US-based fast food underscores the America's economic impact in the UK. Such an impact is nothing very new. In the late 1980s, Grayling and Langdon (1988, 170) observed:

> On a typical day the average Briton will breakfast on American cereal, like shredded wheat or cornflakes, made by Nabisco or Kellogg, perhaps washed down with a mug of Maxwell House coffee (part of General Foods) or a glass of American-produced Florida orange juice. The British may be wearing blue jeans made by Wrangler or Levi Strauss. The family car is likely to be American – a Vauxhall or a Ford – and even the petrol could come from one of the three big American firms: Esso, Mobil and Texaco.

British awareness of American economic penetration has been lessened to the degree to which some US-originated firms are seen as genuinely transnational. Ford is actually one of the few multinational corporations which is, arguably, organized on a genuinely transnational basis. However, as was evident in the Westland affair of 1986, American involvement in the UK economy has occasionally erupted into a major political dispute. The US role in developing North Sea oil resources, along with the increasing importance of information technology, has also intensified awareness in Britain about American involvement and leadership.

In the US, significant political forces have been mobilized against excessive foreign direct investment. Inward investment increased sixfold between 1980 and 1991. Rather extraordinarily, however, the big political and journalistic guns were turned on Japan and the 'Japan lobby' rather than on Britain. Hanson Trust, a major British investor in the US, actually ran an advertising campaign in the late 1980s based on the perception that most Americans presumed it to be a US company. American insouciance about British penetration may be linked to the 'special relationship' and to generally positive appraisals of the UK. In 1981, David Yankelovich and Larry Kaagan (1981, 696) noted how Americans felt 'bullied by OPEC' and 'out-traded by Japan'. Similar resentments were highly unlikely to extend to the UK. Britain's American penetration has, like the Japanese incursions into Hollywood in the 1980s, occasionally been high-profile; an example was the 1987 take-over of the J. Walker Thompson advertising agency. They have not, however, tended to result in the future of large numbers of American jobs depending upon decisions made in London.

The early years of the twenty-first century actually saw a heightening of mutual US–UK economic activity. While over 50 per cent of UK trade in the first years of the new century remained with the European Union, in 2004 the UK exported 46 billion dollars worth of goods and services to the United States. The reciprocal US to UK figure was 36 billion, giving Britain a substantial trade surplus with America. British investment in the US in 2004 was at a level of approximately 252 billion dollars. The figure for US investment in the UK was roughly 303 billion dollars. Britain was the largest foreign investor in the US and *vice versa*. The economic policies directed by Chancellor of the Exchequer Gordon Brown provided a positive framework for close US–UK economic relations. A Congressional Research Service study in 2005 noted : 'US exporters and investors are attracted to the UK because of the common language, similar legal framework and business practices, relatively low rates of taxation and inflation, and access to the EU market' (Archik, 2005, 21).

European Integration

Macmillan to Heath

Between 1947 and the beginning of the Kennedy presidency, the US gave strong support to the concept of European integration. The Marshall Plan, launched in 1947, led to the setting up of the Organisation for Economic Cooperation and Development. Paul Hoffman, who supervised the administration of Marshall aid, called in 1949 for a 'single large market' in Western Europe (Bainbridge,

1998, 444). Despite some early worries about the formation of a Western European trading cartel, American leaders continued to support the idea, increasingly in the context of anti-communist Atlanticism. In 1961, President Kennedy told Chancellor Konrad Adenauer of West Germany: 'It is best for the Atlantic Community if the United Kingdom joined the EEC [European Economic Community] on an unconditional basis' (*Foreign Relations of the US, 1961–63*, vol. 13, 1986, 6, 'memorandum of conversation, Kennedy-Adenauer', 13 April 1961). In July 1962, he declared: 'We do not regard a strong and united Europe as a rival but as a partner. To aid its progress has been the object of our foreign policy for 17 years' (*Public Papers of the Presidents ... John F. Kennedy, 1962*, 1964, 538 (4 July 1961)).

Geir Lundestad (1998) traces US support for European integration to five factors. First, European integration was seen as in the tradition of American federalism. Secondly, integration was seen to further the cause of political and economic rational efficiency. Thirdly, European integration might ease America's defence burden. British policy makers were consistently worried that defence integration might speed US withdrawal from Europe – 'letting them off the hook', as British diplomat Roger Makins called it in the late 1940s (H. Young, 1998, 75) Some Americans also looked to economic benefits from trade with a strong Europe. Fourthly, and unsurprisingly, European integration was seen as furthering the cause of anti-Soviet containment. Lastly, and especially strong in the early years of integration though far from entirely absent thereafter, was the perceived need to contain Germany. In May 1961, Prime Minister Macmillan was informed by JFK: 'We believe that only with growing political coherence in Western Europe can we look to a stable solution of the peace of Germany' (*Foreign Relations of the US, 1961–63*, vol.13, 1986, 20, 'telegram from the Department of State to the Embassy in the United Kingdom', 23 May 1961).

We have already encountered some of these points in the discussion in Chapter 7 of the European multilateral nuclear force proposals in the Kennedy and Johnson years. The MLF advocates represented part of what Pascaline Winand (1993; 1997, 164) has called 'a network of American and European friends and colleagues' who ' "co-inspired" to further the cause of European integration'. The European project could not be sunk so easily as the MLF's mixed-nationality fleet.

Harold Macmillan's own, highly pragmatic, commitment to Europe was profoundly influenced by American pressure. Leo Pliatzsky (1982, 45), leading Treasury civil servant, attributed his 'conversion to Europe' to his 'failure to gain a niche in history by acting as a bridge between the American and Russian superpowers'. By 1960, Macmillan seems to have accepted that a 'new' foreign policy, a European future, still articulated in terms of the 'special relationship', was inevitable. Pressure from JFK, exercised primarily in the person of George Ball, left him in no doubt about where Washington saw London as fitting into its European 'grand design'. Kennedy was not unworried about European protectionism, but saw Britain's entry as a way of alleviating it. And only full entry would do; the US would not be recruited in support of the 'outer seven' solution: the European Free Trade Area. EFTA grew out of the work of a committee chaired by Reginald Maudling, President of the Board of Trade. It derived from British counter-proposals to plans for a West European customs union. Established by the 1960 Stockholm Treaty, EFTA's membership encompassed Austria, Denmark, Norway, Portugal, Sweden, Switzerland and the UK. It did not escape Washington's notice that, of these, at least two – Sweden and Switzerland – followed a declared foreign policy of neutrality. The US was no more impressed by British appeals to Commonwealth ties. (London's original counter to the customs union idea had been a European free trade area limited to manufactured goods. It wished to preserve Commonwealth preferential links in terms of agricultural trade.) David Ormsby-Gore reported from Washington in 1962 that it was 'a source of mystification to Americans that former colonies should be willing to maintain a special and close relationship with Britain'. The Kennedy administration was 'quite openly opposed to many of our ideas for solving the Commonwealth problem in the context of our membership of the European Economic Community'. Ormsby-Gore noted that the US was not, however, reluctant to mobilize the Commonwealth against the influence of communism (FO 371 161648, Ormsby-Gore to Earl of Home, 3 April 1962).

By mid-1961, Macmillan had abandoned the idea of attempting to negotiate a full-scale EFTA entry into the EEC. A simple UK application for membership was proffered. Ormsby-Gore offered a detailed commentary as negotiations continued throughout 1962. The US had 'a heavy stake in the success of the negotiations'. The

Americans 'know as well, if not better than, ourselves how difficult the French can be. They have deep-seated suspicions of possible German domination of the Six'. (The original six members of the European Coal and Steel Community, later the European Economic Community, were France, Belgium, Italy, Luxembourg, the Netherlands and West Germany). Ormsby-Gore repeated the view that European integration might encourage the US to remove European forces to the Pacific. However, the application should be pressed: 'the least reaction we must expect in the United States, should we elect to remain outside the Common Market, is perplexity and disappointment, and an unhelpful neutrality towards the consequences of our decision'. Washington 'would be unlikely to accept failure as final and before long their salvage engineers would be at the scene of the wreck' (FO 371 162648, as above).

Ambassador David Bruce, George Ball and other American 'Europeanists' were sensitive to the charge that they were bullying Britain into action on Europe. In May 1961, Bruce warned Ball of the dangers of stoking British resentment. Ball, however, was still unhappy about what he saw as Macmillan's attempting to 'slide sideways' into Europe (Dobson, 1991b, 85–6). Pressure was applied to the Six to facilitate Britain's entry, while the 1962 Trade Expansion Act gave Kennedy leeway to negotiate tariff reductions with an integrated Europe. Worries about British resentment were reflected in American reassurances to London that diplomatic closeness would continue. They may also have been reflected in the generous Polaris deal of late 1962. Shortly after the Nassau conference, in January 1963, General de Gaulle vetoed British entry. He resolved, in Frank Costigliola's words, 'not to admit the Americans' front man'. Though 'the French shared the Americans' opposition to the Commonwealth preference and the EFTA', de Gaulle 'sought a reborn Carolingian empire', not an anti-communist alliance fashioned by Washington (Costigliola, 1984b, 238; Bange, 2000).

The American salvage engineers could not refloat the wreck. Washington appreciated the role played by Polaris in influencing the French decision. The Americans were also sympathetic to what later became termed the 'Summer argument': the view that Macmillan prevaricated during 1962 and might have closed the deal before the Cuban missile crisis and Polaris intervened. President Lyndon Johnson was not so clearly an advocate of integrated Europeanism as his predecessor had been. As a senator, however, he had listened to Jean Monnet in Paris in 1960; LBJ later told journalists that Monnet was 'a great man' (Winand, 1997, 169). In 1966, he announced: 'Every lesson of the past and every prospect for the future argue that the nations of Western Europe can only fulfil their proper role in the world community if increasingly they act together' (*Public Papers of the Presidents ... Lyndon Johnson*, 1966, 1967, 477 (3 May 1966)). The Johnson administration looked to an Atlanticized integrated Europe. It also became increasingly preoccupied with narrower economic questions. The US succeeded in reducing tariffs on industrial goods in the Kennedy Round of GATT (General Agreement on Tariffs and Trade) talks. It remained concerned, however, about the protectionist implications of the EEC Common Agricultural Policy, and saw UK entry as a way of easing these worries. A paper put before the British Cabinet in the final months of the Tory government in 1964 argued that, especially 'if European unity proceeds on the basis of the Six only', the EEC and the US 'may fall out with each other'. However, its author, Sir Con O'Neill (ambassador to the European Community) concluded:

> I find it hard to see an effective future for the United Kingdom unless we can establish a satisfactory relationship with the Community, at all events as long as the Community continues to develop and to maintain even reasonable relations with the United States.
>
> He also recorded the view that 'the Community has almost succeeded by stealth, in achieving what Napoleon and Hitler failed to achieve by force: a Europe united without Britain and therefore against her'. (CAB 118 (part 2) 96, O'Neill to R. A. Butler, 25 July 1964)

For the Labour leadership at this time, 'a satisfactory relationship' did not mean membership. Hugh Gaitskell had opposed the 1961 application. Harold Wilson in the early 1960s was also an anti-integrationist. Richard Crossman (1963, 743), a leading figure in the then Labour opposition, wrote for an American audience in 1963: 'Surely it is a good thing that one of Britain's two great parties is still passionately convinced that this country has a future – outside the Common Market.' The 1964 and 1966 Labour manifestos were ambiguous about membership and emphasized the importance of Commonwealth ties. Shortly after Wilson's second general election, in April 1966, Cecil King, *Daily Mirror* chairman, recorded a conversation with the prime minister: 'About Europe, he said he thought we should be in in two or three years' (H. Young 1998, 187).

How far was Wilson's conversion due to American pressure? Hugo Young (1998, 222) deplored what he saw as Wilson's 'cringing submission to Lyndon Johnson'. George Ball was still urging Britain to 'sign the Treaty of Rome with no ifs and buts' (Ziegler, 1993, 241). In November 1966, President Johnson told Wilson: 'Your entry would certainly help to strengthen the West.' The US would contribute 'anything we might do to smooth your path' (Ziegler, 1993, 332). Yet this was not quite JFK's 'grand design'. As Ambassador Patrick Dean reported to Foreign Secretary Brown in January 1967, 'The days of Grand Designs and American nostrums like the MLF for European diseases appear to be over.' LBJ was preoccupied with reconciling the needs of the Great Society with those of the Vietnam War. He tended, according to Dean, to think in less grandiose terms than JFK and 'to judge the value of United States-European relations in terms of the benefits which they bring to United States national interests' (FCO 7 769, P. Dean to G. Brown, 23 Jan. 1967). Wilson was arguably subjected to as much, or more, American pressure to send British troops to Vietnam as to enter the EEC. US–UK interactions over European integration were only part of the complex mix of issues which swirled around Wilson's relationship with Washington: issues ranging from Rhodesia, to devaluation, to the German offset. Rather than American pressure per se, what seems to have convinced Wilson of the wisdom of renewing the bid to enter the Community was the economic argument. Britain's economic future seemed to depend on close European relations. As the Wilson government did its sums, Britain's imperial legacy seemed far more of a burden than an asset which could be developed. Wilson was generally regarded as a 'Commonwealth man'. He also once famously defended a British presence in the Indian Ocean in terms of the inadvisability of leaving it 'to the Americans and Chinese, eyeball to eyeball, to face this thing out' (Ziegler, 1993, 219). By 1966, however, the Rhodesian issue had cast a shadow over the Commonwealth's future, while, in more general terms, Britain's absence from the Community appeared increasingly unappealing.

The real problem, as both London and Washington acknowledged, was de Gaulle. In January 1967, Brown and Wilson visited the Six in preparation for that year's entry bid. They deliberately sought to convince their interlocutors that Britain was breaking loose from the US. In Strasbourg, Wilson denounced 'an industrial helotry under which we in Europe produce only the conventional apparatus of a modern economy, while becoming increasingly dependent on American business for the sophisticated apparatus which will call the industrial tune in the 70s and 80s'. In Wilson's account of their meeting, de Gaulle even acknowledged that 'things had changed' in regard to British subservience to the US (H. Wilson, 1971, 334, 336). De Gaulle still objected, however, to Anglo-American monetary cooperation, indeed to the whole Bretton Woods system, and issued his second veto on British entry to the EEC in May 1967.

Acute insights into British thinking about the intersection of Europeanism and the 'special relationship' emerge from Ambassador Dean's report of January 1967. Surveying various plans, including those advanced by Senator Jacob Javits of New York, for transatlantic free trade, Dean concluded:

> A weak Britain, whether going it alone or seeking some closer (and necessarily subordinate) special link with the United States in an English Speaking Union, or an Atlantic Free Trade Area of the Javits pattern, is likely to cost the Americans more than it is worth. A strong Britain within a European Community will, it is hoped, be a net asset even if we do not choose to act (as the Americans would not expect us to act) as a 'trojan horse' and if the policies of the Community to which we belong diverge from those of the United States. The Americans have sufficient confidence in us to believe that we can keep Western Europe on the tracks, but not enough to believe that they can continue to derive net benefit from our partnership with them if we remain outside Europe. (FCO 7 769, P. Dean to G. Brown, 23 Jan. 1967)

Following the 1967 rebuff, it seemed as if further progress would have to await de Gaulle's departure from the political stage. A 1968 Cabinet paper noted that the general's 'anti-Americanism clearly worried the Germans' (CAB 129 136, 23 Feb. 1968). A series of shifts in scene and personnel prepared the way for British entry into the Community in January 1973.

From British Entry to the End of the Cold War

Charles de Gaulle retired from politics in 1969, following the domestic student and labour activism of 1968. In 1970, Edward

Heath, leading Tory Europeanist and veteran of the Macmillan era entry negotiations, became Britain's leader. British opinion remained divided over the virtues of entry. However, by 1970 there was at least something approaching a consensus that the falling away of Britain's options – collapse of empire, East of Suez withdrawals, the failure of the Commonwealth to cohere and develop, continued economic difficulties – pointed to a commitment to Europe. As John Young has argued (1993, 174): 'Entry to the EC did *not* mean the abandonment of traditional policies, it was a reaction to their collapse.' The damage caused to the 'special relationship' by devaluation and by Wilson's failure to commit troops to Vietnam actually enhanced the prospects for a successful British entry bid. Henry Kissinger recalled Heath's conduct in Washington in 1970: 'he wished neither to negotiate Common Market issues bilaterally with us nor to appear – on, for that matter, to be – America's Trojan Horse in Europe' (Kissinger, 1979, 937). Not least in importance, President Nixon's destruction of the Bretton Woods system in 1971, ironically initially opposed by Heath's government, removed a traditional French objection to British entry. It was no longer possible to argue that the very structure of the international financial system enshrined a coordinated US–UK dominance.

The Nixon-Kissinger years saw a reappraisal of elite American attitudes towards European union. In 1969, before he became Nixon's National Security Adviser, Kissinger wrote: 'We have sought to combine a supranational Europe with a closely integrated Atlantic Community under American leadership. These objectives are likely to prove incompatible' (Kissinger 1969, 30). Nixon's speeches on Europe began to reflect domestic anxieties about burden sharing. In 1974, he announced that the Europeans 'cannot have the United States' participation and cooperation on the security front and then proceed to have confrontation and even hostility on the economic and political front' (*Public Papers of the Presidents ... Richard M Nixon, 1974* (1975, 276)). While Washington remained in favour of European integration, it developed in this period a new scepticism about supranationalism in Europe which made the Kennedy 'grand design' seem very far away.

Washington's new distancing from the processes of European integration suited the purposes of the Heath government. Heath further assured French President Georges Pompidou in 1970 'that there could be no special partnership between Britain and the

United States even if Britain wanted it, because one was barely a quarter the size of the other'. He reassured Pompidou that Britain would be prepared 'to defend European interests in the face of likely economic and political onslaughts from outside' – including the US (Heath 1998, 364). Soon after entry, Heath pressed for the Community to adopt a common external policy towards the US.

The entry negotiations, though complex and difficult, were eased by Heath's acceptance both of the Treaty of Rome as it stood and of the current operation of the Common Agricultural Policy. From January 1973, Britain was a Community member, and the context of US–UK relations radically altered.

President Jimmy Carter in the late 1970s proclaimed himself a strong supporter of greater integration. A strong, united Europe was a precondition of the 'trilateralism' (a new capitalist world balance between the US, Japan and Western Europe) favoured in the early years of the Carter administration. As foreign secretary and as prime minister, James Callaghan presented himself as a salesman for Carter's plans for international economic cooperation. In March 1974, Callaghan told the House of Commons: 'I must emphasise that we repudiate the view that a united Europe will emerge only out of a process of struggle against America' (Central Office of Information, 1975, 58). He held to this line in his dealings with Britain's EC partners. Even in the Carter years, however, US-EC trade disputes, notably over textiles, did occur.

Such disputes increased in number and severity during the 1980s. US interest rates, rising deficits and anti-Sovietism opened further rifts between America and Europe. As we have seen, London did not always side with the US in these transatlantic storms, yet the Thatcher-Reagan friendship was strong enough to weather them. London was not, in this period, subjected to significant pressure to be more European-minded. Indeed, European integration in the 1980s developed out of a feeling of hostility to the US, rather than as part of any American 'grand design' (George, 1994, 169). Thatcher and Reagan exchanged anecdotes concerning the lunacy of the Common Agricultural Policy. When Margaret Thatcher delivered her anti-integrationist Bruges speech in 1988, Secretary of State George Shultz commented: 'She's trying to have an impact on the shape of [Europe], and a lot of things that she's battling for have sense in them' (G. Smith, 1990, 249). Britain's leader was always careful to link her Euroscepticism with a stout defence of American leadership in NATO. Following Reagan's departure from the White House, there was a rapid switch in Washington's tone. During 1989, both President Bush and Secretary of State James Baker made strong public commitments to the acceleration of European integration. The US was now looking to a post-Cold War Atlantic architecture and to the 'containment' of a unified Germany. Margaret Thatcher, of course, held that a 'united Europe would augment, not check, the power of a united Germany' (Thatcher, 1993, 784.) In a fairly clear reference to Reagan's attitudes, Bush himself spoke of the 'absurdity' of future historians attributing 'the demise of the Western alliance to disputes over beef hormones and wars over pasta' (Lundestad, 1998, 10–11).

This section will conclude with a consideration of three themes in the post-1970 history of Europeanized US–UK relations between accession and the end of the Cold War: the changing economic relationship between the US and Europe, developing political and defence relations, and the link between the 'special relationship' and British attitudes towards Europe. At the heart of the first of these themes is the fact of greatly increased economic interdependence. By the early 1990s, over 18 per cent of European Community imports came from the US, while 16.8 per cent of exports from the EC went to the United States. By 1989, about one third of service exports from the US went to the EC. Over half of foreign direct investment in the US came from the EC, much of it, of course, from Britain (Archer and Butler, 1996, 191). Two-way trade and investment, including sales accruing from investment, was valued at over one trillion dollars in 1990. Alongside growing interdependence went the trade disputes. Kevin Featherstone and Roy Ginsberg (1996, 115, 168–9) identified 15 major disputes between Britain's accession and 1990. The majority were settled following punitive action. (The Featherstone-Ginsberg list included the Soviet natural gas pipeline dispute of 1981–2 and rows over Spanish and Portuguese accession. It also included US complaints over EC subsidies on wheat flour and canned fruit, and EC complaints about US cuts in European steel imports.)

It is difficult to generalize about Britain's role in these disputes. Most of them involved, in some form or another, the Common Agricultural Policy, of which the UK was a consistent critic. Often, for example in the context of aviation diplomacy, British negotiators sought bilateral contacts with the US, even when American negotiators preferred to operate on an integrated European basis. Following the 1974 Trade Act, the US became increasingly prepared to take unilateral action in respect of what were regarded as unfair European trade practices. According to Smith and Woolcock (1993, 51), for ' "unfair trade" practices' one might read 'systemic differences'. Such action generally emanated from the US Congress, often associated with amendments bearing the name of Congressman Richard Gephardt of Missouri. The Reagan administration, however, was sympathetic to more aggressive use of trade law. The fear of an economic 'fortress Europe' in this period reinforced the Reagan administration's disquiet about European supranationalism. As European institutions geared up to the launch of the single market in 1992, US negotiators frequently voiced fears of being excluded from rule drafting, of having no say in the establishment of new reciprocity standards between the US and Europe (Colchester and Buchan, 1990, 195–7). Again, in many respects, Britain was sympathetic to US worries. However, since 1973, the UK has, at least formally and often wholeheartedly, stood on the anti-American side of transatlantic trade disputes.

Our second theme concerns Britain's place in the developing foreign policy and defence relations between the US and an integrating Europe. Featherstone and Ginsberg discovered that between 1973 and 1990, there were 20 major US–EC foreign policy disputes, mainly deriving either from the conflict in the Middle East or from the global anti-communism of the Reagan administration. Here, especially in relation to Reagan's Central American policies, the UK, of course, took a pro-American line. Data on bilateral contacts between US and European leaders (including ministerial contacts) revealed high levels of US–UK contact. During the years following 1973, however, US-West German contacts began to outnumber those between Washington and London (Featherstone and Ginsberg, 1996, 101, 104–5).

Writing in the early 1990s, and surveying events over the previous twenty years, former Labour Foreign Secretary David Owen recalled the consistent American view 'that the sooner the United Kingdom signed up for a United States of Europe the better':

> A glazed look would come over American diplomats and commentators
> if one as much as hinted that part of Britain's reluctance to sacrifice our
> independent foreign policy had its roots in history; that Britain's

refusal to countenance majority voting (in European institutions) was a necessary safeguard for their security and ours. (Owen, 1992, 806)

The US was certainly not sympathetic to the view that Britain, through some combination of history and the 'special relationship', might be allowed to shirk its European responsibilities. However, this is not equivalent to arguing that, following Britain's accession, the US was committed to the vision of supranationalism promoted by Jacques Delors (president of the European Commission from 1985 to 1995). The Nixon and Kissinger doubts have already been mentioned. Interestingly, James Callaghan recorded a reassurance given him by Kissinger during the Ford presidency. As the Wilson government renegotiated terms with the EEC prior to the 1975 referendum on continued British membership, Kissinger expressed his support for Britain in Europe. However, if the decision went the other way, we could 'be sure that the United States would do all it could to help Britain and to sustain the relationship between our two countries' (Callaghan, 1981, 319–20).

The main structural change between 1970 and 1990 was a move by the US away from 'guardianship' of the Atlantic system – including an integrating Europe – towards greater ambivalence about the economic and defence implications of Europeanism (Smith and Woolcock, 1993, 5). The post-1984 French efforts to revive the Western European Union, the defence arm of the European countries in NATO, stimulated particular American unease. In March 1985, Assistant Secretary of State Richard Burt warned the WEU membership that the US would not tolerate a repositioning of defence policy outside the framework and command structure of NATO (Lundestad, 1998, 111). Unsurprisingly, Margaret Thatcher endorsed Burt's view, though she was persuaded to take a slightly less hostile line to the French action by Foreign Secretary Geoffrey Howe and Defence Secretary Michael Heseltine. Howe later wrote of the difference between 'Margaret's instinctive reaction' and his own to 'the permanent British dilemma: how far are we, will we in the future be, wise to base our security on a transatlantic or on a European foundation?': (Howe, 1995, 387.) The characteristic American attitude was to berate Britain for lagging behind the integrationist project, while simultaneously questioning both the credibility and desirability of a European defence identity.

Our final theme in this section is the role which invocations of the 'special relationship' played in the quarter of a century or so after the UK's accession in forming British attitudes towards Europe. The European issue has long formed the central cross-cutting debate in British politics, throwing up all manner of paradoxes and strange allegiances. Conventional wisdom holds that the 'special relationship' is no alternative to integration in Europe. According to Anthony Barber (1996, 77), chancellor of the exchequer in the Heath government, 'the hard fact is that it is largely because of our membership of the European Union that we still count in Washington'. Yet attitudes towards the US have long affected, and continue to affect, British views on Europe. Anti-American attitudes have been associated with both pro- and anti-integrationist positions. In 1973, Tom Nairn (1973, 46) offered a leftist defence of Europeanism, and linked it to the desirability of escaping US domination:

> Whether and in what sense the Common Market stands for a 'capitalist conspiracy' of narrow nationalists or an Iron Heel of monopolists is a peculiarly debatable question. What really cannot be questioned at all is that there is a great – the greatest – capitalist power in close alliance with the British nation-state; that this power has exercised a virtual stranglehold over Britain's foreign policy.

Yet, during the 1975 referendum on British membership, many leftists in the 'No' campaign were convinced that their opponents were being funded by the Central Intelligence Agency (*Time*, 9 June 1975). The CIA had certainly bankrolled the European Movement, a British pro-integrationist group, in the 1950s. On the right, Enoch Powell interpreted British membership as an act of *subservience* to the US. In his view, Washington saw the EC as the 'political-economic counterpart to NATO' (Shepherd, 1997, 250). Surveying the 1975 campaigns, Anthony King (1977, 38) concluded that many 'anti-European moderates' had particular links either with the US or with the Commonwealth.

Following the referendum, arguments for and against greater integration tended to be based on issues of sovereignty and economic advantage, rather than on pro- or anti-Americanism. Nevertheless, the American argument sometimes surfaced: for example, in Margaret Thatcher's view that European defence integration was a threat to US leadership in NATO. Emotional invocations of English language ties also occasionally emerged. Peter Shore, Labour anti-integrationist, for example, once remarked: 'There are more people of European origin outside the continent of Europe than in the EC and they all speak English' (Radice, 1992, 164–5). Advocates of integration sometimes argued that the failure to achieve unity would be a sign to Washington that European countries cannot work together, and that the Atlantic alliance would be thereby weakened. Some anti-Europeanists in the Conservative Party argued in the 1990s that Britain should tie itself to America, the global economic hegemon, perhaps even applying to join the North American Free Trade Area . For Tory MP Michael Spicer, the whole European project reeked of anti-Americanism. For France, in particular, the European Union was 'about cocking a snoot at the Americans'. 'The only practical argument advanced by the supporters of the common European security policy', according to Spicer, 'is based upon the fact of withdrawal of US troops from Western Europe' (Spicer, 1992, 25, 73, 127).

After the Cold War

As indicated previously, the end of the Cold War prompted a major debate about the future of America's commitment to Europe. Could NATO survive the end of the Soviet threat? How long would public and congressional opinion in the US tolerate an expensive American military presence in Europe? How long would it be before the integrative momentum of European development came to countenance the exclusion of the US from Europe's diplomatic and military future? What was NATO *for*?

Against the argument that the US was bound to pull away from Europe was the demonstrable concern of American political elites to retain European leadership, almost as a 'test' of American internationalism. During the Bush Senior administration, Washington seemed to oppose the emergence of a clearly institutionalized European defence identity for fear of playing into the hands of domestic isolationism. Williams and Schaub (1995, 182) observed that official Washington had, since the Cold War ended, showed no signs of wishing to relinquish its European role: 'The main reason is that the NATO framework offers the United States a crucial seat at the table on European affairs – a seat that, even if it does not enable Washington to exert as much influence in the future as in the past, is irreplaceable.'

Publicly, the George H. W. Bush administration resumed the pre-Nixon American enthusiasm for European integration. Margaret Thatcher was horrified at the president's 1989 suggestion that 'the events of our time call for a continued, and perhaps intensified, effort by the Twelve to integrate' (P. Sharp, 1999, 209). On the economic front, the US position was bolstered by the settlement of various transatlantic disputes arising from the Single European Act, and by US achievement of a trade surplus with the EC. In early 1990, Washington achieved a newly regularized schedule of high-level US–EC consultations. The schedule was incorporated into the Transatlantic Declaration, negotiated by US Secretary of State James Baker and promulgated in November 1990. The Declaration listed rather vague 'common goals' and 'challenges'. The US and EC would, for example, work to strengthen the 'multilateral trading system'. Both would bear 'in mind the accelerating process by which the European Community is acquiring its own identity in economic and monetary matters, in foreign policy and in the domain of security' (Featherstone and Ginsberg, 1996, 295–7).

Despite (or in some senses because of) domestic uncertainty about NATO's future, Washington remained strongly committed to US leadership in NATO. The 'European defence identity' preferred by Washington, however, was, as indicated previously, clearly one in which Europe spent more, rather than enjoyed much greater decisional independence. In February 1991, the Bush administration issued the so-called 'Dobbins demarche' to European capitals. This was an expression of unease over any Western European Union or other European defence identity which was not clearly integrated into NATO structures of US leadership (Lundestad, 1998, 115). The warning was formally issued by Undersecretary Reginald Bartholomew and Assistant Secretary of State for European Affairs James Dobbins. Later, in November 1991, Bush himself referred directly and publicly to these issues: 'if, my friends, your ultimate aim is to provide independently for your own defense, the time to tell us is today' (Lundestad, 1998, 115; Hoffman, 1993). Such statements seemed to point Washington away from the concept of American 'followership': US willingness, especially in circumstances where European capitals might pick up more of their own defence bill, to accept European responses to (primarily) European security problems (Nye, 1993).

Washington's unwillingness to condone a de-Americanized NATO was very welcome in London. On non-security issues, however, the George H.W. Bush administration remained true to the goals of the 1990 Transatlantic Declaration. As Europe debated eventual monetary union in 1991, Bush declared firmly: 'A more united Europe offers the United States a more effective partner, prepared for larger responsibilities.' The 'historic steps towards economic and political union' made at Maastricht were publicly applauded by Bush in 1991 (Lundestad, 1998, 116).

The 1990–91 Maastricht deliberations on economic and political union unsurprisingly saw Britain as the most vigorous defender of Atlanticism in security issues. London succeeded in having statements about the centrality of the American security relationship written into the Maastricht Treaty. NATO would 'remain the essential forum' for European defence decisions. During the Maastricht negotiations, Britain joined Denmark and Portugal in favouring a clearly Atlanticist defence future, with decisions undertaken via intergovernmental negotiations. (France favoured a Europeanist future along intergovernmental lines, while Germany was more integrationist, but was prepared to admit a stronger role for NATO.) At the Maastricht European Council of December 1991, London effectively secured a postponement of any common defence policy. Various French and German positions, including the establishment of a European defence academy and of a common defence timetable, were shelved. NATO's Rome summit of November 1991 combined acceptance of European multinational forces 'in the context of an emerging European Defence Identity', with a commitment to Atlantic Alliance primacy (Blair, 1998, 97).

Throughout the mid-to-late 1990s, Washington continued to offer public support for a real European defence identity, linked of course to the survival of NATO as the 'primary institution'. Changing British attitudes were important here. A European Security and Defence Identity (ESDI) was not credible without a strong British commitment. In its early incarnation, however, the Blair government continued the traditional British suspicion of ESDI. By the end of 1998, however, London's position had shifted. The change reflected a reworking of views on the likely shape and pace of European defence integration, and the possibility of reinventing the 'Atlantic intermediary' role in the new climate. The British initiative was matched by a changing mood in Paris: a continuation of the new French warming to NATO and some diminution of French fears about US domination in the post-Cold War era. At the St Malo summit in December 1998, France and Britain agreed both that the European Union 'must have the capacity for autonomous action, backed up by credible military forces, the means to decide to use them, and the readiness to do so' and that 'the Atlantic Alliance is the foundation' of Europe's collective security (Walker, 1999, 28). This doctrine was adopted as NATO strategy at the 1999 Washington summit. European Commission President Romano Prodi indicated that the establishment of a new identity for European defence would be the main priority for his period in office. The 1999 Cologne summit of European powers approved the appointment of Javier Solana as the first integrated European foreign policy leader. At last there would be 'someone to answer the phone' when Washington called (Medley, 1999, 18). At century's end, the rush to military integration was evident. Solana's first job appeared to be the fusing of the Western European Union with the European Union itself. The Helsinki summit of December 1999 left it to a summit, to be held in Paris one year on, to see the EU provided with its own integrated military organisation.

Blair's switch to enthusiasm for ESDI was accompanied by some characteristic glances over his shoulder towards Washington. Important here has been British support for a Rapid Reaction Corps. This body would be both more mobile and more genuinely pan-European than the Eurocorps. In late 1998, Britain suggested that it might number around 40 000. Blair's line was that the RRC would be suitable for efforts approved by the US administration, but lacking direct support by US public and congressional opinion. 'In other words,' as *The Economist* (20 November 1999) reported, 'a more robust Europe would be doing America a sort of favour.'

The Rapid Reaction Corps was designed in part to remedy the weaknesses in European defence, and abject dependence on the US, exposed during the Kosovo campaign of 1999. European air power was not only incapable of leading the bombing campaign; European nations also found themselves stretched to supply peacekeeping forces in the war's later stages. Generally, however, the problems of European defence so clearly revealed in 1999 served to ignite the fuse of military reform and integration. The Cologne summit accepted the need to repair deficiencies in EU 'intelligence, strategic transport and command and control'. Blair himself wrote in the *New York Times:* 'We need to identify the gaps in our capability and plug them. We need to do more to plan our defense together at a

European rather than a national level ... We need to reconstruct our forces together and make sure spending on defense matches the need' (Medley, 1999, 21).

Britain's argument, that European defence spending should be both increased and reoriented towards procurement and research, could hardly fail to find a welcome in Washington. American worries attached rather to the concept of 'autonomy' and to the possibility of NATO being superseded as the 'primary institution' of European defence. And, indeed, not only defence; the Kosovo conflict involved a redefinition of NATO roles, beyond strictly defined defence, and towards 'out-of-area' policing. The US was also very concerned about the position of NATO allies (notably Turkey) who were not, or not yet, members of the European Union. The Blair government's stance on military integration was designed to meet these various worries, thereby prolonging and transforming the 'Atlantic intermediary' role.

The early Blair period saw a series of economic disputes, inevitably involving Britain, between the US and the EU. The Blair government's caution on monetary union primarily reflected both the ambivalence of British domestic opinion on the issue and a desire to observe the process in action before making irretrievable commitments. To some extent, however, the policy also reflected the perceived need to weigh and take account of evolving American concerns. Blair's domestic defence of Europeanism involved the clear statement that Britain must stop seeing the future in terms of a choice between Europe and America. A joint 1999 statement from Blair and Gordon Brown described the need for any such choice as a 'myth': 'It is clear that Britain in Europe enjoys greater success in America and elsewhere than Britain apart from Europe ever would' (*The Independent*, 14 October 1999).

Britain, European Integration and the Post-9/11 Transatlantic Rift

The transatlantic rifts of the early years of the twenty-first century have already been surveyed in some detail. Some commentators have made the point that the quarrels between Washington and London on the one hand, and Paris, in particular, on the other, was to some degree manufactured (MacShane, 2006). According to

Clare Short: 'The vilification of France and the misrepresentation of its position was the fig-leaf for the failure' of the second UN resolution on Iraq, specifically endorsing military action in February/ March 2003 (Short, 2004, 229). As noted in the previous chapter, London and Washington did seek concertedly to blame French intransigence for the confusions and bitterness that attended the run-up to the invasion. However, the rifts were real and profound. They were not even simply about policy. In a sense they were existential, with a considerable literature emerging on the roots, nature and likely future for two continents so clearly at odds with one another (Judt, 2005; Kagan, 2003; Rifkin, 2004).

Blair's attempts to balance US–UK 'special relations' with his commitment to Europe occasionally bordered on the desperate. A reasoned attempt to explain and resolve his dilemma was made in a speech delivered to a conference of British ambassadors in January 2003, some two months before the invasion of Iraq. Describing anti-Americanism as 'foolish indulgence', he defended the alliance with Washington in terms not only of the sharing of values, but also because of the advantages which it bestowed on Britain: 'Bluntly, there are not many countries who wouldn't wish for the same relationship as we have with the US and that includes most of the ones most critical of it in public' (Geddes, 2004, 91). According to Blair's analysis, the United Kingdom's influence in, and commitment to, Europe are enhanced by the 'special relationship'; London brings its special relations, particularly its special defence relations, to the European bargaining table.

Tony Blair's 'transatlantic bridge' leverage in defence matters was arguably illustrated in his first meeting with President George W. Bush at the so-called 'Colgate summit' in February 2001. Blair secured American approval for the St Malo defence integration agenda, provided it did not sideline NATO. As something of a *quid pro quo*, Blair reaffirmed UK willingness to assist the US in its National/Ballistic Missile Defence programme, with the agreement also that some kind of negotiations be opened with Russia over the Anti-ballistic Missile Treaty (Seldon, 2004, 612). (The ABM Treaty, an obvious obstacle to the American missile defence initiative, was abrogated by the US later in 2001). On European defence more generally, the post-9/11 transatlantic rows greatly increased the momentum, if not the credibility, of ESDI. US Secretary of Defense Donald Rumsfeld's denunciations of irresponsible Europeanism served only to encourage it further; as did General Henry Shelton's quip that Europeans were meeting their defence obligations by sending their boys to assist old ladies to cross busy roads in Pristina; (this as the EU was edging towards its first operational deployment in Bosnia) (*The Guardian*, 11 February 2002).

NATO was more or less ignored by Washington in the immediate aftermath of 9/11 (Vlasek, 2001–2); the European Union, however, as a transnational institution with ambitions extending beyond the arena of economics, seemed to play no part whatsoever even in Washington's medium to long-term reaction. President Chirac of France argued that Europe must develop as a counter-hegemon to the US, a view very different from Blair's commitment to making Europe 'a proper strategic partner' to the US (Goodhart, 2002, 18). In February 2005, Chancellor Schroeder of Germany indicated that 'NATO is no longer the primary venue where transatlantic partners discuss and co-ordinate strategies' (*The Economist*, 26 February 2005, 48). By early 2005, both NATO and the EU were developing rapid reaction forces. Blair's insistence that EU defence integration should and would complement, not rival, NATO really failed to square this particular circle, though the intra-European strength of the British military did lend weight to his Atlanticist case. The new EU members from East and Central Europe tended also to back the UK line, as did, less reliably, Italy and the Netherlands. Even more damaging to the Chiaracist agenda was its sheer implausibility in military terms. In 2002, Michael Clarke and Paul Cornish argued: 'In both NATO and the EU the Europeans are struggling: struggling to meet the defence commitments they have already undertaken; struggling to develop a genuinely multifaceted approach to the new security challenges we all face, terrorist and otherwise; and struggling to remain relevant to a determined US which will not put alliance unity ahead of other national needs as Washington interprets them' (Clarke and Cornish, 2002, 786). The EU itself lacks both a strategic concept and even a basic military capability. EU forces are not geared towards power projection. 'Combat support capabilities (particularly airlift, sealift, and air-to-air refuelling), precision-guided munitions, command and control, interoperable secure communications, and intelligence are among the chronic deficiencies of European military organizations' (Oudraat, 2004, 181).

Post-9/11 transatlantic rows also broke out over policy towards China, especially regarding the European desire to resume arms sales in defiance of the embargo. Throughout 2005, London appeared to be in favour of lifting the embargo, while linking it to a strengthened EU export control regime (Archik, 2005, 18). Conflicting US-European perspectives on China reflected a difference of outlook: the US tending to focus on Chinese military advancement, Europe on the need to assist and (if possible) control wider Chinese adjustment to global power (Shambaugh, 2005). As in all these debates about competing transatlantic outlooks and cultures, however, US-European difference often centres on issues of interest and power. With no strategic interest in Asia, the EU tends inevitably to focus on trade. As Richard Bernstein (2005) put it: 'The Europeans know and can count on the fact that whatever the consequences of its decision on arms to China, the responsibility to deal with them will be left to America alone'.

Blair's exposed position on the wobbling Atlantic bridge was made a little easier by the second term George W. Bush administration's efforts to mend at least some US-European fences. London took the opportunity of the EU dialogue with Teheran, part of the European effort to effect a peaceful resolution of the Iranian nuclear proliferation crisis, to distance itself from any further direct military action in the region. In the post-9/11 era, as before, US-EU trade disputes continued. London continued to support the US trade liberalization agenda, but naturally continued to develop trade policies within the EU framework. Disputes arose, for example, over (US and European) government subsidies to civil aircraft production and over EU bans on genetically modified food production. Even in these various trade disputes, problems were frequently traced to differing value systems. A Congressional Research Service study in 2004 noted: 'disputes now involve clashes in domestic values, priorities, and regulatory systems where the international rules of the road are inadequate to provide a sound basis for effective and timely dispute resolution' (Ahearn, 2004, 3). The putative 'values debate' also underpinned rifts (again, actually as much traceable to interests as to values) over climate change at the Montreal negotiations in December 2005.

The debate over the transatlantic rifts that occurred during the junior Bush's presidency will be taken up again in this book's concluding chapter. The present chapter will end simply with a reminder of the extreme uncertainty of the entire European future. In 2005–6, with the rejection of the constitutional treaty – a treaty which, whatever its uncertainties and ambiguities would have enhanced European foreign policy identity – the EU's future became impossible to predict. The assumption that the new Eastern members (Romania and Bulgaria are also due to join in 2007) would constitute a bloc of Atlanticist allies for London also looked far from certain. During 2005, public opinion in the new states swung clearly against US foreign and military policy, while generational change and the rise of new nationalisms added more layers of uncertainty (Bugajski and Teleki, 2005). The American public debate continues to be dominated by simultaneous calls to 'wake up' to the new Europe (Reid, 2004) and to resist French agendas of countering American hegemony. In truth, the counter-hegemonic agenda is not credible; contemporary Europe is too divided and complex to mount much of a threat to America. The real question seems to be whether an integrating Europe can even aspire to being a valuable partner to the US. As John Peterson and Mark Pollack (2003, 140) put it: 'In a contest to determine the "biggest threat" to the transatlantic relationship, American unilateralism and European disarray would probably finish tied in a dead heat'. Further disarray would enhance the George W. Bush administration's tendency to work with Europe on a bilateral, country-by-country basis. As far as the concerns of this chapter are concerned, the US–UK 'special relationship' would have come full circle.

10
Ireland

Many standard histories of Anglo-American relations ignore Ireland. Historians of the relationship have tended to acknowledge the potential for US–UK tension mounted by Irish issues in general, and by the activity of various Irish American lobbies in general. The Irish dimension to the London-Washington relationship, however, has not fitted in very easily to analyses of UK–US relations centred on the high diplomatic and military politics of the Cold War. Following the end of the Cold War, however, and certainly by the early 1990s, Irish issues emerged as the most public source of tension between London and Washington. Following Tony Blair's election in 1997, conspicuous tension was transformed into conspicuous cooperation. Still, Ireland manifestly constituted a central issue in Anglo-American relations.

Notwithstanding appearances to the contrary, the 'American dimension' to the Northern Irish troubles, indeed to the Irish troubles generally in the 19th and 20th centuries, had always been of far more than marginal importance. The 'American dimension' operated at various levels, posing complex problems for Anglo-American relations. James Joyce's metaphorically one-eyed 'citizen' in *Ulysses* (1922) encapsulated a common dream or fear of those caught in the troubles: the entry of a *deus ex machina* in the shape of the Irish-American Catholic diaspora. Joyce's 'citizen' informs the drinkers in Barney Kiernan's bar: 'We have our greater Ireland beyond the sea ... twenty thousand of them died in the coffinships'. Those that made it to the American 'land of the free remember the land of bondage'. They 'will come again and with a vengeance, no cravens, the sons of Granuaile, the champions of Kathleen ni Houlihan' (Joyce, 1992, 427–8).

In recent times, American politicians who have sought to intervene in Northern Irish issues, whether in response Irish-American opinion or for other motives, have faced a formidable obstacle in the shape of the 'special relationship'. As James Schlesinger, former member of President Carter's Cabinet, reminded President Clinton in 1995, 'Northern ireland is, after all, a province of the United Kingdom' (*Congressional Record* S5679, 25 April 1995). A different view of the interaction between the 'special relationship' and American desires to intervene in Northern Ireland's problems was expressed by Kevin Cahill and Hugh Carey (1984, 564) in 1979: 'It is not easy to rebuke a friend like Britain. Yet it is not noble to ignore another friend, one in need.' Cahill edited the Irish-American journal, *The Recorder*. Carey, sometime governor of New York, was a leading figure among Irish-American political leaders who sought to establish a legitimate and substantive US interest in the affairs of the Northern Irish 'friend in need'. For its part, London has traditionally and intensely resented outside interference in sovereign British affairs. Patrick Mayhew, Northern Ireland secretary in John Major's Conservative government, responded icily to President Clinton's interest in the province in 1993: 'We do not need a peace envoy, thank you very much' (*The Observer*, 21 February 1993).

The main focus of this chapter is on the intense and controversial activism of the Clinton presidency in Northern Irish issues. We begin with the social and historical context for Clinton's peace offensive.

Irish America and the Northern Irish Conflict

Many commentators on, and indeed many participants in, Northern Irish affairs take the ignorance and unreflecting nationalism of Irish America as a given and largely irredeemable condition. Brian Faulkner (1978, 19), the last Northern Irish prime minister under the 1920 constitution, recalled shortly before his death in 1977 a 1949 TV debate in New York City with a Judge Troy. Upon being asked where he originated, Troy replied: 'County Westmeath ... though I haven't been there since the age of three. But I do have to get an Irish vote'. James Prior (1986, 219), secretary of state for Northern Ireland between 1981 and 1984, noted urban America's 'large numbers of Irish constituents who still harbour views which originate from the potato famine of the 1840s' and accused American politicians like Senator Edward Kennedy of pandering to them. Margaret Thatcher (1993, 58) herself wrote in her memoirs of Irish-American 'emotions and loyalties' being 'manipulated by Irish Republican extremists'.

Prominent Irish-Americans who sought a voice in the peace process of the 1990s rejected the common stereotype of what Bruce Morrison called 'naive romantics, dreaming of 1916' (*The Guardian*, 22 August 1994). Morrison, former Democratic Congressman and Clinton associate, led a group of Irish-Americans who became closely involved in peace diplomacy after 1992. The stereotype ignores a number of important factors which affect the 44 million or so Americans who claim some kind of Irish ancestry. It ignores the large number of Irish *Protestant* immigrants. In 1994, Congressman Joseph Kennedy (son of Robert) declared in a BBC interview broadcast on 22 September 1994 that around one-quarter of Irish-Americans in his Massachusetts constituency were of Protestant background. Though Protestants, who mostly arrived in the US earlier, have generally assimilated to a greater degree than their Catholic counterparts, deracination has affected Irish America generally. The backers of Morrison's group in the 1990s represented a new Irish-American business elite, far removed from the world of ward and boss politics. The effect of suburbanization and generational change should be recognized. Also relevant here is the academic literature on ethnic group influence on foreign policy. This tends to deny the notion of a cohesive Irish-American 'vote', geared to American stances on Ireland. It also argues that ethnic group influence on US foreign policy succeeds only when group aims coincide with other, usually strategic, US foreign policy goals (McCaffrey, 1992; Siegal, 1978; Thompson and Rudolph, 1987).

This is not to suggest that the 'naive romantics' stereotype is entirely mistaken. Especially during the 1970s and early 1980s, the Provisional Irish Republican Army (PIRA) was able to look to the US for money and guns . The promise of access to clearly legalized fund raising was an important factor in the changing tactics of Sinn Fein in the 1990s. When the 32-County Sovereignty Committee was founded in protest against Sinn Fein participation in peace talks, its leaders naturally embarked on transatlantic fund-raising expeditions almost as a rite of passage.

A large number of Irish-American organizations have sought some kind of influence over Northern Irish issues since the modern 'troubles' began in 1968. These range from the Ancient Order of Hibernians, the traditional cultural defence organization, to various socialist, reconciliationist and civil rights groups. The main organization supporting the Provisional IRA has been the Irish Northern Aid Committee (NORAID). Spreading out from its Bronx (New York City) base, NORAID provided the Provisionals with money and access to gun-running networks. Its impact was dissipated in the late 1980s, by splits, notably over the issue of Sinn Fein involvement in elections in the Irish Republic. By the early 1990s, it was being challenged by groups like Friends of Irish Freedom, more in tune with the developing strategies of Sinn Fein. More geared to elite political lobbying in the US was the Irish National Caucus (INC), led by Father Sean McManus and Fred Burns O'Brien. The INC, whose influence remained strong in the 1980s and early 1990s, was associated with the establishment in 1977 of the Congressional Ad Hoc Committee on Irish Affairs. Though less directly associated with the Provisionals than NORAID, the Ad Hoc Committee and the INC essentially presented the case for militant republicanism .

Beyond the various organizations, Irish-American opinion on Northern Ireland has fluctuated considerably since 1969. The changing dollar totals collected by NORAID provide some guide, however unreliable, to changing opinion (Dumbrell, 1995b, 111). For some Catholic Irish-Americans, the events of 1968–9 reawakened a commitment to Irish nationalism which had been buried as a result of Eamon da Valera's policy of Irish neutrality in World War Two. The stationing of 120,000 US troops in Northern Ireland in 1944 dramatized this situation, and arguably made many older Irish-Americans more sympathetic to the unionist position (Farrell, 1976, 163). The association of early Northern Irish civil rights groups with the US civil rights movements, however, energized a new generation of Irish-Americans. Predictably, Irish America looked more favourably upon the PIRA following human rights violations by the British authorities, the various miscarriages of justice and the hunger strikes of the early 1980s. The cause of militant nationalism suffered in response to IRA violence, peace initiatives and perceptions of flexibility by London, and generally in response to positive views on Britain's role as a dependable US ally.

John Kennedy to George H. W. Bush

Ireland and Anglo-American Relations, 1960–81

President Kennedy's visit to Ireland in 1963 was, as described in a contemporary CIA briefing, 'a triumphal homecoming' (Keogh, 1994, 251). Kennedy's speech to a joint session of the Irish parliament, the Oireachtas, touched key green themes and showed little concern for British sensibilities. He quoted James Joyce's description, in the context of Irish emigration, of the Atlantic as 'a bowl of bitter tears'. He linked the theme of British imperialism with that of Ireland's growing internationalism (under Sean Lemass) and apparent rejection of Cold War neutrality. According to Kennedy, it was 'fitting' that Ireland 'played a leading role in censuring the suppression of the Hungarian revolution' in 1956: 'how many times was Ireland's quest for freedom suppressed, only to have that quest renewed by each succeeding generation?' Leaving Shannon airport to meet Macmillan at Birch Grove, Kennedy announced he was off 'to another country' (FO 371 168414).

The outbreak of violence in the North in 1968–9 was analysed for the US Embassy in London by Neil McManus, the American consul-general in Belfast. McManus was briefed by Terence O'Neill, Northern Irish premier. He reported: 'Finally the pot has boiled over.' The early troubles were seen as products of the peculiar circumstances of the province, rather than touching directly on questions of London's jurisdiction. In October 1968 McManus reported on the disturbances: 'participation few IRA or Communist types' (*sic*) (Cronin, 1987, 285, 283).

As the situation deteriorated, the role of London came under attack in the US press, notably by the journalists Pete Hamill and Jimmy Breslin, and in the US Congress. A shifting coalition of Members of Congress emerged to protest British policy. In 1971, Senator Edward Kennedy supported a motion calling for the immediate withdrawal of British troops. Yet the State Department's position was made clear in these early years: the US had no right or duty to intervene. As a State Department spokesman declared in

1969: 'The United Kingdom is a friendly country which, unlike certain other countries with civil rights problems, has a basic structure of democratic institutions and political freedom' (Cronin, 1987, 291).

Congressional pressure on the executive to take some kind of initiative on Ireland continued during the late Nixon and Ford years. It was led by Irish-American members from New York and Massachusetts, though by no means confined to them. The cause appealed also to those members who asserted a 'human rights' orientation in foreign policy in the context of the Vietnam War. Edward Kennedy argued in 1972:

> So long as Britain pursues the phantom of victory over the IRA ... the violence will continue. ... Fifty thousand Americans died before we learned that lesson in Vietnam, and there can be no excuse for Britain to have to learn that lesson now in Ulster. (House of Representatives Hearings, 1972, 153)

Nixon was unresponsive. NORAID was investigated by the Federal Bureau of Investigation in 1971 and forced to register as a 'foreign agent'. In 1976, President Ford and Irish Taoiseach Liam Cosgrave issued a joint communiqué calling on Irish-Americans to stop giving money which 'is helping to kill and maim Irish men and women of every religious persuasion' (A. J. Wilson, 1995, 119–20).

The 1976 communiqué, and the setting up of the Ireland Fund in the same year, reflected a Dublin diplomatic initiative which was to have a significant impact on Washington's role (the Ireland Fund, directed by businessman Tony O'Reilly, was designed to divert Irish-American dollars away from NORAID and towards peaceful and reconciliationist Irish causes). Irish Republic diplomats Sean Donlon and Michael Lillis recruited leading Irish-American politicians to the cause of constitutional nationalism. This was designed to put them in a better position to lobby the executive to push London in the direction of some kind of constitutional, power-sharing solution to the troubles. The key Irish-American players were the so-called 'four horsemen': Edward Kennedy, Hugh Carey, House of Representatives Speaker 'Tip' O'Neill and Senator Daniel Patrick Moynihan of New York. The Carter administration's espousal of a foreign policy outlook based on human rights also helped the Donlon-Lillis project. Carter, in search of urban northern votes in the 1976 election campaign, had already rather clumsily become involved in the American politics of Irish nationalism, and now sought a clear identification with peaceful change. In a 1977 statement, he dangled the prospect of 'increased investment' in the event of a 'peaceful settlement' rooted in power sharing. The 1977 statement was praised by John Hume of the Northern Irish Social Democratic and Labour Party, and leading figure in Dublin's diplomatic initiatives, as showing 'the people what the real prize of agreement can be' (*The Times*, 31 August 1977; Hume, 1996,136; Donlon, 1993). John Hume used his time as an associate fellow at Harvard University in the mid-1970s to develop a resilient network of contacts with leading Irish-American politicians. Carter had also become the first president to assert a clear and substantive American interest in the province's affairs.

London's reaction to the 1977 statement combined lukewarm condescension with resentment. Carter had been condemned by Northern Ireland Secretary Roy Mason for his unwise involvement in INC-sponsored events during the 1976 campaign. Yet, however much London might resent Carter's 'interference', it could hardly oppose that part of the Dublin 'four horsemen' strategy which sought to cut the ground from under NORAID. The New York-based UK government agency, the British Information Service, was already trying to do this itself, with some limited success. Directed by Hamilton Whyte in the mid-1970s, the BIS had an annual budget of around one and a half million dollars and a staff approaching one hundred. Its most successful activity was the production of 'news spots' for American television, designed to head off the putatively sympathetic treatment accorded the IRA by the US media. The BIS effort was supplemented by Harold Wilson when he visited the US in December 1975. He addressed the Association of American Correspondents, condemning contributors to NORAID as 'splashing blood' on the shamrock (A. J. Wilson, 1995, 109–11; Bowyer-Bell, 1993, 512).

The Dublin initiative was, at least on one level, a welcome addition to these efforts. London applauded Taoiseach Jack Lynch's 1977 attacks on the Congressional Ad Hoc Committee on Irish Affairs, led by Congressman Mario Biaggi. Roy Mason was briefed in Washington in October 1977 by Edward Kennedy and 'Tip' O'Neill. He began noticeably to temper his hostility to Carter's intervention, embracing the idea of a 'peace dividend'. He was impressed by plans announced by the US firm Du Pont to upgrade its plant in Derry (*The Times*, 20 November 1977). Following the 1977 statement, the 'four horsemen', in alliance with Dublin and John Hume, continued to press on Carter the virtues of a new power-sharing initiative – of, in effect, a revival of the failed Sunningdale agreement of 1974, with its devolved executive and Council of Ireland. Edward Kennedy urged a 'Marshall Plan' for Ireland. The final year of James Callaghan's premiership (1978–9) saw frequent American expressions of frustration at the lack of progress, usually blamed on Callaghan's reliance on unionist votes at Westminster. In August 1979, the Congressional Ad Hoc Committee led a successful move to ban arms sales to the Royal Ulster Constabulary. The failure of the Carter administration to oppose the ban in any direct way reflected Washington's irritation with London during this period.

Nicholas Henderson, British ambassador in Washington, felt that 'discretion is the better part of valour on arms sales'. Henderson appreciated that the State Department opposed the ban, and was successful in persuading London to finesse the situation. London sources were at this time quoted as implying that no protest need be made and that, once the fire of extremists in Congress died down, Washington would 'quietly ... resume' sales (*Daily Telegraph*, 4 August 1979). Such a strategy did not directly appeal to Margaret Thatcher who was, as Henderson noted, 'in her fighting mood' (Henderson, 1994, 284). Nonetheless, an open row with Washington was averted in respect of the ban, which lasted into the early 1980s, and the era of the hunger strikes.

The 'four horsemen' continued their lobbying. Edward Kennedy told Carter in June 1979 that he should convey to Thatcher that:

> a British policy that emphasised 'security' concerns while ignoring a political initiative could inflame Irish-American opinion, undercut the responsible leadership that Speaker O'Neill and the rest of us are trying to provide; upset other important aspects of the US and British relationship; fuel anti-British sentiment in America; and even become a hair- curling issue in the 1980 election. (Kennedy to the President, 21 June 1979, box CO–64, White House Central Files: Subject File: CO-167, executive, JCL)

Kennedy's urging was given added poignancy by his own imminent challenge to Carter in the Democratic primaries. A handwritten note from the president to Kennedy, available in the Carter Presidential Library, indicates that he pressed the American case on Northern Irish reform with Margaret Thatcher at the Tokyo summit in June 1979. Kennedy suggested to Carter that a new initiative should eschew the term, 'power-sharing' (Kennedy preferred the phrase, 'participatory democracy'); that it be made clear that a united Ireland was 'not likely to occur in the foreseeable future'; and that the 'pure negativism of [Ian] Paisley and his faction' should be marginalized (Kennedy to the President, 21 June 1979; Carter to Kennedy, 25 June 1979, box CO–64, White House Central Files: Subject File: CO–167, executive). In October, an initiative associated with Northern Irish Secretary Humphrey Atkins, involving a plan for devolved government based on 'the highest possible level of agreement', did broadly follow the Kennedy formula, and indeed was widely seen as reflecting American pressure (Guelke, 1988, ch. 7). Ulster Unionist leader James Molyneaux even suggested that British policy was being driven by undertakings made in a 'high powered conference ... in London', between Foreign Secretary Lord Carrington and Secretary of State Cyrus Vance, and held in June 1979 (Arthur and Jeffrey, 1988, 86–7).

Reagan and Bush

By the time Reagan, an Irish-American on his father's side, came to the White House, Irish issues had moved firmly up the Anglo-American agenda. The Dublin 'four horsemen' strategy proceeded with the formation of the Friends of Ireland (prominent Members of Congress committed to constitutional nationalism) in 1981. Sean Donlon persuaded Reagan publicly to endorse the Friends on St Patrick's Day, 1981, when he also strongly condemned American abettors of violence in Ulster. Donlon especially cultivated William Clark, Reagan's second national security adviser, as well as other Irish-American presidential advisers.

Yet problems for the Donlon programme were also emerging. At the level of Catholic Irish America, a rift was appearing between what Tim Pat Coogan has called the 'consular circuit', led by Donlon, and broader Irish-American opinion. The rift was exacerbated by the IRA hunger strikes, and by various interventions from Fianna Fail leader Charles Haughey. Haughey declared during a 1985 US visit that 'Americans who wished only to offer genuine support' on Irish issues were 'met with suspicion, rebuff and disapproval' (Coogan, 1995, 348–9.) There were also doubts about Reagan's willingness to intervene with London. Would a Republican in the White House see any need to listen to Irish America? Perhaps Reagan would set himself against any change in Ireland, interpreting instability there, as some on the Republican right did, as threatening 'another Cuba'? More significantly, Dublin saw the 'special relationship' and Reagan's admiration for Thatcher as major obstacles (Bowyer-Bell, 1993, 648).

The first test came in relation to the prisoners on hunger strike. The Friends of Ireland, Charles Haughey and Fine Gael leader Garret Fitzgerald, elected Taoiseach in June 1981, pressed Reagan to intercede. Donlon requested Reagan in July 1981 to send an emissary to negotiate directly with the prisoners over the key issue of 'special status' for 'political prisoners'. Reagan did not respond. Fitzgerald found him poorly informed on the issue, reluctant to offend London and unwilling 'to aid prisoners detained for terrorism' (Fitzgerald, 1991, 373). In October 1983, Reagan directly rejected a Friends of Ireland call to appoint an American 'peace envoy' for the province.

Yet Donlon, now as Irish ambassador to Washington, persuaded Reagan to visit Ireland in 1984. The elite Irish-American lobby continued to work, not only for some 'power-sharing' solution, but also for the incorporation of an all-Ireland dimension into any settlement. The hunger strikes, the hostility shown by Dublin to Britain's conduct in the Falklands conflict, and electoral gains made by Sinn Fein, made the task difficult, but gave it increased urgency. The Reagan administration was urged to support the New Ireland Forum (NIF) process and report (May 1984) and Reagan himself was lobbied on this issue during his trip to the Irish Republic. William Clark was recruited to intercede with Reagan over Thatcher's emotional rejection of the NIF report, with its espousal of all-Ireland initiatives. The president raised the NIF rejection with Thatcher at Camp David in December 1984, occasioning an almost immediate change of heart, notably in her February 1985 address to a joint session of the US Congress.

Reagan's willingness to intervene was matched by new attitudes at the State Department. Richard Burt, secretary for European affairs, was persuaded by Donlon and Irish Foreign Minister Peter Barry to take up the NIF initiative. At Burt's request, progress in

Ulster was put on the agenda for talks with Thatcher at the State Department following the February 1985 congressional address. Via his boss, George Shultz, Burt also succeeded in recruiting Reagan to the view that 'Margaret Thatcher should be given one more nudge' in the NIF direction, whereupon 'the United States might be willing to give financial backing to an agreement' (Fitzgerald, 1991, 535).

Pressure was applied by Reagan at a meeting with Thatcher at Camp David in December 1994 and 'one more nudge' given when the British leader visited Washington the following February, to address the two houses of Congress. John Campbell (2004, 434) quotes a draft document, actually giving the old actor-president his script for his Camp David meeting with Thatcher: 'I am concerned that unless there is the appearance of progress at the next Anglo-Irish summit, a radicalisation will occur in Irish-American opinion which would endanger the current bipartisan support our Northern Ireland policy enjoys'. Margaret Thatcher's own worries about the NIF agenda were made plain in her memoirs, where she described it as alienating 'Unionists without gaining the level of security co-operation' expected from the South (Thatcher, 1993, 415). It seems likely that American lobbying was decisive in securing her support for the Anglo-Irish Agreement, with its recognition of a role for Dublin in the affairs and future of the North. The Agreement was signed by Margaret Thatcher and Garret Fitzgerald in November 1985. American pressure was acknowledged by Geoffrey Howe (foreign secretary from 1983 to 1989), though he insisted: 'Only rarely were we under direct pressure from the other side of the Atlantic specifically to change our policies' (Howe, 1995, 422).

Britain expected some American financial backing for the Agreement, though London was sensitive, as Garret Fitzgerald (1991, 561) recalled, 'lest the promise of official aid by the United States be interpreted as a bribe'. The American reception. of the Agreement, and the passage through Congress of an aid package associated with it, became entangled in a variety of complications: attempts by Charles Haughey to sabotage the Agreement; its rejection by NORAID, as well as by Sean McManus and the INC, as a Dublin 'sell out'; even in presidential-congressional tensions over Central America. Congress eventually voted a three-year 120 million dollar package, the new International Fund for (all) Ireland. This sum fell short of the expectations generated by Reagan immediately following the Agreement. In July 1986, the US Senate also approved a new extradition treaty, which London hoped would facilitate procedures regarding Irish terrorists residing in the US. The treaty was directly linked to the 1985 Agreement. Richard Lugar, Senate Foreign Relations Committee chairman, pressured opponents of the treaty by linking its passage to release of the International Fund money. The treaty's passage also reflected America's response to London's cooperation in the 1986 Libyan air raid. White House lobbyists joined the Northern Irish Office in pointing up IRA links with Libya (A.J. Wilson, 1995, 255).

Between 1985 and 1992, the American dimension to the Northern Irish conflict was dominated by extradition issues, notably involving Joe Doherty, and by the INC-led campaign for 'fair employment' requirements for US firms operating in Ulster (the MacBride principles). The MacBride principles, setting quotas for Catholic employment, had been adopted by 10 states by 1987. The MacBride campaigns energized many younger Irish-Americans outside the 'consular circuit', as did the campaigns for regularizing the status of illegal Irish immigrants (McKittrick, 1989, 12025). The MacBride principles were opposed by the George H. W. Bush administration, as indeed by Senator Kennedy and John Hume. Although Bush's State Department made clear its support for new initiatives, it essentially interpreted the situation as 'unripe' for significant American intervention (Haass, 1990, ch. 6). Interested parties in Congress continued to press for a US 'peace envoy' and to denounce British conduct in connection with the Guildford Four and Birmingham Six cases, along with the John Stalker affair and the 1988 Gibraltar shootings (Kennedy, 1991).

Clinton

Bill Clinton's first acquaintance with Northern Irish issues came during his time as a student at Oxford in the late 1960s. He later commented: 'I could see it coming, that religious differences were likely to lead to the same kinds of problems that racial differences had in my childhood' (*The Times*, 9 December 1995). His first political involvement, however, came, as with Jimmy Carter, during a presidential election campaign. Like Carter, Clinton in 1992 was a candidate, seeking to widen his support base from that associated with his former incarnation as governor of a southern state. Rather than the INC, however, Clinton became involved with a group centred on Bruce Morrison, Niall O'Dowd (editor of *The Irish Voice*) and several representatives of corporate Irish America. The group, Americans for a New Irish Agenda, supported the 'peace envoy' idea and the MacBride principles. In a speech made in New York City in April 1992, Clinton told the ANIA that 'our longstanding special relationship with Great Britain' had made the US 'too reluctant to engage ourselves' on Northern Ireland (O'Clery, 1996, 8). (Clinton was engaged in the New York Democratic primary race, and was facing a major challenge from Jerry Brown.) Ten days before the 1992 general election, Clinton issued a statement on Northern Ireland, embracing the ANIA policy positions and condemning the 'wanton use of lethal force by British security services'. The statement was addressed to 'Irish Americans for Clinton and Gore', a body formed by Clinton campaign aide Chris Hyland with O'Dowd's group, and drafted by Nancy Soderberg, who had spent 10 years on Edward Kennedy's staff (*The Observer*, 8 November 1992).

A coming together of Kennedy forces with the O'Dowd group, under White House sponsorship, was a key feature of the early Clinton period. Ted Kennedy's sister, Jean Kennedy Smith, was appointed as US ambassador to Dublin. Raymond Seitz, US ambassador to London until 1994, later commented: 'If giving Mrs Smith the Dublin post made Senator Ted happy, it was cheap at the price' (Seitz, 1998, 286). The White House also drew close to Albert Reynolds, who replaced Charles Haughey as Taoiseach in February 1992. Tim Pat Coogan comments: 'Not even in Parnell's time, when ... the Fenians, the Land League and the forces of constitutionalism joined together under his leadership, had such a powerful coalition been formed' (Coogan, 1995, 355). The Irish-American dynamic of 1992 was maintained, with O'Dowd and Bruce Morrison leading delegations to Belfast. In August 1993, they were actually greeted by a short IRA ceasefire, in a gesture which underlined the significance of their initiative. O'Dowd later recalled:

> It had been obvious to me for some time Sinn Fein were looking for another, wider outreach in America ... I met Clinton in September 1992 and raised the question of a visa for [Gerry] Adams with him then. From January 1993 I had a series of meetings with Sinn Fein

about bringing America into the equation. (Mallie and McKittrick, 1996, 280)

The situation was further complicated by a coolness between the White House and Downing Street which led back to various clumsy attempts by London to aid the Bush cause in the 1992 elections.

The main issues in the 1993–4 period concerned the 'peace envoy' idea, and the issuing of a visa to allow Sinn Fein leader Gerry Adams to visit the US. In a February 1993 meeting with Prime Minister John Major, Clinton indicated that he was not especially committed to the idea. One of the major candidates for the post, House Speaker Tom Foley, considered it a 'cockamamie' idea (Seldon, 1997, 364); and Albert Reynolds also urged Clinton against it. Reynolds was concerned to consolidate his good relationship with Major, as part of the developing peace initiative (Coogan, 1995, 355).

The issue of Gerry Adams' visa was more difficult. He had already been rebuffed eight times. Seitz, the State Department, the Justice Department, the Federal Bureau of Investigation, the CIA and Speaker Foley all opposed the visa. London succeeded in its lobbying against Adams in 1993. In November 1993 Clinton responded to pressure from New York City Mayor David Dinkins on the visa issue in words that might have been written in London: 'Credible evidence exists that Adams remains involved at the highest level in devising PIRA strategy ... despite his recent talks with John Hume, Adams has still not publicly renounced terrorism' (Mallie and McKittrick, 1996, 282). Roderick Lyne, Major's Downing Street foreign policy adviser, told Clinton bluntly in January 1994: 'Tell Adams that if there is a cessation of violence, then he can have the visa' (Seldon, 1997, 443).

By this time, the 1993 Downing Street Declaration, with its denial of selfish British interest in the province and commitment to democratic majority wishes, had been issued. Albert Reynolds told Clinton that the Declaration was 'a big leap forward' and that Adams should now be admitted to the US as a way of getting him to 'join the peace train' (O'Clery, 1996, 90). Jean Kennedy Smith and Nancy Soderberg (now staff director on the National Security Council) pressed for the visa; other key pro-visa NSC figures were National Security Adviser Tony Lake and European specialist Jane Holl. They faced intense opposition from Seitz and from Britain's

Washington ambassador, Robin Renwick. On the pro-visa side, John Hume's role remained central. Vice-President Al Gore reportedly informed British Foreign Secretary Douglas Hurd that 'we have taken advice from John Hume and he has not misled us for twenty years'. A two-day visa was issued to enable Adams to attend a conference, organized by the O'Dowd-Morrison group, in early February 1994. In publicly overruling the State Department and ignoring Raymond Seitz, the White House was prioritizing Irish policy to an unprecedented degree. The visa was issued following receipt of a fax from Adams, transmitted to the *Irish Voice* and conveyed to the White House, declaring: 'I don't advocate violence' (O'Clery, 1996, 97, 98). To Bruce Morrison, the invitation was Sinn Fein's opportunity to 'come in from the cold' (*Newsweek*, 12 September 1994). Nancy Soderberg later described Clinton's position as 'win-win': if the visa 'helped foster a ceasefire, then Clinton's actions would be vindicated'. However, if 'Adams failed to deliver a ceasefire after Clinton had risked such political capital on him, then Clinton would be in a strong position to turn Irish America against Adams and undermine the IRA' (Soderberg, 2005, 72). For Clinton, the visa 'would boost Adams's leverage within Sinn Fein and the IRA, while increasing American influence with him' (Clinton, 2005, 580).

The issuing of the visa took place amid intense bitterness. *A Daily Telegraph* headline on 2 February 1994, proclaimed the 'worst rift since Suez'. A leader in the *Sunday Times* declared that 'Clinton does not really care what Major thinks', and linked the granting of the visa to profound changes in US foreign policy. The US was decoupling from Europe and 'Pacificizing' its foreign policy. It would involve itself in European affairs, so the *Sunday Times* argued on 6 February 1994, only – as with Northern Ireland – to placate important domestic lobbies. John Major kept a brave face in public, but vented his anger against Clinton in a Cabinet meeting on 3 February (Seldon, 1997, 444–5). Bitterness was also evident among various American participants. White House adviser George Stephanopoulos was quoted as saying: 'It obviously ticks off the Brits but equally obviously that is acceptable to a lot of us' (O'Clery, 1996, 98). Seitz derided White House 'munchkins' (*The Guardian*, 16 April 1994) describing the visa issuance in his memoirs as 'a fiasco of political amateurism'. For Seitz, Soderberg was merely the 'in-house coach for the Irish lobby'. As for Kennedy

Smith, 'Too shallow to understand the past and too naive to anticipate the future, she was an ardent IRA apologist.' Seitz considered National Security Adviser Tony Lake, initially neutral on the visa issue, as motivated by an antipathy to colonialism. From February 1994, Lake emerged to lead the Clinton administration's Irish policy, claiming to devote around one-quarter of his time to it. Most spectacularly, Seitz alleged in his memoirs that at this time 'London even stopped passing sensitive intelligence to the White House because it often seemed to find its way back to the IRA' (Seitz, 1998, 286, 289–91; Stevenson, 1996–7).

From February 1994, Clinton made efforts to restore relations with Major. Though not apologizing, Clinton smoothed some ruffled feathers over Ireland during Major's visit to Washington at the end of February. Tony Lake later admitted: 'I don't think that we understood at the time fully British sensitivities'. Clinton also seems to have been disappointed by Adams' conduct in the US, and his failure to make any announcement about a ceasefire (Seldon, 1997, 445–6).

When the ceasefire eventually came, in August 1994, Washington felt vindicated. A Downing Street aide retorted that the visa 'took the pressure off Adams ... Without it, we'd have had the ceasefire sooner' (Seldon, 1997, 444; Cox, 1998; 1999). By August 1994, however, the American role was a fact of life. The ANIA group (O'Dowd, Morrison, William Flynn and Charles Feeney) visited Belfast immediately before the ceasefire, accompanied by Irish-American labour leaders. Their importance in securing the ceasefire was palpable. The IRA Army Council itself insisted that Joe Cahill, the veteran republican, be in the US to explain the cease-fire to NORAID. (The successful fight for Cahill's visa reopened the battles of January. Albert Reynolds, who communicated with the IRA via Fr. Alex Reid of Belfast's Clonard monastery, informed Clinton that Cahill's visa was essential to the ceasefire (A.J. Wilson, 1997, 32)). Lake opened a direct line of communication with Adams, demanding some move on the ceasefire. Despite Seitz's depiction of her as 'a promotion agent for Adams' (Seitz, 1998, 289), it is also clear that Kennedy Smith attempted to bring along moderate unionists. The Clinton team were anxious to avoid the kind of united unionist opposition which had followed the 1985 Anglo-Irish Agreement. Official Unionist leader James Molyneaux was invited into a dialogue with Al Gore, while the ANIA group took pains to include the Protestant paramilitaries in the ceasefire negotiations. As early as spring 1994, Robin Renwick, who in January 1994 had called Adams a 'Goebbels figure', advised the prime minister that it was time to swallow pride and accept American mediation (O'Dowd, 1996; Walker, 1996, 279).

Adams visited the US twice more in 1994. In November, he met Lake and Gore at the White House, which gave him, in O'Dowd's words, 'the same status as Unionists in terms of contact' (Coogan, 1995, 382; A.J. Wilson, 1995). On St Patrick's Day 1995, Adams actually received an unphotographed presidential handshake at Clinton's annual reception for Irish-Americans. The declared 'decontamination' period for contacts with Sinn Fein was over. US policy during the 1994–6 IRA ceasefire was to talk up the economic benefits of peace, to integrate Sinn Fein into high-level political networks and to encourage London to press ahead with negotiations. Clinton welcomed the February 1995 Framework Document as promising 'all-inclusive' talks, 'with all issues on the table' (Baylis, ed., 1997, 238–9). In December 1994, retiring Senate Majority Leader George Mitchell became 'special adviser for economic initiatives in Ireland'. Announcing Mitchell's appointment, Clinton declared: 'There must be a peace dividend in Ireland for the peace to succeed' (*Public Papers of the Presidents ... 1995*, 2129). A major investment conference was organized in Washington in May 1995. Commerce secretary Ron Brown noted that change 'can be profound' in the event of significant private investment in the province. He noted that Catholic unemployment rates in Northern Ireland were virtually identical to those affecting African-Americans (Cullen, 1996; Oliver, 1995).

London, of course, was happy to support economic initiatives. It noted, however, that the administration was requesting only modest additions to the International Fund for Ireland. The Republican Congressional take-over of January 1995 also pointed decisively against rises in public investment. Far more irritating to London were the increasingly close overtures to Adams, and the removal of restrictions on Sinn Fein fund raising in the US. William Crowe, Seitz's successor as ambassador to London, announced his support for removing the ban in January. John Major argued that Clinton should not even consider such a step until Sinn Fein moved significantly on the arms decommissioning issue. Washington lifted the ban in early March 1995, arguing that Adams' promise to discuss decommissioning was sufficient. The White House made no secret of its view that delay in the peace process was less the product of Sinn Fein intransigence than of John Major's reliance, like that of James Callaghan in 1979, on Unionist support at Westminster. The fundraising announcement outraged Downing Street. Anthony Seldon quotes a Major aide: 'The White House having done the wrong thing, typically the next thing they did was to try getting on the phone to say they were sorry.' The call went unreturned (O'Clery, 1996, 214; Seldon, 1997, 538). Richard Holbrooke, European specialist at the State Department, announced that Clinton had 'taken a risk on behalf of peace' and that Sinn Fein should now reciprocate (*The Independent*, 11 March 1995). In early April 1995, Clinton was again trying to conciliate Major: 'I was very clear … that there must be an agreement entered in good faith to seriously discuss arms decommissioning' (*The Guardian*, 5 April 1995). By 1996, Sinn Fein was operating a major fund-raising operation in downtown Washington, and resisting attempts to have its accounts audited.

Between the summer of 1994 and spring 1995 it became clear to all participants and observers that Washington was intimately woven into the peace process. Official Unionist leader David Trimble visited the White House. A loyalist paramilitary visit of October 1994, following the loyalist paramilitaries' ceasefire, was organized by the White House and O'Dowd's forces. Former Conservative minister Michael Mates was despatched to put London's case both to official Washington and on American TV.

Clinton's November 1995 Northern Irish trip was a major publicity success, the moment when 'hope and history rhymed'. The president was the first US leader ever to visit the province. He asked an audience in Derry: 'Are you going to be someone who defines yourself in terms of what you are against or what you are for?' (Clinton, 2005, 687). Clinton's team was reported as objecting to the tone taken by British officials. One member was quoted to the effect that the British hosts 'talked about Northern Ireland as if it was a third world country'. The British attitude was: 'those people, they're impossible' (O'Clery, 1996, 230). Clinton's public remarks in Belfast made clear his commitment to the 'twin track' approach (begin talks while simultaneously finding a way around the decommissioning problem): 'honest dialogue is not an act of surrender' (R. Wilson, 1995).

Despite the tensions noted above, Clinton's November 1995 meeting with Major did salve some wounds opened up earlier in the year. Anthony Seldon suggests that the White House was becoming increasingly irritated by Gerry Adams' wavering on decommissioning, and more willing to listen to the unionist case. Gore's talks with the unionists seemed to have involved a temporary decline in the stock of John Hume. Ambassador Crowe also was increasingly reflecting and explaining London's position (Seldon, 1997, 622). On 28 November, Major and Taoiseach John Bruton, with US backing, announced that an international board would handle the decommissioning issue, with talks commencing in February 1996. The international commission would be led by George Mitchell.

At the time of Clinton's Belfast visit, Nancy Soderberg expressed her anxiety over excessive expectations about 'the president pulling a rabbit out of the hat' (*Fortnight*, 4 December 1995, 23). The breaking of the IRA ceasefire in February 1996 seemed to indicate that Clinton had run out of rabbits. Mitchell's commission had just reported to the effect that decommissioning should occur in parallel with talks. When the talks began, at Stormont Castle, under Mitchell's chairmanship, in June 1996, Sinn Fein was excluded. David Trimble's proposal to elect an assembly seemed further to damage Clinton's line. Important tensions appeared in the US. O'Dowd's group split over the question of continued Sinn Fein US fund raising, which was banned again following IRA violence in 1996.

Washington seemed to have had its fingers burned. Some leading Irish-American figures, like Senator Christopher Dodd, were prepared to call the whole Clinton strategy into question. The departure from the administration of Tony Lake and Nancy Soderberg seemed to underpin a new caution in Washington, which the new secretary of state (Madeleine Albright, appointed in January 1997) seemed to favour. During 1996, Adams was allowed into the US, but conspicuously not invited to the White House. By 1997, the approaching British general election held centre stage. Labour's victory in May unfroze the situation and led to an IRA ceasefire restoration in July 1997. While a degree of American influence can be assumed, the restoration was more the product of intra-republican politics, and the prospect of the Blair government, unconstrained by unionist pressures at Westminster, finessing the decommissioning issue.

White House support for the peace dynamic in 1997–8 was far less controversial than in the Major years. Under Blair, Downing

Street welcomed US involvement. Taoiseach Bertie Ahern noted on US television on St Patrick's Day 1998 that Dublin, London and Washington were now 'extremely close'. As journalist John Carlin noted around this time: 'Every public declaration made by Mr Clinton, Mr Ahern and [Northern Irish Secretary] Mo Mowlam appeared almost as if it had been carefully orchestrated and jointly rehearsed' (*The Independent on Sunday*, 22 March 1998). Trimble, Adams, Hume, Lord Alderdice of the Alliance Party and Gary McMichael of the Ulster Democratic Party (linked to the loyalist paramilitaries) attended a White House 17 March reception. Clinton declared his wish to 'give them a perfectly harmless ... cold, which would require them all to be quarantined in the Green Room' (*The Independent on Sunday*, 22 March 1998). All five were seen by Clinton in a '30 hour marathon' negotiation. The White House's concern to be even-handed was conceded by Anne Smith, US representative for the Ulster Unionists, and by Tony Cullen-Foster, a Virginia businessman cultivated at this period as an American ally of unionism. During the final Stormont negotiations, Clinton contacted Mitchell and was put to work (around 3 to 4 a.m. Washington time), directly lobbying the leading players. Mitchell (1999, 178) later emphasized that Clinton 'wasn't making cold calls. He knew the people he was calling'. The personal presidential contact with Ahern, Trimble and Adams on 10 April was widely reported as decisive in securing a positive outcome (Cox, 2006, 436). Personal lobbying by the head of the world's one remaining superpower was indeed difficult to resist.

Following the signing of the 1998 Good Friday Agreement, the White House continued to urge a 'vote for peace' in the referendum and assembly elections. Clinton was also dissuaded from campaigning in person in the province, despite his presence in Britain for an economic summit during the referendum campaign. Trimble's advice was that a visit would be counter-productive (*National Journal*, 23 May 1998, 1184). Clinton welcomed enthusiastically both the referendum and assembly election results, interpreting both as victories for the peace process. In August 1998, Bernadette Sands-McEvitt, member of a prominent republican family and now associated with the 32-County Sovereignty Committee, was denied renewal of her US visit, following the Omagh bombing. (Sands-McEvitt was sponsored in the US by Martin Galvin, former NORAID public relations chief and John McDonaugh, host of the

'Radio Free Ireland' talk show in New York.) Clinton visited Ireland in September 1998 and remained close to negotiations designed to implement the Good Friday Agreement. During 1999, the White House continued to pressure Sinn Fein to do all it could to begin the process of IRA arms decommissioning. (The need for the IRA to make such a start was known as 'Washington Three'.) Clinton maintained his lobbying during the June 1999 talks which proved unable to secure implementation of the 1998 Agreement. Meanwhile, congressional pressure continued. In April 1999, the House International Relations Committee passed an amendment designed to end Federal Bureau of Investigations involvement in the training of Royal Ulster Constabulary officers. The move was connected to allegations of RUC complicity in the murders of solicitors Rosemary Nelson and Pat Finucane. Implementation of the 1998 Good Friday Agreement eventually came late in 1999, with the White House maintaining a close, if understated, involvement. Into early 2000, the White House continued direct contacts with the paramilitaries in order to persuade them to decommission weapons.

Clinton's Irish Activism and its Aftermath

One point in the preceding paragraph bears repeating. In 1998, the American head of state had to be actively dissuaded from campaigning personally in a democratic referendum held in a sovereign, foreign country. Clinton's Irish policy achieved a great deal. The precise importance of Clinton's interventions in securing the Belfast Agreement is a matter of intense debate. Paul Dixon (2006, 420) argues, for example, that Clinton's interventions, even before 1997, certainly did not amount to anything approaching the coercion of London into a process of which it did not generally approve. Key features of the process – war weariness, the working out of various debates within both republicanism and loyalism – clearly owed little or nothing to Clinton. Yet, Clinton's activism was still a central aspect of the dynamic which led to the 1998 Agreement. Yet, it should also be recognised that Clinton's Irish activism involved an extraordinary level of intrusion into internal UK affairs. During 1993 and 1994, before Tony Lake's emergence as the policy's bureaucratic principal, the O'Dowd-Morrison group operated for the White House, albeit unofficially. Clinton was able to enjoy the benefits of plausible deniability: claiming credit, leaving failures unacknowledged. Supporters of the general 'peace' thrust of Clinton's policy have tended to understate the novelty and implications of these interventions. As Raymond Seitz (1998, 285) has written, only 'the British government had the constitutional responsibility for bridging the historic mistrust between majority and minority'. Usurpation of this responsibility by Washington, however desirable in the short term, did set some contentious precedents.

By the same token, opponents of the Clinton policy tended either to couch their criticisms in extreme and abusive terms or to trace everything to White House pursuit of Irish-American votes. In 1994, British journalist Simon Jenkins suggested that London should 'give the Americans a taste of their own crassness' by inviting Haiti's leader, 'General Cedras to a taco party on the British embassy lawn in Washington' (*The Spectator*, 15 October 1994, 29). (Jenkins was writing in the month following the US landings on Haiti.) Michael Mates wrote in August 1996 of 'Clinton's cynical playing to the green Irish vote' and charged the president with being in thrall to a 'small group of advisers whose vote-winning agenda is not so much peace, as giving Irish Republicans what they want at almost any price' (*The Mail on Sunday*, 25 August 1996).

Such comments do violence to the complexity of the post-1992 transatlantic interactions. Parallels between Northern Ireland and Haiti are more rhetorical than real. The strength of the entire post-1975 US constitutionalist strategy, from the 'four horsemen' to O'Dowd and Morrison, lay in the appreciation that a negotiated settlement would mean no clear victories. Nor should the policy be damned as a Dickensian Eatanswill of vote grubbing. It is certainly true that Irish-Americans have disproportionately been identified as 1980s 'Reagan Democrats': the voters that Clinton wished to woo back to his party in 1992. Yet, as was noted above, Irish America is diverse and concerned, as are most voters, with a wide range of issues. Senator Christopher Dodd, Democratic National Committee chairman in 1996, concluded that Irish initiatives alone would be a swing issue only for those few Irish-Americans 'who will consider everything else being equal'. Democratic attempts to woo Irish-American voters in 1996 emphasized a wide range of policy positions (A.J. Wilson, 1997, 26). Many of Clinton's policy stances actually upset sections of Irish-American opinion. In June 1996, the Ancient Order of Hibernians withdrew an invitation to Clinton to address its annual convention in protest at his stance on abortion. The INC broke with Clinton in 1996 over his lukewarm attitude towards the MacBride principles. Fr. Sean McManus rather implausibly described Bob Dole, Republican presidential candidate in 1996, as standing to the 'green' side of Clinton (Cullen, 1996). It has also been pointed out that, in 1992, Clinton won those states with high Irish-American populations fairly easily. There was no obvious reason why he should make extraordinary efforts regarding those states for 1996 (Brady, 1995).

Clinton became involved with the Irish issue during the 1992 New York primary election. Subsequently, he wished to attract votes, and financial contributions from Irish America. Such obvious truths do not explain the strength of the Clinton administration's commitment. Some commentators, again those largely hostile to the US initiatives, have sought to emphasize American security and economic interests. Where Republican Senator John McCain criticized Clinton's involvement in a conflict that has 'never ... remotely, affected our security interest' (McCain 1996), others have tried to give the policy a security rationale. For many years, Enoch Powell argued that the goal of American policy was a united Ireland in NATO (*Parliamentary Debates*, 612 Series, vol. 87, 27 Nov. 1985, 954–5; Powell 1992, 189; Powell, 1994). From a vastly different perspective, Sean Cronin concluded that Washington's Cold War goal was the compromising of Irish neutrality in the context of bargaining over US support for Irish nationalism (Cronin, 1987; Davis, 1998, 135–73; Hume, 1979–80). Writing in 1996, well into the post-Cold War era, Robert Fisk argued that US involvement 'will not produce a fair settlement – merely the victory of those whom America chooses to regard as future allies in the furthest north-west corner of Europe'. Among the ' "has beens" in Ireland,' argued Fisk, 'the Americans might well number the Brits' (Fisk, 1996). The US also clearly does have real, though limited, economic interests in investment in a peaceful Northern Ireland. George Mitchell and Commerce Secretary Ron Brown frequently made the point in the mid-1990s about Northern Ireland constituting a bridgehead into the European Union market (Brinkley, 1997, 117; O'Brien, 1995; Spillane, 1995).

These arguments, based on narrowly conceived American 'interests', are not entirely wide of the mark; they partake of the strength of realist theory in international relations generally.

However, they again fail to explain the intensity of the Clinton concern with a region that is, as McCain argued, only of marginal security concern, especially in post-Cold War conditions. The argument about the US wishing to create pliant allies also overstates American hopes and expectations regarding Irish unity. Figures like Tony Lake and Senator Mitchell were sufficiently sophisticated in Irish issues to appreciate that complex problems require complex solutions. US policy on Ireland has not merely been camouflaged nationalism.

The most convincing explanation for Clinton's intense activism lies in the conjunction of post-Cold War foreign policy priorities, and changing assumptions concerning the 'special relationship'. Viewed from the White House, Northern Ireland offered a promising opportunity to practise the 'peace promotion' facet of its post-Cold War internationalist agenda. Success there, if some success could be claimed, would help silence domestic calls for a neo-isolationist or unilateralist foreign policy. Nancy Soderberg points up the US role as 'indispensable intermediary', also emphasising, in connection with US economic incentives for the Irish peace process, Clinton's predilection for 'commercial diplomacy' (Soderberg, 2005, 69, 73). In contrast to other regions in the world, involvement in Northern Ireland ran no risk of military engagement or casualties. There was a real possibility for success, while failure would not be catastrophic for the White House. The policy was, of course, bound to be criticized by political opponents in the US. Former Secretary of State James Baker declared in 1996 that Clinton's Irish policy had produced 'the worst relationship with our closest ally, Britain, since the Boston Tea Party' (*The Times*, 16 August 1996). However, there were unlikely to be too many domestic objections to peace activism in Ireland.

The policy was made easier still by Clinton's ability to ignore inhibitions imposed by the Cold War 'special relationship'. Nancy Soderberg attempted to turn this (and Baker's) point around, arguing that 'it is precisely because of the special relationship that we can afford to have disagreements and get over them and continue to work together' (*The Sunday Times*, 2 April 1995). However, Niall O'Dowd's gloss on this issue rings truer: 'We were taking on forty-five years of Anglo-American relations' (Cox, 1997, 687–9; *The Guardian*, 1 December 1995). Freed from the Cold War relationship, Clinton operated with little concern for British sensibilities. The degree to which Major's government came to accept this illustrated, not so much the strength of the 'special relationship', as the triumph of *force majeure*. Clinton's Irish policy indicated that it was now unnecessary even to invoke core American interests to justify uninvited dabbling in the international affairs of Washington's closest ally. By the later 1990s, British opinion tended to the view that Clinton had played a valuable part in the peace process that, whatever its ultimate outcome, had of itself saved many lives. An indication, however, of the affront to British diplomatic sensibilities caused generally by America's Irish policy was given in various remarks made in 1997 by Nicholas Henderson. The Irish experience, according to the former ambassador, illustrated the *limits* of influence enjoyed by HM embassy at Washington: 'This is a major problem for the embassy in Washington, and I cannot say that they have been very successful in diverting the American government from allowing, permitting, or not preventing, the continuation of arms, money and supplies to the IRA' ('Witness Seminar', 1998, 121).

Evaluation of Clinton's Irish policy should also take account of the polarization in Northern Irish politics which stretched into the new century. Admitting Sinn Fein into the democratic, power-sharing party was always liable to contribute to the collapse of the Northern Irish centre. By the time of the 2005 British general election, the Social Democratic and Labour Party had given way to Sinn Fein as the representative of the nationalist and Catholic tradition, while the Democratic Unionist party had taken much of the ground previously occupied by the Official Unionists. The 2005 electoral defeat of David Trimble exemplified the new order. The Clinton team accepted that Irish issues were complex; however, Nancy Soderberg's insistence that the bestowal of 'political legitimacy' on Trimble increased his 'political power at home' did betray at least a degree of naivety about Ulster politics (Soderberg, 2005, 72). As with the peace process generally, electoral polarization was not entirely a product of Clinton's policy, but was certainly a partial, and foreseeable, effect of it.

Unsurprisingly, Northern Ireland did not figure prominently in the foreign policy agenda of Clinton's presidential successor. A Republican president, following a fairly narrow 'interests' agenda was unlikely to see Northern Ireland as a major priority. In the case of Ireland, however, there was no real question of the new administration distancing itself from Clinton and his legacy. It was quite prepared to accept that Washington had indeed played a valuable and historic role in securing the Belfast Agreement. America's proper course now was cautiously to encourage and facilitate progress on the promises made in 1998 (Dumbrell, 2006). Richard Haass, Director of Policy Planning in the State Department, was appointed as unofficial 'ambassador' to the province in 2001. 'Peace in Northern Ireland', declared Bush on St Patrick's Day 2001, 'is in America's strong national interest' (Haass, 2002). Irish issues became more prominent following the arrest in Colombia in August 2001 of three members of the Provisional IRA. A *Washington Post* editorial (16 August 2001) reported that the IRA men were assisting Colombia's 'drug-trafficking terrorists in mastering explosives'. The potential damage to Sinn Fein' American fund-raising accruing from association between Irish republicans and the Colombian Revolutionary Armed Forces (FARC) was vast. On the actual morning of September 11, 2001, Richard Haass was apparently engaged in talks with Gerry Adams, involving a US threat to withdraw fund-raising and visa rights if the IRA did not proceed with arms decommissioning (Special Report, 2001).

The unfolding events of that September day compounded the weak American position of Sinn Fein. Haass was quoted in early 2002 that there was now ' "zero tolerance" in this country for terrorism of any sort' (Dunphy, 2002). Some of Sinn Fein's most prominent American supporters changed tack in this period. New York Congressman Pete King – confounding stereotypes, King is actually a Republican – warned the IRA in connection with the Colombian arrests: 'you're only allowed one mistake in this business' (House of Representatives hearings, 2002, 113). The IRA's continued involvement with bank robbery and murder, especially in the period of late 2004 and early 2005 further weakened its US base. The potential and actual loss of Irish-American sympathy for their cause was a significant factor in the slow process of internal IRA acceptance, by mid-2005, of the need to make a public declaration of the end of the armed struggle.

The George W. Bush administration maintained a degree of Irish activism, even in the midst of the War on Terror. Stopping in Belfast to meet Blair in Belfast shortly after the 2003 invasion of Iraq, the US president presided over an unlikely meeting of Northern Irish representatives from across the political spectrum. The official

American line was on the one hand that Sinn Fein must renounce any connection with terrorism, and on the other that 'inclusiveness' was the key to progress. In Haass's phrase, Northern Ireland must be 'a house that is warm for all those who live there' (Haass, 2002). On Haass's departure from the administration prior to the 2004 elections, Mitchell Reiss continued his role. President Bush continued to take a personal role; for example, speaking directly on the telephone to both Gerry Adams and Ian Paisley in late 2004 when a decommissioning and power-sharing solution seemed feasible. Bush publicly welcomed the IRA peace declarations and decommissioning later in 2005, always emphasising that words and deeds must move together (Archick, 2005, 23). The extent of Bush's Irish activism is to some degree explicable in terms of Tony Blair's enhanced post-9/11 status in Washington. Here perhaps was something concrete which Blair did manage to extract from Bush in return for loyalty over the War on Terror and the Iraqi invasion. More important for our enquiry into Anglo-American relations, however, is the apparent extent to which White House concern with Northern Irish affairs was actually continued, even institutionalized, following Clinton's presidency.

11
Conclusion

Themes of mutuality and domination, sovereignty and surrender recur in the relatively short history of the US–UK 'special relationship'. As we have seen, these themes are regularly overlaid and distorted by emotion, whether of the hands-across-the-sea variety, or of the death-knell-of-British-sovereignty hue. Historian A. J. P. Taylor declared in the course of a 1946 BBC radio programme on US–UK relations, just as the 'special relationship' was changing from its anti-Nazi to its anti-communist form, that US foreign policy would become 'increasingly selfish, harsh and self-interested'. Britain must end the 'present policy of becoming an economic and military satellite of the United States' (Burk, 2000, 379). Taylor's words echoed down the decades and were reiterated by those who protested against President George W. Bush in the state visit to London described in the first chapter of this book. For Mark Curtis (2003, 112), 'Britain under Blair' was 'so clearly the apologist for US foreign policy, that the relationship seriously resembles that between the former Soviet Union and its satellite republics of Belorussia and Ukraine'. According to Labour MP Alan Simpson (2004) the contemporary US–UK relationship 'is a twenty-first century replica of the relationship between Britain and its colonies during the days of empire'. Harold Pinter took the opportunity of his Nobel Prize acceptance speech in 2005 to denounce US selfishness, harshness and self-interest, as well as Britain's spineless support of the American empire.

It is not unreasonable to posit a distinct 'American' model of empire. The American dialectic of republic *versus* empire sits at the centre of American political discourse. In one of the more thoughtful analyses of the problem of American empire, Andrew Bacevich (2003, 243) notes: 'although the United States has not created an

269

empire in any formal sense – what would be the point of doing so? – it has most definitely acquired an imperial problem'. The American imperial model embraces Geir Lundestad's concept of 'empire by invitation' (Lundestad, 1986). It is not primarily an empire, if indeed it is an empire at all, of coercion. The concept of 'empire', rooted in American and Anglo-American economic and geopolitical interests, has been reworked and reinvigorated by a variety of leftist and neo-Marxist critics of recent US foreign policy (Colas and Saull (eds) 2005; Engdahl, 2004). It has also famously been revived by US neo-conservatives like Max Boot (2002) in a positive context. Let us consider one or two points relevant to the debates over American empire, especially in so far as they relate to the US–UK 'special relationship'.

The point is often made that the American empire, if indeed it does exist, is not like the formal, coercive British empire. Joseph Nye reminds us that in 2003, the US could not even coerce Mexico to support a second UN resolution on Iraq, noting: 'The British Empire did not have that kind of problem with Kenya or India' (Nye, 2004, 136). Anti-imperialist Charles Beard wrote at the beginning of the Second World War: 'America is not to be Rome or Britain. It is to be America' (Bacevich, 2003, 242). The exceptionalist tradition is a strong one, and the temptation always is to argue that if America has an empire, it has one in a peculiarly and exceptionally American way. Yet the British empire was, for most of its history, a fairly loose and even ramshackle organization. In India, it also depended on the cooperation of princely states whose conduct and compromised independence may, perhaps not too fancifully, be compared to contemporary Britain's. Michael Cox reminds us that imperial America, like imperial Britain, 'has often tolerated a good deal of difference; and it has been careful, though not always, not to undermine the authority of friendly local elites' (Cox, 2004, 601). What does need to be borne in mind, however, is, as Nye again writes, that 'power depends on context'. The US is military top dog. The Final Report of the 9/11 Commission (2004, 95) noted of the US Defense Department: 'With an annual budget larger than the gross domestic product of Russia, it is an empire'. Military power does give the US unilateral, and indeed, imperial options. In respect of its economic power, however, the US has to operate – certainly as regards Europe – in a much more reciprocal and concessionary fashion. Other dimensions of power in a globalized information age are 'chronically dispersed' (Nye, 2004, 136–7). Globalization is far too complex and decentralized a process (even if we merely consider its impact on the UK) simply to be equated with American empire. Even American military power is not limitless. No doubt like British power before it, US military power depends on continued economic strength, good decisions and national will. The American empire certainly cannot rely on good decisions being made. There is also the problem of what Nye calls 'imperial understretch': a type of 'overstretch' resulting from 'having to police more and more peripheral countries with nationally resistant publics than foreign or American public opinion will accept' (Nye, 2004, 138). Democracy and imperialism are not natural allies.

More directly on the issue of US–UK relations, we confront the perennial problem of structure and agency. Robert Jervis (2005, 98) argues that the US–UK 'special relationship' does exist, though primarily in a way that demonstrates that the structures of international power always leave 'room for choice'. The US–UK relationship is explicable, according to this line of argument, to a considerable extent in terms of elite views about the best way to sustain Britain's own post-imperial global standing, as well as the orientation towards American power displayed by individual British leaders. Again and again, from the era of Jack and Mac to the war decisions of Tony Blair, we have encountered the characteristic, though generally tacit, assumptions of British diplomacy: the view, deriving ultimately from Macmillan's 'Greeks and Romans' analogy, that the UK benefits from propinquity to American power, and that British influence over US foreign policy (to the extent that it enjoys any at all) makes that policy better. A lesson of the recent traumas in the 'special relationship' is surely that these assumptions need to be examined critically, if not entirely abandoned. 'Greeks and Romans' thinking insults America, reinforces British unrealism, and distorts rational calculations about British interest.

Robert Jervis also argues that 'only one ally can have a "special relationship" with the hegemon, and Britain's having taken this role makes it harder for others to emulate it' (Jervis, 2005, 98). Here is worth re-emphasizing that the concept of the US-UK 'special relationship' has, from its inception in the middle years of the twentieth century, been primarily a British one. As noted in this book's first chapter, Mexico and Israel are prime candidates to rival Britain's claim to specialness. David Schoenbaum has argued that

since the American Revolution, the US has also 'entertained, cultivated, endured, and suffered special relationships, with countries as
diverse as Canada, Panama, France, Germany, Russia, South Korea,
'one Vietnam and two Chinas', Guatemala, Nicaragua and El
Salvador (Schoenbaum, 1998, 273). Even confining our list to
countries with whom the US has, at least during the past half
century or so, enjoyed generally cordial relations, we are still left
with several rivals to the UK's 'special relationship'. Academic
books and articles on American relations with countries as various
as China, Israel, Germany. Canada, and no doubt many more, have
the phrase, 'special relationship', in their titles (Gatzke, 1980; Hunt,
1983; Little, 1993; Morici, 1991). Clearly a case can be made for
the US-Israeli relationship as the most special of all special cases.
In the case of Israel, the relationship is existential. President Carter
declared in 1977: 'We have a special relationship with Israel ... our
number one commitment in the Middle East is to protect the right of
Israel to exist' (Bar-Simon-Tov, 1998, 231). It is also worth pointing
out that, as this study has shown, if Britain and the US have enjoyed
a generally friendly alliance in the years of what this book, rather
pompously, calls *the* 'special relationship', the Anglo-American
ride has been an extremely bumpy one. However, Anglo-American
tension has, fortunately, never in recent times reached the level of
actual combat. Even this modest achievement eludes some other
friendly 'special relationships': in 1967, towards the climax of the
Six Day War, as Israeli forces were advancing towards Damascus
against the wishes of Washington, Israel actually attacked the US
ship *Liberty* (Oren, 2002).

The conclusion that emerges from the preceding chapters is that,
in the Cold War and, rather surprisingly, afterwards as well, a
US–UK 'special relationship' did indeed exist. Its 'specialness'
resided primarily in military and intelligence cooperation, but it did
draw importantly on culture, history, shared outlook and habits of
cooperation. 'Specialness' was also reflected in the, admittedly
sometimes very limited, mutuality in the relationship. From
Britain's viewpoint, the Cold War relationship with the US, may
have fostered delusions about the UK's international status, as well
as disguising Britain's European interests. It did, however, have
some benefits. It provided something of a soft landing for Britain's
post-imperial fall. The old adage about Britain being able to punch
above its diplomatic weight was not entirely wrong. Provided that

British diplomats and leaders recognized the radical asymmetry at the relationship's heart – above all, provided they made decisions which reflected the wide and complex spectrum of British interests – successes could be achieved in the house that Jack and Mac built. Despite its economic difficulties and despite the Cold War defence dependency, the UK never sank entirely to the status of client, vassal or satellite. The Cold War 'special relationship' was an important aspect of anti-communist Atlantic security. Whether it was the threat of premature devaluation in the 1960s or the promise of acting as a pro-American force in European for a in the 1980s, London did have important cards to play. On occasion, as we have seen, London did oppose Washington: over the Multilateral Nuclear Force, over the Siberian pipeline; over a host of economic and trade issues over the period since 1973. From a slightly different perspective, it can be emphasized, of course, that Britain's contribution to the cause of American 'soft power' actually depended on the retention of credibility and independence. When the relationship was so dramatically renewed by Tony Blair after 9/11, the driving factor was Blair's own contingent belief system. Structures of power and the inclinations of history played only subsidiary, supporting roles.

Looking to the future, we can only counsel caution. In the concluding chapter of this book's first edition, I wrote: 'to risk a strangulated metaphor, the writing for the "special relationship" was on the (Berlin) Wall as it fell' (Dumbrell, 2001, 220). The geopolitical ties of anti-communism and the 'shared fate' were indeed removed in 1989, but special relations continued regardless, only to be vigorously resuscitated after 2001. As noted already, inertia and shared culture to some degree were responsible for this survival, as were the particular post-9/11 decisions of Tony Blair's government. Inertia cannot last forever. Particular governments come and go. Shared culture – Margaret Thatcher's 'ties of blood, language, culture' (Howe, 1995, 559) – is changing, rather than disappearing. Cheap, if not always convenient, air travel has had an impact; so has the growth of a young, transatlantic army of corporate professionals, commuting between London and major US (and European) cities. Shared culture will nevertheless have to contend with rapid demographic change in the US, as well as with the complexities and uncertainties of British involvement in the affairs of continental Europe.

There certainly is such a thing as 'Anglo-American culture', rooted to some degree in history and language, to some degree in the economic convergence of the US–UK model of contemporary capitalism. In many ways, however, the US – culturally as well as in power terms – is very different from the Britain. The illusion of 'knowing' America through familiarity with its popular culture bedevils real understanding, which can only be achieved through immersion in *American* history and culture. In the early 1950s, Walter Gifford, the US ambassador to London felt it necessary to emphasize to his bosses in Washington that 'we are two different peoples with different reactions, different modes of operation and at times transitory differences in interest' (*Foreign Relations of the United States, 1951*, vol. 4, part 1, 895). The memory of a later counterpart to Gifford, British Ambassador Christopher Meyer, is similarly instructive. Recalling his first visit to the US, Meyer wrote in 2005: 'So much was intensely familiar from movies and television; but so much was alien'. America was indeed 'a foreign country, not Britain writ large' (Meyer, 2005, 5). In certain respects, and crucially in terms of their democratic polities and purposes, the US has arguably more in common with universalist, post-Enlightenment France than with unmessianic Britain. Charles de Gaulle spoke of a 'certain idea' of France 'dedicated to an exalted and exceptional destiny' (*The Economist*, 24 December 2005, 51). Such words could readily be transposed to the lips of an American political leader; they do not find an obvious home in prosaic British political discourse.

Turning to prospects for US–European relations, it is tempting to declare that everything in the future of Europeanism and consequently in the future of US-European relations, is uncertain, and to leave it at that. European expansion and public disquiet about the whole European project throws all into doubt. The future of NATO, if indeed it has one, again is unknowable. Alongside a multi-speed integrated Europe, there is the possibility of a similar division within NATO, with its European and American components taking on distinct military roles. It may be objected that the possibility of US-European collision has been with us for a long time, and certainly was a staple of the post-Cold War debates of the 1990s. The Iraq invasion of 2003, however, took all this to a new level. In the wake of the invasion, it was not difficult to find commentators seriously considering the possibility of an American military exit from Europe (Trachtenberg, 2005). Clearly, the future of US–UK relations depends upon how these tensions are resolved.

Most academic analyses conclude that the Atlantic alliance can and should be preserved through mutual adjustment and reconfigured understanding. Thus Simon Serfaty (2005, 144) argues that, for Europe 'its longing for a compassionate America is an inducement for an American strategy of restraint that would serve both sides of the Atlantic well'. For the US, 'its hopes for a stronger, larger, and more united Europe is also compatible with a more active role of Europe in the world, which would also serve both sides of the Atlantic well'. Sustained American unilateralism and Chiracist counter-hegemony projects are equally unhelpful to a renewal of the Atlantic alliance. There needs to be a fundamental rethinking of the purposes and modalities of NATO and of the EU and its relationship to the US; what David Andrews calls the reheating of 'this plate of Cold War leftovers' will not suffice (Andrews, 2005, 72).

It would be naïve to suppose that British support for the Iraqi invasion of 2003 amounted to a choosing of the pro-American path over a European one. The 2003 transatlantic dispute, especially in one considers the role of Eastern and Central Europe, was, after all, primarily a US/Franco-German, rather than a US–European rift *per se*. Memories of the problems that surrounded Blair's decisions could arguably drive Britain more in a European than in an American direction in any future disputes. Just as there was a 'Suez generation' and a 'Vietnam generation', so the possibility of a lasting generational dimension to the events of 2003–4 needs to be recognized. In the short term, and pending any reformed Atlantic settlement, London has little option but to seek to rebuild the 'Atlantic bridge', attempting to use its putative custody of the bridge as a lever in respect both of the US and the European allies. Timothy Garton Ash (2005, 52–3) puts the point well: 'Britain's connections with both Europe and America are so thick and vital that to "choose Europe" or "choose America" would be to cut off the country's left or right leg'. It is still vital for all parties to recognize that, for London, partnership with the United States is not possible. Even with all the contemporary uncertainties, an active future in Europe is.

Appendix:
Key Events and American/British Office-Holders

1 Some key events: 1956–2006

1956	Suez crisis
1957	Sandys White Paper
1958	Repeal of McMahon Act
1961	Berlin Wall crisis
1962	Cuban missile crisis
	Polaris deal
1964	Effective abandonment by Washington of Multilateral Nuclear Force proposals
1965–6	Harold Wilson refuses to send British forces to Vietnam
1967	Major defence cuts announced by London (especially East of Suez)
	Currency devaluation
1968	Nuclear Nonproliferation Treaty
1971	Indo-Pakistan War
1972	Heath government approves Chevaline production
1973	Britain accedes to Treaty of Rome
1974	Cyprus crisis
1976	IMF crisis
1980	Rhodesian settlement
1980–2	Trident deal
1981	Siberian pipeline project cancellation
1982	Falklands War
1983	Grenada invasion
1985	Anglo-Irish Agreement
1986	Libyan bombing
	Westland affair
1989	Fall of Berlin Wall
1990	Transatlantic Declaration (James Baker)
1990–91	Gulf crisis and war
1993	US rejects Vance-Owen plan for division of Bosnia
1994	Gerry Adams admitted to US
1995	First Clinton visit to Belfast
1997	Hong Kong handover to China
1998	Good Friday (Belfast) Agreement
	Air bombardment of Iraq
1999	Blair address to the Economic Club of Chicago
	Air bombardment of Kosovo and Serbia
2001	9/11 terror attacks on New York and Washington DC
	Start global of War on Terror

	Invasion of Afghanistan
2002	Passage of United Nations Resolution 1441 on Iraq
2003	Invasion of Iraq
	State visit to London of President George W. Bush
2005	G8 summit (Gleneagles)

2 British prime ministers, 1957–2006

1957–63	Harold Macmillan (Conservative)
1963–4	Sir Alec Douglas-Home (Conservative)
1964–70	Harold Wilson (Labour)
1970–74	Edward Heath (Conservative)
1974–76	Harold Wilson (Labour)
1976–79	James Callaghan (Labour)
1979–90	Margaret Thatcher (Conservative)
1990–97	John Major (Conservative)
1997–	Tony Blair (Labour)

3 American presidents, 1961–2006

1961–63	John Kennedy (Democrat)
1963–69	Lyndon B. Johnson (Democrat)
1969–74	Richard Nixon (Republican)
1974–77	Gerald Ford (Republican)
1977–81	Jimmy Carter (Democrat)
1981–89	Ronald Reagan (Republican)
1989–93	George Bush (Republican)
1993–2001	Bill Clinton (Democrat)
2001–	George W. Bush (Republican)

4 British foreign secretaries, 1960–2006

1960–63	Earl of Home
1964	Richard Austen (Rab) Butler
1964–5	Patrick Gordon Walker
1965–6	Michael Stewart
1966–8	George Brown
1968–70	Michael Stewart
1970–74	Sir Alec Douglas-Home
1974–76	James Callaghan
1976–77	Anthony Crosland
1977–79	David Owen
1979–82	Lord (Peter) Carrington
1982–83	Francis Pym
1983–89	Sir Geoffrey Howe
1989	John Major
1989–5	Douglas Hurd
1995–7	Malcolm Rifkind
1997–2001	Robin Cook
2001–2006	Jack Straw
2006–	Margaret Beckett

5 US secretaries of state, 1961–2006

1961–69	Dean Rusk
1969–73	William Rogers
1973–77	Henry Kissinger
1977–80	Cyrus Vance
1980–81	Edmund Muskie
1981–82	Alexander Haig
1982–89	George Shultz
1989–92	James Baker
1992–93	Lawerence Eagleburger
1993–97	Warren Christopher
1997–2001	Madeleine Albright
2001–2005	Colin Powell
2005–	Condoleezza Rice

Bibliography

Primary Materials

This book draws on standard primary sources, such as *The Public Papers of the Presidents of the US, Foreign Relations of the United States, Parliamentary Debates, Documents on British Policy Overseas: Series III* and various other governmental and private publications. It rests also on research done at the National Archives at Kew, London. Most National Archives references are to Foreign Office (FO), Foreign and Commonwealth Office (FCO), Cabinet (CAB) or PREM material. Research was also undertaken at the Jimmy Carter Presidential Library (Atlanta, GA) and the Lyndon B Johnson Presidential Library (Austin, TX). Most Presidential Library references are to National Security File (NSF) material.

Books and articles

Acevedo, D. E. (1984) 'The US Measures against Argentina Resulting from the Malvinas Conflict', *American Journal of International Law*, 78: 4, 323–43.

Acheson, Dean (1970) *Present at the Creation: My Years in the State Department* (London: Hamish Hamilton).

Adams, C. F. (ed.) (1853) *The Works of John Adams* (Boston: Little Brown).

Adams, D. K. (1989) 'Preface' to Adams, D. K. (ed.), *Studies in US Politics* (Manchester: Manchester University Press).

—— (ed.) (1995) *British Documents on Foreign Affairs: Reports and Papers from the Confidential Print, Series C: North America, 1919–1939, vol. 23, Annual Reports 1933–1936* (Washington, DC: University Press of America).

Adonis, A. and Tim Hames (eds) (1994) *A Conservative Revolution? The Thatcher–Reagan Decade in Perspective* (Manchester: Manchester University Press).

Ahearn, R. J. (2004) *US–European Trade Relations: Issues and Policy Challenges* (Washington, DC: Congressional Research Service Brief).

Ahrar, M. E. (ed.) (1987) *Ethnic Groups and US Foreign Policy* (New York: Greenwood).

Aldous, R. (1996) ' "A Family Affair": Macmillan and the Art of Personal Diplomacy', in R. Aldous and S. Lee (eds) *Harold Macmillan and Britain's World Role*.

Aldous, R. and S. Lee (eds) (1996) *Harold Macmillan and Britain's World Role* (London: Macmillan).

Aldrich, R. J. (1994) 'The Value of Residual Empire: Anglo-American Intelligence Cooperation in Asia after 1945', in Aldrich and Hopkins (eds) *Intelligence, Defence and Diplomacy*.

—— (1998) 'British Intelligence and the Anglo-American "Special Relationship" During the Cold War', *Review of International Studies*, 24: 3, 331–51.

—— (2001) *The Hidden Hand: Britain, America and Cold War Secret Intelligence* (London: John Murray).

—— and M. F. Hopkins (eds) (1994) *Intelligence, Defence and Diplomacy: British Policy in the Post-war World* (Ilford: Cass).

Allen, D. J. (2002) 'A Competitive Relationship: the Maturing of the EU–US Relationship, 1980–2000', in Ramet and Ingebritsen (eds) *Coming in from the Cold War*.

Allen, H. C. (1954) *Great Britain and the United States: A History of Anglo-American Relations 1783–1952* (London: Odhams Press).

Allin, D. H. (2003) *NATO's Balkan Interventions* (Oxford: Oxford University Press).

Alterman, Eric (1998) *Who Speaks for America? Why Democracy Matters in Foreign Policy* (Ithaca, NY: Cornell University Press).

Amato, G. *et al.* (2005) *Initiative for a Renewed Transatlantic Partnership* (Washington, DC: Center for Strategic and International Studies).

Anderson, Perry (1992) *English Questions* (London: Verso).

Andrew, Christopher (1995) *For the President's Eyes Only* (London: HarperCollins).

Andrews, D. M. (ed.) (2005) *The Atlantic Alliance under Stress: US–European Relations after Iraq* (Cambridge: Cambridge University Press).

—— (2005) 'The United States and its Atlantic Partners', in Andrews (ed.) *The Atlantic Alliance under Stress*.

Applebaum, A. (2005) 'In Search of Pro-Americanism', *Foreign Policy*, 149, 32–41.

Archer, Clive and F. Butler (1996) *The European Union: Structure and Process* (London: Pinter).

Archik, Kristin (2005) *The United Kingdom: Issues for the United States* (Washington DC: Congressional Research Service Report).

Art, R. J. (1996) 'Why Western Europe Needs the United States and NATO', *Political Science Quarterly*, 111: 1, 1–39.

Arthur, P. and K. Jeffrey (1988) *Northern Ireland since 1968* (Oxford: Blackwell).

Artis, M. J. (ed.) (1996) *The UK Economy* (Oxford: Oxford University Press).

Ascherson, N. (1993) 'The Republican Virtue of Leaving Yesterday Behind', *The Independent on Sunday*, 24 January.

Ashdown, Paddy (2002) *The Ashdown Diaries: Volume 2, 1997–99* (London: Penguin).

Ashton, N. J. (2002) *Kennedy, Macmillan and the Cold War: the Irony of Interdependence* (Basingstoke: Palgrave)

—— (2005) 'Harold Macmillan and the "Golden Days" of Anglo-American Relations Revisited, 1957–63', *Diplomatic History*, 29: 4, 691–724.

Atkinson, R. (1994) *Crusade: The Untold Story of the Gulf War* (London: HarperCollins).

Attlee, C. R. (1954) 'Britain and America: Common Aims, Different Opinions', *Foreign Affairs*, 32: 1, 190–202.

Auger, V. A. (1996) *The Dynamics of Foreign Policy Analysis: The Carter Administration and the Neutron Bomb* (Lanham: Rowman and Littlefield).

Bacevich, A. J. (2003) *American Empire: the Realities and Consequences* (Cambridge, MA: Harvard University Press).

Badger, Tony. (1992) 'Confessions of a British Americanist', *Journal of American History*, 79: 3, 515–23.

Bainbridge, T. (1998) *The Penguin Companion to the European Union* (London: Penguin).

Baker, D. and D. Seawright (eds) (1998) *Britain For and Against Europe* (Oxford: Clarendon Press).

Baker, James A. (1995) *The Politics of Diplomacy* (New York: Putnam's Sons).

Balen, M. (1994) *Kenneth Clarke* (London: Fourth Estate).

Ball, George (1982) *The Past Has Another Pattern* (New York: Norton).

Ball, S. and A. Seldon (eds) (1996) *The Heath Government: 1970–74: A Reappraisal* (London: Longman).

Bamford, J. (1983) *The Puzzle Palace* (London: Sidgwick & Jackson).

Bange, O. (2000) *The EEC Crisis of 1963: Kennedy, Macmillan, de Gaulle and Adenauerin Conflict* (Basingstoke: Macmillan).

Bar-Simon-Tov, Y. (1998), 'The United States and Israel since 1948: A "Special Relationship"?', *Diplomatic History*, 22: 2, 231–62.

Barber, Anthony (1996) *Taking the Tide: A Memoir* (Norwich: Michael Russell).

Barnett, Joel (1982) *Inside the Treasury* (London: Andrew Deutsch).

Barry, J. and C. Dickey (1999) 'Warrior's Reward', *Newsweek*, 9 August.

Bartlett, C. J. (1992) *'The Special Relationship'* (London: Longman).

Baudrillard, J. (1988) *America* (London: Verso).

Baylis, John (1984) *Anglo-American Defence Relations, 1939–1984: The Special Relationship* (London: Macmillan).

—— (1985) 'The Anglo-American Relationship and Alliance Theory', *International Relations*, 4: 4, 368–79.

—— (ed.) (1997) *Anglo-American Relations since 1939: The Enduring Alliance* (Manchester: Manchester University Press).

—— (1998) 'The "Special relationship": A Diverting Myth', in Buffet and Heuser (eds) *Haunted by History*.

—— (2001) 'Exchanging Nuclear Secrets: Laying the Foundations of the Anglo-American Nuclear Relationship', *Diplomatic History*, 25: 1, 55–61.

—— and Stoddart, K. (2001) 'Britain and the Chevaline Project: the Hidden Nuclear Programme, 1967–82', *Journal of Strategic Studies*, 26: 4, 134–55.

BBC News (2005a) 'Global Poll Slams Bush Leadership', 19 January (via BBC website).

BBC News (2005b) 'World Press Electrified by Bush Vision', 21 January (via BBC website).

Beck, P. (1988) *The Falkland Islands as an International Problem* (London: Routledge).

Beck, R. J. (1993) *The Grenada Invasion: Politics, Law and Foreign Policy Decisionmaking* (Boulder, CO: Westview).

Beer, S. H. (1982) *Britain Against Itself. The Political Contradictions of Capitalism* (London: Faber and Faber).

Bellamy, A. J. and Williams, P. D. (2005) 'Who's Keeping the Peace?', *International Security*, 29: 4, 157–95.

Benn, Tony (1987) *Out of the Wilderness: Diaries 1963–67* (London: Hutchinson).

—— (1988) *Office Without Power: Diaries 1968–72* (London: Hutchinson).

—— (1989) *Against the Tide: Diaries 1973–76* (London: Arrow Books).

—— (1991) *Conflicts of Interest: Diaries 1977–80*, ed. R. Winstone (London: Arrow Books).

Bennett, Alan (1994) *Writing Home* (London: Faber and Faber).

Bennett, G. and K. A. Hamilton (eds) (1997) *Documents on British Policy Overseas*, Series III: Vols 1–2 (London: The Stationery Office).

—— (eds) (2001) *Documents on British Policy Overseas*, Series III: Vol. 3 (London: Cass).

Bennett, J. (2004) *Anglosphere: the Future of the English-speaking Nations in the Internet Era* (Lanham: Rowman and Littlefield).

Bergsten, C. Fred (1999) 'America and Europe: Clash of the Titans', *Foreign Affairs*, 78: 2, 20–34.

Bernstein, Robert (2005) 'EU *vs.* US *vs.* China: Partnership Paradoxes', *International Herald Tribune*, 21 January.

Bert, Wayne (1997) *The Reluctant Superpower: United States Policy in Bosnia, 1991–95* (Basingstoke: Macmillan).

Beschloss, M. (ed.) (1997) *Taking Charge: The Johnson White House Tapes, 1963–64* (New York: Simon and Schuster).

Bevan, Aneurin (1957) 'Britain and America at Loggerheads', *Foreign Affairs*, 36: 1, 60–67.

Bill, J. A. (1997) *George Ball: Behind the Scenes in US Foreign Policy* (New Haven, CT: Yale University Press).

Billings-Yun, M. (1977) *Decision Against War: Eisenhower and Dien Bien Phu, 1954* (New York: Columbia University Press).

Bishop, P. and E. Mallie (1987) *The Provisional IRA* (London: Heinemann).

Blair, A. (1998) 'Swimming with the Tide? Britain and the Maastricht Treaty Negotiations on Common Foreign and Security Policy', *Contemporary British History*, 12: 3, 87–102.

Blair, Tony (2004) 'Doctrine of the International Community', in Stelzer (ed.) *Neoconservatism*.

Blix, Hans (2004) *Disarming Iraq: The Search for Weapons of Mass Destruction* (London: Bloomsbury).

Bluth, C. (2004) 'The British Road to War: Blair, Bush and the Decision to Invade Iraq', *International Affairs*, 80: 5, 871–92.

Boot, Max (2002) *The Savage Wars of Peace: Small Wars and the Rise of American Power* (New York: Basic books).

Boren, D. (1994) 'The Trident Missile and Britain's 1981 Defence Review', in R. J. Aldrich and M. F. Hopkins (eds) *Intelligence, Defence and Diplomacy*.

Botsford, K. (1990) 'With a Little Help from Dr Death', *The Independent*, 18 August.

Bowyer-Bell, J. (1993) *The Irish Troubles: A Generation of Violence, 1967–1992* (Dublin: Gill and Macmillan).

Boyle, Peter G. (1996) 'The British Government's View of the Cuban Missile Crisis', *Contemporary Record*, 10: 3, 22–38.

—— (2005) *Eisenhower* (Harlow: Pearson Education).

Bradbury, Malcolm (1980) 'How I Invented America', *Journal of American Studies*, 14: 1, 110–21.

Brady, M. J. (1995) 'Democratic Audit', *Fortnight*, December.

—— (1996) 'The Fraying of the Green', *Fortnight*, June.

Brandon, Henry (1988) *Special Relationship: A Foreign Correspondent's Memoir from Roosevelt to Reagan* (London: Macmillan).

Brands, H. W. (1993) *The Devil We Knew: Americans and the Cold War* (New York: Oxford University Press).

—— (1995) *The Wages of Globalism* (New York: Oxford University Press).

Brinkley, Douglas (1992) *Dean Acheson: The Cold War Years, 1953–1971* (New Haven, CT: Yale University Press).

—— (1997) 'Democratic Enlargement: The Clinton Doctrine', *Foreign Policy*, 106, 110–21.

Brivati, Brian (1998) *Hugh Gaitskell* (London: Richard Cohen).

Brogan, D. W. (1959) 'From England', in F. Joseph (ed.) *As Others See Us* (Princeton: Princeton University Press).

Brosio, M. (1971) 'Will NATO Survive Detente?', *The World Today*, June.

Brown, George (1971) *In My Way* (London: Gollancz).

Brown, N. (1969) 'Anglo-French Nuclear Collaboration?', *The World Today*, August.

Brugioni, D. A. (1991) *Eyeball to Eyeball: The Inside Story of the Cuban Missile Crisis* (New York: Random House).

Bryson, Bill (1996) *Notes from a Small Island* (London: Black Swan).

Brzezinski, Z. (1983) *Power and Principle* (London: Weidenfeld & Nicolson).

Buffet, C. and Heuser, B. (eds) (1998) *Haunted by History: Myths in International Relations* (Providence: Berghahn Books).

Bugajski, J. and Teleki, I. (2005), 'Washington's New European Allies: Durable or Conditional Partners?', *The Washington Quarterly*, 28: 2, 95–107.

Bulmer, S., S. George and A. Scott (eds) (1992) *The United Kingdom and EC Membership Evaluated* (London: Pinter).

Bulmer, S. and G. Edwards (1992) 'Foreign and Security Policy', in Bulmer and Scott (eds) *The United Kingdom and EC Membership Evaluated*.

Burk, Kathleen (1998) 'Our Dangerous Reliance on America', *The Independent*, 27 August.

Burk, Kathleen (2000) *Troublemaker: the Life and History of A. J. P. Taylor* (New Haven, CT: Yale University Press).

Burk, Kathleen and A. Cairncross (1992) *'Goodbye Great Britain': The 1976 IMF Crisis* (New Haven, CT: Yale University Press).

Burns, Nicholas (2005) 'A Transatlantic Agenda for the Year Ahead', speech delivered at the Royal Institute for International Affairs (Chatham House, London), 6 April.

Burns, R. A. (1997) 'Strengthening the Transatlantic Partnership', in D. Eden (ed.) *The Future of the Atlantic Community*.

Busch, P. (2003) *All The Way With JFK? Britain, the US, and the Vietnam War* (Oxford: Oxford University Press).

Butler, R. (2004) 'Butler Review of Intelligence on Weapons of Mass Destruction' (www.butlerreview.org.uk/)

Byrd, P. (ed.) (1991) *British Defence Policy: Thatcher and Beyond* (London: Philip Allan).

Cable, J. (1994) 'Foreign Policy-making: Planning and Reflex', in C. Hill and P. Beschoff (eds) *Two Worlds of International Relations* (London: Routledge).

Cahill, K. M. and H. L. Carey (1984) 'America's Role in Northern Ireland', in K. M. Cahill (ed.) *The American Irish Revival* (Port Washington: Associated Faculty Press).

Cairncross, A. and B. Eichengreen (1983) *Sterling in Decline: The Devaluations of 1931, 1949 and 1967* (Oxford: Blackwell).

Callaghan, James (1981) *Time and Chance* (London: Collins).

Callaghan, John (1997) *Great Power Complex* (London: Pluto).

Campbell, C. S. (1974) *From Revolution to Rapprochement: The United States and Great Britain, 1783–1900* (New York: Wiley).

Campbell, David (1992) *Writing Security* (Manchester: Manchester University Press).

Campbell, Duncan (1984) *The Unsinkable Aircraft Carrier: American Military Power in Britain* (London: Michael Joseph).

Campbell, John (1993) *Edward Heath: A Biography* (London: Pimlico).

—— (2004) *Margaret Thatcher: Volume 2, The Iron Lady* (London: Pimlico).

Capet, A. and Sy-Wonyu, A. (eds) (2003) *The 'Special Relationship': La 'Relation Speciale'* (Rouen: University of Rouen).

Carrington, Peter (Lord) (1988) *Reflect on Things Past* (London: Collins).

Carroll, F. M. (2005) *The American Presence in Ulster: A Diplomatic History, 1796–1996* (Washington, DC: The Catholic University of America Press).

Carter, Jimmy (1982) *Keeping Faith* (London: Collins).

Castle, Barbara (1984) *The Castle Diaries, 1964–70* (London: Weidenfeld & Nicolson).

Ceaser, J. (2004) 'The Philosophical Origins of Anti-Americanism in Europe', in Hollander (ed.) *Understanding Anti-Americanism*.

Central Office of Information (1975) *Britain in the European Community* (London: COI).

Chace, J. (1973–74) 'The Concert of Europe', *Foreign Affairs*, 52: 1, 96–108.

Chalmers, M. (1984) *Trident: Britain's Independent Arms Race* (London: CND).

Chancellor, Alexander (1999) *Some Time in America* (London: Bloomsbury).

Charlton, M. (1983) *The Price of Victory* (London: BBC).

Charmley, John (1995) *Churchill's Grand Alliance: The Anglo-American Special Relationship 1940–57* (London: Hodder & Stoughton).

Cheney, S. A. (1998) 'The General's Folly', *Foreign Affairs*, 77: 1, 155–7.

Chichester, M. and J. Wilkinson (1982) *The Uncertain Ally: British Defence Policy, 1960–1980* (Aldershot: Gower).

Citrin, J., E. B. Haas, C. Muste and B. Reingold (1994) 'Is American Nationalism Changing? Implications for Foreign Policy', *International Studies Quarterly*, 38: 1, 1–31.

Clark, Alan (1993) *Diaries* (London: Phoenix).

Clark, Ian (1994) *Nuclear Diplomacy and the Special Relationship: Britain's Deterrent and America, 1957–1962* (Oxford: Oxford University Press).

Clark, W. K. (2001) *Waging Modern War: Bosnia, Kosovo and the Future of Combat* (New York: Public Affairs).

Clarke, M. (1985) 'American Reactions to Shifts in European Policy', in J. Roper (ed.) *The Future of British Defence Policy* (Aldershot: Gower).

—— (2004) 'The Diplomacy that led to War in Iraq', in Cornish (ed.) *The Conflict in Iraq, 2003*.

—— and Cornish, P. (2002) 'The European Defence Project and the Prague summit', *International Affairs*, 78: 4, 777–89.

Clarke, R. A. (2004) *Against All Enemies: Inside America's War on Terror* (New York: Free Press).

Clinton, Bill (2005) *My Life* (London: Arrow Books).

Coates, David (1980) *Labour in Power?: A Study of the Labour Government, 1974–79* (London: Longman).

—— and Krieger, J. (2004) *Blair's War* (Cambridge: Polity Press).

Cohen, W. I. and L. Zhao (eds) (1997) *Hong Kong under Chinese Rule: The Economic and Political Implications of Reversion* (Cambridge: Cambridge University Press).

Coker, C. (1992) 'Britain and the New World Order: The Special Relationship in the 1990s', *International Affairs*, 68: 3, 407–21.

Colas, A. and R. Saull (eds) (2005) *The War on Terror and the American 'Empire' after the Cold War* (London: Routledge).

Colchester, N. and D. Buchan (1990) *Europe Relaunched: Truths and Illusions on the Way to 1992* (London: Hutchinson).

Coleman, P. (1989) *The Liberal Conspiracy: The Congress for Cultural Freedom and the Struggle for the Mind of Postwar Europe* (New York: Free Press).

Colman, J. (2003) 'Harold Wilson, Lyndon Johnson and Anglo-American "Summit Diplomacy", 1964–1968', *Journal of Transatlantic Studies*, 1: 2, 131–51.

—— (2004) *A 'Special Relationship'?: Harold Wilson, Lyndon B. Johnson and Anglo-American Relations 'at the Summit'* (Manchester: Manchester University Press).

Coogan, Tim Pat (1995) *The Troubles* (London: Hutchinson).

Cook, Robin (2003) *The Point of Departure* (London: Simon and Schuster).

Cooley, J. (1999) *Unholy Wars: Afghanistan, America and International Terrorism* (London: Pluto).

Cooper, Chester L. (1970) *The Lost Crusade* (London: MacGibbon & Kee).

Cooper, Robert (2003) *The Breaking of Nations: Order and Chaos in the 21st Century* (London: Atlantic Books).

Coopey, R., S. Fielding and N. Tiratsoo (eds) (1993) *The Wilson Governments 1964–1970* (London: Pinter).

Cordesman, A. (1985) 'The Use of Force in the Middle East', in J. Coffey and G. Bonvicini (eds) *The Atlantic Alliance and the Middle East* (Basingstoke: Macmillan).

Cornish, Paul (1996) 'European Security: the End of Architecture and the new NATO', *International Affairs*, 72, 751–69.

—— (1997) *Partnership in Crisis: the US, Europe and the Fall and Rise of NATO* (London: Pinter/RIIA)

—— (ed.) (2004) *The Conflict in Iraq, 2003* (Basingstoke, Palgrave).

Cornwell, R. (1999) 'What Did Bill and Tony Argue About?', *The Independent*, 22 May.

Cosgrove, P. (1985) *Thatcher: The First Term* (London: The Bodley Head).

Costigliola, F. (1984a) *Awkward Dominion: American Political, Economic and Cultural Relations with Europe, 1919–1933* (Ithaca: Cornell University Press).

—— (1984b) 'The Failed Design: Kennedy, de Gaulle, and the Struggle for Europe', *Diplomatic History*, 8, 227–51.

—— (1995) 'Kennedy, the European Allies and the Failure to Consult', *Political Science Quarterly*, 110: 2, 105–24.

Cox, Michael (1997) ' "Bringing in the International": the IRA Ceasefire and the End of the Cold War', *International Affairs*, 73: 4, 671–94.

—— (1998) ' "Cinderella at the Ball": Explaining the End of the War', *Millennium*, 27: 3, 325–47.

—— (1999) 'The War that came in from the Cold', *World Policy Journal*, 16: 1, 59–67.

—— (2004) 'Empire. Imperialism and the Bush Doctrine', *Review of International Studies*, 30: 1, 585–608.

—— Guelke, Adrian, and Fiona Stephen (eds) (2006) *A Farewell to Arms? Beyond the Good Friday Agreement* (second edition) (Manchester: Manchester University Press).

—— (2006) 'Rethinking the International and Northern Ireland', in Cox, Guelke and Stephen (eds) *A Farewell to Arms?* (second edition).

Cradock, P. (1997) *In Pursuit of the British Interest: Reflections on Foreign Policy under Margaret Thatcher and John Major* (London: Murray).

Crick, Bernard (1978) 'The Pale Green Internationalists', *The New Statesman*, 11 May.

Critchley, J. (1991) 'Tories Need a Touch of the Showboat Style', *The Observer*, 25 August.

Crockatt, Richard (2003) *America Embattled: September 11, Anti-Americanism and the Global Order* (London: Routledge).

Crocker, Chester A. (1992) *High Noon in Southern Africa* (New York: Norton).

Croft, S. (2001) 'Britain's Nuclear Weapons Discourse', in Croft, *Rees and Uttley* (eds) *Britain and Defence 1945–2000*.
—— Dorman, A., Rees, W. and M. Uttley (eds) (2001) *Britain and Defence 1945–2000* (London: Longman).
Cronin, Sean (1980) *Irish Nationalism* (Dublin: Academy Press).
—— (1987) *Washington's Irish Policy*, 1916–1986 (Dublin: Anvil).
Crossman, Richard H. S. (1963) 'British Labor Looks at Europe', *Foreign Affairs*, 41: 4, 732–43.
—— (1975) *The Diaries of a Cabinet Minister*, ed. J. Morgan, Vol. 1 (London: Hamish Hamilton/Jonathan Cape).
—— (1976) *The Diaries of a Cabinet Minister*, Vol. 2 (London: Hamish Hamilton/Jonathan Cape).
Cullen, K. (1996) 'Ireland's Friends', *Fortnight*, May.
Cunliffe, Marcus (1986) 'The Anatomy of Anti-Americanism', in Kroes and Van Rossem (eds) *Anti-Americanism in Europe*.
Curtis, Mark (1998) *The Great Deception: Anglo-American Power and World Order* (London: Pluto Press).
—— (2003) *Web of Deceit: Britain's Real Role in the World* (London: Vintage).
Daalder, I. (2000) *Getting to Dayton* (Washington, DC: Brookings Institution).
—— and Lindsay, J. M. (2003) *America Unbound: the Bush Revolution in Foreign Policy* (Washington, DC: Brookings Institution).
Daddow, O. (ed.) (2002) *Harold Wilson and European Integration* (London: Cass).
Danchev, Alex (ed.) (1992) *International Perspectives on the Falklands Conflict* (New York: St Martin's Press).
—— (1996) 'On Specialness', *International Affairs*, 72: 4, 737–51.
—— (1998) *On Specialness: Essays in Anglo-American Relations* (Basingstoke: Macmillan).
—— (2005) 'How Strong are Shared Values in the Transatlantic Relationship?', *The British Journal of Politics and International Relations*, 7: 3, 429–36.
—— and MacMillan, J. (eds) (2005) *The Iraq War and Democratic Politics* (London: Routledge).
Davis, Troy D. (1998) *Dublin's American Policy: Irish-American Diplomatic Relations, 1945–1952* (Washington, DC: The Catholic University of America Press).
Dawson, R. and R. Rosencrance (1966) 'Theory and Reality in the Anglo-American Alliance', *World Politics*, 19: 1, 21–51.
DeConde, A. (1992) *Ethnicity, Race and American Foreign Policy* (Boston: Northeastern University Press).
Deighton, A. (2001) 'Why St Malo Matters', in Gardner, H. and Stefanova, R. (eds) *The New Transatlantic Agenda* (Aldershot: Ashgate).
de la Billière, Peter (1992) *Storm Command* (London: HarperCollins).
Denman, R. (1996) *Missed Chances: Britain and Europe in the Twentieth Century* (London: Cassell).
Dent, C. M. (1997) *The European Economy in the Global Context* (London: Routledge).

Dickie, John (1992) *Inside the Foreign Office* (London: Chapmans).
—— (1994) *'Special No More': Anglo-American Relations: Rhetoric and Reality* (London: Weidenfeld & Nicolson).
Dillon, G. M. (1989) *The Falklands: Politics and War* (Basingstoke: Macmillan).
Dillon, M. (1992) *Killer in Clowntown* (London: Arrow).
Dimbleby, Jonathan (1997) *The Last Governor: Chris Patten and the Handover of Hong Kong* (Boston: Little, Brown).
Divine, R. A. (1967) *Second Chance: The Triumph of Internationalism in America* (New York: Atheneum).
Dixon, Paul (2006) 'Rethinking the International: a Critique', in Cox, M., Guelke, Adrian, and Stephen, F. (eds) *A Farewell to Arms?* (second edition).
Dobson, Alan P. (1988) 'The Kennedy Administration and Economic Warfare against Communism', *International Affairs*, 64, 599–618.
—— (1990a) 'Labour or Conservative: Does It Really Matter in Anglo-American Relations?', *Journal of Contemporary History*, 25: 3, 387–407.
—— (1990b) 'The Years of Transition: Anglo-American Relations 1961–67', *Review of International Studies*, 16: 2, 239–58.
—— (1991a) *Peaceful Air Warfare: The USA, Britain and the Politics of International Aviation* (Oxford: Clarendon Press).
—— (1991b) 'The Special Relationship and European Integration', *Diplomacy and Statecraft*, 2: 1, 79–102.
—— (1995a) *Anglo-American Relations in the Twentieth Century* (London: Routledge).
—— (1995b) *Flying in the Face of Competition: Diplomacy and Airline Policy in Britain, the USA and the European Community 1968–94* (Aldershot: Ashgate).
Dockrill, M. (1988) *British Defence Policy since 1945* (Oxford: Blackwell).
Dockrill, S. (2001) 'Forging the Anglo-American Global Defence Partnership: Harold Wilson, Lyndon Johnson and the Washington Summit, December 1964', *Journal of Strategic Studies*, 23: 4, 107–29.
—— (2002) *Britain's Retreat from East of Suez: the Choice between Europe and the World?* (Basingstoke: Palgrave).
Donlon, Sean (1993) 'Irish-American Relations', *The Irish Times*, 25 January.
Dorrill, S. and R. Ramsay (1991) *Smear: Wilson and the Secret State* (London: Grafton).
Dowds, L. and K. Young (1996) 'National Identity', in Jowell, Curtis, M. Park Brook and Thomson (eds) *British Social Attitudes: the 13th Report*.
Duke, Simon (1987) *US Defence Bases in the United Kingdom* (London: Macmillan).
—— (1989) *United States Military Forces and Installations in Europe* (Oxford: Oxford University Press).
Dumbrell, John (1995a) *The Carter Presidency: A Reevaluation* (Manchester: Manchester University Press).
—— (1995b) 'The United States and the Northern Irish Conflict, 1969–74: From Indifference to Intervention', *Irish Studies in International Affairs*, 6, 107–25.

—— (1996) 'The Johnson Administration and the British Labour Government: Vietnam, the Pound and East of Suez', *Journal of American Studies*, 30: 2, 211–31.

—— (1997) *American Foreign Policy: Carter to Clinton* (Basingstoke: Macmillan).

—— (2001) *A Special Relationship: Anglo-American Relations in the Cold War and After* (first edition) (Basingstoke: Palgrave).

—— (2004) 'The US-UK "Special Relationship" in a World Twice Transformed', *Cambridge Review of International Affairs*, 17: 3, 437–50.

—— (2005) 'Winston Churchill and American Foreign Relations: John F. Kennedy to George W. Bush', *Journal of Transatlantic Studies* (Supplement), 3: 1, 31–42.

—— (2006) 'The New American Connection: President George W. Bush and Northern Ireland', in Cox, M., Guelke, A. Stephen, F. (eds) *A Farewell to Arms?* (second edition).

—— and S. Ellis (2003) 'British Involvement in Vietnam Peace Initiatives, 1966–1967: Marigolds, Sunflowers, and "Kosygin Week"', *Diplomatic History*, 27: 1, 11–42.

Dunne, T. (2004) ' "When the Shooting Starts": Atlanticism in British Security Strategy', *International Affairs*, 80: 5, 893–909.

Dunphy, E. (2002) 'Interview with Eamon Dunphy, March 2002', www.usembassy.org.uk/nil69.html (accessed 4 September 2004).

Eden, Anthony (1960) *Full Circle* (London: Cassell).

Eden, Douglas (ed.) (1997) *The Future of the Atlantic Community* (London: Middlesex University Press).

Edmonds, Robin (1986) *Setting the Mould: The United States and Britain, 1945–1950* (Oxford: Clarendon Press).

Elie, J. B. (2005) 'Many Times Doomed But Still Alive: An Attempt to Understand the Continuity of the Special Relationship', *Journal of Transatlantic Studies* (Supplement), 3: 1, 63–83.

Elkins, Caroline (2005) 'The Wrong Lesson', *The Atlantic Monthly*, July/August, 34–8.

Ellis, Sylvia (2001) 'Lyndon Johnson, Harold Wilson and the Vietnam War: a *Not* So Special Relationship', in Hollowell, J. (ed.) *Twentieth Century Anglo-American Relations*.

—— (2004) *Britain, America, and the Vietnam War* (Westport, CT: Praeger).

Engdahl, W. A. (2004) *A Century of War: Anglo-American Oil Politics and the New World Order* (London: Pluto Press).

Evans, Harold (1981) *Downing Street Diary: The Macmillan Years, 1957–1963* (London: Hodder and Stoughton).

Farrell, M. (1976) *Northern Ireland: The Orange State* (London: Pluto).

Faulkner, Brian (1978) *Memoirs of a Statesman* (London: Weidenfeld & Nicolson).

Fay, S. and H. Young (1978) 'How the Hard Money Men Took Over Britain', *The Sunday Times*, 14 May.

Featherstone, K. and R. H. Ginsberg (1996) *The United States and the European Union in the 1990s: Partners in Transition* (Basingstoke: Macmillan).

Final Report of the 9/11 Commission (2004) (National Commission on Terrorist Attacks on the United States) (New York: Norton).

Fisher, D. H. (1989) *Albion's Seed: Four British Folkways in America* (New York: Oxford University Press).

Fisher, Nigel (1982) *Harold Macmillan: A Biography* (London: Weidenfeld & Nicolson).

Fisk, R. (1996) 'No Use Relying on Uncle Bill', *Fortnight*, January.

Fitzgerald, Garret (1991) *All in a Life: An Autobiography* (London: Macmillan).

Foreign Relations of the United States, 1946, Vol.1 (1972) (Washington, DC: US Government Printing Office).

Foreign Relations of the United States 1951, Vol. 4, Parts 1–2 (1985a) (Washington, DC: USGPO).

Foreign Relations of the United States 1961–63, Vol. 13 (1985b) (Washington, DC: USGPO).

Foreign Relations of the United States 1964–1968, Vol. 5 (2002) (Washington, DC: USGPO).

Forster, A. and Wallace, W. (2001–02) 'What is NATO For?', *Survival*, 43: 4, 107–22.

Fowler, Norman (1991) *Ministers Decide* (London: Chapman).

Fox, R. (1997–98) 'Too Much Memory', *The National Interest*, 50, 57–65.

Frankel, Joseph (1974) 'Britain's Changing Role', *International Affairs*, 50: 4, 574–85.

Franks, Oliver (1995) 'The "Special Relationship", 1947–1952', in Wm. R. Louis (ed.) *Adventures with Britannia* (Austin: University of Texas Press).

The Franks Report (1992) (London: Pimlico).

Freedland, Jonathan (1998) *Bring Home the Revolution: The Case for a British Republic* (London: Fourth Estate).

—— (2005) 'Yes, They Did Lie To Us', *The Guardian*, 22 June.

Freedman, Lawrence (1980) *Britain and Nuclear Weapons* (London: Macmillan).

—— (2005) *The Official History of the Falklands Campaign: volumes 1 and 2* (London: Routledge).

—— and V. Gamba-Stonehouse (1990) *Signals of War: The Falklands Conflict of 1982* (London: Faber & Faber).

—— and E. Karsh (1992) *The Gulf Conflict, 1990–1991* (London: Faber & Faber).

Freeman, J. P. G. (1986) *British Nuclear Arms Control Policy in the Context of Anglo-American Relations* (London: Macmillan).

Fursenko, A. and T. Naftali (1997) *'One Hell of a Gamble' – Khrushchev, Kennedy and the Cuban Missile Crisis, 1958–1964* (London: Murray).

Gaiduk, I. N. (1996) *The Soviet Union and the Vietnam War* (Chicago: Dee).

Galbraith, J. K. (1981) *A Life in Our Times* (Boston: Houghton Mifflin).

The Gallup International Public Opinion Poll: Great Britain, 1937–1975 (1976) (New York: Random House).

The Gallup Poll: Public Opinion, 1972–1977 (1978), vol. 1, 1972–1975 (Wilmington: Scholarly Resources).

The Gallup Poll: Public Opinion, 1982 (1983) (Wilmington: Scholarly Resources).
The Gallup Poll: Public Opinion, 1984 (1985) (Wilmington: Scholarly Resources).
The Gallup Poll: Public Opinion, 1989 (1990) (Wilmington: Scholarly Resources).
The Gallup Poll: Public Opinion, 1994 (1995) (Wilmington: Scholarly Resources).
The Gallup Poll: Public Opinion, 1995 (1996) (Wilmington: Scholarly Resources).
The Gallup Poll: Public Opinion, 1996 (1997) (Wilmington: Scholarly Resources).
Gamble, Andrew (1998) 'The European Issue in British Politics', in D. Barker and D. Seawright (eds) *Britain For and Against Europe* (Oxford: Clarendon Press).
—— (2003) *Between Europe and America: the Future of British Politics* (Basingstoke: Palgrave).
Gardner, Lloyd (1995) *Pay Any Price: Lyndon Johnson and the Wars for Vietnam* (Chicago: Dee).
—— (2005) ' "Damned High Wire": on the Special Relationship that Unites Bush and Blair in Iraq', *Journal of Transatlantic Studies* (Supplement), 3: 1, 43–62.
Garthoff, Raymond (1989) *Reflections on the Cuban Missile Crisis* (Washington, DC: Brookings).
Garton Ash, T. (2003) 'Anti-Europeanism in America', *New York Review of Books*, 13: February, 13–18.
—— (2005) *Free World* (London: Penguin).
Gatzke, H. (1980) *Germany and the United States: a "Special Relationship"?'* (Cambridge, MA: Harvard University Press).
Gearson, J. P. S. (1998) *Harold Macmillan and the Berlin Wall Crisis, 1958–62* (Basingstoke: Macmillan).
Geddes, A. (2004) *The European Union and British Politics* (Basingstoke: Palgrave).
Geertz, Clifford (1973) *The Interpretation of Culture* (New York: Basic Books).
George, S. (1994) *An Awkward Partner: Britain in the European Community* (Oxford: Oxford University Press).
Gill, S. (1988) 'The Rise and Decline of the Great Powers', *Politics*, 8: 1, 3–9.
Gilmour, Ian (1992) *Dancing with Dogma: Britain under Thatcherism* (London: Simon & Schuster).
—— (1995) 'Time to Shut Up, Maggie', *The Independent*, 14 June.
—— and M. Garnett (1998) *Whatever Happened to the Tories?* (London: Fourth Estate).
Godson, D. (2005) *Himself Alone: David Trimble and the Ordeal of Unionism* (London: Perennial).
Godson, G. (1987) 'British Attitudes towards the United States', in M. Holmes, G. Frost, C. Ciker, D. Greenwood, M. Edligton, D. Godson,

J. Davis and R. Pfaltzgraff (eds) *British Security Policy and the Atlantic Alliance* (Washington, DC: Pergamon/Brassey).

Gombert, D. C. (1985) 'American Diplomacy and the Haig Mission', in A. R. Coll and A. C. Arend (eds) *The Falklands War* (Boston: Allen & Unwin).

Goodhart, D. (2002) 'Tony's World' (interview with Tony Blair), *Prospect*, August, 16–19.

Goodman, Geoffrey (1979) *The Awkward Warrior: Frank Cousins* (London: Davis-Poynter).

Gould, P. (1998) *The Unfinished Revolution: How Modernisers Saved the Labour Party* (London: Abacus).

Gowing, Margaret (1986) 'Nuclear Weapons and the "Special Relationship" ', in Louis and Bull (eds) *The 'Special Relationship, Anglo-American Relations since 1945*.

Grant, Charles (2003) *Transatlantic Rift: How to Bring the Two Sides Together* (London: Centre for European Reform).

Granville, B. (1999) 'Bananas, Beef and Biotechnology', *The World Today*, April.

Grasselli, G (1996) *British and American Responses to the Soviet Invasion of Afghanistan* (Aldershot: Dartmouth).

Gray, C. S. (1996) 'The Continued Primacy of Geography', *Orbis*, 40: 2, 247–59.

Grayling, C. and C. Langdon (1988) *Just Another Star? Anglo-American Relations since 1945* (London: Harrap).

Green, C. J. (1996) 'The Balance of Payments', in Artis (ed.) *The UK Economy*.

Greenberg, S. (1990) 'Reconstructing the Democratic Vision', *The American Prospect*, June.

Greene, Graham (1977) *The Quiet American* (London: Penguin).

Greig, G. (1994) 'Why Clinton's "Rhodies" Hate Britain', *The Sunday Times*, 27 February.

Guelke, Adrian (1984) 'The American Connection to the Northern Irish Conflict', *Irish Studies in International Affairs*, 1, 27–36.

—— (1988) *Northern Ireland: The International Perspective* (Dublin: Gill and Macmillan).

—— (1991) 'British Policy and International Dimensions of the Northern Ireland Conflict', *Regional Politics and Policy*, 1: 2, 140–60.

—— (1996) 'The United States, Irish Americans and the Northern Ireland Peace Process', *International Affairs*, 72: 4, 521–36.

Haass, R. N. (1990) *Conflicts Unending: The United States and Regional Disputes* (New Haven, CT: Yale University Press).

—— (2002) 'Address to the National Committee on American Foreign Policy, 9 January 2002', www.usembassy.org.uk/nil67.html (accessed 4 September 2004).

Haftendorn, H. (1996) *NATO and the Nuclear Revolution: A Case of Credibility* (Oxford: Clarendon Press).

—— and C. Tuschhoff (eds) (1993) *America and Europe in an Era of Change* (Boulder, CO: Westview).

Haig, Alexander M. (1984) *Caveat: Realism, Reagan and Foreign Policy* (London: Weidenfeld and Nicolson).

Halper, Stefan and Jonathan Clarke (2004) *America Alone: the Neoconservatives and Global Order* (Cambridge: Cambridge University Press).

Hames, Tim (1994) 'The Special Relationship', in Adonis and Hames (eds) *A Conservative Revolution?*

Hamilton, Adrian (1994) 'Long Live a New Relationship', *The Observer*, 9 January.

Hammond, P. Y. (1992) *LBJ and the Presidential Management of Foreign Relations* (Austin: University of Texas Press).

—— (1997) 'The 1976 UK-IMF Crisis: the Markets, the Americans and the IMF', *Contemporary British History*, 11: 1, 1–17.

Hannah, N. B. (1987) *The Key to Failure: Laos and the Vietnam War* (Lanham: Madison Books).

Hare, David (2004) *Stuff Happens* (London: Faber and Faber).

Harrington, R. L. (1996) 'The UK Economy in Context', in Artis (ed.), *The UK Economy*.

Haseler, S. (1985) *Varieties of Anti-Americanism* (Washington DC: Ethics and Public Policy Center).

—— (1996) *The English Tribe: Identity, Nation and Europe* (Basingstoke: Macmillan).

Hastings, Max (2003) 'Why Britain is Furious with America', *The Spectator*, 8 November, 16–17.

Hathaway, R. M. (1981) *Ambiguous Partnership: Britain and America, 1944–1947* (New York: Columbia University Press).

—— (1990) *Great Britain and the United States: Special Relations since World War II* (Boston: Twayne).

Hawthorn, G. (1999) 'Pinochet: The Politics', *International Affairs*, 75: 2, 253–8.

Heale, M. J. (1985) 'Writing in Great Britain on United States History, 1945–1980', in L. Hanke (ed.) *Guide to the Study of United States History Outside the US, 1945–1980* (White Plains: Kraus).

Healey, Denis, (1989) *The Time of My Life* (London: Michael Joseph).

Heath, Edward (1969–70) 'Realism in British Foreign Policy', *Foreign Affairs*, 48: 1, 39–51.

—— (1998) *The Course of My Life: My Autobiography* (London: Hodder & Stoughton).

Henderson, Nicholas (1987) *Channels and Tunnels: Reflections on Britain and Abroad* (London: Weidenfeld and Nicolson).

—— (1994) *Mandarin: The Diaries of an Ambassador, 1969–82* (London: Weidenfeld & Nicolson).

Hennessy P. and C. Anstey (eds) (1990) *Moneybags and Brains* (Glasgow: Strathclyde University/BBC).

Henning, C. R. (1996) 'Europe's Monetary Union and the United States', *Foreign Policy*, 102, 83–100.

Heren, Louis (1970) *No Hail, No Farewell* (London: Harper and Row).

Herring, G. C. (ed.) (1983) *The Secret Diplomacy of the Vietnam War: The Negotiating Volumes of the Pentagon Papers* (Austin: University of Texas Press).

Hersh, Seymour (1997) *The Dark Side of Camelot* (London: HarperCollins).
Heseltine, Michael (1987) *Where There's a Will* (London: Hutchinson).
Heuser, Beatrice (1996) *Transatlantic Relations: Sharing Ideals and Costs* (London: Pinter/RIIA).
Hill, C. and C. Lord (1996) 'The Foreign Policy of the Heath Government', in Ball and Seldon (eds) *The Heath Government*.
Hindley, B. (1999) 'New Institutions for Transatlantic Trade', *International Affairs*, 75: 1, 45–60.
Hiro, D. (1992) *Desert Shield to Desert Storm* (London: Paladin).
Hirst, P. and G. Thompson (1996) *Globalization in Question* (Oxford: Polity).
Hitchens, Christopher (1990) *Blood, Class and Nostalgia* (London: Chatto & Windus).
—— (1993) 'Say What You Will about Harold', *London Review of Books*, 2 December.
Hocking, B. and M. Smith (1995) *World Politics* (London: Prentice-Hall).
Hodder-Williams, R. (2000) 'Reforging the "Special Relationship": Blair, Clinton and Foreign Policy', in Little and Whickham-Jones (eds) *New Labour's Foreign Policy*.
Hoffman, Stanley (1993) 'America and Europe in an Era of Revolutionary Change', in Haftendorn and Tuschhoff (eds) *America and Europe in an Era of Change*.
Hogan, M. (1987) *The Marshall Plan: America, Britain and the Reconstruction of Western Europe, 1947–1952* (Cambridge: Cambridge University Press).
Hoggett, P. (2005) 'Iraq: Blair's Mission Impossible', *The British Journal of Politics and International Relations*, 7: 1, 418–28.
Holland, Jack (1989) *The American Connection: US Guns, Money and Influence in Northern Ireland* (Dublin: Poolbeg Press).
Holland, Mary (1992) 'Irish Notebook', *The Observer*, 8 November.
Hollander, Paul (1992) *Anti-Americanism: Critiques at Home and Abroad* (New York: Oxford University Press).
—— (ed.) (2004) *Understanding Anti-Americanism: its Origins at Home and Abroad* (Chicago: Dee).
Hollowell, J. (ed.) (2001) *Twentieth Century Anglo-American Relations* (Basingstoke: Palgrave).
Hopkins, M. F. (2003) *Oliver Franks and the Truman Administration: Anglo-American Relations, 1948–1952* (London: Cass).
Horne, A. (1988) *Macmillan, 1894–1956* (London: Macmillan).
—— (1989) *Macmillan: Volume 2, 1957–1986* (London: Macmillan).
House of Commons (1985) *Third Report from the Foreign Affairs Committee, 1984–85 Events Surrounding the Weekend of 1–2 May 1982* (London: HMSO).
House of Representatives Hearings (1972) Before the Subcommittee on Europe of the Committee on Foreign Affairs, *Northern Ireland*.
—— (2002) before the Committee on International Relations, *International Terrorism, Its Links with Illicit Drugs as Illustrated by the IRA and Other Groups in Colombia*.

Howard, Anthony (1990) *Crossman: The Pursuit of Power* (London: Jonathan Cape).

Howorth, J. (2005) 'The Euro-Atlantic Security Dilemma: France, Britain and the ESDP', *Journal of Transatlantic Studies*, 3: 1, 39–54.

—— and Keeler, J. T. S. (eds) (2003) *Defending Europe: the EU, NATO and the Quest for Autonomy* (New York: Palgrave).

Howe, Geoffrey (1990) 'Sovereignty and Interdependence: Britain's Place in the World', *International Affairs*, 66: 4, 675–95.

—— (1995) *Conflict of Loyalty* (London: Pan).

Hume, John (1979–80) 'The Irish Question: A British Problem', *Foreign Affairs*, 58: 2, 300–13.

—— (1996) *Personal Views: Politics, Peace and Reconciliation in Northern Ireland* (Dublin: Roberts Rinehart).

Hunt, M. H. (1983) *The Making of a Special Relationship: the United States and China to 1914* (New York: Columbia University Press).

—— (1987) *Ideology and US Foreign Policy* (New Haven: Yale University Press).

Huntington, S. P. (2005) *Who Are We?: America's great Debate* (London: The Free Press).

Hurd, Douglas (1979) *An End to Promises* (London: Collins).

Hutchinson, George (1980) *The Last Edwardian at No. 10* (London: Quartet).

Hutton, D. (2004) 'Report of the Inquiry Into the Circumstances Surrounding the Death of Dr David Kelly' (www.the-hutton-inquiry.org.uk).

Hutton, Will (1996) *The State We're In* (London: Vintage).

Hyland, W. G. (1999) *Clinton's World* (Westport: Praeger).

Ignatieff, Michael (1998) *Isaiah Berlin* (London: Chatto & Windus).

Ikenberry, G. K. (1998–99), 'Institutions, Strategic Restraint and the Persistence of American Postwar Order', *International Security*, 23: 3, 58–72.

Independent Profile (1990) 'Alan Clark: High Tory of the Old School', 2 June.

Inglehart, R. (1994) *Culture Shift in Advanced Society* (Princeton: Princeton University Press).

Jackson, I. (1999) 'The Kennedy Administration, Britain and East-West Trade', paper presented to Society of Historians of American Foreign Relations Conference, Princeton, June.

Jakub, J. (1995) 'The Anglo-American "Special Relationship" in the Post-Cold War World', *Defence Analysis*, 11: 3, 318–21.

Jay, A. (ed.) (1996) *The Oxford Dictionary of Political Quotations* (Oxford: Oxford University Press).

Jay, Peter (1980) 'Why President Carter has Clearly Proved His Right to a Second Term', *The Times*, 27 October.

Jenkins, Roy (1972) *Afternoon on the Potomac* (New Haven: Yale University Press).

—— (1991) *Life at the Centre* (London: Macmillan).

—— (2002) *Churchill* (London: Pan Macmillan).

Jentleson, B. W. (1992) 'The Pretty Prudent Public', *International Studies Quarterly*, 36: 1, 49–74.

Jervis, Robert (2005) *American Foreign Policy in a New Era* (London: Routledge).

Johnes, G. and J. Taylor (1996) 'The Structure of the Economy', in Artis (ed.) *The UK Economy*.

Johnman, L. (1989) 'Defending the Pound: The Economics of the Suez Crisis', in Gorst, Johnman and Lucas (eds), *Post-war Britain, 1945–64* (London: Inter).

Johnson, Boris (2003) *Lend Me Your Ears* (London: Harper Perennial).

Johnson, Lyndon B. (1971) *The Vantage Point* (New York: Rinehart and Winston).

Jones, Peter (1997) *America and the British Labour Party: The Special Relationship at Work* (London: I. B. Tauris).

Jowell, R., S. Witherspoon and L. Brook (eds) (1989) *British Social Attitudes: Special International Report* (Aldershot: Gower).

Jowell, R., J. Curtice, A. Park, L. Brook and K. Thomson. (eds) (1996) *British Social Attitudes: the 13th Report* (Dartmouth: Gower).

Joyce, James (1992) *Ulysses* (London: Penguin).

Judt, T. (2005) 'Europe vs. America', *The New York Review of Books*, 10 February.

Kagan, Robert (2003) *Paradise and Power: America and Europe in the New World Order* (London: Atlantic Books).

Kahler, M. and W. Link (1996) *Europe and America: A Return to History* (New York: Council on Foreign Relations Press).

Kampfner, J. (2003) *Blair's Wars* (London: Free Press).

Kaplan, L. S. (1996) 'NATO after the Cold War', in Wiener (ed.), *The Transatlantic Relationship*.

Kavanagh, D. and A. Seldon (eds) (1989) *The Thatcher Effect* (Oxford: Clarendon Press).

Kennan, G. F. (1974) 'Europe's Problems, Europe's Choices', *Foreign Policy*, 41, 3–16.

—— (1986) 'Reciprocity in International Relations', *International Organization*, 23: 1, 1–29.

Kennedy, Joseph (1991) 'Its the British People Who Hold the Key', *The Guardian*, 22 October.

Kennedy, Paul (1988) *The Rise and Fall of the Great Powers* (London: Unwin Hyman).

Kennedy, Robert (1968) *Thirteen Days* (New York: Norton).

Kent, J. (1993) *British Imperial Strategy and the Origins of the Cold War, 1944–49* (Leicester: Leicester University Press).

Keogh, D. (1994) *Twentieth Century Ireland* (Dublin: Gill and Macmillan).

Keohane, D. (1993) *Labour Party Defence Policy since 1945* (Leicester: Leicester University Press).

—— (2005) 'The United Kingdom', in Danchev and MacMillan (eds) *The Iraq War and Democratic Politics*.

Kettle, M. (1999) 'The Great American Disaster', *The Guardian, 17* September.

Kiger, P. J. (1998) *Squeeze Play: The United States, Cuba, and the Helms-Burton Act* (Washington, DC: Center for Public Integrity).

Kilfoyle, P. (2003) 'US and Them', *The Guardian*, 18 November.

Kimball, W. F. (2000), ' "Fighting with Allies": the Hand Care and feeding of the Anglo-American Special relationship – from WW11 to the Falklands War', in Schmitz and Jespersen (eds) *Architects of the American Century.*

—— (2005a) 'The "Special" Anglo-American Special Relationship: "A Fatter, Larger Underwater Cable" ', *Journal of Transatlantic Studies* (Supplement), 3: 1, 1–6.

—— (2005b) 'Dangerously Contagious? The Anglo-American Special Relationship', *The British Journal of Politics and International Relations*, 7: 3, 437–41.

Kindleburger, C. (1973) *The World in Depression* (Berkeley: University of California Press).

King, Anthony (1977) *Britain Says Yes: The 1975 Referendum on the Common Market* (Washington, DC: American Enterprise Institute).

King, C. (1972) *The Cecil King Diary, 1965–1970* (London: Jonathan Cape).

Kinney, D. (1989) *National Interest/National Honor: The Diplomacy of the Falklands Crisis* (New York: Praeger).

Kissinger, Henry A. (1969) 'What kind of Atlantic partnership?', *The Atlantic Community*, 7: 1, 18–38.

—— (1979) *The White House Years* (Boston: Little, Brown).

—— (1982) *Years of Upheaval* (London: Weidenfeld & Nicolson).

—— (1999) *Years of Renewal* (London: Weidenfeld & Nicolson)

KR Washington Bureau (2003) 'Bush's Image in Europe Takes Sharply Negative Turn', (release, 24 February).

Krasner, S. D. (1978) *Defending the National Interest* (Princeton: Princeton University Press).

Kroes, R. (1996) *If You've Seen One, You've Seen Mall* (Urbana: University of Illinois Press).

—— (1999) 'Commentary: World Wars and Watersheds', *Diplomatic History*, 23: 1, 71–7.

Kroes, R. and M. Van Rossem (eds) (1986) *Anti-Americanism in Europe* (Amsterdam: Free University Press).

Kull, S. (2005) 'It's lonely at the Top', *Foreign Policy*, 149, 36–7.

Kunz, D. (1999) ' "Somewhat Mixed up Together": Anglo-American Defence and Financial Policy during the 1960s', *Journal of Imperial and Commonwealth History*, 27: 2, 213–32.

The Labour Party (1987) *Britain Will Win* (London: The Labour Party).

Lacorne, D., J. Rupnik and M. Toinet (eds) (1990) *The Rise and Fall of Anti-Americanism: A Century of French Perception* (Basingstoke: Macmillan).

Lamb, Richard (1995) *The Macmillan Years, 1957–1963: The Emerging Truth* (London: Murray).

Lane, Ann (2004) 'Foreign and Defence Policy', in Seldon and Hickson (eds) *New Labour, Old Labour.*

Langford, P. (2000) 'Manners and Character in Anglo-American Perceptions, 1750–1850', in Leventhal and Quinault (eds) *Anglo-American Attitudes.*

Lankford, N. D. (1996) *The Last American Aristocrat: The Biography of David K. E. Bruce, 1898–1977* (Boston: Little, Brown).

Larres, Klaus (2002) *Churchill's Cold War: the Politics of Personal Diplomacy* (New Haven: Yale University Press).

Larsen, S. R. and J. L. Collins (1975) *Allied Participation in Vietnam* (Washington, DC: Department of the Army).

Lauter, P. (ed.) (1982) *The Heath Anthology of American Literature* (Lexington: Heath).

Lawrence, D. H. (1977) *Studies in Classic American Literature* (Harmondsworth: Penguin).

Lawson, Nigel (1992) *The View from No. 11* (London: Bantam).

Lawson, S. (1998) 'The Culture of Politics', in R. Maidment and C. McKerras (eds) *Culture and Society in the Asia Pacific* (London: Routledge).

Lee, Donna (1998) 'Middle Powers in the Global Economy: British Influence during the Opening Phase of the Kennedy Round Negotiations 1962–64', *Review of International Studies*, 24: 4, 515–28.

—— (1999) *Middle Powers and Commercial Diplomacy: British Influence at the Kennedy Trade Round* (Basingstoke: Macmillan).

Lee, S. (1996) 'Staying in the Game? Going into the Game? Macmillan and European Integration', in Aldous and Lee (eds) *Harold Macmillan and Britain's World Role*.

Leigh, D. (1988) *The Wilson Plot* (London: Heinemnan).

Leuchtenberg, W. E. (1979) 'The Jubilee in the Bicentennial Era', in Leuchtenberg *et al., Britain and the United States*.

—— *et al.* (1979) *Britain and the United States: Views to Mark the Silver Jubilee* (London: Hutchinson).

Leventhal, F. M. and R. Quinault (eds) (2000) *Anglo-American Attitudes: from Revolution to Partnership* (Aldershot: Ashgate).

Lewis, M. (1991) 'Not Angels but Anglophobes', *The Spectator*, 17 August, 8–9.

Lipset, Seymour M. (1996) *American Exceptionalism: A Double-Edged Sword* (New York: Norton).

Little, D. (1993) 'The Making of a Special Relationship: the United States and Israel, 1957–1968', *International Journal of Middle East Studies*, 25: 4, 563–85.

Little, R. and Whickham-Jones (eds) (2000) *New Labour's Foreign Policy: A New Moral Crusade?* (Manchester: Manchester University Press).

Livingstone, Ken (1998) 'Uncle Sam's Patsy', *New Statesman and Society*, 12 June.

Lock-Pullan, R. (1999) 'Defence for a New Era?', *Talking Politics*, 11: 3, 148–53.

Louis, William R. (ed.) (1995) *Adventures with Britannia* (Austin: University of Texas Press).

—— and Hedley Bull (eds) (1986) *The 'Special Relationship': Anglo-American Relations since 1945* (Oxford: Clarendon Press).

Lundestad, Geir (1986) 'Empire by Invitation? The United States and Western Europe, 1945–1952', *Journal of Peace Research*, 13: 1, 263–77.

—— (1998) *'Empire' by Integration: The United States and European Integration, 1945–1997* (Oxford: Oxford University Press).

Lynch, T. J. (2004) *Turf War: the Clinton Administration and Northern Ireland* (Aldershot: Ashgate, 2004).

McCaffrey, L. J. (1992) *Texture of Irish America* (New York: Syracuse University Press).

McCain, John (1996) 'Imagery or Purpose? The Choice in November', *Foreign Policy*, 103, 25–31.

McCarthy, J. F. (1995) *Dissent from Irish America* (Lanham: University).

Macintyre, Ben (2005) 'When Rimbaud Meets Rambo', *The Times*, 4 June.

McEwan, Ian (1998) *The Innocent or the Special Relationship* (London: Vintage).

—— (2005) *Saturday* (London: Jonathan Cape).

McGiffert, M. (ed.) (1964) *The Character of Americans* (Chicago: Dorsey).

McInnes, C. (1986) *Trident: The Only Option?* (London: Brassey's).

—— (1991) 'Trident', in Byrd (ed.) *British Defence Policy*.

—— (1998) 'Labour's Strategic Defence Review', *International Affairs*, 74: 4, 837–54.

Macintyre, D. (1999) *Mandelson: The Biography* (London: HarperCollins).

McKittrick, D. (1989) *Despatches from Belfast* (Belfast: The Blackstaff Press).

Macmillan, Harold (1971) *Riding the Storm, 1955–1959* (London: Macmillan).

—— (1972) *Pointing the Way, 1959–1961* (London: Macmillan).

—— (1973) *At the End of the Day, 1961–1963* (London: Macmillan).

—— (1984) *War Diaries* (New York: St Martin's Press).

McNamara, R. S., J. Blight, R. Brighma, T. Biersteker and H. Schardler, (1999) *Argument without End: In Search of Answers to the Vietnam Tragedy* (New York: Public Affairs).

McRae, H. (1999) 'America – the Gentle Giant?', *The Independent*, 22 July.

MacShane, Denis (2006) 'No, Ambassador', *Prospect*, January, 64–5.

Magee, Brian (1990) 'New World Symphony', *The Guardian*, 22 September.

—— (1998) *Confessions of a Philosopher* (London: Phoenix).

Maidment, R. and M. Dawson (eds) (1994) *The United States in the Twentieth Century: Key Documents* (London: Hodder & Stoughton).

Major, John (1999) *John Major: The Autobiography* (London: Harper Collins).

Mallie, E. and D. McKittrick (1996) *The Fight for Peace: The Secret Story behind the Irish Peace Process* (London: Heinemann).

Mandelbaum, M. (1990–91) 'The Bush Foreign Policy', *Foreign Affairs*, 70: 1, 5–22.

Marchetti, V. and J. D. Marks (1975) *The CIA and the Cult of Intelligence* (London: Cape).

Marquand, David (2003) 'The End of the Affair', *New Statesman*, 24 November, 18–20.

Marshall, A. (1999) 'Changing the Ground Rules', *The Independent on Sunday*, 23 May.

Martin, Laurence W. (1969) 'British Defence Policy: The Long Recessional', *Adelphi Papers*, 61, 18–30.

—— (1997) 'Risky Rush for a Doubtful Goal', *The World Today*, February.

Martin, Laurence W. and J. Garnett (1997) *British Foreign Policy: Challenges and Choices for the 21st Century* (London; Pinter/RIIA).

Martin, P. and M. R. Brawley (eds) *Allied Forces or Forced Allies? Kosovo and NATO's War* (New York: St Martin's).

Maudling, Reginald (1978) *Memoirs* (London: Sidgwick & Jackson).

Mauer, V. (1998) 'Harold Macmillan and the Deadline Crisis over Berlin', *Twentieth Century British History*, 9: 1, 54–85.

May, E. R. and P. D. Zelikow (eds) (1997) *The Kennedy Tapes: Inside the White House during the Cuban Missile Crisis* (Cambridge Mass.: Harvard University Press).

Meacher, Michael (2003) 'This War on Terrorism is Bogus', *The Guardian*, 6 September.

Medley, Richard (1999) 'Europe's Next Big Idea', *Foreign Affairs*, 79: 5, 18–22.

Melissen, J. (1992) 'The Restoration of the Nuclear Alliance: Great Britain and Atlantic Negotiations with the United States, 1957–58', *Contemporary Record*, 6, 72–100.

Menaul, S. (1980) *Countdown: Britain's Strategic Nuclear Forces* (London: Hale).

Meyer, Christopher (2005) *DC Confidential* (London: Weidenfeld and Nicolson).

Middeke, M. (2000) 'Anglo-American Nuclear Weapons Co-operation after the Nassau Conference: the British Policy of Interdependence', *Journal of Cold War Studies*, 2: 2, 69–96.

—— (2001) 'Britain's Global Military Role, Conventional Defence and Anglo-American Interdependence after Nassau', *Journal of Strategic Studies*, 24: 1, 143–64.

Minkin, L. (1978) *The Labour Party Conference* (London: Allen Lane).

Mitchell, George (1999) *Making Peace* (London: Heinemann).

Monk, R. *Bertrand Russell: The Ghost of Madness, 1921–1970* (London: Vintage).

Moorhouse, Geoffrey (1977) *The Diplomats: The Foreign Office Today* (London: Macmillan).

Morgan, K. O. (1990) *The People's Peace* (Oxford: Oxford University Press).

—— (1993) 'Hugh Gaitskell and International Affairs', *Contemporary Record*, 7: 4, 312–20.

—— (1997) *Callaghan: A Life* (Oxford: Oxford University Press).

Morici, P. (1991) *A New Special Relationship: Us-Canada Economic Relations in the 1990s* (Ottawa: IRPE).

Moser, J. E. (1999) *Twisting the Lion's Tail* (Basingstoke: Macmillan).

—— (2003) 'The Decline of American Anglophobia', in Capet and Sy-Wonyu (eds) *The 'Special Relationship'*.

Mowlam, M. (2002) *Momentum: the Struggle for Peace, Politics and the People* (London: Coronet Books).

Mowle, T. S. (2004) *Allies at Odds? The United States and the European Union* (New York: Palgrave Macmillan).

Murray, D. (2000) *Kennedy, Macmillan and Nuclear Weapons* (Basingstoke: Macmillan).

Nairn, Tom (1973) *The Left against Europe?* (Harmondsworth: Penguin).

Naughtie, J. (2004) *The Accidental American: Tony Blair and the Presidency* (London: Macmillan).

Neustadt, Richard E. (1970) *Alliance Politics* (New York: Columbia University Press).

Newsom, D. D. (1996) *The Public Dimension of Foreign Policy* (Bloomington: Indiana University Press).

Nicholas, H. G. (1975) *The United States and Britain* (Chicago: University of Chicago Press).

Nordlinger, E. A. (1995) *Isolationism Reconfigured: American Foreign Policy for a New Century* (Princeton: Princeton University Press).

Northedge, F. S. (1970) 'Britain as a Second-Rank Power', *International Affairs*, 46: 1, 37–47.

Nott, John (2002a) *Here Today, Gone Tomorrow: Recollections of an Errant Politician* (London: Politico's).

—— (2002b) 'Introduction', *Revue Francaise de Civilisation Britannique* ('La "Relation Speciale" '), 12: 1, 7–9.

Nunnerly, D. (1972) *President Kennedy and Britain* (London: The Bodley Head).

Nye, J. S. (1981) *Bound to Lead: The Changing Nature of American Power* (New York: Basic Books).

—— (1993) 'Patrons and Clients: New Roles in the Post-Cold War Order', in Haftendorn and Tuschhoff (eds) *America and Europe in an Era of Change*.

—— (2004) *Soft Power: the Means to Success in World Politics* (New York: Public Affairs).

Oborne, P. (2003) 'Hail to the Chief', *The Spectator*, 15 November, 14–15.

O'Brien, C. C. (1995) 'The Wearing of the Greenbacks', *National Review*, 17 April.

O'Clery, C. (1996) *The Greening of the White House* (Dublin: Gill and Macmillan).

O'Dowd, N. (1996) 'Peace is Strongest Weapon in IRA Armoury', *The Irish Times*, 4 April

Oliver, Kendrick (1997) *Kennedy, Macmillan and the Nuclear Test Ban Debate, 1961–63* (Basingstoke: Macmillan).

Oliver, Q. (1995) 'Working with Bill', *Fortnight*, July–August.

O'Malley, Brendan and Ian Craig (1999) *The Cyprus Conspiracy* (London: I. B. Tauris).

Orde, Anne (1996) *The Eclipse of Great Britain* (London: Macmillan).

Oren, M. B. (2002) *Six Days of War: June 1967 and the Making of the Modern Middle East* (New York: Oxford University Press).

Oudraat, C. de J. (2004) 'The Future of US-European Relations', in T. G. Weiss, M. E. Crahan and J. Goering (eds) *Wars on Terrorism and Iraq*.

Ovendale, Ritchie (ed.) (1994) *British Defence Policy since 1945* (Manchester: Manchester University Press).

Ovendale, Ritchie (1996) *Britain, the United States and the Transfer of Power in the Middle East* (London: Longman).
—— (1998) *Anglo-American Relations in the Twentieth Century* (Basingstoke: Macmillan).
Owen, David (1979) 'Britain and the United States', in Leuchtenberg *et al., Britain and the United States*, 68–79.
—— (1992) *Time to Declare* (London: Penguin).
—— (1995) *'Balkan Odyssey'* (London: Gollancz).
Page, B. I. and R. Y. Shapiro (1992) *The Rational Public* (Chicago: University of Chicago Press).
Papacosma, S. V. and M. A. Heiss (eds) (1995) *NATO in the Post-Cold War Era: Does It Have a Future?* (Basingstoke: Macmillan).
Parmar, Inderjeet (1995) *Special Interests, the State and the Anglo-American Alliance, 1935–45* (London: Cass).
Parris, M. (2003) *Chance Witness* (London: Penguin).
Parsons, A. (1983) 'The Falklands and the United Nations', *International Affairs*, 59: 2, 165–79.
—— (1989) 'Britain and the World', in Kavanagh and Seldon (eds) *The Thatcher Effect*.
Paterson, R. H. (1997) *Britain's Strategic Nuclear Deterrent* (London: Cass).
Patten, Chris (1999) *East and West* (London: Pan).
—— (2005) 'History Will Judge Blair as a Defender of Bush's Agenda above Britain's', *The Guardian*, 19 September.
Pearce, E. (2002) *Denis Healey* (London: Little, Brown).
Pearce, R. (ed.) (1991) *Patrick Gordon Walker: Political Diaries, 1932–1971* (London: The Historian's Press).
Pells, Richard (1997) *Not Like Us: How Europeans Have Loved, Hated and Transformed America* (New York: Basic Books).
Peterson, J. (2002) 'Europe, America and the War on Terrorism', *Irish Studies in International Affairs*, 13, 23–42.
—— and Pollack, M. A. (eds) (2003) *Europe, America, Bush: Transatlantic Relations in the Twenty-first Century* (London: Routledge).
Pfaff, W. (1998–99) 'The Coming Clash of Europe with America', *World Policy Journal*, 15: 1, 1–9.
—— (2005) 'Why Bush Will Fail in Europe', *The Observer*, 20 February.
Phythian, Mark (1997a) *Arming Iraq* (Boston: Northeastern University Press).
—— (1997b) 'The Arms Trade', *Parliamentary Affairs*, 50: 1, 41–54.
Pickering, J. (1998) *Britain's Withdrawal from East of Suez* (Basingstoke: Macmillan).
Pierre, A. J. (1972) *Nuclear Politics: The British Experience with an Independent Strategic Force* (London: Oxford University Press).
Pimlott, Ben (1993) *Harold Wilson* (London: HarperCollins).
Plesch, Dan (2004) 'This Relationship Isn't Working', *The Guardian*, 6 April.
—— (2005) 'Britain's "Independent" Deterrent is in American Hands', *The Independent*, 21 November.
Pliatzsky, Leo (1982) *Getting and Spending: Public Expenditure, Employment and Inflation* (Oxford: Blackwell).

Pond, E. (2004) *Friendly Fire: the Near-death of the Transatlantic Alliance* (Washington DC: Brookings Institution).
—— (2005) 'The Dynamics of the Feud over Iraq', in Andrews (ed.) *The Atlantic Alliance under Stress*.
Ponting, Clive (1989) *Breach of Promise: Labour in Power 1964–70* (London: Hamish Hamilton).
Potter, Stephen (1970) *The Complete Upmanship* (London: Hart-Davis).
Powell, Colin (1995) *A Soldier's Way: An Autobiography* (London: Hutchinson).
Powell, J. Enoch (1972) *Still to Decide* (London: Batsford).
—— (1992) *Reflections*, R. Collings (ed.) (London: Bellew).
—— (1994) 'Aligned with the IRA', *The Times*, 10 August.
Prados, John (1986) *Presidents' Secret Wars* (New York: Morrow).
Priest, A. (2005) 'In American Hands: Britain, the United States and the Polaris Nuclear Project 1962–1968', *Contemporary British History*, 19: 3, 353–76.
Prior, James (1986) *A Balance of Power* (London: Hamish Hamilton).
Public Papers of the Presidents of the United States: John F. Kennedy, 1962 (1964) (Washington, DC: USGPO).
Public Papers of the Presidents of the United States: Lyndon B. Johnson, 1966 (1967) (Washington, DC: USGPO).
Public Papers of the Presidents of the United States: Richard M. Nixon, 1974 (1975) (Washington, DC: USGPO).
Public Papers of the Presidents of the United States: William J. Clinton, 1994, vols 1 and 2 (1995) (Washington, DC: USGPO).
Public Papers of the Presidents of the United States: William J. Clinton, 1995, vol. 1 (1996) (Washington, DC: USGPO).
Public Papers of the Presidents of the United States: William J. Clinton, 1997, vol. 1 (1998) (Washington, DC: USGPO).
Puchala, D. J. (2005) 'The Atlantic Community in the Age of International Terrorism', *Journal of Transatlantic Studies*, 3: 1, 89–104.
Pym, Francis (1984) *The Politics of Consent* (London: Hamish Hamilton).
Raban, Jonathan (1990) *Hunting Mr. Heartbreak* (London: Picador).
Rachman, G. (2001) 'Is the Anglo-American Relationship Still Special?', *The Washington Quarterly*, 24: 1, 7–15.
Radice, Giles (1992) *Offshore: Britain and the European Idea* (London: I. B. Tauris).
Ramet, S. P. and C. Ingebritsen (eds) (2002) *Coming in from the Cold War: Changes in US-European Interactions since 1980* (Boulder: Rowman and Littlefield).,
Ramsay, R. (1993) 'Wilson and the Secret State', in Coopey, Fielding and Tiratsoo (eds) *The Wilson Governments*.
—— (1998) *Prawn Cocktail Party: The Hidden Power behind New Labour* (London: Verso).
Ramsbotham, O. (ed.) (1987) *Choices: Nuclear and Non-Nuclear Options* (London: Brassey's).
Rasmussen, J. and J. M. McCormick (1993) 'British Mass Perceptions of the Anglo-American Special Relationship', *Political Science Quarterly*, 108: 3, 515–41.

Rawnsley, G. D. (1995) 'How Special is Special? The Anglo-American Alliance during the Cuban Missile Crisis', *Contemporary Record*, 9, 586–601.

Reagan, Nancy (1989) *My Turn: The Memoirs of Nancy Reagan* (London: Weidenfeld & Nicolson).

Reagan, Ronald (1990) *An American Life* (London: Hutchinson).

Redwood, John (2001) *Stars and Strife* ((Basingstoke: Palgrave).

—— (2005) *Superpower Struggles: Mighty America, Faltering Europe, Rising Asia* (Basingstoke: Palgrave).

Reed, B. and G. Williams (1971) *Denis Healey and the Policies of Power* (London: Sidgwick & Jackson).

Rees, G. Wynn (1996) *Anglo-American Approaches to Alliance Security, 1955–60* (Basingstoke: Macmillan).

—— (1998) *The Western European Union at the Crossroads: between Trans-Atlantic Solidarity and European Integration* (Boulder: Westview).

Reid, T. R. (2004) *The United States of Europe: the New Superpower and the End of American Supremacy* (New York: Penguin).

Rentoul, J. (1997) *Tony Blair* (London: Warner).

Renwick, Robin (1996) *Fighting with Allies: America and Britain in Peace and War* (Basingstoke: Macmillan).

—— (1981) *The Creation of the Anglo-American Alliance, 1937–41* (London: Europa).

—— (1989) 'Rethinking Anglo-American Relations', *International Affairs*, 59: 2, 89–111.

Reynolds, David (1989) 'The Special Relationship: Rethinking Anglo-American Relations', *International Affairs*, 65: 1, 64–81.

—— (1991) *Britannia Overruled: British Policy and World Power in the 20th Century* (London: Longman).

Richardson, Louise (1996) *When Allies Differ: Anglo-American Relations during the Suez and Falklands Crises* (Basingstoke: Macmillan).

Richelson, J. T. and D. Ball (1990) *The Ties that Bind: Intelligence Cooperation between the UKUSA Countries* (London: Unwin Hyman).

Riddell, Peter (2003) *Hug Them Close: Blair, Clinton, Bush, and the 'Special Relationship'* (London: Politico's).

Ridley, N. (1991) *'My Style of Government': The Thatcher Years* (London: Hutchinson).

Rifkin, J. (2004) *The European Dream: how Europe's Vision of the Future is Quietly Eclipsing the American Dream* (New York: Tarcher/Penguin).

Rielly, J. E. (1991) 'Public Opinion: The Pulse of the 90s', *Foreign Policy*, 82, 79–96.

Risse-Knappen, Thomas (1995) *Cooperation among Democracies: The European Influence on US Foreign Policy* (Princeton: Princeton University Press).

Roger, P. (2005) *The American Enemy: the History of French Anti-Americanism* (Chicago: University of Chicago Press).

Roosa, R. V. (1968) 'Where is Britain Heading?', *Foreign Affairs*, 46: 3, 503–18.

Roper, J. (ed.) 1985 *The Future of British Defence Policy* (Aldershot: Gower).

Rossiter, C. (ed.) (1961) *The Federalist Papers* (New York: New American Library).

Routledge, P. (1997) *John Hume* (London: HarperCollins).

Rubin, B. (1987) *Secrets of State* (New York: Oxford University Press).

—— and Rubin, J. C. (2004) *Hating America: a History* (New York: Oxford University Press).

Russett, B. and D. Deluca (1983) 'Theater Nuclear Forces: Public Opinion in Western Europe', *Political Science Quarterly*, 98: 2, 171–90.

Ryan, David (2003) *The United States and Europe in the Twentieth Century* (London: Pearson Longman).

Said, E. W. (1978) *Orientalism* (London: Penguin).

Sanders, D. (1990) *Losing an Empire, Finding a Role: British Foreign Policy since 1945* (Basingstoke: Macmillan).

Saunders, F. S. (1999) *Who Paid the Piper? The CIA and the Cultural Cold War* (London: Granta).

Sawyer, M. (1996) 'Industry and Its Structure and Policies Towards It', in Artis (ed.) *The UK Economy*.

Schlaim, A., P. Jones and K. Sainsbury (1977) *British Foreign Secretaries since 1945* (Newton Abbott: David and Charles).

Schlesinger, Arthur M. (1965) *A Thousand Days* (London: Deutsch).

—— (1996) 'E Pluribus Unum', in A. Breidlid, F. Brogger, G. Guliksen and T. Sirevag (eds), *American Culture* (London: Routledge).

Schmitz, D. and T. C. Jesperson (eds) (2000) *Architects of the American Century: Individuals and Institutions in Twentieth-century U.S Foreign Policymaking* (Chicago: Imprint).

Schneider, W. (2003) 'Unilateralism Wins Few Friends', *National Journal*, 4 January, 66.

Schoen, D. E. (1977) *Enoch Powell and the Powellites* (New York: St Martin's Press).

Schoenbaum, D. (1998) 'Commentary: Special Relationships', *Diplomatic History*, 22: 2, 273–84.

Schulte, J. W. (1986) 'Anti-Americanism in European Culture', in Kroes and Van Rossem (eds) *Anti-Americanism in Europe*.

Schwabe, K. (2005) 'Three Grand Designs: the USA, Great Britain, and the Gaullist Concept of Atlantic Partnership and European Unity', *Journal of Transatlantic Studies*, 3: 1 (Supplement), 7–30.

Schwarzkopf, Norman (1992) *'It Doesn't Take a Hero'* (New York: Bantam).

Scott, L. V. (1991) 'Close to the Brink? Britain and the Cuba Missile Crisis', *Contemporary Record*, 3: 4, 507–18.

—— (*1999*) *Macmillan, Kennedy and the Cuban Missile Crisis* (Basingstoke: Macmillan).

Seitz, Raymond (1993) 'Britain and America: towards Strategic Coincidence', *The World Today*, May, 85–7.

—— (1998) *Over Here* (London: Weidenfeld & Nicolson).

Seldon, Anthony (1997) *Major: A Political Life* (London: Weidenfeld & Nicolson).

—— (2004) *Blair* (London: The Free Press).

Seldon, Anthony and Hickson, K (eds) (2004) *New Labour, Old Labour: the Wilson and Callaghan Governments, 1974–79* (London: Routledge).

Serfaty, S. (2005) *The Vital Partnership: Power and Order: America and Europe after Iraq* (Lanham: Rowman and Littlefield).

Shambaugh, D. (2005) 'The New Strategic Triangle: US and European Reactions to China's Rise', *The Washington Quarterly*, 28: 3, 7–26.

Sharp, Jane. (2004) 'The US-UK "Special Relationship" after Iraq', in Cornish (ed.) *The Conflict in Iraq, 2003*.

Sharp, Paul (1999) *Thatcher's Diplomacy: The Revival of British Foreign Policy* (Basingstoke: Macmillan).

Shaw, Eric (1988) *Discipline and Discord in the Labour Party* (Manchester: Manchester University Press).

Shawcross, W. (2003) *Allies: the United States, Britain, Europe and the War in Iraq* (London: Atlantic Books).

Shepherd, R. (1997) *Enoch Powell: A Biography* (London: Pimlico).

Sherr, A. B. (1988) *The Other Side of Arms Control* (London; Unwin Hyman).

Sherry, N. (1990) *The Life of Graham Greene: Volume 1* (London: Penguin).

Short, Clare (2004) *An Honourable Deception? New Labour, Iraq, and the Misuse of Power* (London: The Free Press).

Short, Edward (1989) *Whip to Wilson: The Crucial Years of the Labour Government* (London: Macdonald).

Shultz, George P. (1993) *Turmoil and Triumph: My Years as Secretary of State* (New York: Scribner's Sons).

Siegal, M. A. (1978) 'Ethnics: A Democratic Stronghold?, *Public Opinion*, 19, 47–8.

Simon, S. (1982) 'How Britain is Losing the Irish Argument', *The Listener*, 2 December.

Simpson, A. (2004) 'Missile Defence: the Parliamentary Challenge', *Red Pepper*, 116, v.

Singh, R. (2001) 'Teaching American Politics', *Politics*, 21: 2, 130–36.

Sloan, S. R. (1995) 'US Perspectives on NATO's Future', *International Affairs*, 71: 2, 217–31.

Smith, Geoffrey (1990) *Thatcher and Reagan* (London: The Bodley Head).

Smith, Michael and S. Woolcock (1993) *The United States and the European Community in a Transformed World* (London: Pinter/RIIA).

Smith, T. W. (1989) 'Inequality and Welfare', in Jowell, Witherspoon and Brook (eds) *British Social Attitudes*.

Snyder, G. H. (1990) 'Alliance Theory: A Neorealist First Cut', *Journal of International Affairs*, 44: 2, 103–23.

Soderberg, Narcy (2005) The Supopower Myth: *The Use and Abuse of American Might* (Hoboren NJ: John Wiley)

Solomon, R. (1977) *The International Monetary System, 1945–1976* (New York: Harper & Row).

Sorensen, Theodore (1965) *Kennedy* (New York: Harper & Row).

Sorman, G. (1990) 'United States: Model or *bête noire*?', in Lacorne, Rupnik and Toinet (eds) *The Rise and Fall of Anti-Americanism*.

Speakes, Larry (1988) *Speaking Out: The Reagan Presidency from Inside the White House* (New York: Scribner's Sons).

Special Report (2001) 'How America Held the IRA over a Barrel', *The Observer*, 28 October.

Spender, S. H. (1974) *Love-Hate Relations: A Study of Anglo-American Sensibilities* (London: Hamish Hamilton).

Spicer, M. (1992) *A Treaty Too Far: A New Policy for Europe* (London: Fourth Estate).

Spillane, M. (1995) 'Northern exposure', *The Nation*, 19 June.

Spiro, H. J. (1988) 'Anti-Americanism in Western Europe', *The Annals of the Academy of Political and Social Sciences*, 497, 120–33.

Starobin, Paul (1999) 'The Liberal Hawk Soars', *National Journal*, 15 May.

Steinbruner, J. D. (1974) *The Cybernetic Theory of Decision* (Princeton: Princeton University Press).

Steiner, Z. (1987) 'Decision-making in American and British Foreign Policy', *Review of International Studies*, 13: 1, 1–18.

Steininger, R. (1997) ' "The Americans are in a hopeless position": Great Britain and the War in Vietnam, 1964–65', *Diplomacy and Statecraft*, 8: 3, 237–85.

Stelzer, I. (ed.) (2004) *Neoconservatism* (London: Atlantic Books).

Stephens, A. (1990) 'Britannia Loses Reputation as a Classy Broad', *The Observer*, 31 May.

Stevenson, J. (1996–97) 'Northern Ireland: Treating Terrorists as Statesmen', *Foreign Policy*, 105, 125–40.

Stodhard, P. (2003) *Thirty Days: A Month at the Heart of Blair's War* (London: HarperCollins).

Stokes, B. and M. McIntosh (2002) 'How They See Us', *National Journal*, 21 December, 3720–6.

Storry, M. and P. Childs (1997) 'Conclusion', in M. Storry and P. Childs (eds) *British Cultural Identities* (London: Routledge).

Sundquist, J. L. (1986) *Constitutional Reform and Effective Government* (Washington DC: Brookings).

Sussman, L. (1992) *The Culture of Freedom: The Small World of Fulbright Scholars* (Maryland: Rowman and Littlefield).

Thatcher, Margaret (1993) *The Downing Street Years* (London: HarperCollins).

Thomas, J. (1988) 'Bloody Ireland', *Columbia Journalism Review*, 27: 1, 31–7.

Thompson, E. P. (1980) *Writing by Candlelight* (London: Merlin).

Thompson, R. J. and J. R. Rudolph (1987) 'Irish Americans in the American Foreign Policy-making Process', in Ahrar (ed.) *Ethnic Groups and US Foreign Policy*.

Thorne, C. (1979) *Allies of a Kind: The United States, Britain and the War against Japan* (London: Hamish Hamilton).

Thornton, T. P. (1988) 'Preface', *The Annals of the American Academy of Political and Social Science*, 497, 9–19.

Thorpe, D. A. (1996) *Alec Douglas-Home* (London: Sinclair-Stevenson).

Trachtenberg, M. (1999) *A Constructed Peace: the Making of the European Settlement 1945–1963* (Princeton: Princeton University Press).

—— (2005) 'The Iraq Crisis and the Future of the Western Alliance', in Andrews (ed.) *The Atlantic Alliance under Stress*.

Tratt, J. (1996) *The Macmillan Government and Europe* (Basingstoke: Macmillan).

Treverton, G. F. (1990) 'Britain's Role in the 1990s: An American View', *International Affairs*, 60: 4, 703–10.

Tucker, Nancy B. (1994) *Taiwan, Hong Kong, and the United States, 1945–1993* (New York: Twayne).

—— (1997) 'Hong Kong as a Problem in Chinese-American Relations', in Cohen and Zhao (eds), *Hong Kong under Chinese Rule*.

Tugendhat, C. and W. Wallace (1988) *Options for British Foreign Policy in the 1990s* (London: Routledge/RIIA).

Turner, A. C. (1971) *The Unique Partnership: Britain and the United States* (New York: Pegasus).

Turner, Stansfield (1983) 'The Unobvious Lessons of the Falklands Wars', *Proceedings of US Naval Institute*, 50–56.

Urban, G. R. (1996) *Diplomacy and Illusion at the Court of Margaret Thatcher: An Insider's View* (London: I. B. Tauris).

Urban, Mark (1996) *UK Eyes Alpha: The Inside Story of British Intelligence* (London: Faber & Faber).

Valasek, T. (2001–02) 'The Fight against Terrorism: Where's NATO?', *World Policy Journal*, 18: 3, 19–25.

Vance, Cyrus (1983) *Hard Choices* (New York: Simon & Schuster).

Vidal, Gore (1994) *United States: Essays, 1952–1992* (London: Abacus).

Vivekanandan, B. (1991) 'Washington Must Rely on London, Not Bonn', *Orbis*, 35: 4, 411–22.

Vlahos, M. (1991) 'Culture and Foreign Policy', *Foreign Policy*, 82, 59–78.

Walden, George (1999) *Lucky George* (London: Allen Lane).

Walker, Martin (1996) *Clinton: The President They Deserve* (London: Fourth Estate).

—— (1999) 'The New European Strategic Relationship', *World Policy Journal*, 16: 2, 23–30.

Wall, I. M. (1991) *The United States and the Making of Postwar France, 1945–1954* (Cambridge: Cambridge University Press).

Wallace, William (1975) *The Foreign Policy Process in Britain* (London: RIIA).

—— and Oliver, T. (2005) 'A Bridge Too Far: the United Kingdom and the Transatlantic Relationship', in Andrews (ed.) *The Atlantic Alliance under Stress*.

Walt, S. (1998–99) 'The Ties That Fray: Why Europe and America are Drifting Apart', *The National Interest*, 54: 1, 3–11.

War Department (2004) *Instructions for American Servicemen in Britain 1942* (Oxford: Bodleian Library).

Warner, G. (1988) 'The Settlement of the Indochina War', in J. W. Young (ed.) *The Foreign Policy of Churchill's Peacetime Administration, 1951–1955*.

—— (1989) 'The Anglo-American Special Relationship', *Diplomatic History*, 13: 4, 479–99.

Watt, D. C. (1984) *Succeeding John Bull: America in Britain's Place 1900–1977* (Cambridge: Cambridge University Press).

—— (1993) 'The Special Relationship is Knowing When to Say You're Sorry', *The Independent on Sunday*, 16 May.

Weinberger, Caspar (1990) *Fighting for Peace: Seven Critical Years at the Pentagon* (London; Michael Joseph).

Weiss, T. G., Crahan, M. E. and J. Goering (eds) (2004) *Wars on Terrorism and Iraq* (New York: Routledge).

Weller, M. (1999) 'The Rambouillet Conference on Kosovo', *International Affairs*, 75: 2, 211–52.

Weller, P. (1998) 'Britain and the First Cold War', *Twentieth Century British History*, 9: 1, 127–38.

Wheatcroft, G. (1998) 'The Special Relationship: One-Sided and Foolish', *The Independent on Sunday*, 23 August.

Wheen, F. (1996) 'Spun Out of Thin Air', *The Guardian*, 10 April.

Wiener, J. (ed.) (1996) *The Transatlantic Relationship* (Basingstoke: Macmillan).

Wilford, H. (2003) *The CIA, the British Left and the Cold War: Calling the Tune?* (London: Cass).

Wilkes, G. (ed.) (1997) *Britain's Failure to Enter the European Community 1961–63* (London: Cass).

Williams, A. (2003) 'Before the Special Relationship: the Council on Foreign Relations, the Carnegie Foundation and the Rumour of an Anglo-American War', *Journal of Transatlantic Studies*, 1: 2, 233–51.

Williams, Phil (1985) *The Senate and US Troops in Europe* (London: Macmillan).

—— and Schaub, G. (1995) 'NATO and the "Special Relationship" ', in Papacosma and Heiss (eds) *NATO in the Post-Cold War Era*.

Williams, Shirley (2001) 'In Bed with Bush', *The Guardian*, 5 May.

Wilson, A. J. (1995) *Irish America and the Ulster Conflict: 1968–1995* (Belfast: The Blackstaff Press).

—— (1997) 'The Clinton Administration, Sinn Fein and the Northern Ireland Peace Process', *New Hibernia Review*, 1: 1, 23–39.

Wilson, Harold (1971) *The Labour Government 1964–70* (London: Weidenfeld & Nicolson).

—— (1979) *Final Term: The Labour Government, 1974–1976* (London: Wiedenfeld & Nicolson and Michael Joseph).

Wilson, R. (1995) 'Days Like These', *New Statesman and Society*, 15 December.

Winand, P. (1993) *Eisenhower, Kennedy and the United States of Europe* (London: Macmillan).

—— (1997) 'American "Europeanists", Monnet's Action Committee and British Membership', in Wilkes (ed.) *Britain's Failure to Enter the European Community 1961–63*.

Windrich, E. (1978) *Britain and the Politics of Rhodesian Independence* (London: Croom Helm).

—— (1979) 'The Anglo-American Initiative in Rhodesia', *The World Today*, July.

Windsor, Philip (1983) 'Diplomatic Dimensions of the Falklands Crisis', *Millennium*, 83: 2, 88–96.

Wintour, P. and Kettle, M. (2003) 'Special Investigation: Blair's Road to War', *The Guardian*, 26 April.
—— (2005) 'Britain Faces Long-term Nuclear Threat and Must Plan for It, Says Reid', *The Guardian*, 13 September.
Witness Seminar (1993) 'The East of Suez Decisions', ed. P. Catterall, *Contemporary Record*, 7: 4, 612–53.
—— (1998) 'The Role of the British Embassy in Washington' ed. G. Staerck, *Contemporary British History*, 12: 2, 115–38.
Wolfe, Tom (1987) *The Bonfire of the Vanities* (New York: Farrar, Straus, Giroux).
Woodward, Bob (2003) *Bush at War* (New York: Simon and Schuster).
—— (2004) *Plan of Attack* (New York: Simon and Schuster).
Woodward, N. (1993) 'Labour's Economic Performance', in Coopey, Fielding and Tiratsoo (eds) *The Wilson Governments*.
Worcester, R. M. (1997) 'Its Foreign and Off the Agenda', *The World Today*, April.
Wright, J. (1999) 'Trusting Flexible Friends: the Dangers of Flexibility in NATO and the Western European Union/European Union', *Contemporary Security Policy*, 20: 2, 111–29.
Wrigley, C. (1993) 'Now You See It: Now You Don't: Harold Wilson and Labour's Foreign Policy 1964–70', in Coopey, Fielding and Tiratsoo (eds) *The Wilson Governments*.
Wybrow, R. J. (1989) *Britain Speaks Out, 1937–87: A Social History as Seen Through the Gallup Data* (Basingstoke: Macmillan).
Yankelovich, D. and L. Kaagan (1981) 'Assertive America', *Foreign Affairs*, 59: 4, 696–713.
Young, Hugo (1990) *One of Us: A Biography of Margaret Thatcher* (London: Pan).
—— (1994) 'Sleeping with America When We Should Be Courting Europe', *The Guardian*, 1 March.
—— (1998) *This Blessed Plot: Britain and Europe from Churchill to Blair* (London: Macmillan).
—— (2002a) 'Perhaps a Russian-British Lobby against War on Iraq?', *The Guardian*, 19 February.
—— (2002b) 'This Good Cop, Bad Cop Routine is Working – So Far', *The Guardian*, 21 October.
Young, John W. (ed.) (1988) *The Foreign Policy of Churchill's Peacetime Administration, 1951–1955* (Leicester: Leicester University Press).
—— (1993) *Britain and European Unity, 1945–1992* (Basingstoke: Macmillan).
—— (1996) 'The Heath Government and British Entry Into the European Community', in Ball and Seldon (eds) *The Heath Government*.
—— (1997) *Britain and the World in the Twentieth Century* (London: Arnold).
—— (1998) 'The Wilson Government and the Davies Peace Mission to North Vietnam', *Review of International Studies*, 24: 4, 545–62.
—— (2003) *The Labour Governments, 1964–1970: volume 2, International Policy* (Manchester: Manchester University Press).

—— (ed.) (2005) 'The Diary of Michael Stewart as British Foreign Secretary, April–May 1968', *Contemporary British History*, 19: 4, 481–510.

Zeldin, T. (1990) 'The Pathology of Anti-Americanism', in Lacorne *et al.* (eds) *The Rise and Fall of Anti-Americanism.*

Zelikow, P. and C. Rice (1995) *Germany Unified and Europe Transformed* (Cambridge, Mass.: Harvard University Press).

Ziegler, P. (1993) *Wilson: The Authorised Life* (London: Weidenfeld & Nicolson).

Zuckerman, S. (1988) *Monkeys, Men and Machines* (London: Collins).

Index